THE CASE FOR DISCRIMINATION

THE CASE FOR DISCRIMINATION

WALTER E. BLOCK

I owe a great debt of gratitude to Lew Rockwell for publishing this book (and for much, much more) and to Scott Kjar for a splendid job of editing.

Ludwig von Mises Institute
518 West Magnolia Avenue
Auburn, Alabama 36832
mises.org

ISBN: 978-1-933550-81-7

CONTENTS

FOREWORD

EVERY AGE OFFERS ITS OWN VERSION OF A FALSE MORAL CODE.
Just as Tom Sawyer thought that he was surely evil for being tempted
to free a slave, we too live with incredible illusions about right and
wrong as it applies to the civic realm. A firm principle of our age
is that we must never discriminate. With Professor Block's book,
however, we are encouraged to be free at last.

The very title of Professor Block's book is likely to set off alarm
bells. Is he really saying that what we've been taught to be immoral
is perfectly fine? Is he defending the undefendable, again? If he is a
libertarian, why not stick to defending the right to discriminate rather
than actually making a case for it?

The confusion deals with language first and economic theory
second, and both points are critical. The word discrimination means
nothing other than to choose between options in an environment of
scarcity. If you can only have one car, and both a mini-van and SUV
are available, you must choose between them, even if you don't
have strong feelings about either option. You must discriminate, and
therefore you must have the freedom to discriminate, which only
means the freedom to choose. Without discrimination, there is no
economizing taking place. It is chaos.

But of course the controversy over discrimination does not involve
vehicles. It pertains to people, groups of people, and groups of people
who have successfully lobbied for special protection. The law says
they may not be excluded from jobs or admission or whatever on

grounds of race, sex, religion, disability, or any other trait that the law may stipulate.

How does the state know for sure? It can pretend to read minds and motives, which is probably impossible. As a means of discovery, it listens for complaints and decides if they are valid by counting bodies. That's where quotas come in, and there are few forms of central planning more egregious than this. It creates group resentment and fuels conflict and hatred where none need exist—all in the name of resolving conflict and forbidding hatred. Here we have a classic case of the stated aim of the state turning out to accomplish the very opposite.

But rather than offer a more detailed critique—Walter Block does that brilliantly in this exciting book—let me address a more fundamental problem. What is the theoretical basis of discrimination law? Think back to the age of Marxism, and its core idea that capitalism introduced an intractable conflict, woven into the very fabric of society, between the owners of capital and the workers. The gain of one could only come at the expense of the other. In the free market, they believed, capital would exploit labor to the point of death. The role of the revolutionaries, then, was to turn the historical trajectory on its head and enable workers—the masses of people—to exploit capital to the point of death. The expropriators would be expropriated.

Of course most people realize that this is a silly way to look at the labor market. Workers and owners make agreements based on the prospect of mutual benefit. They are benefactors of each other through an act of human cooperation. The essential conflict in society is not between labor and capital, but between them and the agency that exploits them both, namely the state, which taxes and regulates them. The expropriators who should be expropriated are the bureaucrats and politicians who make life a living heck for the multitudes.

Marxism is old hat; hardly anyone takes it very seriously anymore. But the conflict model of society that is at its core—valid insofar as it pertains to the state—has been changed to an endless stream of other implausible scenarios. We are told that women and men are always and everywhere at odds, that blacks and whites are going to be forever at each others' throats, that people of different religions will forever attempt to drive each other into the ground, that people with a disability will always suffer at the hands of those with full abilities, and so on. This is the view of society that the proponents of discrimination law have inherited from the Marxists. The irony of policy based on this idea is that it creates the conflict itself—as all violations of the freedom to associate do—and thus the alleged evidence that this confused view of society is actually true.

The alternative to all this is the one accepted by Walter Block, the old liberal view, nowadays called libertarian, that society on its own is not rooted in conflict but cooperation, and that no central administration is necessary to bring about social peace. Yes, there are problems and conflicts, but there is no institution more likely to resolve them than the free market itself. People must be permitted to work out their own problems, and the result will be a flourishing of all groups. This is his view, and it is also the one held and defended by the whole liberal tradition from the late Middles Ages to the current day.

Walter Block's book is a specialized application of the libertarian perspective on society, as applied to a particular controversy in our times. It is supremely rare in tackling this issue head-on and offering a no-compromise alternative: abolish all anti-discrimination law on grounds that it makes no economic sense and only generates conflict where none need exist. Will this book cause controversy? Most assuredly. But that is not its goal. Its goal is the uprooting of a flawed and failed social theory and its replacement by a realistic one that is rooted in a genuine concern for human rights and the good of all.

Llewellyn H. Rockwell, Jr.
Auburn, Alabama

PREFACE

SOME OF THE ESSAYS INCLUDED IN THIS BOOK DEAL WITH EVENTS
as they arose in Canada. This is due to the fact that I worked at
the Fraser Institute, located in Vancouver, British Columbia from
1979–1991, when a portion of these pieces were written. But, let
me assure readers from other nations, the issues of discrimination
which arose there and then were global issues having implications
for most places in the world, particularly the U.S., in the modern era.
In many ways, Canada was then and is now "ahead" of the U.S., at
least insofar as the march downward toward socialism and economic
interventionism are concerned.

Walter E. Block
New Orleans, September 2010

PART ONE

DISCRIMINATION IS EVERYWHERE

EVERYONE HAS HEARD ABOUT SEX DISCRIMINATION, RACIAL discrimination, and age discrimination, but what about height discrimination or language discrimination? What about beard discrimination? Or discrimination against people who kneel in church? This section of the book shows that discrimination exists in obvious, and sometimes not-so-obvious, places. In short, discrimination is everywhere.

Further, families come in all shapes and sizes, from single-parent households to traditional two-parent families, from blended families to extended families. But when government steps in, it brings along coercive elements that destroy the voluntary and beneficial nature of families.

1. Discrimination Runs Rampant

"If you're so smart, why aren't you rich?" This challenge shows only that there are exceptions to every rule. Other things equal, smarter people are richer than the rest of us, and this bit of folk wisdom is well-known to most people.

Statistical analyses have shown, too, that height is correlated with pay. As a matter of fact, every extra inch added to a businessman's stature translates into roughly $1,000 of extra income. Pity the poor but short executive officer.

Now comes a University of Manitoba study which shows that people also discriminate in favor of good looks (as if this facet of human nature were not already fully documented). According to a survey conducted by the psychology department, respondents are more likely to consider an unattractive person guilty of a crime.

The study first asked 40 students to rate head-and-shoulders photographs in terms of attractiveness. Then, they were asked to determine which were most likely to have committed murder or armed robbery. The resulting correlation between guilt and ugliness was statistically significant.

It will come as no surprise whatsoever that tall, smart, and handsome people earn more than their short, stupid, and homely counterparts. Few will deny that they are more successful, for that

Fraser Forum (March 1989): 22–23.

matter, in all other aspects of life as well. Indeed, merely to state this is to belabor the obvious.

Is there a need, then, for affirmative action for these groups? According to one vision of social propriety, there certainly is. Individuals are short through no fault of their own. No matter how hard they try, some people will always be wiser than others. And, the best efforts of the cosmetic and fitness industries notwithstanding, the ugly stepsister can never attain the beauty of Cinderella.

If it is no one's fault that he or she is short, dull, and plain, and if such people almost always get the short end of the stick due to the discriminatory behavior of others, then the case for government interference with such results is all but made. Given that quotas and other systems of preferential treatment are justified for groups on the basis of race, national origin, gender, sexual orientation, and handicap status, there would seem to be no reason not to make such programs available to these other victims of discrimination.

But there is a competing philosophical perspective that can guide public policy prescriptions in such matters. In this view, the role of the state is at most to protect persons and property. Its responsibility is to set up rules so that all can compete, but not to attempt to ensure equal outcomes. If a tall but ugly and blind lesbian Protestant with bad breath earns more than a short deaf divorced but smart Catholic homosexual, or if an atheistic bald male Jew confined to a wheelchair is promoted to a job coveted by a beautiful but fat Jewish female with no sense of humor, it should be no business of the state.

People, in other words, should have the right to voluntarily associate with others on whatever terms they find mutually agreeable. They should be allowed to indulge their prejudices, no matter how unsavory they appear to the rest of us. The right of free association is simply incompatible with a program that forces employers, or anyone else, to hire workers based on ethnicity, gender, or any other criterion.

Even if such a policy were possible to administer fairly, which it is not, even if it did some good, which it does not, it is always open to the charge of hypocrisy, for there is no difference in principle between the characteristics which are presently protected (race, gender, nationality) and those that are not (height, weight, intelligence, beauty). And further, the characteristics we have so far considered are only the tip of the iceberg of those upon which people discriminate. In addition, to mention only a few more, there is hair color, the side of the head upon which people part their hair, fastidiousness, neatness, strength of handshake, biliousness, loudness, shyness, considerateness, reliability, left or right handedness—the list goes on and on.

A government intent upon eliminating all forms of discrimination, if it perseveres in this madness, will turn us into a society fit only for the Brave New World.

2. AFFIRMATIVE ACTION CHICKENS FINALLY COME HOME TO ROOST

IT WAS ONLY A MATTER OF TIME. IT HAD TO HAPPEN. AND FINALLY, it did. Two pink-skinned, fair-haired firemen have created quite a ruckus in Boston. They were hired under a minority preference plan, and therein lies a sad tale of woe.

Twins Phillip and Paul Malone have now been suspended from the Boston Fire Department. It is alleged that they misrepresented their race as a minority in order to qualify for acceptance in their jobs. As a result of this brouhaha, no less than 36 other firemen are under investigation. According to department officials, they, too, may have misled authorities as to their racial background in order to obtain employment. So far, 11 of them face disciplinary hearings.

The story of the Malones goes back a few years. They first applied to the Boston Fire Department in 1975. At that time, they identified themselves as white. But their scores on the state civil service exam were below the cut-off point for acceptance for this racial group; thus, they were not hired. In 1977, they took the test again, this time identifying themselves as black, and passed, due to the lower requirements demanded of members of this group. (They later explained that in the interim, their mother had told them that their maternal great-grandmother was black.)

Fraser Forum (October 1989).

According to a fire department spokesman, the two brothers "look like 6'2" white guys, Irish guys, maybe a little German." And, stated a Boston City Councilman, "it's a very serious situation." Very serious? More like all but intractable, at least in terms of people who may or may not have in them that proverbial "one drop" of black blood, as claimed by these firemen. How do you tell the difference between blacks and whites of this sort? Do you look deeply into their eyes or ears or other orifices? No differences have been discovered there either. Maybe athletic tests can accomplish this goal. Do you put candidates on a basketball court or watch them run a 100-meter dash or throw them in a swimming pool and record the differences?

Merely to mention these possibilities is to show how ludicrous an enterprise it is. People on the borders, such as these, cannot be scientifically distinguished on the basis of race, and any attempt to do so is to leave the realm of science and enter that of superstition. In fact, before our own, there were only two societies of note in which this distinction was a burning issue. The first was in the U.S., during the slavery and post-Civil War, Jim Crow period. In order to enforce these institutions, it was crucially important to determine who was white and who was black. So imperative was this distinction that a whole literature arose out of this question. Distinctions such as "octoroon," "quadroon," "mulatto," and "high yeller" were brought to the fore. Black people tried to "pass" for white and were sometimes blackmailed due to these efforts.

Then, of course, there is South Africa. How can a system of apartheid be run if those in charge cannot even tell who is white and who is black? Here, too, a plethora of rights depends intimately upon race: where one can live, what kind of job one is qualified for, and what restaurant one can legally be admitted to. Again, we find people trying to "pass" as a member of a certain racial group, with all the concomitant chaos which inevitably follows in the wake of legislated racism.

It is to the eternal shame of the U.S. and Canada and other western democracies that we have now joined the Confederacy and the Republic of South Africa in legally imposing racism. Now here too there will be people trying to "pass." True, they will not be blacks trying to pass as whites. Instead, it will be whites, such as the Malone brothers, trying to pass as blacks. But the principle is the same. This is something the human rights, civil liberties, and other such groups who favor racial quotas and affirmative action have not yet incorporated into their world view. It is time that this whole spate of legislation be reconsidered.

3. RACISM FLARES ON BOTH SIDES

WHOEVER SAID THAT POLITICS MAKES STRANGE BEDFELLOWS must have been thinking of Doug Collins and Harry Rankin.

On the one hand, we have a man with impeccable left-wing credentials. An ex-Committee of Progressive Electors Vancouver alderman, a stalwart supporter of the NDP, a card-carrying member of the British Columbia Civil Liberties Association, lawyer Harry Rankin yields to no one in his devotion to left-wing causes; radical environmentalism, feminism, government controls over the economy, peace marches, economic nationalism, he has fought for them all.

On the other hand, there is a man with equally impeccable right-wing credentials. Doug Collins is a long-time west coast columnist now writing for the *North Shore News*. A rejected candidate for the newly formed Reform Party (by leader Preston Manning after the local constituency had nominated him), Collins has been highly visible as a witness for Mr. Zundel at their hate literature court trials. Drawing his ire are feminists, multi-culturalists, the immigration lawyers, and radical environmentalists.

What on earth could these two very different political animals have in common—apart from the fact they happen to reside in British Columbia?

Both have recently criticized the purchase of Vancouver real estate by foreign investors from Hong Kong. In the words of Mr. Rankin,

---

Daily Townsman (Cranbrook, British Columbia), January 24, 1989.

"When money floods in from individuals buying four or five houses for investment purposes instead of for living in, you heat up and inflate the economy. We have to check the source of the inflation—the foreign speculators—by not allowing anyone other than Canadians and landed immigrants to purchase residential property."

In chillingly similar language, Mr. Collins strongly objects to the practice of the Block Bros. real estate firm in "taking out whole-page ads in the Hong Kong press inviting Hong Kongers to buy homes on the North Shore. "Recently," he stated, "a woman in Woodcroft was offered a fancy price for her apartment by an Asiatic. When she asked him why he wanted her place, he told her he had already bought every other apartment on that floor.

"Regulations to prevent the mass selling of residential real estate to foreigners would not be unusual. The Australians have already put the clamps on such sales. So have some other jurisdictions, including P.E.I. and Hawaii."

These statements are very objectionable, even frightening. They harken back to the discredited and discreditable era of the "yellow menace" and "yellow peril." One would have hoped that never again would a presumably civilized society such as ours be subjected to such carryings on, but it appears that we are not to be spared.

Adding insult to injury, there is a small matter of hypocrisy. Collins is himself an immigrant to Canada from the U.K., while Rankin's forebears hail from Europe. It comes with particular ill grace, then, for these two gentlemen to engage in blatant foreigner bashing.

Further, it is simply untrue, as both imply, that Hong Kong investments in Canada will harm the inhabitants of this country. When a person of Chinese descent (or any other, for that matter) purchases a home in British Columbia, he offers consideration which, in the eye of the seller, is worth more than the property in question. For example, if a British Columbian sells a domicile to a resident of Hong Kong, for $300,000, it must be true that the vendor values the money he receives more highly than he values the residence he gives up. Otherwise, he would scarcely agree to the sale!

Collins and Rankin go wrong in that they liken the foreign investment to a takeover of real estate. As a moment's reflection will convince us, the Hong Kong Chinese are not seizing property; they are trading for it.

As for the similarity of belief way out on the fringes of the left-right spectrum, this is only paradoxical to those who do not realize that both extremes, not just one or the other, fail to comprehend the subtleties of voluntary social arrangements. Both, unfortunately, are all too willing to call for the coercive power of government to do their bidding, to impose their will on the rest of society.

4. EXCLUSION OF BISEXUAL IS JUSTIFIED

THE BIG BROTHERS OF GREATER LOS ANGELES IS IN TROUBLE with the forces of law and order.

This organization—dedicated to matching fatherless boys with adult males who can guide, counsel, and advise them—has had the temerity to exclude homosexuals and bisexuals from its pool of potential candidates on the grounds that they will be improper role models.

For this sin against the "human rights" philosophy, Big Brothers has been made the defendant in a lawsuit by the American Civil Liberties Union of Southern California. The ACLU is suing in order to end this act of blatant discrimination against its client, one Richard Stanley, an avowed bisexual.

Can't happen here in Canada, you say? Nonsense. There is nothing in the law of this "true north strong and free" land of ours which would preclude such an eventuality. The only surprise is that this particular bit of imbecility first came to light south of our border. (However, in a related case, a Beaver Scout leader in Solstead, Alberta has recently been demoted by Boy Scouts of Canada officials because of her atheism.)

Make no mistake about it. If Mr. Stanley and the ACLU prevail in this case, it will spell the death knell for groups such as Big Brothers. If these organizations can no longer guarantee the female heads of

---

Alaska Highway News (Fort St. John, British Columbia), March 19, 1988.

single-parent families that their sons will not be placed in an intimate situation with adult male homosexuals or bisexuals, they will soon enough be unwilling to have anything to do with the program.

But do not homosexual and bisexual men have the "right" not to be discriminated against in this matter? That is, do they not have the "right" to have innocent young boys placed in their tender care, against the wishes of their parents or guardians if need be? Even to ask such a question is to see the utter ludicrousness of it.

No one has the "right" to impose himself on an unwilling victim. If anything, the bisexual man has more of a "right" to enter into a dating relationship with the boy's mother against her will than into a Big Brother relationship with her son without her permission.

For at least she is an adult; he is not. And of course, no man, of whatever sexual preference or practice, has a "right" to utilize the law of the land to force a woman to enter into a relationship with him. Even less so, then, can he properly use the courts to become Big Brother to her son.

And this has nothing to do with the question of whether or not the homosexual or bisexual will use his Big Brother status to seduce the youngster. Rape and other abuse of position are certainly not unknown in the heterosexual world.

Our conclusion follows solely from the fact that in a free society, all relationships should be based on mutual consent. Every person thus has the right to ignore, or boycott, or discriminate against those one would rather avoid.

5. Catholic Kneelers

A BATTLE HAS BEEN BREWING AT OUR LADY OF LOURDES ROMAN Catholic Church in Stellarton, an eastern Nova Scotia mining town. Six parishioners have insisted upon kneeling, not standing, while receiving communion, despite an explicit determination to the contrary by Bishop William Power of Antigonish.

The "Stellarton Six" have been convicted in Nova Scotia last summer for violating Section 172(3) of the criminal code, which makes it an offence to "disturb the order or solemnity" of a religious service. But Roseanne Skoke-Graham, a lawyer and one of the six, will appeal the decision this autumn before the Supreme Court of Canada. She will argue, among other things, that no disturbance was caused by kneeling, nor any interference with the order and solemnity of a religious service.

The Nova Scotia Court of Appeal has already rejected this claim. It held that the trial court was correct in finding that kneeling constituted a disturbance, given the bitter dispute concerning this practice. How the Supreme Court will deal with the matter, under the new Charter of Rights and Freedoms, is anyone's guess.

It is highly unfortunate that this case has turned so far on whether or not kneeling constitutes the disturbance of a religious ceremony. For there are really no objective criteria which can help us make a determination one way or another. What is one person's disturbance

---

The Daily Bulletin (Kimberley, British Columbia), October 17, 1983.

(Bishop Power) is another person's solemn practice (Roseanne Skoke-Graham).

Fortunately, however, there exists a point of law upon which an unambiguous determination can be made. This is the law of trespass.

Suppose I were to make it a rule that anyone who comes into my living room must remain standing (i.e., cannot kneel). And now, suppose that you enter my living room and insist upon kneeling. It would be impossible to even claim that your action disturbs the order or solemnity of a religious service, since my living room is patently not a house of worship. Am I thus without legal remedy?

Of course not. It is my living room, and I and I alone may determine the criteria for entry. I may insist, for example, that in order to stay on the premises, one must do a handstand, a cartwheel, or behave in any other outlandish manner I deem appropriate. Your only choice is to comply, or to leave.

In much the same way, what is proper behavior in church can only be determined by its owner. And in the case of Our Lady of Lourdes Roman Catholic Church, the owner is Bishop William Power, as the representative of the parishioners. If the bishop wishes, he may require all those who enter this church to come in crawling, pushing a peanut in front of their noses. (Of course, if he acts in so capricious a manner, he may destroy the parish and lose his job; for these and other reasons, he is extremely unlikely to act in such a way. But as long as he is in charge, he has a right to determine the rules for entry.)

Now in the event Bishop Power, in consultation with his associates, has determined that standing, not kneeling, is the proper demeanor at communion service, it is completely beside the point whether kneeling in violation of this ruling disturbs the solemnity of the service. We may even concede, for the sake of argument, that kneeling is somehow more "solemn" than standing. Despite this, the bishop is completely within his rights to insist that his own ruling be upheld.

If a man's home is his castle, then a church is the castle of the bishop. It would be a travesty of justice for the Supreme Court of Canada to make any other finding this fall.

6. Human Rights Commissions Interfere with Individual Rights

There is a political maxim that runs something like this: "If a man is not a socialist in his twenties, he has no heart. If he is still a socialist in his forties, he has no brain."

While I don't entirely agree with this maxim, it comes to mind in considering a situation at the University of British Columbia (UBC) where Andre Sobolewski, a 27 year old UBC biology student, has been fasting for human rights. That is, he has been fasting for the restoration of the British Columbia Human Rights Commission—which is quite a different kettle of fish.

This is why Sobolewski's effort is such a shame. If he were really fasting for human rights, well and good. We can use all the human rights we can get.

But this young student has been trying to launch moral pressure on behalf of the British Columbia Human Rights Commission, which is, despite its self-acclaimed and self-serving title, in direct opposition to human rights, correctly understood.

It is always important to talk about human rights. But it is particularly important to analyze the concept of human rights because of the political brouhaha surrounding the cutbacks on the British Columbia Human Rights Commission imposed by Bill Bennett's Social Credit

The Whig-Standard (Ontario, Canada), January 27, 1984, Religion Section.

government. And given actions such as Andre Sobolewski's fast, it becomes more crucial than ever.

Let's begin with some of the recent activities of the British Columbia Human Rights Commission. First, it has plagued a man called Bill Konyck because he wanted to name his business *Hunky Bill's Perogies*. The Commission made him go through the courts for months and lose an inordinate amount of money in those bureaucratic red tape snafus.

In another example, the British Columbia Human Rights Commission refused to allow a golf course to refuse service to women on Saturdays. When women prohibited male attendance at a UBC conference called *Women and Words*, however, there was no pressure from the Commission.

Then there was the case of a little old lady who advertised for a "good Christian boarder" to live in a basement suite. She was told that this is against human rights legislation. Presumably she was discriminating against "bad non-Christian boarders."

Another human rights case, this one in Alberta, involved a Tall Girls Shop, which catered to women 5 feet 10 inches and taller in height. They were advertising for a tall woman sales clerk. "No!" said the Human Rights Commission, this is discrimination. Obviously, the reason for the store's action was that a tall woman sales clerk would be better able to empathize with the problems of tall women shoppers. But this, presumably, discriminates against short people and males, and was not allowed.

Consider as well the fact that the Roman Catholics, the Russian Orthodox Church, and Orthodox Jews all refuse to ordain women. That is, they will not hire women for certain jobs in the priesthood.

Here is a conflict of the so-called human rights law with the rights of religious liberty. And people must have the liberty to practice religion as they wish.

But what of the bread-and-butter issues? Are not discrimination laws needed, for example, to protect women? Well, the usual argument is that females earn something in the order of 55 percent to 60 percent of male earnings, and that this is due to private sector employer discrimination.

Nonsense.

The Fraser Institute published a book called *Discrimination, Affirmative Action, and Equal Opportunity*, which reported some interesting discoveries. First of all, we were unable to find any substantial private employer discrimination against females. Actually, this cannot occur in the private sector to any great degree.

Let's consider the following case. Suppose there are a man and a woman, each with a productivity of $10 an hour. Assume that the man is paid $10 an hour and that the woman is only paid $6 an hour because she is being discriminated against. In such a situation, it is as if the woman has written on her forehead a little sign saying, "hire me and you'll make an extra $4 profit over and above that which you would make if you hired a man."

How long can such a situation exist in the private market?

A person who started hiring women at $6.25 or $6.50 or $7 an hour would have a severe competitive advantage over people who were sexist and only employed men, or who refused to pay women more than $6.

These discriminators would go bankrupt, so such an occurrence is extremely unlikely to take place in the private sector.

The contrast with the public sector is very clear here. How many women are there in legislative assemblies? How many women are there in Parliament? How many women are there in the senior civil service? The point is that there is no profit and loss incentive which works against discrimination in the public sector.

But we still face an interesting question: If there is no discrimination in the private sector, why is it that women earn so much less than men?

Statistical material collected for the book *Discrimination, Affirmative Action, and Equal Opportunity* revealed that one of the most important explanations for male/female earnings differentials is the asymmetrical effect of marriage on incomes.

The institution of marriage enhances male incomes and reduces those of females. Married women do more housework than their husbands, more childrearing than their husbands, and the migration patterns of married couples are such that they enhance male incomes, and reduce female incomes.

For example, suppose there is a married couple in Victoria and both are Ph.D. chemists. The male receives a far better employment opening in New Brunswick where his wife has no job offer whatsoever. If they relocate, she will have to pick up whatever job she can. Can employer discrimination really be blamed for the great disparity of income which will develop as a result of this relocation choice? Moreover, research shows that the couple is much more likely to make this move if it is the male who has received the offer rather than the female.

Then, too, is the case where a wife refuses a raise or refuses a promotion on the grounds that she will end up earning more than her husband—and this will threaten her marriage. As well, there is the whole question of the socialization of little girls who are taught not to beat Johnny in tennis, otherwise he will not date or marry them.

There has even been research that demonstrates high school girls do much better in tests when there are only other girls in the room. Now this is a serious problem. I'm not trying to sweep it under the rug and say it's unimportant. It *is* important. And we as a society have to deal with it. But not by blaming employers for discriminating against women. That just doesn't wash.

The Fraser Institute made a statistical test. Using Canadian data, we calculated male and female income ratios based on marital status. We divided our sample into two groups. First, there were those who had been married—which included those who were married, divorced, separated, or widowed. Second, there were people who were never married.

The statistics were very instructive. Women who were married, divorced, separated, or widowed earned 33.2 percent as much as men in the same situation. But among people who had never been married, females were found to earn 99.2 percent of male income.

This is why we say that the asymmetrical effects of marriage are very important factors in understanding income distribution among the sexes. This has nothing to do with private employer discrimination, the *bête noir* of the British Columbia Human Rights Commission.

The Fraser Institute's study was based on data from the 1970s, but recent investigations have had the same results. A report on research completed late in 1983 states:

> To their surprise, the sociologists discovered that the social and economic gains borne by so many women during the past decade have had remarkably little impact on the traditional gender roles assumed by the more than 3,600 married couples in the study.
>
> Although 60 percent of the wives had jobs, only about 30 percent of the husbands believed that both spouses should work—and only 39 percent of wives thought so.
>
> *No matter how large their paycheque, the working wives were still almost entirely responsible for the couple's housework. Husbands so hated housework, the researchers found, that wives who asked them to help out could sometimes sour the marriage.*
>
> Most women, on the other hand, even executives, do not consider housework demeaning.[1]

Well, if women do all the housework and the men are busy studying or preparing for promotions, is it any wonder that given equal talents, the male will outpace the female income?

---

[1] Philip Blumstein and Pepper Schwartz, *American Couples: Money, Work, Sex* (New York: William Morrow, 1983).

7. Watch Your Language

Language is crucial to clear communication. It makes distinctions. We can hardly express ourselves without it. Our very thoughts can either be brought forth, or not, depending upon whether we have sufficient verbiage with which to attain this end. If the pen is mightier than the sword because it can determine the direction in which this weapon is aimed, then words are even mightier than the pen, for without the former, the latter is useless.

Which words have we lost? Which have been thrust down our throats by the forces of socialism, statist feminism, and political correctness? What changes are imperative, if we are to even have a chance to turn things around in a more freedom-oriented direction?

Ms.

Mrs. and Miss have been all but taken from us, and we have been given the execrable Ms. in their place. This is a crucial loss, for the modern language in this regard papers over, nay, obliterates, the distinction between the married and unmarried state for women, while the "archaic" words positively exult in this distinction. This alteration has become so well entrenched by the "inclusive" language movement that even some ostensibly conservative writers and periodicals have adopted it.

Original article appeared on mises.org.

Why is this a tragedy? Because it is a disguised attack on the family. Whether the feminists accept this or not, virtually all heterosexual bondings are initiated by the male of the species. (There are good and sufficient sociobiological reasons why this should be the case.) Anything that promotes this healthy and life-affirming trend must be counted as a good; anything that impedes it as a bad. If it is easy to distinguish between married and unmarried females, male initiative is to that extent supported; if not, then the opposite.

If unmarried males are given incentive to approach unmarried females, this supports the institution of marriage and heterosexuality. To the extent they approach married women, this not only undermines marriage, one of the main bulwarks of society, but directly attacks civilization by exacerbating jealousy and intra-male hostility.

Why have the feminists urged Ms. upon us? Ostensibly, because it is "unfair" to distinguish between women on the basis of marital status, but not men. If so, then far better to urge the analogous distinction Mister and Master for married and unmarried men, than to lose that for women. We live in a complex age; surely any institution which simplifies it, by costlessly giving us more information, not less, is to be applauded.

But the softening of this distinction between Mrs. and Miss has implications far removed from any questions of "fairness." This can be seen by asking "*Cui bono*" from Ms.? Those who benefit from making single women less available to heterosexual men are homosexual women, plus all those concerned with the so-called overpopulation problem. In economics, when there are large numbers of people or anything else involved, it is commonly assumed that at least some are on the margin.

In this case, there are males on the margin between approaching a female or not, and females on the margin between hetero- and homosexuality. Ms. moves society in the diametric opposite direction from the desirable in both these dimensions.

One argument against refusing to adopt to this modern consensus is that people should have the right to choose their own names. If someone wants to change from Cassius Clay to Muhammad Ali, or from Don

McCloskey to Dierdre McCloskey, that is their business. Polite people will refer to them by their chosen not their given names.

But this does not at all apply to titles. If I call myself King Block or Emperor Block, no one need follow suit on this out of considerations of etiquette. Ms. is a title, not the name of any person. When in doubt, always use Miss, not Mrs. The latter is, or at least should be, an honorific, not lightly to be bestowed in ignorance.

And the same analysis applies to using "he" to stand for "he" or "she," or "him" for "him" or "her." Our writing has become convoluted, and singular and plural no longer match, in an attempt to defer to the sensibilities of self-styled feminists. There is nothing more pathetic than a conservative magazine attempting to score points against a feminist idea, and yet feeling constrained to use such "inclusive" language.

Could we have as successfully criticized Marxism had we felt constrained to couch our attacks in Marxist language?

8. SEXIST ADVERTISING AND THE FEMINISTS

THE WAR BETWEEN THE SEXES IS STILL RAGING.

The city council of Kamloops, British Columbia, placed an ad in its tourism brochure featuring an attractive bikini-clad woman kneeling at the feet of a businessman who was reclining in a beach chair. Accompanying the ad is the message "Where Business and Pleasure Come Together—in Super, Natural High Country, Kamloops, B.C."

According to the local woman's resource center, the ad clearly implies that the barely dressed female represents the sexual pleasure, while the almost fully dressed male is mixing a little business with his pleasure.

But Kamloops Mayor John Dormer is having none of that. "To me, it's a non-issue and I don't think members of the general public would be offended either. It's tastefully done, and the complaints about it are ridiculous." And a majority of the aldermen are hanging tough, too. They like the ad because it is "eye-catching," although a minority, including the lone female member of council, find it "offensive."

It is of great interest to contrast this case with a superficially similar one which took place in Vancouver a few years ago. At that time, Eaton's department store had placed an exhibit in its sidewalk window that was also deemed sexist by spokespersons for the local feminist movement. (It featured a male doctor manikin holding a probe aimed at the crotch of a female patient manikin.)

Chronicle Journal (Thunder Bay, Ontario), December 17, 1988.

But in the aftermath of the protest, all similarity between the two cases dramatically disappears. Eaton's management, instead of stonewalling, and insisting upon maintaining its vision of propriety, caved in with alacrity. Within a matter of hours, the offensive exhibit was withdrawn, to the accompaniment of profuse apologies.

How can we explain the two very divergent reactions? At first glance, this would appear to be exceedingly difficult, since both protests were undertaken by much the same people, feminists, objecting to essentially identical occurrences.

The difference lies not in the offense, nor in the identity of the protestors, but in the people against whom the complaint was made. In Kamloops, the perpetrators of the transgression are part of the public sector; in Vancouver, they were a private business. As such, they are confronted with very different incentives:

- The Kamloops mayor and Council do not have to face voters in the polling booth for another few years; Eaton's, in sharp contrast, had to face its "dollar" voters the very next day, and every day thereafter.

- On that far-off day when the politicians shall finally be called upon to defend their actions, they will be judged not only by how well they acquitted themselves in this one case, but by how well they collected the garbage, filled the pot-holes, ran the recreation centers, distributed patronage, conducted library services, etc. In addition, if they are telegenic, or particularly well spoken, they will effortlessly be able to explain away their acts.

- In sharp contrast, the shoppers could easily focus their entire dissatisfaction on the businessmen they held responsible. Nor could the latter squirm out. All the protestors needed to do was to patronize a competitor. This potential threat was more than enough to quickly bring to heel the capitalists who owned Eaton's.

The point of this little civics lesson is that we as consumers are able to exercise a far greater degree of control over private businesses, even though we do not own them, than we can exert over politicians, despite the fact that we are theoretically their employers and they ostensibly act in our behalf. Paradoxically to some people, the marketplace is far more responsive to our needs and desires than is the cumbersome and inefficient political system.

We can easily see from these two cases that if feminists truly had the interests of their constituency at heart, they would urge a greater role for the private sector. Instead, their biases run toward more government intervention. This is highly unfortunate from the perspective of those of us who favor the goals of the women's movement, if not their means.

9. NO MALES NEED APPLY

THE MANITOBA HUMAN RIGHTS COMMISSION STRIKES AGAIN. Only this time, not on behalf of a discrimination-free society, but in favor, it would appear, of one segregated on the basis of gender.

Claudia Wright, head of the MHRC, attended a female-only conference on the media, and participated in one of the workshops, despite her acknowledgement of the fact that the Manitoba Human Rights Act prohibits sex discrimination. Talk about sending in the fox to guard the chicken coop.

The event was put on by the Manitoba Action Committee on the Status of Women and Media Watch, groups which at least heretofore had been opposed to sexual segregation. But according to conference organizer Lynne Gibbon, men were excluded because a number of male journalists had already been interviewed on the subject of the media.

Evidently, the male reporter who had tried to cover a weekend session, but was told to leave, was not one of those who had "already been interviewed." Ms. Gibbon went on to explain that this occurrence "was an attempt to include women rather than exclude men." Put that in your pipe and smoke it, male, chauvinist pigs of the world.

Nor did this bit of illogic exhaust the explanatory powers of the women's movement. According to one Debbie Holmberg-Schwartz, managing editor of *Herizons* (sic), a national women's news magazine

---

Alberni Valley Times (Port Alberni, British Columbia), May 16, 1985.

located in Winnipeg, the decision to exclude men was a form of affirmative action: "It's really important that women catch up in this field, and of course the logical place to give them opportunity is at a women's conference."

Can anyone imagine the response of the Manitoba Human Rights Commission, and all others in the human rights biz, had a group of male white Anglo-Saxon protestants used a similar line of argument to justify the exclusion of females, or gays, or native peoples, or handicapped persons, or francophones, or indeed, any other group favored by current prejudices?

The double standard, so long reviled in Canada, would appear to be alive and well, at least in some parts of Winnipeg.

10. WE OUGHT TO HAVE SEX EDUCATION IN THE SCHOOLS

THIS HAS BEEN A VERY DIVISIVE ISSUE OF LATE. SOME PARENTS want very much for their children to be fully educated, and they see learning about human sexuality as crucial to the well developed person. Others are equally vociferous—but on the other side. In their view, such matters should be left to the home or to the church, or not be discussed at all.

How can such disputes be resolved? Well, there are two and only two ways to accomplish this; all others are simply combinations and permutations of these polar solutions.

The first method is the use of physical force. The matter is decided by a dictator, or by a democratic election of the entire populace, or by a school board or a mayor or a city council or a parent-teacher association. However it is determined, the decision is enforced upon the losers. Whichever way it goes, we either have sex education in the schools, or we do not. One group, either the opponents or the proponents, must of necessity be dissatisfied.

The other method is called the free-enterprise system. Here, there are no such things as public schools. All are private. Each one determines its own policy on this issue. In some, sex education is totally banned.

Appeared in *Clichés of Politics*, ed. Mark Spengler (Irvington-on-Hudson, N.Y.: Foundation for Economic Education, 1994), pp. 240–42.

In others, it forms the central focus of the entire learning experience. In most cases, this subject plays a more intermediate role.

Under such circumstances, everyone can be satisfied. Parents can patronize the schools that most nearly reflect their own views on the matter. Given dozens—if not hundreds—of educational enterprises in each city, there is little doubt that all tastes on the spectrum can be accommodated.

Let us now consider an analogy. Instead of considering the proposition "We ought to have sex education in the schools," let us contemplate "We ought to have pizza in the restaurants."

Were this question solved in the manner presently used for sex education, our system would be very different. Most restaurants would be run by the government. All citizens would be forced to pay for these public restaurants, whether they used them or not. Those who patronized private ones would have to pay twice: once in fees for meals, and then again through taxes. People, moreover, would be assigned to the public restaurant located nearest to them.

As to the pizza question, all public restaurants would either stock this foodstuff, or they would not. There could be no such thing as restaurants specializing in different cuisines, and people sorting themselves out according to their tastes. Thus, either the pizza lovers, or the pizza haters, would be disappointed.

The point is, the market is almost infinitely flexible compared to government. And this holds true even when a free market in education is compared to educational socialism. In addition, the profit-and-loss system of free enterprise tends to weed out those entrepreneurs who cannot satisfy their customers. Let a business firm supplying elementary school services answer the sex educational question in a way at variance with a parent, and that is one customer gone to patronize a competitor. In contrast, the state educational bureaucrats have very little incentive to satisfy the demands of their captive audience; if the parents don't like the policy, it is just too bad for them: they must continue to pay their school taxes in any case.

The proof of this contention is that there simply is no "pizza in restaurants" issue now bedeviling society. The very idea is ludicrous. But the reason we have escaped this particular vexation is that the market functions, in large part, without our appreciation or even knowledge. The best way to answer the challenge of sex education in the schools is to privatize the entire industry, and allow each parent to decide this issue for him- or herself.

There is the objection that schooling is too important to be left to free enterprise, and that the government must therefore take it over.

It is certainly true that education is crucial to living a good life. The ignorant man is only half alive. But food, too, is important. And if we have found a way to feed people—efficiently and affordably—without emulating the Soviet system of collectivized farms, restaurants, grocery stores, and so on, surely we can do so with regard to education as well.

We conclude that the way to address the issue of sex education (as well as other seemingly intractable issues such as school busing, prayer in the schools, and debates over educational philosophy) is to allow the market to function. It is the most productive and moral economic institution known to man; surely it can suffice in this particular case.

11. ANOTHER ROLE FOR WOMEN

DURING THE AMERICAN MILITARY ACTIVITY IN CENTRAL AMERICA, U.S. Army Captain Linda Bray commanded a 30-man platoon in an attack on a Panamanian Defense Forces guard dog kennel.

West Point, that bastion of the U.S. army, recently chose a female student as first captain of its Corps of Cadets.

Female soldiers have been placed in potential combat positions in the armies of Canada, Israel, and other countries.

These and other such occurrences have once again focused public attention on the question of women in the military.

Why is it that we commonly have this deeply embedded "sexist" idea that women are to be spared military duty? That "women and children" have first priority in the lifeboats? Why place women on a pedestal in this way? Why not make the military an "equal opportunity employer," as far as men and women are concerned?

In the widely popular "feminist" analysis, this is because men regard women as little better than children in terms of intelligence, physical strength, and maturity: if children should be saved first from a sinking ship, or protected during war, because of their relative weakness, then so should women.

The sociobiological explanation of this event provides a sharp contrast. In this view, the women-and-children-first rule came about

The Vancouver Sun, February 16, 1990.

because this philosophy ensured the survival of our species. Women are biologically far more precious than men, and any species that does not base its actions on this rule is thus far less likely to survive than one that does. This is why chivalrous notions are so deeply embedded in our psyches: the human race has been acting on these principles for eons.

Suppose that there were two races of apes, otherwise equally fit to survive, which had different customs regarding warfare. One group of apes (call them the human apes) did not allow their females to fight. Instead, they tried to protect them as much as possible. When fighting took place, it was with the expendable males in the front lines. The other group of apes (call them extinct) either pushed the women forward to the front lines of battle or were egalitarian— no "spurious" distinctions were made between the males and the females: they all went out and fought on an equal basis.

Which group would more likely survive? Obviously, the first, the "human" apes, because women are far more important—when it comes to survival of the species. A dramatic illustration of this is that one male and 25 females can leave as many progeny as 25 males and 25 females. That is, 24 of the males are biologically extraneous to the process. It may be nice to have them around—at the very least they can furnish added protection, but, biologically speaking, their roles are as necessary for the survival of the human species as are drones for the survival of bees.

That is why farmers commonly keep one bull for 25 cows, and not the other way around. However incompatible with the "feminist" view of the world, this biological fact simply cannot be denied.

Consider Germany, Poland, and the Soviet Union after the Second World War; an entire generation of men in these countries was decimated; the lives of the women were by and large spared, at least relatively speaking. How noticeable is this in the modern day, in terms of demographic implications?

Compare that scenario to the following hypothetical case. Suppose that a high proportion of the women of the Soviet Union of child-bearing age were killed, but hardly any of the men, roughly the reverse of what actually occurred. What would be the demographic results in such a case? They would be no less than catastrophic. Not only would there be great danger for the next generation in these countries, the real question is whether there would be any next generation.

When women enter in the military in any great numbers, it will be a threat to the entire human race.

12. Female Golfer

ANNIKA SORENSTAM HAS ACCEPTED HER INVITATION TO PLAY in the men's Professional Golf Association tournament in Fort Worth, Texas, and everyone and his uncle (excuse me, his aunt) has practically dropped their teeth over this wondrous occurrence.

Headlines range from "Let's hear it for Sorenstam," to "She's an inspiration," to "Why this Swede is 'da woman' of golf." If there has been a critical reaction to this phenomenon in the mainstream press, I have not heard about it.

Her first-day 71 score (one over par) at the Bank of America Colonial was good enough to beat out or tie several of her male competitors. This set off even more paroxysms of self-congratulation and high-fiving amongst the politically correct sports commentators. According to one low-key journalist, this accomplishment "made golf fans around the world scream with joy." A commentator has even gone so far as to characterize Annika's accomplishment "as one of the all-time greatest performances by a female athlete in any sport." There may be a glass ceiling in the business world (that is a bit of economic illiteracy that shall have to be discussed on another occasion), but the "grass ceiling" in athletics in general, and golf in particular seems to have been pierced.

Before we get caught up in the general hysteria, let us recognize a few worms in this particular apple. If females can enter male

Original article appeared on lewrockwell.com.

competitions on the grounds that they are just as good as men, then, based on this egalitarian "logic," the latter will no longer be able to be kept out of those that have previously been limited to women. After all, why have different sections of an athletic event, if there are no relevant differences? No one organizes special matches for left- and right-handed people, for the blue eyed and the brown eyed, because these differences are not thought to be relevant to ability. If the internal plumbing of human beings is now likewise determined to be of no moment, competitively speaking, thanks to Annika's marvelous accomplishments, why, then, there would be no reason to exclude males from female competitions. There would no longer be separate track and field, swimming, basketball, golfing or tennis leagues for men and women. In this one-size-fits-all new world order, all separations between the LPGA and the PGA, between the NBA and the WNBA would disappear. Segregation, after all, is invidious.

But this would pretty much spell the death knell for women's sports. With the possible exceptions of sports that call more for finesse than strength (think billiards, bowling, and, ok, maybe, golf), females would be all but frozen out of professional top-flight competition (and even here, it would be the rare woman who could effectively compete with men). In the present left-wing feminist frenzy, this may not be readily apparent in basketball, tennis, soccer, baseball and other team sports. The two genders rarely if ever meet each other in sanctioned official matches. Although even here, there is some supportive evidence. E.g., the top speed for a male tennis serve is 149 mph; the female counterpart is only 127.4 mph. Yes, yes, (a young) Billie Jean King beat (an old) Bobby Riggs in a tennis match. This is just the exception that proves the rule.

However, there is a plethora of data, emanating from sports in which success can be measured objectively, which indicates that few or no women would be able to compete effectively against men. For example:

• The high jump world record for men is 8'5"; for women it is only 6'10.25". In contrast, the boys' high school record is 7'6".

- The best male long jump is 29'4.5"; the top female can do only 24'8". The long jump record in high school (male, of course) is 26'9.25".
- The mile can be run by a male athlete in 3:43.1; a female takes 4:12.6; a high-schooler can do this distance in 3:53.
- The male record for the 100-meter run is 9.78 seconds, the female, 10.49; the high school record is 10.13.

Forget competing against world class male athletes; the top women would not even be able to garner medals in a robust high school setting.

This pattern of male dominance holds true for all sports where a premium is enjoyed by possessing strength, speed and endurance. And in quite a few "sports" where it is not. For example, this applies to virtually all chess grandmasters.

These points are made not to demonstrate male superiority in athletics. Their dominance is so well established by the facts that only hysterical left-wing feminists (of both sexes) must be reminded of them. No. We take cognizance of them because of the danger to women's sports posed by allowing Annika Sorenstam to compete with men. If we are logically consistent and allow the genders to play against each other in such environments, there will be (virtually) no athletic contests where girls and women will have any chance of victory.

In boxing and other martial arts, there are commonly weight divisions. This doesn't mean that a pugilist weighing 120 pounds can never triumph over someone at the 190 pound level. We engage in such segregation because weight gives such a clear advantage to the heavier athlete, other things equal, that a match between two such competitors would be too one sided. It would be boring to watch. Most people would consider it "unfair."

It is precisely the same with men and women.

13. Silver Lining Part IV:
Term Limits and Female Politicians

This is the fourth in a series of columns dealing with silver linings: the phenomenon that unwarranted and unjustified acts can sometimes have positive elements. This of course does not justify them, but we do ourselves a disservice if we ignore these benefits.

In the first of these columns, "A Silver Lining in Drug Prohibition,"[1] I noted that real criminals who might not otherwise be caught are sometimes jailed for engaging in the drug trade, which they have every right to do. But fewer murderers and rapists at large is surely a good thing. In the second of these columns, "A Silver Lining in Unjust Executions,"[2] I observed that those executed for murders for which they are innocent (a travesty of justice if ever there was one) were sometimes guilty of committing other capital crimes for which they were not charged. Thus, a critique of the death penalty was not as powerful as otherwise thought. In the third,[3] I tried to clarify my position on this issue *vis-à-vis* several objections that had been made of it.

Today, we consider the silver lining involved in term limits: it reduces the percentage of female politicians.

Original article appeared on lewrockwell.com.

[1] See lewrockwell.com.

[2] See lewrockwell.com.

[3] See lewrockwell.com.

There is much wailing and gnashing of teeth at this phenomenon on the part of our friends on the Democratic side of the aisle. According to an editorial appearing in the *Seattle Times* (8/17/03, p. A6; okay, okay, this statement doesn't appear on the editorial pages, but rather is disguised as "news"): "Fewer female legislators in statehouses: Term limits are seen as culprit in curtailing women's progress in winning seats, which has stalled since the early 1990s." The editorial, sorry, the story, goes on to say that in states with term limits, female politicians are very rare. For example, 9.4 percent of South Carolina legislators were female, in Alabama it was 10 percent, and in Kentucky the figure was 10.9 percent. In contrast, in the non-term-limit states, the percentages were much higher, e.g., 36.7 percent in Washington, 52 percent in Michigan, 33 percent in both Colorado and Maryland. (The overall average in 2003 was 22.3 percent, down from a high of 22.7 percent in 2002.)

So much for the facts. Where is the silver lining?

In order for there to be a silver lining, there has to be an evil, and, also, some good must come out of it. I am already on record[4] in taking the position that term limits are highly problematic. I did so on grounds blazed by Professor Hans Hoppe.[5] His argument is based on time preference: other things equal, the longer a politician is in office, the more of a long-run viewpoint he can afford to take. If he can leave the office to his children (e.g., a monarchy), he will act even more responsibly; he doesn't want to kill the golden goose, otherwise there will be nothing left for his progeny to exploit.

In the other direction, if a politician could only be in office for, say, one month, then "make hay while the sun shines," even more so than at present, would become his motto. That is, he would have very little incentive to reign in his natural rapaciousness, for he would be turned out all too soon. There would only be the thinnest veneer of

---

[4] "The Evil of Term Limits," lewrockwell.com.

[5] See Hans-Hermann Hoppe, *Democracy—The God That Failed: The Economics and Politics of Monarchy, Democracy, and the Natural Order* (New Brunswick, N.J.: Transaction, 2001).

"public service" to cover the theft-as-usual policies. Why leave much of anything for the next officeholder, certainly not if it interferes with your own pillage?

Term limits, then, are a disaster, in that they enhance the already very great incentives for politicians to loot.

But there is a silver lining: females appear to be booted out by this initiative to an even greater degree than males. Why is this to be considered a good thing?

On the economic front, it is clear that women on average favor social welfare schemes more than do men, and I extrapolate from females in general to their sister politicians. It is surely no accident that programs such as social security, welfare, and unemployment insurance came after the "weaker sex" was given the right to vote. This phenomenon might stem from women being more risk averse than men, and seeing such coercive socialistic policies as somehow "safer."

Further evidence: there is a large "gender gap" between the Republican and Democratic parties on domestic issues; females favor the latter over the former; as well, the membership of the Libertarian Party is overwhelmingly male. (As against this, I must concede that on matters of imperialism and foreign military adventurism, female timidity probably inclines them to a less-aggressive stance.)

Second, apart from considerations of this sort, there is no intrinsic reason to favor male over female politicians. With the exception of Ron Paul and only a few others, all are hypocritical and pompous mountebanks, not content with merely robbing us, but determined to convince us they do it for our own good. However, another issue arises: one of the strongest motivating forces behind the leftish push for female politicians is the quaint notion that apart from under-handed skullduggery, all groups would be exactly equal. That is, in the truly just society, both genders, all races and nationalities, all ages, people of all sexual orientations, etc. bloody, etc., would be equally represented in all callings. If they are not, this is due to exploitation, or injustice, or some such. That is, absent improprieties such as racism, sexism, look-ism (I kid you not), able-ism, etc., since males and females comprise roughly 50 percent each of the electorate, this would also be their representation amongst office-holders. (Also, the National Basketball Association would employ as players tall, strong, athletic blacks, and short, fat Jews, in proportion to their overall numbers in the population; it is only due to racial discrimination against Orientals that so few of them are on National Football League team rosters.)

There is no one who has done more to combat this pernicious fallacy than Tom Sowell.[6] But he needs all the help he can get on this mission. It is incumbent upon all men of good will to help him in this regard. And one way that we can do so is to recognize one of the side order benefits of that otherwise insidious policy of term limits: that it disproportionately penalizes female politicians.

To clarify matters, I do not favor term limits. However, I do recognize that there is a silver lining in this particular cloud.

---

[6] See, e.g., Thomas Sowell, *Race and Culture: A Worldview* (New York: Basic Books, 1994).

14. ARM THE COEDS

THERE HAS BEEN A SPATE OF ROBBERIES AND SEXUAL ASSAULTS aimed at university coeds in uptown New Orleans. A single, typically black man approaches girls walking in the street in pairs at night and then proceeds to rob, confine, and sexually assault them.

The reaction on the part of the police authorities is the usual blather about being "street smart," not carrying a weapon, not resisting, and not venturing out at night. If going unarmed was such great advice, why don't they follow it themselves? Further, why should the victims have to pay twice, once in the form of being robbed and raped, and then, again, in the form of having their liberties to walk on the public streets curtailed?

The response from school authorities is, if anything, even worse: holding candlelight vigils, praying, having "take back the night" marches, and organizing teach-ins attempting to indoctrinate the students with the usual leftist feminist and liberal shibboleths, *ad nauseam*. If these things give university students any comfort, it is a false sense of security which could prove to be their undoing. Quite possibly, the assailant joins the very parade set up against him, biting his lip to keep from laughing outright, which might well be the only harm that befalls him from these events. Such tactics might make some people feel good, but they do nothing to address the problem.

Walter Block and William Barnett II at lewrockwell.com.

ARM THE VICTIMS

In contrast, we offer a five-point program of arming the victims, virtually guaranteed to solve the problem.

1. Take down those signs on campuses announcing they are "gun-free" zones. That is the worst possible message to be sent to potential perpetrators of violence against our community. We might as well post a sign saying, "C'mon in, attackers, we've disarmed ourselves and will be easy prey." This no-gun policy, thank God, does not apply to campus police, who can't be everywhere, as is the case with their city counterparts.

2. Require that all female students own a pistol or other means of self-defense (e.g., pepper spray or mace, stun gun or other electric shock device) and carry it with them at all times. The women of Kennesaw, Georgia, an affluent northern suburb of Atlanta Georgia, were once plagued by rapists. This town not only allowed, but required its citizens to be armed. You'll never guess what happened to the rape rate after this progressive policy was enacted. ("Guns" 2001)

The law, however, was compulsory, and, as such, violated the rights of pacifists and other local citizens who might have objected. But this would not at all apply to Loyola, a private institution. This change in policy would have to be "grandfathered in" so as to avoid contractual violations, but in the future, females who do not wish to protect themselves in this way would be perfectly free to attend other universities. They would have no right to be on campus unless they obey all rules and regulations (in contrast, the citizenry of Kennesaw did have a right to remain there, in violation of the law). In the meantime, this enlightened policy could be introduced on a voluntary basis, and encouraged by the administration.

3. Packing a weapon is necessary, but not sufficient. All women at Loyola ought to be required to take a course in gun safety. The last thing we want are accidental shootings. Leftists bruit about statistics on accidents where children are killed with revolvers. But these data are wildly exaggerated by including the shooting deaths of young, teenaged gang-bangers, whose deaths are certainly purposeful.

4. Volleyball, basketball, cross-country, and baseball teams are all well and good, but a sports organization aimed at improving marksmanship would be far more helpful in present circumstances. (When is the last time a Loyola student won an Olympic medal in target shooting? Never, that's when. It is time, it is long past time, for a change.) All students don't have to be sharp shooters. Reasonable accuracy even at 10 to 15 feet will be more than enough to scare off potential rapists. Heck, even the presence of an automatic in a co-ed's hand bag or pocket fully accomplishes this task.

5. When the new student center at Loyola is erected, it should include an indoor shooting range, just as the old field house did. The new rifle and pistol team would practice there, as would every woman student who so wished. The muffled sounds of target practice would alone give pause to all ne'er-do-wells in the neighborhood.

It will undoubtedly be objected against this modest proposal that arming young girls will not protect them; that their weapons will be seized by their attackers. Logic, common sense, and vast hordes of empirical evidence give the lie to all such negativism. Put yourself in the position of a New Orleans mugger and rapist: would you really want to engage in your usual depredations in the uptown area, knowing full well that you could do so on no more than even terms? Not bloody likely. The uptown predator has already come armed; let his victims face him on even terms. As to the facts of the matter, world class economist John Lott has done a series of studies linking gun ownership with increased personal safety.

After this forward-looking policy proves a success in the collegiate uptown area, it could be implemented by private organizations throughout the entire city. Then and only then would the scourge of raping and robbing have a good chance of being vastly decreased throughout our whole community.

15. Free Market Would Alleviate Poverty and Strengthen Family Relations

GOVERNOR BLANCO IS NOW HOLDING HEARINGS ON THE PROBLEM of poverty. Since she is a mainstream politician, she will likely arrive at the wrong answers for its cause and adopt fascistic solutions for its cure. Worse, this initiative will cost hundreds of thousands of dollars or more, and thus exacerbate the very poverty she is supposedly fighting.

In 1776, Adam Smith wrote *An Inquiry into the Nature and Causes of the Wealth of Nations*. The governor might do worse than cancel her meetings and read this book instead. Smith said that those countries that rely mainly on the free enterprise system of private property rights and the rule of law prosper, while those that do not are consigned to a life of grinding poverty.

Research I conducted[1] finds a statistically significant relationship not only between the degree of economic freedom in a country and its *per capita* income but also between liberty and income equality.

Smith, who was not as free-enterprise oriented as his reputation implies, hedged on this basic insight with too many exceptions and too many concessions to government, but the general rule he

---

Loyola University New Orleans *The Maroon*, January 21, 2005, p. 5.

[1] James Gwartney, Robert Lawson, and Walter Block, *Economic Freedom of the World, 1975–1995* (Vancouver, British Columbia: The Fraser Institute, 1996).

articulated was as true in the 18th century as it is in our own, and applies as much to countries as to states and cities.

Why do markets work to alleviate poverty and governments fail?

The main reason is the profit and loss system, the automatic feedback loop mechanism of free enterprise. If an entrepreneur does a bad job, people avoid his firm. If he does not mend the error of his ways, bankruptcy is the inevitable and usually swift result. In sharp contrast, if a politician makes mistakes in satisfying a constituency, he can stay in office for up to four years; a bureaucrat, practically forever.

The situation regarding pizza, pens, and pickles is pretty satisfactory; those who could not provide these goods at a competitive quality and price went broke. But what of the post office and the motor vehicle bureau? Poor service for decades, and nothing we consumers can do about it.

Why do free markets tend toward income equality? The only legitimate way to earn vast sums of money under free enterprise is by enriching others. Yes, Bill Gates, Sam Walton, Henry Ford, and Ray Kroc make billions, but they do so by economically uplifting all those they deal with. If people did not benefit from dealing with Microsoft, Wal-Mart, Ford, and McDonalds, they would not continue to do so.

In contrast, in politics, vast fortunes are made not by attracting customers but by raising taxes and siphoning off the lion's share of them. The wealth of the politician rises, and that of everyone else falls.

But do governments not give money to the poor in the form of welfare? Doesn't that help the poor? First, only the crumbs go to the poor. The rich, after all, run the government. It would take quite a bit more benevolence than they have for them to orchestrate things against their own interests.

Second, what little money does go to the poor impoverishes them; it does not lift them out of poverty. The key to understanding the direction of causation in this paradoxical situation is the family. Anything that supports this vital institution reduces poverty; anything that undermines it increases poverty.

Family breakdown is causally related to all sorts of poverty indices besides lack of money: imprisonment, lack of educational attainment, unemployment, lower savings, illegitimacy, etc.

And what is the effect of welfare on the family? To ask this is to answer it. As Charles Murray has shown in his insightful book *Losing Ground*, the social worker makes a financial offer to the pregnant girl that the father of her baby cannot even come close to matching. But they do so on the condition that this young man be out of the picture. A recipe for family disaster if ever there was one.

Slavery was not able to ruin the black family (poverty is dispro-portionately a black problem), but insidious welfare had that very effect. The black family was just about as strong as the white in the years following the War of Northern Aggression, but fell apart after Johnson's War on Poverty.

Similarly, Social Security weakens intergenerational family ties. Public housing, with its income cutoff points, evicts intact families. The remaining female heads of families are no match for gangs of teenage boys lacking adult male role models.

The government is also a direct source of poverty. Its minimum wage and union legislation make it difficult if not impossible for poor youth to get jobs. Its rent control makes cheap housing scarce. Its tariffs make all basic necessities more expensive, and its subsidies to business have the same effect.

Want to cure poverty, Governor Blanco? Reduce government interference with the free enterprise system.

16. RACISM: PUBLIC AND PRIVATE

WHEN AN INDIVIDUAL OR A GROUP OF PERSONS IN THE PRIVATE
sector discriminates against a racial or ethnic minority, the results
can be debilitating. Psychological harm, feelings of isolation, and a
sense of hostility are likely to result.

Fortunately, in the private sector, there is a little-recognized
phenomenon which helps to protect minorities from great economic
harm: the fact that private individuals tend to pay for their discrimination.
For example, if a segment of the population is discriminated against
in employment, this tends to drive down their wage rates. However,
the lower wages they now command act as a magnet, inducing other
employers to make them job offers. Employers who discriminate pass
up these lower wages. Other things equal, competition will tend to
drive the discriminating employers out of business.

This is hardly an ideal situation from the viewpoint of the
minority—they would be better off with no discrimination. But at
least this aspect of the free market tends to reduce the injury which
would otherwise accompany discrimination.

Things are far worse for the minority victimized by government
discrimination. For one thing, the incomes of prejudiced bureaucrats
and politicians are protected from market forces. Their incomes do not
tend to fall, as they do for prejudiced businessmen in the private sector.

The Freeman, January 1989. Reprinted in *The Lincoln Review: A Quarterly
Journal* 9, no. 3 (Spring-Summer 1989).

For another, civil servants do not run the risk of bankruptcy at the hands of non-discriminating competitors—their jobs are guaranteed.

Consider, for example, the "back of the bus" rules which discriminated against blacks in the South. This aspect of Jim Crow was part and parcel of government. The buses were part of the public sector; they were subsidized, and no competition was allowed. As a result, blacks had to suffer discrimination for many years, until the "back of the bus" rules finally were changed through massive demonstrations. Had blacks been told that they could ride only in the back of the bus in a market situation, other bus companies would have been formed, and would have enjoyed an inside track in competing for black customers.

Sometimes discrimination in the public sector is so well camouflaged that few people realize it is taking place. For example, the Hutterites were victimized by discriminatory legislation in the Canadian province of Alberta that did not even mention them by name! These people commonly live in colonies of 100 families or more. But the economics of farming in this part of the prairie are such that each colony needs two or three square-mile sections to support itself. An Alberta law which restricted holdings by size thus made it very difficult for the Hutterites to form colonies.

But well hidden public discrimination is by no means limited to rural areas. In Vancouver, there is a crackdown on illegal suites, and a ban is in the works for second kitchens in areas zoned for single-family occupancy. None of the laws mentions the Sikh community by name; nonetheless, this spate of legislation singles out the East Indian community for discriminatory treatment. The reason is not difficult to fathom. Like the Hutterites, Sikhs live in very large groups. According to Gurnam Singh Sanghera of the East Indian Workers Association of Canada, many ethnic communities live with three or four generations under one roof—and with an extended family in each generation of aunts, uncles, cousins, and so on.

Were the private sector discriminating against the Sikhs or Hutterites, these groups could find accommodations, albeit perhaps at slightly higher prices. But when they are victimized in the public sector, their plight is far more serious. They must convince a majority of the electorate—many of whom are hostile to them—of the injustice in discriminatory laws. History tells us this is no easy task.

Given that public-sector discrimination is far more harmful to minorities than is private discrimination, those who sympathize with racial and ethnic victims should think twice before entrusting human rights to the state. The market is a far better alternative.

17. STABBING THE HUTTERITES IN THE BACK

ALBERTA'S TREATMENT OF ITS HUTTERITE COMMUNITIES GIVES the lie to any residual claim it may have as a bastion of free enterprise and fair play.

The Hutterites are the followers of non-conformist Protestant martyr Jacob Hutter. Since arriving in Alberta in 1918, they have founded 110 communal farm colonies throughout the province. The Hutterites live on an extended family or communal basis. They are quiet, law-abiding, and God-fearing citizens. They pay their taxes, don't brawl in public, and don't make pests of themselves to their neighbors. On the contrary, they keep to themselves.

Nevertheless, they have a history of persecution in Alberta. According to the 1944 Communal Property Act, their colonies were limited to 10 square miles in size. Now this may not sound like much of an interference to most city folk. It sounds like limiting the average middle class family to no more than 25 Mercedes-Benz limousines. But such a law has serious repercussions in Alberta, where the typical farm works on two-, three- and even four-square-mile sections. A cutoff point of 10 square miles thus severely limits the number of families who may join a given colony, at a level far below the size the Hutterite community would otherwise take.

Compiled from a series that was published in *Grainews* (Winnipeg, Manitoba): "Stabbing the Hutterites in the Back," October, 1983; "Part 1, The Hutterite Question," February 28, 1984; "Part 2, The Hutterite Question," March 19, 1984; and "Is This Really a 'Free Market?'," March 31, 1984.

The Communal Properties Act struck a responsive chord in the minds of those who fear "business concentration." If large size is evil, it seems easy to nip it in the bud through legislation, But as the experience of the Hutterites shows, there is a strong connection between economic and political liberties. When government interferes with one thing a person has every right to do (grow, expand his business through completely legitimate practices, "concentrate") it violates rights in other ways, too.

Happily, this evil law was repealed in 1973. But ever since then, complaints about Hutterite expansion have multiplied. Last year, Municipal Affairs Minister Julian Koziak received a letter from Willow Creek farmer Edward Menzies, asking for legislation banning any new land purchases by Hutterites.

This abomination, of course, was resisted. After all, Alberta has not quite descended to blatant government discrimination on religious grounds. But what happened instead was even worse. In a measure that reached new heights of hypocrisy, a group of political hacks have asked the province to pass legislation limiting any "person, family, cooperative, corporation, church, or affiliated communal living group" from owning or controlling more than 10 percent of the land in any municipality. Responsible for this quest, by a 24-21 vote, were local politicians representing the 10 counties and districts between Calgary and the U.S. border.

The "beauty" of this request is that it never mentions the Hutterites by name! But there is more than one way to skin a cat. It is never explicitly stated in typical zoning law that its purpose is to discriminate against the poor. But by requiring that each home, say, must be built on a half-acre plot, the poor are effectively precluded from entry. As shown in a Fraser Institute book *Zoning: Its Cost & Relevance for the 1980s*, this hypocritical law may be even more effective than "honest" discriminatory legislation, in that it is difficult to prove it in violation of our human rights guarantees.

WHY IS ALBERTA PERSECUTING THE HUTTERITES?

Complaints are rife. These "communal-living groups" keep to themselves too much. They make their own clothing, grow most of the food they eat, don't patronize local bars, restaurants, pool halls, and bowling alleys. They pay school taxes, but as they attend their own colony schools, the locality does not receive the per-pupil provincial grants to which it would otherwise be entitled.

Regarding the latter charge, it would be easy to alter the law. In any case, it is the Hutterites, not their neighbors, who are the real victims here. They are forced to pay double for education: once for their own schools, and a second time via school taxes for other people's children.

As to the former, it is just hard cheese on the Alberta retailers. This, after all, is one of the risks of doing business. Passing discriminatory legislation against the Hutterites for this reason—or for any other—is unjustified. The sooner this blot on its record is erased, the sooner Alberta can reclaim its otherwise reasonably justified reputation as a land of freedom and free enterprise.

But, it will be objected, the Hutterites are a communal group not deserving of protection from free enterprise institutions. Stuff and nonsense. The Hutterites are a *voluntary commune* (similar to the monastery, the kibbutz in Israel, the food cooperative). No one is forced to join against his will. They may not live according to strict free market principles, but their underlying philosophy is entirely in keeping with that of *laissez-faire* capitalism. They live, after all, according to the principle that all social and economic action shall take place strictly on a voluntary basis.

The Hutterites do not seek special treatment. Nor do they deserve any. But simple and elemental justice requires that their private property rights be respected. That no law be passed which violates their right to buy and own property. Private property rights—the recent Canadian Constitution to the contrary notwithstanding—are the bulwark of all human rights and liberties.

The philosopher-economist Ludwig von Mises wrote of private property as follows:

> Private ownership of the means of production is the fundamental institution of the market economy. It is the institution the presence of which characterizes the market economy as such. Where it is absent, there is no question of a market economy.

Ownership means full control of the services that can be derived from a good. This catallactic notion of ownership and property rights is not to be confused with the legal definition of ownership and property nights as stated in the laws of various countries. It was the idea of legislators and courts to define the legal concept of property in such a way as to give to the proprietor full protection by the governmental apparatus of coercion and compulsion to prevent anybody from encroaching upon his rights.

However, nowadays, there are tendencies to abolish the institution of private property by a change in the laws determining the scope of the actions which the proprietor is entitled to undertake with regard to the things which are his property. While retaining the term private property, these reforms aim at the substitution of public ownership for private ownership. Private ownership means that the proprietors determine the employment of the factors of production, while public ownership means that the government controls their employment.

Private property is a human device. It is not sacred. It came into existence in early ages of history, when people with their own power and by their own authority appropriated to themselves what had previously not been anybody's property. Again and again proprietors were robbed of their property by expropriation.

The history of private property can be traced back to a point at which it originated out of acts which are certainly not legal. Virtually every owner is the direct or indirect legal successor of people who acquired ownership either by arbitrary appropriation of ownerless things or by violent spoilation of their predecessor.

However, the fact that legal formalism can trace back every title either to arbitrary appropriation or to violent expropriation has no significance whatever for the conditions of a market society. Ownership in the market economy is no longer linked up with the remote origin of private property.

These events in a far-distant past, hidden in the darkness of primitive mankind's history, are no longer of any concern for our day. For in an unhampered market society the consumers daily decide anew who should own and how much he should own. The consumers allot control of the means of production to those who know how to use them best for the satisfaction of the most urgent wants of the consumers. Only in a legal and formalistic sense can the owners be considered the successors of appropriators and expropriators. In fact, they are mandataries of the consumers, bound by the operation of the market to serve the consumers best. Under capitalism private property is the consummation of the self-determination of the consumers.

The meaning of the private property in the market society is radically different from what it is under a system of each household's autarky. Where each household is economically self-sufficient, the privately owned means of production exclusively serve the proprietor. He alone reaps all the benefits derived from their employment.

In the market society the proprietors of capital and land can enjoy their property only by employing it for the satisfaction of other people's wants. They must serve the consumers in order to have any advantage from what is their own. The very fact that they own means of production, forces them to submit to the wishes of the public. Ownership is an asset only for those who know how to employ it in the best possible way for the benefit of the consumers. It is a social function.[1]

BLOCK REPLIES TO CRITICS

A number of letters and commentaries have been published in the last several issues regarding my columns in *Grainews*. I have not answered them, preferring to finish a series on the economics and morality of the Christian Farmers Federation of Ontario, without interruption. But now that my analysis of the CFFO has been completed, it is time for a reply to all these letters.[2]

ALICE GREEN

I begin with a letter from Alice Green of Mossleigh, Alberta in the November *Grainews*, entitled "Block Knows Little of Hutterites." As

---

[1] Ludwig von Mises, *Human Action*, 3rd ed. (Chicago: Regnery, 1963), pp. 82–84.

[2] *Grainews* (Winnipeg, Manitoba), November 1983 to February 9, 1984.

a matter of fact, this title is quite accurate. I *do* know very little of the actual day-to-day lives of the Hutterite Brethren. I have never been to one of their farms, I have never met one in person, I have never even spoken to any Hutterite for any length of time. Actually, except for one brief phone conversation with a member of the Brethren who thanked me for my articles in *Grainews*, I have no relationship with the Hutterites whatsoever.

But I do know something of injustice. And I know that the personal habits, mores, folkways of a people are completely irrelevant to questions of justice. I did not know, personally, a single solitary Jew out of all the millions who were slaughtered in the Nazi concentration camps, nor one Ibo of all the millions killed in Biafra, nor any kulak of the millions murdered by Stalin, nor any of the millions of Chinese who perished during the Cultural Revolution in China. I do not know if these people locked their doors, or even if they had doors in the first place. All this is entirely irrelevant to the question of justice.

Moreover, it might well be the case that, were I to be introduced to these Jews, Ibos, Russians, or Chinese, I might actually have hated them. I might find their personal habits disgusting, their appearance unsavory, their smell repugnant, their intelligence non-existent, their personalities unappealing. And this, of course, applies to the Hutterites, to Alice Green, to the other citizens of Mossleigh, Alberta and, for good measure, to the entire staff of *Grainews*.

But this is all so irrelevant. If the personal or property rights of any of these people were violated, I would defend them. The lover of justice need not love, admire, or even like those victimized by injustice. He may know absolutely *nothing* of their personal lives; or, knowing them, may detest them. It is all beside the point. The only question is, have the rights of a people been violated? And if so, a moral analysis requires a critique of the injustice.

As to the Hutterites, they have been "stabbed in the back" by the Alberta officials, as I claimed in my column (*Grainews*, October 1983), and nothing regarding "the actual workings of the Hutterite Brethren," or whether or not they lock their doors, can change that fact by one iota.

PETER HOFER

Likewise, the Reverend Peter K. Hofer of Raymond, Alberta, writing in the January 13 *Grainews* also seeks to set Alice Green along the straight and narrow path. A Hutterite himself, the Reverend Hofer denied the charge of communism, and then went on to explain why his community does lock their doors.

I find this letter to be positively *dripping* in kindness, concern, humanity, and good sense. I, too, share Reverend Hofer's dismay that Alice Green should know so little of her neighbors, and empathize with them even less.

However, and perhaps Reverend Hofer can correct me if I am wrong, from what little I know of the Hutterites, I must disagree with his denial on the communism description. That is, as far as I am concerned, the Hutterites *do* practice a form of communism. On this question, I agree with Alice Green.

But there is nothing at all wrong with the form of communism practiced by the Hutterites! As a long-time advocate of the free market system, I hasten to explain this, lest misunderstanding arise.

As I view the long, broad scope of political economy, the main danger to innocent people comes from those individuals who seek to achieve their ends by force, or by the threat of force, violence, and aggression. Certainly, coercive communism, as practiced in Russia, mainland China, Cuba, Eastern Europe, and elsewhere behind the Iron Curtain are all examples of this. In these societies, people are forced to give their be-all and end-all to the state apparatus. Virtually all property has been seized by the government, and the people are little better than slaves to their masters.

But force, coercion, and institutionalized violence are by no means limited to communist countries. Western democracies (such as Canada) and right-wing dictatorships also utilize such measures, albeit to a lesser degree. Legislation underlying tariffs, Crown corporations, unions, rent control, marketing boards, business subsidies and bailouts, minimum wages, socialized medicine, and agricultural land reserves are just as much violation of person and property—even if to a lesser degree—as the government exploitation which occurs behind the Iron Curtain.

In stark contrast to coercive systems—whether of the left or the right—are voluntary ones. Here, all, or at least virtually all, interactions between adults take place on a strictly voluntary basis, with no violation of person or property. One such is the institution of free enterprise, where the scope of government is severely restrained and all capitalist "acts between consenting adults" are allowed. Although we human beings have never on this earth fully reached so exalted a state, present reasonably close examples might be Hong Kong and several other free trade zones; in the past, the United States and Great Britain during much of the 19th century.

Another such system is that of voluntary communism. Examples include the monastery, the kibbutz in Israel, the average Canadian family, various "utopias" and "communes" in the past, and, I am convinced, the present day Hutterites. In each of these cases is practiced the communist dictum "from each according to his ability, to each according to his need." There is nothing, repeat *nothing*, reprehensible about this dictum—provided it is done on a strictly voluntary basis. Take the typical family as a case in point. The working father may earn all the income, but certainly does not use it all up himself. The 2-year-old child, in contrast, earns no income at all; nevertheless it eats in accordance with its needs.

Voluntary communism, together with *laissez-faire* capitalism, has nothing to be ashamed of on moral and economic grounds. They can each hold up their heads, high. Far from enemies, they are merely opposite sides of the same voluntaristic coin. Together, they must battle state coercion, whether called State Capitalism or State Socialism. The point is, "left" vs. "right" is a red herring. The reddest and perhaps most misleading red herring in all political-economic theory.

The true debate is *not* between left and right. It is, rather, between voluntarism (whether of left or right) and coercivism (whether of left or right). The sooner this lesson is learned, the sooner can we make sense of our otherwise paradoxical political debates.

SOCIETY FOR THE PRESERVATION OF THE FAMILY FARM

I next take up a lengthy, unsigned letter written by someone purporting to be of the "Society for the Preservation of the Family Farm" (December, 1983 *Grainews*). But before answering in detail, I wish to recognize the eminent good sense of Al Nickel of Winnipeg, who wrote in *Grainews*, January 13, 1984, of the "strangeness" that this "society" has no officers willing to accept responsibility for the letter. Well, I suppose we live in strange times.

SPFF starts off by separating the ducks and geese: no one really complains that the Hutterites don't patronize local businesses. This claim, actually, is quite false. And for evidence, all we need do is turn to the pages of *Grainews* itself. For example, see letters by F.F. Wark and Ronald F. Bender (January 1983). The problem, in the view portrayed here, is not the Hutterites themselves, but their concentration. (Can't you hear the local bigot saying, "It's not individual Jews—or Catholics, blacks, Indians, French—that are the problem, it's that there are just so darn many of them around.") This is the "true" issue, the one which I have "skirted," according to SPFF.

Then this person launches into a description of a 1972 Alberta study on communal property, recommended "by nine prominent MLAs" who shall—surprise, surprise—remain nameless. What has this untitled "study" to say for itself? There are five "guidelines":

1. Contiguous Lands

Hutterites should buy land contiguously, not spread out all amongst normal people's holdings. "This guideline would prevent neighboring farms from experiencing inconvenience from being surrounded on three or four sides by Hutterite lands."

How nice. But why shouldn't the non-Hutterites be "guided" to plan *their* land purchases so as to conform to this contiguity principle? That is, why shouldn't non-Hutterites refrain from surrounding Hutterites on "three or four sides?" This contiguity idea sounds like nothing but the Nazi plan for ghettoizing Jews in pre-World War II Germany. With the

Jews all conveniently tucked away out of sight of the Aryans this reduced the "experience" of "inconvenience" on the part of the Germanic peoples.

2. Distance from Colonies

More of the same bigotry here. Hutterite colonies shouldn't be located too close to each other, lest this isolate small family farms, and thereby give them offense.

There is a problem here, even apart from the bigotry. Guidelines No. 1 and No. 2 are inconsistent with each other! No. 1 says, in effect, "Hutterites, locate all together, don't go spreading all around, now." But according to No. 2, these people should *not* locate next to each other. Rather, when possible, they should stay at least "15 miles" away from each other.

What kind of racists have we got here, anyway? Illogical ones, that's what. Even the South African government doesn't pass downright self-contradictory legislation.

As well, guideline No. 2, a real gem, this, states that "too many colonies located in a small area would mean that there would be a good deal of intercolony competition for market, a situation which the colonies themselves would prefer to avoid."

There are two difficulties here. First, try as I might, I just can't make sense of this gobbledygook. I am simply unable to understand what "competition for market" is. And even if it actually meant something, I cannot fathom, for the life of me, why Hutterites would provide more such "competition" to each other than would non-Hutterite farmers.

Second, if the "colonies themselves would prefer to avoid" this situation (whatever the devil it is) why, pray tell, do we need a guideline to tell them to do what is, in any case, in their best interest?

3. Size of Colonies

Small is beautiful, seems to be the message here. The Hutterite holdings shouldn't get too large. Eight sections seems to be about right, according to the Hutterites themselves (the Lehrerleut and Dariusleut sects).

Fiddlesticks. Why should any group of people consent to size limits of their land holdings? Suppose we were to construct guidelines along similar lines pertaining not to Hutterites, but to Anglicans, Catholics, members of the United Church, people who like hockey, bowling, or curling. Is there any doubt that were such guidelines offered, those responsible would be run out of Canada on a rail of the type they so richly deserve?

4. Activities of Land Agents

Real estate land agents should consult with "the liaison officer before purchasing land in the name of the Hutterites." Another legal violation of the rights of a downtrodden minority. Is there to be no privacy for these people? On what ground are they singled out for special violations of their rights? On the ground that they annoy other people? Which of us is willing to throw the first stone on that particular issue?

5. Local Consultation

Before setting up a new colony, the Hutterite Brethren should "consult" with the local municipal authorities. Not that the "Select Committee" would interfere with the property rights of the Hutterites. Oh, no! Perish the thought! Pay it no mind! Of course not! However would we have supposed that to be the case? It's just that many of the "problems encountered" in such circumstances could be avoided. Come, let us all sit down and reason together, the lion and the lamb, the fox and the chicken...

There is a saying: "The lion and the lamb may lie down together peacefully, but the lamb won't get too much rest." True. Too true. Sit down and consult, indeed. Why don't we pass a law saying that Progressive Conservatives or Liberals or NDPers have to sit down and "consult" with municipal authorities before buying land? Because such legislation would be a violation of their civil liberties, that's why!

To answer the SPFF's initial question: No, sir, I have not taken the time to read this 1972 study on communal property in Alberta. But if you, or any other *Grainews* reader, would send me a copy of this bilge, I would certainly read it (no matter how distasteful) and then, perhaps, devote a future "Understanding Free Enterprise Economics" column to eviscerating it. I'm far more than passing curious about this document. I would dearly love to learn how much taxpayer money was spent on creating it, among other things.

After regaling us with these five guidelines, SPFF plaintively calls for "a little voluntary cooperation," and for reducing "tensions." But there is an iron fist in this velvet glove: a law limiting a person or group to owning 10 percent of the land in any municipality. Let's give one Ted Menzies credit for this abomination; it "applies fairly and equally to all."

Well, I've got another bright idea which "applies fairly and equally to all." Let's string up the members of all organizations with initials SPFF based in Drumheller, Alberta. What could be fairer? It applies to *all* such groups. It doesn't single out any one group. Nonsense. One need not mention proper names in order to single out certain persons or groups. There are always "objective specifications" which apply to only those one wishes to control.

Yes, indeed, I'm a do-gooder, "wanting to protect a minority's rights." Of course, the majority has rights as well. But not, repeat, *not*, to legislatively prohibit or interfere with a minority group member's right to purchase land from willing sellers at mutually agreeable prices.

Nor can I accept the view that, in order to talk sense about problems arising in Alberta, one must live there. Truth is truth, regardless of who states it or where he happens to live. If my analysis is correct, this is a matter of evidence, of logic, of intellectual rigor—not a matter of geography.

What of SPFF's parting shot: that, "at this rate of expansion," the communal groups will soon own the majority of improved land in Alberta? If this is, indeed, the pattern and it continues in full force (both highly doubtful statements), well, then, so be it. If non-communal Alberta farmers are willing to sell their holdings to the Brethren, it only means that they value the sale price more than their land. Under such circumstances (the *only* circumstances in which the proportion of communal land can rise), a prohibition of these purchases would not only harm the Hutterites, it would hurt the family farmers as well.

F.F. WARK

Mr. Wark of Mossleigh, Alberta (January 13 *Grainews*) takes great delight in reminding us that the Hutterites are pacifists—that they refuse, on religious grounds, to participate in wars. Would he contend that all such people be penalized by not being allowed to own land in Alberta, that bastion of free enterprise, private property rights and freedom? If so, why not lock them up and be done with it? If not, what is the relevance of their pacifist beliefs to the land question, except to use as an underhanded smear against them?

Taking the stance of spokesman for Vulcan County, Mr. Wark declares that the seven colonies now located there (and rumors of two more) "should be more than our share." "Our" share? Indeed. Mr. Wark speaks as if he, himself, personally owns *all* the land in Vulcan County. As if the land for the existing seven colonies were given to the Hutterites, free of charge, out of the goodness of Mr. Wark's blessed heart.

And now those ungrateful Hutterite wretches, what do they do? Why, greedy pigs that they are, they demand even more largesse of the poor, put-upon Mr. Wark. But this worthy, although exceedingly generous man, even charitable to a fault, as it were, has had enough. "No," he declares, seven colonies is quite enough, thank you. If these welfare cases, these bums, want more free land, let them go and beg elsewhere.

The facts, of course, are quite different. As we all know well and good, even city slickers from Vancouver know this, the Hutterites do not beg, whimper, and cry for their land. Rather, they go and purchase it, at prices the owners find acceptable. Nor do Mr. Wark and his ilk own all the land. True, some of the land is sold to the Brethren by absentee owners. But do people lose their legitimate land titles in free enterprise Alberta merely by moving away? Or by never venturing forth there in the first place?

It is time that Mr. Wark came down off his high horse and stopped posturing as the benefactor of all mankind. He, of course, is free to refuse to sell to the Brethren 'til the Heavens fall. But if his neighbors, the "traitors," decide to sell, that is none of his business. It is entirely up to them.

RONALD F. BENDER

Next to take up the cudgels in search of Hutterite blood is Mr. Ronald Bender of Hilda, Alberta (January 13 *Grainews*).

Mr. Bender's point has to do with "money-hungry" real estate agents, and their "smooth-talking, two-faced" supporters, who don't have the decency to go around asking if anyone else would like to buy land bid on by Hutterites.

First of all, we are all "money-hungry" here. On this side of the Garden of Eden, that is. Does Mr. Bender himself seek the *lowest* prices available for his farm produce? And when he goes shopping for a bag of feed, a new tractor or some chicken wire, does he seek to pay the *highest* price for an item of standard quality? He, too, then, is "money-hungry."

Second, why should a real estate agent go around asking for other bids on land to undercut his own client? An agent who did that would soon lose all his clients! And why do this only for Hutterites? Why not, as well, for Anglicans, Catholics, or members of the United Church, who are would-be land purchasers?

Next, Mr. Bender launches into a vitriolic attack on the Hutterites for keeping pigs, chickens, ducks, geese, dairy cows, and feeder cattle on their farms, right next to and upwind of his own, thereby "ruining his life."

Now this is a curious charge, indeed, for one farmer to make against another. Whatever else does one keep on a farm but these barnyard animals? Would Mr. Bender wish them to get rid of their present livestock and, instead, maintain crocodiles, hippopotamuses, elephants, kangaroos and brontosauruses?

Mr. Bender's forefathers may have homesteaded Canada, but they subsequently *sold* parts of their land holdings to newcomers. In any case, if length of tenure in this country is any criteria for legitimacy (and it is not!), then Mr. Bender and his ilk should be the ones to consider going elsewhere. For there were people here *long* before the first white settlers arrived from Europe and elsewhere.

The remainder of Mr. Bender's letter is so venomous, mean, petty, and nasty that an appropriate answer has no place in *Grainews*, a decent, respectable family newspaper.

MARY GILBERTSON

It is, indeed, a pleasure to comment on the letter written by Mary Gilbertson of Hughenden, Alberta (February 28 *Grainews*). She, too, is a neighbor of the Hutterites. But, unlike Mr. Bender, she, it would appear, believes in a good-neighbor policy.

Moreover, she makes an insightful point on farmland prices and the family farm; one, I confess, which I failed to note. She points out that, what with high farm prices and interest rates, the children of many farming families are being forced to seek work in the cities. The Hutterites, however, are an exception! There, thanks to help from parent colonies, the young people can remain on the farm.

Now, as is clear from numerous of my "Understanding Free Market Economics" columns, I hold no particular brief for family farming. In my view, it should sink or swim in fair and unbridled competition with all other institutional arrangements. However, it is good to note that the Hutterites are successfully contending with commercial farming, holding their own and even expanding, in scrupulously fair competition.

Her views on education are exactly my own. Public education, in many cases, is a sham and a disgrace. Why should the busy, productive, happy, and skilled Hutterites be forced to waste their time on it? More to the point, why are they now forced to pay for it, when they don't use it?

It is the same with communism. In the same way that I sought to distinguish between the different types of communism on theoretical grounds, Gilbertson does so on practical grounds. As she so eloquently tells it, just as she and her family fled Romania to escape communism, so did the communalistic Hutterites flee, "to start out in a land they felt offered them peace."

Nor does Gilbertson shrink from taking on the pacifism issue, showing that, even though they refuse to bear arms, the Hutterites can still serve this country. And what, she asks, of the American draft dodgers?

Altogether, it was a pleasure to read this letter and an honor for me to be associated with the views of this woman.

PAUL E. GAUTHIER

Mr. Paul E. Gauthier of Lorette, Manitoba weighs in with a letter (Feb. 9 *Grainews*) not, however, related to the Hutterites. Instead, he is unhappy with some of my other columns. He begins his critique with the assertion that a free market never has existed—except in the minds of some economists, such as myself. This, insofar as it goes, is perfectly correct. A pure, free, pristine free market has never existed throughout all of human history, and probably never will.

Mr. Gauthier, moreover, is right on target in pointing out, as impediments to free enterprise, government grants of monopolistic privileges, such as the British India Tea Company, government financing of "private" companies, guild-like trade associations, and labor unions. These are all incompatible with free enterprise.[3]

But so what? Mr. Gauthier wants to derive from the undisputed fact that the marketplace has never fully existed, the highly dubious conclusion that this is an undesirable goal. But this does not follow logically at all. Just because something, call it X, has never existed, does not mean that X is undesirable!

Perfect good health, immense riches for everyone, perfect marriages, perfect golf games (a score of 18, for an 18-hole golf course) have never existed either. Does this mean that people should stop striving for them? No, of course not.

Similarly, the fact that a system of full free enterprise has not so far come into existence should not make us scorn this state of affairs. Rather, we should double, and redouble again, our efforts to bring it about. For by ridding our economic system of government interferences (tariffs, marketing boards, bureaucratic red tape, monopoly privileges) we can enhance freedom *per se*, as well as increase the chances of attaining our other goals (such as better health and more prosperity).

Mr. Gauthier then attempts to justify subsidies to agriculture, on the ground that they are in support of renewable resources. In this way, we can keep our non-renewables (such as iron, coal, gas, and oil) safely to ourselves.

This is a strange view, indeed. First of all, these so-called non-renewables are only in fixed supply in the sense that no more of them are being *created*. Additional sources, however, are continually being *discovered*. And it may well be, who knows, that before present stocks are exhausted, some of these may become obsolete, perhaps due to alternatives such as nuclear energy. Even if not, it

---

[3] There is one exception, however. The fact that many companies have government charters does not necessarily make them illegitimate. For an amplification of this view, see Robert Hesson, *In Defense of the Corporation* (San Francisco, Calif.: Hoover Institution Press, 1980.)

is economically unjustified to insist on no utilization whatsoever of non-renewable resources.

Does it make any sense, in this regard, to urge Mr. Gauthier's advice on the Arabs, as a means of improving their economic condition? Hardly. And if it makes sense to the Arabs to export their non-renewable (but continually increasing, due to new explorations) oil reserves, why is this calamity for Canada?

But let's forget all about new discoveries and possible obsolescence before depletion. These are only minor points.

The major issue is, even if a resource is in strictly fixed supply and will *always* be needed, it *still* can make sense to export it. The only question is *price*. If we can get enough money for this irreplaceable and precious item, nay, more than enough, then surely it pays to sell it, and to buy the other goods and services more valuable to us which these funds alone make possible. If not, no one would sell it anyway, and we wouldn't need government regulations to deter us.

So the question related by Mr. Gauthier is one of *price*, not one of *principle*.

This reminds one of a story told by George Bernard Shaw. A man approached a woman and asked her if she would go to bed with him for $1,000,000. After mulling over this offer, in all its ramifications, she accepted. Whereupon the man asked the woman, would she go to bed with him for $2? At this point the woman drew herself up haughtily, refused, and said, "What kind of woman do you take me for?" And the man's reply? "We have already established *that*, madame, we were merely haggling about price."

Just like the woman in the story, Mr. Gauthier's objection to exporting non-renewable resources is merely a dispute about *price*. His objection in *principle* to such exports vanishes upon the scrutiny of economic analysis.

Nothing daunted, however, Mr. Gauthier presses onward. Next, he treats us to a quote on speculation from *Economics in One Lesson* by Henry Hazlitt, a disciple of the great Ludwig von Mises. For this, we can only thank him. Surely, the world is a better place when it contains more of Hazlitt's economic analysis.

But then, Mr. Gauthier turns on us. He declares, in effect, that Hazlitt is wrong in stating the speculator, on average, loses money and thus, in effect, although not by intention, ends up subsidizing the consumer. Anyone who believes this swill has had a few bricks knocked off his otherwise full load, perhaps by West Coast air currents and inversions, says Mr. Gauthier.

The point is, it is not impossible for the *average* speculator, on net balance, to make financial losses. "Hope springs eternal," "there is a sucker born every day" are statements which have withstood the test of time. The speculator class is composed of professionals, who rarely lose money, and amateurs, who do, eventually, more often than not. (If they don't, they usually become professionals.) Surely, there should be no mystery about the professionals continually making profits, while the amateurs lose. This is an everyday occurrence. And where would the amateurs get their money from? Rich parents? Possibly, but not necessarily.

The point is, this category is composed of a continually changing number of people. They earn their money elsewhere, wherever, lose it in speculation, retire, and make way for new losers who conform to the same pattern. There is nothing incongruous about this. Indeed, the evidence suggests that it is so.

A word or two about the economics and ethics of bigotry may not be amiss in this rejoinder. As must be clear from the foregoing, I find bigotry personally repugnant. Nevertheless, bigots, too, have rights. It might be very nice if we all treated each other with respect, cordiality and kindness. Unfortunately, we do not. Bigots, it would appear, "we shall always have with us."

But it is important, vitally important, to distinguish between two types of bigotry. According to one type, call it coercive bigotry, anything goes. The bigot will resort to lynching, torture, kidnapping, fire bombing, rape, what have you.

In less-extreme cases, the coercive bigot will launch less serious physical attacks upon persons (and their property) in the despised group: assault and battery, theft, relatively minor depredations, such as slashing their tires and burning crosses. But what qualifies a person of either category as a coercive bigot is his willingness to use force, or the threat of force, against his victims.

I do not for a moment believe that any letter writer to *Grainews* falls into either of these above defined categories of coercive bigotry. However, there is a third type of coercive bigot, which, sad to say, does encompass several letter writers. This is the person who advocates that *government* use its force and might to violate the rights of despised minorities.

For example, laws which prohibit (and interfere with) the Hutterites from buying land. Whether or not the Hutterites are ever mentioned by name in such legislation is completely beside the point. These bigots operate once removed from their victims. They do not, themselves, visit the power of the state apparatus against their victims. But they are coercive bigots for all that, because they are the instruments by which unjustified force is used upon their victims.

The Germans who voted for the Nazis are also coercive bigots of this third category, although their guilt is perhaps of a lower order than those who actually perpetrated the killing of the Jews and other non-Aryans. The legislators who enacted the laws forbidding and interfering with Hutterite land purchases are coercive bigots—although, of course, guilty of far less serious a crime than the Nazis—because they unleashed the force of law upon innocent victims.

With regard to coercive bigots, as defined, there is no ethical argument in their behalf, whatever. And this applies to all three types of coercive bigots: the murderer, the petty thief, and he who calls upon government regulations to do his dirty deeds.

But there is another type of bigot as well. Call him, for purposes of identification, the non-coercive bigot. This is a far more complex and subtle case than the ones treated above. The non-coercive bigot may hate and revile the members of the minority group as much as, or even more than, the coercive bigot. But of one thing he is determined: Never, not in any manner, shape or form, shall he either himself launch physical force against the object of his wrath, nor shall he call upon government to do this for him.

What, then, may the non-coercive bigot do? Well, in the case of the Nazi, he may goosestep. He may carry Nazi insignia on his person, he may sing Nazi songs (but not so loudly as to constitute a threat, or even an annoyance, to his victims. For example, he could do all these things in the privacy of his own home). In short, he may do anything and everything to express his hatred and indignation—except for launching attacks of physical aggression, or asking the government to do so, against the objects of his hatred.

In the case of the Hutterites, the non-coercive bigot could boycott them. He could refuse to sell land (or anything else) to Hutterites. He could refuse to buy from them. He could discriminate against them in various and sundry ways. When he saw them on the street, he could "cut them dead."

He could even enter into restrictive covenants with other like-minded people, agreeing never to sell land to Hutterites—offering similarly (non-coercively) bigoted neighbors and friends first rights of refusal on any land he might ever be tempted to sell to a Hutterite.

Now, what are we to make of this non-coercive bigot? From a moral standpoint, hateful as he is, he must at least be distinguished from the coercive bigot. For he refuses, at all cost, to use force on his victim. More, he will not even petition that others do so.

As well, any ethical analysis of the non-coercive bigot must also reckon with the fact that the Hutterites, or other such people, simply have no right to demand of the bigot that he cease his hatred and befriend them.

The Hutterite, of course, has a *moral* right to ask this but, if the non-coercive bigot refuses, it would be improper to put him in jail for the "offense" of merely "hating." (In other words, it would indeed be the highest form of justice to incarcerate the *coercive* bigot. But not for his *thoughts*. For his invasive *actions*.)

What of the economic analysis? Here, too, we insist that a distinction be made between the two different types of bigotry. In the case of the coercive bigot, the economic case is clear. The coercive bigot is no less than a *disaster* for the downtrodden. Not only is there a direct threat to his property, as important as that is, but his very person is in danger as well.

But the (economic) case of the non-coercive bigot is far from clear. In a Fraser Institute book entitled *Discrimination, Affirmative Action, and Equal Opportunity*, the full economic analysis is laid out. It shows definitively and authoritatively that the haters, the non-coercive bigots, are virtually powerless to reduce the economic fortunes of their intended victims. As well, two prominent contributors to that volume, professors Thomas Sowell and Walter Williams, have shown this to be the case in a series of other publications.

It is for this reason that our Canadian human rights industry has been so far off base. They have been deathly silent regarding the outrageous examples of *coercive* bigotry practiced upon the Hutterites, as exemplified by the Alberta legislation interfering with their rights to purchase land. Indeed, they have concentrated on prosecuting non-coercive bigots—those who supposedly "discriminate" in hiring.

But, such non-coercive bigots are unable to effectively harm their intended victims—in the free enterprise system, or even in the private sector of a mixed economy.

THE ECONOMICS OF DISCRIMINATION

IN THE FIRST PART OF THIS BOOK, WE SAW THAT DISCRIMINATION occurs in many ways, shapes, and forms. Often, these forms of discrimination are ironic or even hypocritical.

Yet, many well-meaning people insist that the real problem associated with discrimination is in its economic effects. They bring forth reams of statistics and studies showing that whites are paid more than blacks, men earn more than women, tall people are paid more than short, and so forth. In light of such statistics, they argue, government needs to step in and "solve" the problem.

What such people fail to realize is that there are clear and distinct economic effects on firms that engage in discrimination. In effect, the free market punishes firms that routinely underpay particular classes of employees, thereby providing economic incentives to end such activity.

This section of the book includes four articles—two long and two short—that explain how the market weeds out certain forms of discrimination. Further, these articles will explain why other forms of discrimination should be welcomed. In addition, they will show why many government programs ostensibly designed to alleviate the problems simply make things worse.

18. ECONOMIC INTERVENTION, DISCRIMINATION, AND UNFORESEEN CONSEQUENCES

GOVERNMENT INTERVENTION IN SUCH ISSUES AS HUMAN RIGHTS, discrimination, affirmative action, and equal pay for equal work is commonly seen as productive, efficient, and just—in a word, as on the side of the angels. On the other hand, businessmen, employers, the marketplace, and the profit system are often viewed as the "devil" in the scenario as far as racial, sexual, and other prejudices are concerned. Evidence cited for these evaluations is black-white and male-female earnings differentials, discriminatory behavior on the part of private employers, and the widely trumpeted good intentions of those charged with administering human rights programs. The government, in short, is seen as part of the solution to the predicament of minorities; the private sector is viewed as part of the problem.

Yet, at least with regard to several well-known and highly acclaimed public sector initiatives, this conventional wisdom is suspect. To show this, we will consider the argument that affirmative action, equal pay for equal work, and various anti-discrimination measures have boomeranged: although specifically created to help people who have been the object of discrimination, they have had unintended and negative consequences. We shall also deal with such programs as minimum wage laws, anti-usury provisions, zoning, and rent control

Originally appeared in *Discrimination, Affirmative Action, and Equal Opportunity*, ed. Walter Block and Michael A. Walker (Vancouver, British Columbia: Fraser Institute, 1982), pp. 101–25, notes pp. 240–51.

legislation. While not purposefully aimed at alleviating minority group suffering, these have, nevertheless, had the very opposite results from those intended, and the ills have particularly focused on society's most downtrodden minority group members.

MINIMUM WAGE LAWS

The avowed intention of minimum wage laws is to raise the wage levels of workers at the bottom of the employment ladder. Instead, the actual effect of such legislation has been to cut off the bottom few rungs of this ladder, thus making it far more difficult for lesser skilled workers to achieve high or even moderate-paying jobs.

The explanation for this is straightforward. If, for example, the law compels that a minimum of $3.25 per hour be paid, the employer will suffer grievous losses if he hires a worker with a productivity of, say, $1.25 per hour: the firm will have to forfeit the $2.00 per hour differential between the $3.25 it must pay and the $1.25 value it receives. Naturally, under such circumstances, the employer will be extremely reluctant to hire such an employee. And the fate of low-productivity workers is thus clear—unemployment.

Without the minimum wage law, such a worker could be *employed* at $1.00 or $1.25 per hour, and not *unemployed* at the relatively exalted wage of $3.25—where his actual earnings are, of course, nil (excluding unemployment insurance). Worse, he is thus precluded from learning the skills necessary to command entrance to the higher wage brackets. Under this law, the worker must already be worth $3.25 per hour or more to be employed at all. Thus, the minimum wage law cuts off the bottom rungs of the employment ladder.

COMPENSATING DIFFERENTIALS

What does this have to do with discrimination against racial and other minorities?

Let us assume (1) a minimum wage level of $3.25 per hour, (2) two young lads—one white, one black—each with productivity of $3.25 per hour, competing for the same job, and (3) a white employer prejudiced against hiring blacks. Under such, perhaps typical, circumstances it is easy to see that the white lad will easily be able to out-compete the black for the job. The two prospective employees are economically indistinguishable, and the employer can indulge his taste for discrimination at no cost to himself.

In the absence of the minimum wage law, however, the traditional economic weapon of the downtrodden can come into play: his willingness and ability to accept a lower wage offer. If the white youngster insists on $3.25 per hour, but his black competitor is willing to work for only $3.10, $2.50, or $1.90 per hour, or even less, then it is not at all clear that the white will be hired, even by an employer prejudiced against blacks.

More realistically, and unfortunately, the sad fact is that the productivity of the white youth is likely to be greater than that of the black. The reasons for this are well known. They include differential educational, cultural, and motivational backgrounds, as well as preparation, related work skills, breakdowns of the family unit, and a host of other unquantifiable phenomena.[1] But the effects of the minimum wage law are painfully obvious: if the average productivity of white youth is, say, $3.25 per hour compared to $3.00 per hour or less for black youth (each with some variance), and the law requires that no less than $3.25 be paid in wages per hour, it is easy to see that the black youth will less likely be hired than the white. And this result stands even on the assumption that all employers are "color-blind" (i.e., they seek only to maximize profits). For the law penalizes employers who hire black youngsters (their expected loss is 25 cents per hour) relative to those who hire whites (no expected loss in this numerical example).

The statistical record more than bears out the contention that the

---

[1] See E. Franklin Frazier, *The Negro in the United States* (New York: Macmillan, 1957); E. Franklin Frazier, *Negro Youth at the Crossways* (New York: Schocken, 1967); Leslie H. Fishel, Jr., and Benjamin Quarles, eds., *The Black American* (Glenview, Ill.: Scott Foresman, 1967); Franz Fanon, *The Wretched of the Earth* (New York: Grove Press, 1963); Henrietta Buckmaster, *Let My People Go* (Boston: Beacon Press, 1969), pp. 103–04; Timothy Thomas Fortune, *Black & White: Land, Labor, & Politics in the South* (New York: Arno Press, 1969), pp. 30–31; Frances Fox Piven and Richard A. Cloward, *Regulating the Poor* (New York: Random House, 1971); William H. Grier and Price M. Cobbs, *Black Rage* (New York: Basic Books, 1968); Claude Brown, *Manchild in the Promised Land* (New York: New American Library, 1965).

minimum wage law creates teenage unemployment for both whites and non-whites, but especially for the second group. In 1948, for example, when the effective minimum wage rate was much lower, and when racial prejudice was more widespread, marked, and virulent than today, white teenage unemployment in the U.S. was 10.2 percent, while *black* teenage unemployment was only 9.4 percent. Today, in a much less discriminatory epoch, but where teenagers are "protected" by a more stringent minimum wage law, white youth unemployment is 13.9 percent, while black youth unemployment is an astounding and shameful 33.5 percent.[2]

---

[2] U.S. Department of Labor figures, Bureau of Labor Statistics, for 1948 and 1979. The figure of 33.5 percent is an underestimate of the real human tragedy, for it is based only on black teenagers who are "actively seeking work." But there are workers who are discouraged after having failed to obtain employment and leave the labor force. These people are ignored in the unemployment figures!

There is a substantial body of information on the unemployment effects of the minimum wage law. For more information, see the following by Walter Williams: "Government Sanctioned Restraints that Reduce Economic Opportunities for Minorities," *Policy Review* (Fall 1977): 1–24; *Youth and Minority Unemployment*, commissioned by the U.S. Congress, Joint Economic Committee, 95th Congress, 1st Session (Washington, D. C.: Government Printing Office, 1977); "The New Jim Crow Laws," *Reason* (August 1978), pp. 16–23; "Minimum Wage Maximum Folly," *Newsweek* (September 23, 1979), also in *Wall Street Journal* (September 13, 1979); "The Shameful Roots of Minority Unemployment," *Readers Digest* (October 1979).

Also see Thomas Sowell, *Race and Economics* (New York: David McKay, 1975), pp. 184–86; Walter Block, *Defending the Undefendable* (New York: Fleet Press, 1976), pp. 227–36; Finis Welch, "Minimum Wage Legislation in the United States," *Economic Enquiry* 12, no. 3 (September 1974): 258–318; Henry Hazlitt, *Economics in One Lesson* (New York: Harper & Row, 1946), chapter 18; Douglas K. Adie, "Teen-Age Unemployment and Real Federal Minimum Wages," *Journal of Political Economy* 81, no. 2, part 2 (March–April 1973): 435–41; and Michael C. Lovell, "The Minimum Wage Reconsidered," *Western Economic Journal* 11, no. 4 (December 1973): 529–37.

Further, see Frank G. Steindl, "The Appeal of Minimum Wage Laws and the Invisible Hand in Government," *Public Choice* 14 (Spring 1973): 133–36; Frank G. Steindl, "More on Minimum Wages and Political Clout," *Public Choice* 19 (Fall 1974): 137–38; Douglas K. Adie and Lowell Gallaway, "The

EQUAL PAY FOR EQUAL WORK

There are important implications to be drawn from this insight relevant to the spate of laws now being enacted and implemented in Canada and the U.S. known under the generic term "equal pay for equal work."[3] Although such interferences with the market economy are usually intended to benefit women, analysis of such laws can be applied to blacks, native peoples, francophones, or, for that matter, to redheads.

An essential point brought forth in the previous discussion was that the downtrodden group had one ace-in-the-hole: the ability to work for a lower wage than everyone else. Although perhaps the object of scorn, derision, and hatred, the minority member was able to claw his way back into economic respectability because he was so eminently *employable*; his willingness to work for less made him an economic attraction even to those most prejudiced against him.[4] Take this one advantage away, and he would have been at the mercy of those whose greatest pleasure consisted in his discomfiture.

But this is precisely the effect of "equal pay for equal work"

Minimum Wage and Teenage Unemployment: A Comment," *Western Economic Journal* 11, no. 4 (December 1973): 525–28; J. Houston McCulloch, "The Effect of a Minimum Wage Law in the Labour-Intensive Sector," *Canadian Journal of Economics* 7, no. 2 (May 1974): 317–39; E. G. West, "Vote Earning versus Vote Losing Properties of Minimum Wage Laws," *Public Choice* 19 (Fall 1974): 133–37; E. G. West and Michael McKee, *Minimum Wages: The New Issues in Theory, Evidence, Policy, and Politics* (Montreal: Economic Council of Canada and The Institute for Research on Public Policy, 1980).

[3] See in this regard *Toronto Globe and Mail* (March 4, 1980), p. B2; also *Toronto Globe and Mail* (March 7, 1980); Murray N. Rothbard, *Power and Market* (Menlo Park, Calif.: Institute for Humane Studies, 1970), pp. 157–60; *Alston v. School Board of City of Norfolk*, 112F 2d 992 (4th Cir.), *certiorari* denied, 311 U.S. 693 (1940); *Financial Post* (May 15, 1980), p. 10.

[4] The analogue of biology is compelling. "Mother nature" often grants otherwise weak organisms a saving grace which enables them to survive: the skunk has its smell, the deer fleetness of foot, the porcupine quills, the chameleon the ability to change its skin color to blend in with the environment, and so forth. It seems that "mother economics" has granted her weakest children (the ugly, the different, the scorned, the hated) a similar grace: this ability to be attractive to employers (and hence customers) despite all other drawbacks.

(EPFEW) legislation. Although conceived with perhaps the best intentions, such laws banish, at one fell swoop, the ability of a group, in this case females, to counteract the economic discrimination they may suffer in modern society. The harm to the cause of women is immense, for EPFEW does not require that women be hired. It only mandates that *if* a woman is hired, she be paid the same as men of equal productivity. But what good is a law that can push female unemployment rates up through the roof while ensuring "equal pay" for jobs they don't have and will not be able to attain?[5] EPFEW legislation will create a field day for those who wish to drive women "back into the kitchen." Feminists support this only at the risk of whatever economic gains women have made in recent years.

Perhaps the starkest example of the operation of this particular economic law occurs in South Africa. In that racist society, job reservation laws are presently on the books, which, as the name implies, specifically reserve certain occupations for certain races. That is, the law compels that there be "white jobs," "black jobs," and so on.

But white racist labor union leaders, the beneficiaries of such legislation, are actually on record expressing a willingness to have job reservation laws abolished—*provided EPFEW laws are substituted in their place.*[6] With friends of EPFEW legislation such as Arrie Paulus, the head of the South African (whites only) Mine Workers Union, it surely needs no support of feminists.

---

[5] The government may then turn around and try to combat the rise in female unemployment (or unemployment) created by EPFEW. It may enact additional "equal opportunity" or "affirmative action" legislation enforcing hiring quotas on employers for women. If so, the felt need for such programs will have been brought about by its very own misguided EPFEW policies. As several of the essays in Walter Block and Michael A. Walker, eds., *Affirmative Action and Equal Opportunity* (Vancouver, British Columbia: Fraser Institute, 1982) make clear, this "cure" may actually be worse than the "disease."

[6] Leon Louw, "Free Enterprise and the South African Black" (address to Barclay's Executive Women's Club, Johannesburg, South Africa, July 31, 1980), p. 4.

ARBITRARINESS

Another difficulty is that "equal opportunity" is a subjective, not an objective, phenomenon.[7] Women do not come equipped with a little tag which indicates their productivity, once and for all, in a manner from which no dissent is possible. (Nor, of course, do men.) Productivity, rather, is a continually changing phenomenon which varies with, for example, education, intelligence, age, experience, presence or absence of complementary factors of production, which can only be partially quantified, as well as with such factors as motivation and determination, which are completely incapable of exact measurement.

Productivity must be estimated (or guessed at) by entrepreneurs, who do so every day, and lose money for each mistake they make. They are far more able to make such determinations accurately than are judges and juries who have little experience in this endeavor, and risk no personal funds if they err. Since they assume that productivity measurements are easily ascertainable, EPFEW laws are at variance with the facts. They are thus incapable of fair and non-arbitrary implementation.

THE EARNINGS GAP

This is not to say it is completely implausible to support the position that EPFEW laws are required. There is ample evidence to suggest that male and female compensation and promotion rates differ. For example, the overall female/male wage ratio for all employees in Canada was .485 in 1979. That is, females, on average, earned only 48.5 percent as much as males.[8] The question is whether or not this reflects an inherent problem in the labor market. The proponents of EPFEW apparently think so. But it is an error to conclude, from

---

[7] James Buchanan, *Cost & Choice* (Chicago: Markham Publishing, 1969), especially pp. 47–48; G.F. Thirlby, "Subjective Theory of Value and Accounting Cost," *Economica* 13 (February 1946): 32–49; Ludwig von Mises, *Human Action*, 3rd ed. (Chicago: Regnery, 1963), pp. 242, 395.

[8] A female/male income ratio of .485 can be derived from *Income Distributions by Size in Canada*, 1979, Statistics Canada, Catalogue 13-207 (Ottawa: Statistics Canada, 1979), p. 99.

such information, that the state of affairs is a result of conscious and hostile human design (i.e., employer discrimination against women), that this is disgraceful and unfair, and that therefore a determined effort on the part of government is required to "right these wrongs." Consider, in this regard, the statement of no less an authority than Dr. Ratna Ray, Director, Women's Bureau, Labour Canada:

> Of our three-part series—*Facts and Figures*—this part is the most critical, because it shows the patterns of earnings in the Canadian labour force. Readers will soon notice that women's earnings are still lagging disgracefully behind in a society in which "How Much Is That Doggy In The Window" pretty well rules our lives.
>
> Economic self-sufficiency for women? "We've only just begun!" Despite sporadic progress, there's a long way to go. Canadian employers, economic planners, and decision-makers should take a long hard look at these figures. Because they tell a shocking story, a story of shortsightedness and languorous efforts towards the utilization of human resources in the workforce. Our publication comes hard on the heels of the National Council of Welfare's report *Women and Poverty* which concludes that "After fifty years or so of unpaid, faithful service a woman's only reward is likely to be poverty."[9]

Such an interpretation, no matter how widespread, is far from proven.

The difficulty is that there are several alternative hypotheses which can explain why women's wages, incomes, and salaries lag behind

---

[9] Ratna Ray, *Women in the Labour Force: Facts and Figures*, Catalogue L 38-30/1977-2 (Ottawa: Department of Labour, Women's Bureau, 1977), page i. Other economic studies of interest in this regard include Alan S. Blinder, "Wage Discrimination: Reduced Form and Structural Estimates," *Journal of Human Resources* 8 (1973): 436–55; Morley Gunderson "Male-Female Wage Differentials and the Impact of Equal Pay Legislation," *Review of Economics and Statistics* 57 (1975): 462–70; Morley Gunderson, "Work Patterns," in *Opportunity for Choice: A Goal for Women in Canada*, ed. G. Cook (Ottawa: Statistics Canada, 1976).

Morley Gunderson, "Time Patterns of Male-Female Wage Differentials," *Relations Industrielles/Industrial Relations* 31 (1976): 57–71; R.A. Holmes, "Male-Female Earnings Differentials in Canada," *Journal of Human Resources* 11 (1976): 109–17; Ronald Oaxaca, "Male-Female Wage Differentials in Urban

those of men. When these are acknowledged, it is no longer necessary to resort to discrimination on the part of the employer, business prejudice, or "capitalism" as explanations for the male/female earnings gap.

Men and women differ in a wide range of economic, educational, and sociological characteristics, each of which exerts an independent effect, raising expected male incomes and reducing expected female incomes. For example, working men tend to be older[10] than women,

Labor Markets," *International Economic Review* 14 (1973): 693–709; Roberta Edgecombe Robb, "Earnings Differentials Between Males and Females in Ontario, 1971," *The Canadian Journal of Economics* 11, no. 2 (May 1978): 350–59; James E. Bennett and Pierre M. Loewe, *Women in Business* (Toronto: Financial Post Books, 1975).

Christina Maria Hill, "Women in the Canadian Economy," in *(Canada) Ltd.: The Political Economy of Dependency*, ed. Robert M. Laxer (Toronto: McClelland and Stewart, 1973), pp. 84–106; Lynn McDonald, "Wages of Work: A Widening Gap Between Women and Men," *Canadian Forum* (April/May 1975): 4–7; Neil MacLeod, "Female Earnings in Manufacturing: A Comparison with Male Earnings," *Statistics Canada, Notes on Labour Statistics*, 1971 (Ottawa: Information Canada, 1972).

Sylvia Ostry, "The Female Worker: Labour Force and Occupational Trends," in *Changing Patterns in Women's Employment: Report of a Consultation Held March 18, 1966* (Ottawa: Dept. of Labour Women's Bureau, 1966), pp. 5–24, 25–31; Sylvia Ostry, *The Female Worker in Canada*, Dominion Bureau of Statistics Census Monograph (Ottawa: Queen's Printer, 1968); Sylvia Ostry, "Labour Force Participation and Childbearing Status," in *Demography and Educational Planning*, Conference on the Implications of Demographic Factors for Educational Planning and Research, ed. Betty MacLeod, Monograph Series, no. 7 (Toronto: Ontario Institute for Studies in Education, 1970), pp. 143–56.

R.A.H. Robson, "A Comparison of Men's and Women's Salaries in the Academic Profession," Report to the Royal Commission on the Status of Women, *C.A.U.T. Bulletin* 17 (1969): 50–75; R.A.H. Robson and Mireille Lapointe, *A Comparison of Men's and Women's Salaries and Employment Fringe Benefits in the Academic Profession*, Canadian Association of University Teachers: Studies of the Royal Commission on the Status of Women in Canada, no. 1 (Ottawa: Information Canada, 1971); Gideon Rosenbluth, "The Structure of Academic Salaries in Canada," *C.A.U.T. Bulletin* 15 (1967): 19–27.

[10] The average age of all employed Canadian men was 37 years in 1980. This placed the typical man in the *highest* male earnings age bracket (35–44 years old). The average age of all employed Canadian women was 34 years in 1980. This placed the typical woman in the *fourth* highest *male* earnings

more highly concentrated in the higher-paying professions,[11] more
heavily unionized in the highly skilled and legislatively protected

---

age bracket (25–34 years old). See *The Labour Force*, Statistics Canada,
Catalogue 71-001, (Ottawa: Statistics Canada, 1980), page 75; and *Income
Distributions by Size in Canada, 1979*, Statistics Canada, Catalogue 13-207
(Ottawa: Statistics Canada, 1979), pp. 104–09.

[11] Occupational segregation such as shown in the table below cannot properly
be interpreted as the result of employer discrimination. After all, the employer
cannot hire a nurse as a doctor, nor a person with secretarial training as an
engineer or accountant.

	1971 Earnings	1971 % Male	1971 % Female	1978 Earnings	1978 % Male	1978 % Female
Actors	$39,555	89.9	10.1	$53,422	90.3	9.7
Dentists	25,828	95.2	4.8	45,985	94.2	5.8
Lawyers & Notaries	27,862	95.2	4.8	40,587	90.0(4)	10.0(4)
Accountants	18,631	84.8	15.2	33,440	96.2(5)	3.8(5)
Architects & Engineers	21,648	98.4	1.6	30,825	99.4(6)	0.6(6)
University Instructors(1)	14,700	83.3	16.7	27,235	85.1	14.9
Elementary School Teachers(1)	7,043(2)	17.7(2)	82.3(2)	17,309	33.2	66.8
Nurses(3)	6,934	4.2	95.8	16,037	2.0	98.0

(1) School years 1970–71 and 1977–78.

(2) This information covers eight provinces of Canada, excluding Quebec and Ontario.

(3) Registered nurses employed as nurses.

(4) These figures are rough estimates of the breakdown by sex, and are for
lawyers only.

(5) Figures on all self-employed accountants unavailable in 1978. Registered
membership list in 1978 of the Society of Management Accountants was
used instead.

(6) These figures are for engineers alone. Incomplete 1978 data on architects shows
a breakdown by sex of 95 percent male, 4.1 percent female. Statistics for Ontario
engineers in 1978 were unavailable; the 1981 count was used instead.

Sources: Earnings for self-employed doctors, dentists, lawyers and notaries, accountants, architects and engineers in 1971: *Taxation Statistics, 1973 Edition: Analyzing the Returns of Individuals for the 1971 Taxation Year*, Revenue Canada Taxation, Catalogue RV 44-1973(Ottawa: Revenue Canada, 1971), p. 13; in 1978: *Taxation Statistics 1980 Edition: Analyzing the Returns of Individuals for the 1978 Taxation Year*, Revenue Canada Taxation, Catalogue RV 44-1980 (Ottawa: Revenue Canada, 1971), p. 13; percentages of doctors, dentists, lawyers and notaries, accountants, architects and engineers by sex in 1971: *Census of Canada 1971, Occupation by Sex for Canada & Provinces*, Statistics Canada, Catalogue 94-717 (Ottawa: Statistics Canada, 1971), pp. 1–3; doctors and dentists in 1978: Health Information Division, Department of National Health and Welfare, unpublished statistics received from Revenue Canada Taxation, September 1980; lawyers: *Demographic Survey, 1979* (Ottawa: Canadian Bar Association, Young Lawyers Section, 1979), p. 5; accountants: unpublished material from the Society of Management Accountants; engineers: unpublished material from the Canadian Council of Professional Engineers; architects: unpublished material from the Royal Architectural Institute of Canada; elementary school teachers' earnings and percentages of elementary school teachers by sex in 1971: *1971 Census*, Statistics Canada, Catalogue 94-717 (Ottawa: Statistics Canada, 1971), pp. 2–3, Table 2; in 1978: *Salaries and Qualifications of Teachers in Public, Elementary, and Secondary Schools 1977, 1978*, Statistics Canada, Catalogue 81-202 (Ottawa: Statistics Canada, 1978), p. 35, Table 2; university teachers' earnings and percentages of university teachers by sex in 1971: *Salaries and Qualifications of Teachers in Universities and Colleges, 1970, 1971*, Statistics Canada, Catalogue 81-302 (Ottawa: Statistics Canada, 1971), p. 27, Table 1; in 1978: *Teachers in Universities*, Statistics Canada, Catalogue 81-241 (Ottawa: Statistics Canada, 1978), p. 27, Table 3; nurses' earnings and percentages of nurses by sex in 1978: *Nursing in Canada: Canadian Nursing Statistics, 1978*, Catalogue 83-226 (Ottawa: Canadian Nurses Association, 1978), pp. 37, 96–98; *Annual Salaries of Hospital Nursing Personnel, 1970*, Statistics Canada, Catalogue 83-218 (Ottawa: Statistics Canada, 1971), pp. 18–20, Table 1.

The *private* employer will not, generally speaking, be able to occupationally segregate equally well-trained people on the basis of sex (or any other criteria). Were the employer to try to do so, he would set up profit opportunities which, when exploited, would forestall any such attempt at occupational segregation. (For a more complete explanation, see the analysis of discrimination against redheads—which applies to occupational segregation as well—in "The Plight of the Minority," in *Discrimination, Affirmative Action, and Equal Opportunity*, ed. Walter Block and Michael A. Walker (Vancouver, British Columbia: Fraser Institute, 1982), pp. 9–11.

There are more plausible explanations for occupational segregation by sex than employer discrimination. These include differential ambitions, talents, tastes,

blue-collar industries,[12] and tend to work, to a greater degree, on a full-time, full-year[13] basis.

CORRECTIONS IN THE ESTIMATES

Not unexpectedly, when female/male income comparisons have been corrected for these factors, the ratio tends to rise. If working

---

attachments to the labor force, etc. A very interesting underlying explanation for all these phenomena is offered by Meredith M. Kimball, "Women and Success: A Basic Conflict?" in *Women in Canada*, ed. Marylee Stephenson (Don Mills, Ontario: General Publishing Co., 1978), p. 85, who says:

> We found, as did Horner, that fear of success imagery increases between grade eight and grade twelve for girls. Homer also found an increase between the first and last years of college. *Thus, in both high school and college years, fear of success is highest when women are making their most important occupational decisions.* The last year of high school is when the decision to go to college is finally made, and if a woman decides not to go to college, then she must decide between marriage or occupation or some combination of both. In college, it is in the final year that decisions about graduate or professional school as well as kind of position must be made, again at a time that a woman often must also make a decision about marriage. It seems that it is not so much that women see no value in successful achievement, but rather that they see successful achievement as conflict-provoking, precisely because success is both desired and threatening. [emphasis added]

[12] In 1978, the percentage of female Canadian union members was 28.7 percent; males comprised 71.3 percent of the membership. Source: *Corporations & Labour Unions Returns Act, Part II, Labour Unions*, Statistics Canada, Catalogue 71-202, p. 41. On the question of male/female productivity differentials, see Jacob Mincer and Solomon Polachek, "Family Investments in Human Capital: Earnings of Women," *Journal of Political Economy* 82, no. 2, part 2 (March 1974): 76–108.

[13] In 1980, 94.1 percent of employed Canadian males worked full time, 5.9 percent worked part time; 76.2 percent of employed Canadian females worked full time, 23.8 percent worked part time. In 1979, 72.9 percent of employed Canadian males worked 50–52 weeks, 27.1 percent worked 1–49 weeks; 60.1 percent of Canadian females worked 50–52 weeks, 39.9 percent worked 1–49 weeks. Source: *The Labour Force*, Statistics Canada, December 1980, p. 105, Catalogue 71-001; *Income Distributions by Size in Canada*, 1979, Statistics Canada, Catalogue 13-207, p. 112.

women are assumed to retain their own income levels, but to take on the same age pattern as working men, the female/male income ratio rises from .485 to .521; if we assume that females are divided among elementary and university teaching in the same manner as males, the ratio increases from .743 to .814; if the female/male income ratio is corrected in a similar manner for full-year or part-year status, it increases from .528 to .575. See Table 1.[14]

As important as these variables are, the strongest determinant of the so-called male/female earnings "gap" is none of these things. Rather, it is marital status, and the asymmetric effects of marriage on

TABLE 1 | ADJUSTED CANADIAN FEMALE-MALE INCOME RATIOS

	(1)	(2)	(3)	(4)	(5)	(6)
Adjustment made for	Annual Male Income	Annual Female Income (Before Correction)	Annual Female Income (After Correction)	Annual $ Gain to Females (3) / (2)	Female/ Male Income Ratio (Before Correction) (2) / (1)	Female/ Male Income Ratio (After Correction) (3) / (1)
Age Pattern	$15,143	$7,342	$7,593	$+251	.485	.521
Full Year/ Part Year Status	16,440	8,679	9.451	+772	.528	.575
University & Elementary School Employment Patterns	26,141	19,414	21,280	+1.886	.743	.814

Source: The Labour Force, December 1980, Catalogue No. 71-001, Statistics Canada, pp. 75–105. *Teachers in Universities*, Catalogue No. 81-241, Statistics Canada, p. 57. *Income Distributions by Size in Canada*, 1979, Catalogue No. 13-207, Statistics Canada, pp. 99, 104–09.

---

[14] These figures are derived from computations based on data cited for elementary school teachers' earnings and percentages of teachers by sex: *Salaries and Qualifications of Teachers in Public, Elementary & Secondary Schools, 1979–80*, Statistics Canada, Catalogue 81-202, p. 25; university

male and female earnings. That is, marriage increases male earnings, and reduces female earnings.[15]

This occurs for many reasons. Wives, to a greater degree than husbands, take on a higher and disproportionate share of child care[16] and the housework and homemaker tasks.[17] They are more likely to quit

---

teachers' earnings and percentages of university teachers by sex: *Teachers in Universities, 1978–1979*, Statistics Canada, Catalogue 81-241, p. 57. Note that while we have corrected the female/ male income ratio for several phenomena not related to discrimination, a still more accurate assessment would have to normalize for all of these variables, together, and include other variables such as continuity of employment, earned degrees, labor force participation, location, industrial concentration, public or private employment, productivity, seniority, as well as such imponderables as motivation, "stick-to-it-iveness," resourcefulness, ambition, expectations, etc.

[15] Thomas Sowell, *Affirmative Action: Reconsidered* (Washington, D.C.: American Enterprise Institute, 1975), pp. 23–34.

[16] Jesse Bernard, *Academic Women* (University Park: Pennsylvania State Univ. Press, 1964), pp. 220–26; Jesse Bernard, *The Future of Motherhood* (New York: Penguin Books, 1974), pp. 165–70; Bryan and Boring, *American Psychologist* 2 (January 1947): 18; Lee Rainwater, *And the Poor Get Children* (Chicago: Quadrangle Books, 1960), pp. 67–69; Wayne R. Bartz and Richard A. Rasor, *Surviving With Kids* (San Luis Obispo, Calif.: Impact, 1978), p. 147; Martin Meissner, "Sexual Division of Labour and Inequality: Labour and Leisure," in *Women in Canada*, pp. 166–74; Nancy Chodorow, "Being and Doing: A Cross Cultural Examination of the Socialization of Males and Females," in *Women in Sexist Society*, ed. Vivian Gornick and Barbara K. Moran (New York: Basic Books, 1971), pp. 183–84; Roslyn S. Willett, "Working in 'A Man's World': The Woman Executive," in *Women in Sexist Society*, p. 368; Jean Tepperman, "Two Jobs: Women Who Work in Factories," in *Sisterhood is Powerful*, ed. Robin Morgan (New York: Random House, 1970), pp. 115, 121.

[17] Gail C.A. Cook, "Opportunity for Choice: A Criterion," in *Opportunity for Choice: A Goal for Women in Canada*, ed. Gail C.A. Cook (Ottawa: Statistics Canada and C.D. Howe Research Institute), Catalogue IC 23-15/1976, p. 4; Gail C.A. Cook and Mary Eberts, "Policies Affecting Work," in *Opportunity for Choice*, p. 145; Richard A. Lester, *Antibias Regulations of Universities* (New York: McGraw-Hill, 1974), p. 39; Willett, "Working in 'A Man's World'," p. 368; Pat Mainardi, "The Politics of Housework," in *Sisterhood Is Powerful*, pp. 447–54; Jesse Bernard, *The Future of Motherhood*, pp. 157–65;

their jobs if their partner receives a better job elsewhere,[18] to interrupt their careers for domestic reasons,[19] to place their homes and families ahead of their jobs or professions,[20] and even to purposefully attempt to keep their earnings below that of their spouses.[21] It is

---

Kathryn E. Walker, "Time Used by Husbands for Household Work," *Family Economics Review* (June 1970): 8–10; M. Meisner, E.W. Humphries, S.M. Meis, and W.J. Scheu, "No Exit for Wives: Sexual Division of Labour and the Cumulation of Household Demands," *Canadian Review of Sociology and Anthropology* 12 (1975): 424–39.

[18] Barbara B. Reagan, "Two Supply Curves for Economists? Implications of Mobility and Career Attachment of Women," *American Economic Review* 65, no. 2 (1975): 102; Jacquelyn S. Crawford, *Women in Middle Management* (Ridgewood, N.J.: Forkner, 1977), p. 63.

[19] E.W. Burgess and Paul Wallin, *Engagement and Marriage* (New York: Lippincott, 1953), pp. 614, 618; and Reagan, "Two Supply Curves," p. 104. See also Beth Neimi, "The Female-Male Differential in Unemployment Rates," *Industrial and Labour Relations Review* 27, no. 3 (April 1974): 331–50.

[20] Alan E. Bayer, " Marriage Plans and Educational Aspirations," *American Journal of Sociology* 75 (1969): 239–44; Reagan, "Two Supply Curves," p. 103; Bernard, *The Future of Motherhood*, pp. 91, 151, 181; Jean Tepperman, "Two Jobs," p. 123; Betty Friedan, *The Feminine Mystique* (New York: Dell, 1974), p. 31; Meg Luxton, *More Than a Labour of Love: Three Generations of Women's Work in the Home* (Toronto: Women's Educational Press, 1980), p. 16; Margaret Luxton, "Urban Communes and Co-ops in Toronto," (M. Phil. dissertation, University of Toronto, 1973), cited in Luxton, *More Than a Labour of Love*; Ann Oakley, *Women's Work: The Housewife Past and Present* (New York: Vintage Books, 1976); Eli Zaretsky, *Capitalism, The Family, and Personal Life* (New York: Harper & Row, 1976), p. 17; Simone de Beauvoir, *The Second Sex* (New York: Vintage Books, 1974), p. 482.

[21] Let us imagine an experiment. We offer a large number of employed married couples the following option: jobs in city A, where the husband will earn $200,000 per year and the wife $150,000, or in city B, where the wife will earn $200,000 per year, and the husband $150,000. (The type of employment and the amenities of the cities are assumed to be identical in each case.) How many of the husbands would prefer city B? How many wives would prefer city A? Although there is only casual evidence on this, since such an experiment has not yet been done, one may speculate that there will be more wives who will prefer city A than there will be husbands who will prefer city

B. The motivations behind these choices may vary. Some husbands may feel "less of a man" if their wives earn more than they do; others may feel it is just "not fitting" that their incomes should be lower; some wives may feel less damaged psychologically from earning less than their spouses; others may subscribe to the societal pressures which teach, at a young age, that "nice girls don't outcompete boys." But whatever the reason, there is abundant anecdotal evidence that many women have great psychological and other personal difficulties in competing with men, and are thus, when married, more likely than men to purposefully keep their earnings below those of their spouses—with important implications for the low female/male earnings ratios for married people.

See, for example, Bernard, *Academic Women*, p. 216, who speaks of "a determined effort" on the part of academic women "not to outshine [their] husband[s]"; Vivian Gorlick, "Why Women Fear Success," in *Essays in Feminism* (New York: Harper & Row, 1978), p. 87, who reports the typical response of a woman who "deliberately lower[s] her academic standing ... while she does all she subtly can to help [her future husband]"; Dorothy Jongeward and Dru Scott, *Women as Winners* (London: Addison-Wesley, 1976), p. 15, who cites the following woman's statement about her and her husband as typical: "I would never take a job where I earned more than Bob. If I start being really successful, that means I'm making him less of a man"; Betty Friedan, *The Feminist Mystique*, pp. 29, 30, who discusses the contents of an early 1960s issue of *McCalls*, "the fastest growing of the women's magazines," which, in her opinion, "are a fairly accurate representation of the image of the American woman." The article in question describes a "nineteen-year-old girl sent to charm school to learn how to bat her eyelashes and *lose at tennis*" (emphasis added) by never "volleying to the backhand of male opponents." Betty Friedan also relates how she herself, as a young woman, gave up a graduate fellowship to study for a doctorate, upon being told by her male companion that "Nothing can come of this, between us. I'll never win a fellowship like yours" (pp. 62–63); Judith M. Bardwick and Elizabeth Douvan, "Ambivalence: The Socialization of Women," in *Women in Sexist Society*, p. 150, who discuss social pressures which interfere with pubescent girls' successfully competing against boys; Mary Ann Zasylycia-Coe, "Canadian Chief Librarians by Sex," *Canadian Library Journal* 38, no. 3 (June 1981): 162, who points to the lower marriage rate of female than male chief librarians, and states, "this would seem to indicate that more females than males perceive marriage and a high level position as incompatible"; Margaret Hennig and Anne Jardim, *The Managerial Women* (New York: Simon & Schuster, 1976), p. 23, who cite the difficulties undergone by women students in participating in the case study method at the Harvard

impossible to quantify the effects of such phenomena in driving a wedge between married male and female incomes, but there is little doubt that they are important.

The asymmetrical effects of marital status on earnings by sex can be seen by a perusal of Table 2, which abstracts from such variables as age, occupation, location, full time or part time, and unionization.

Here, the female/male income ratios diverge widely, based on marital status. Throughout the 12-year span covered, the married

MBA program, and attributes this, in part, to "their own doubts as to whether they could *or even wanted to compete with the men in the class* (emphasis added); Meredith M . Kimball, "Women and Success: A Basic Conflict?" in *Women in Canada*, pp. 73, 74, who tells us that "girls are socialized, especially from early adolescence on, to see achievement as unfeminine ... success for women has negative *as well as* positive value."

See also M.S. Horner, "Fail: Bright Women," *Psychology Today* 3 (November 1969): 36; M.S. Horner, "Femininity and Successful Achievement: A Basic Inconsistency," in *Feminine Personality and Conflict*, ed. J.M. Bardwick et al. (Belmont, Calif.: Wadsworth, 1970), p. 60; M.S. Horner, "Sex Differences in Achievement Motivation and Performance in Competitive and Non-Competitive Situations," Ph.D. diss., University of Michigan, 1968, cited in Meredith M. Kimball, "Women and Success: A Basic Conflict?" p. 89; Roslyn S. Willett, "Working in 'A Man's World'," p. 369; and Jacquelyn S. Crawford, *Women in Middle Management*, pp. 63–65. See also *Psychology of Women*, ed. Juanita H. Williams (New York: W.W. Norton, 1979), esp. Lisa A. Serbin and K. Daniel O'Leary, "How Nursery Schools Teach Girls to Shut Up," pp. 183–87; Grace K. Baruch and Rosalind C. Barnett, "Implications and Applications of Recent Research on Feminine Development," pp. 188–99; and Julia A. Sherman, "Social Values, Femininity, and the Development of Female Competence," pp. 200–11. In addition, see V. O'Leary, "Some Attitudinal Barriers to Occupational Aspirations in Women," *Psychological Bulletin* 81 (1974): 809–26; A. H. Stein and M. Bailey, "The Socialization of Achievement Motivation in Females," *Psychological Bulletin* 80 (1973): 345–66; Juliet Mitchell, *Woman's Estate* (New York: Vintage Books, 1973), pp. 124–29; Simone de Beauvoir, *The Second Sex*, pp. 368–72.

category has consistently shown the lowest ratios, the singles show the highest, and "other" (widowed, divorced, separated) has occupied an intermediate position.

So stark is the difference that the female/male income ratio actually doubles (or more) as we move from married to single status. This ratio even approaches unity, although without ever quite reaching it, in eloquent testimony to the differential effects of marriage on earnings.

There is, however, a difficulty with these data: they are not precise enough. They include not only wages and salaries, which can, perhaps, serve as a basis for employer discrimination, but also income from self-employment, investments, pensions, and government transfers, which clearly are unrelated to employer discrimination.

WAGES AND SALARIES ONLY

In order to remedy this situation, we turn to Table 3, which includes *only* wages and salaries and specifically excludes all other income. As a test of the hypothesis that marital status has widely asymmetrical effects on earnings by sex, Table 3 is an improvement over Table 2 in yet another way: it collapses the categories of "married" and "other" into "ever-married," which, as the name implies, includes all people who were *ever*-married, regardless of the marital status they now occupy. That is, it compares people presently married, divorced, widowed, *or* separated, with those who were never married in their entire lives. Table 3 thus furnishes a comparison of people who have

---

Many of these inferences about income-earning capacities apply, of course, to never-married women as well as to ever-married women. That never-married women have nevertheless been able to register at .992 income ratio with their male counterparts, despite these obstacles, is all the more evidence of their great earning capacity. True, never-married women have slightly higher educational preparations than never-married men (10.9 vs. 9.3 years—see Kuch and Haessel, cited in Table 3). But it is unlikely that this slight advantage would more than offset all the other psychological and sociological disadvantages to their income-earning ability.

TABLE 2 | AVERAGE INCOME OF INDIVIDUALS IN CANADA BY
MARITAL STATUS, 1971–79

Males	Single	Married(1)	Other	Total(1)
1967	2,665	6,210	3,492	$5,334
1969	2,697	7,300	4,394	6,162
1971	3,192	8,322	5,117	7,004
1972 (2)	3,889	9,008	—	7,633
1973	4,024	10,051	6,992	8,410
1974	4,805	11,630	7,776	9,749
1975	5,437	12,919	8,365	10,865
1976	5,876	14,736	10,146	12,430
1977	6,850	15,050	10,105	12,698
1978	7,079	16,654	12,239	13,871
1979	8,331	18,002	12,575	15,143
Females				
1967	2,380	2,241	2,259	$2,283
1969	2,574	2,435	2,738	2,524
1971	2,817	2,994	2,985	2,948
1972 (2)	3,231	3,253	—	3,243
1973	3,409	3,658	3,720	3,604
1974	3,902	4,362	4,403	4,255
1975	4,511	4,845	4,983	4,788
1976	4,761	5,373	5,658	5,285
1977	5,967	6,032	6,410	6,085
1978	6,035	6,825	7,411	6,749
1979	6,847	7,403	7,800	7,342
Ratio Female:Male				
1967	.89	.36	.65	.43
1969	.95	.33	.63	.41
1971	.88	.36	.58	.42
1972 (2)	.83	.36	—	.43
1973	.85	.36	.53	.43
1974	.81	.37	.56	.44
1975	.83	.37	.60	.44
1976	.81	.36	.56	.43
1977	.87	.40	.63	.48
1978	.85	.41	.61	.49
1979	.82	.41	.62	.49

(1) Married and Total figures are published in each year's Income Distribution by Size (Statistics Canada, Catalogue 13-207). Single and Other averages are from unpublished tables. Survey of Consumer Finances, Statistics Canada.[22]

(2) In 1972, "Single" figure includes Single and Other.

[22] Unfortunately, only the "married" and "total" columns are widely published in official Canadian Statistics. To say the least, this gives rather a biased account of the true state of the female/male earnings ratio, and its basic cause (marital status and its widely diverging effects on male and female earnings).

been touched in some way by the institution of marriage with those who have not.[23]

TABLE 3 | FEMALE/MALE EARNINGS RATIOS BY MARITAL STATUS, CANADA, 1971

	Never Married Female	Never Married Male	Ever Married Female	Ever Married Male	Total Female	Total Male
Sample Size	2,117	2,439	14,060	27,800	16,177	30,239
Income	$4,169.72	$4,201.24	$2,216.58	$6,674.91	$2,407.70	$6,430.30
Income Differential (Male-Female)		$31.52		$4,458.33		$4,022.60
Income Ratio (Female:Male)		.992		.332		.374

Source: This table is based on calculations made from the empirical record compiled by Peter Kuch and Walter Haessel, who used the Public Use Sample Tape as a source (computed for individuals aged 30 years and over). See their Census Analytical Study written on behalf of Statistics Canada and entitled: *An Analysis of Earnings in Canada* (Ottawa: the Ministry of Industry, Trade, and Commerce, 1979 Catalogue No. 99-758E), pp. 113, 206.

---

[23] Not only does *marriage* have asymmetrical effects on earnings by sex, but it is reasonable to believe that so does "living together" or "cohabitation"—and for similar reasons. Moreover, this category has become more statistically significant in recent years, though actual data are lacking. Table 3, in distinguishing between the ever married and the never married, cannot separate those who have ever lived together—whether married or unmarried—from those who have never lived together. If cohabitation as well as ever-married status could be controlled for, one would thus expect the female/male ratio to be *higher* than .992. There is also, however, a reason for believing that .992 may be somewhat of an *overestimate* of the "true" female/male earnings ratio: never-married females are older than never-married males (46.2 years vs. 43.7 years old), have more schooling (10.9 vs. 9.3 years), work more weeks (45.6 vs. 42.3 weeks), and work on a part-time basis to a lesser degree (10.6 percent vs. 11.8 percent). (All figures based on calculations made from data presented by Kuch and Haessel; see Table 3 for full citation.)

And the results are truly staggering! Never-married females in Canada earned $4,169.72 in 1971, while their male counterparts registered earnings of $4,201.24. The differential by sex for those who have never been married amounted to only $31.52 for an entire year; this translates into a female/male earnings ratio of 99.2 percent!

We can see, too, that the poor earnings record of all females compared to all males (a ratio of 37.4 percent) is almost entirely a function of "ever-married" status (a ratio of 33.2 percent). As of 1971, at least, Canadian women who have never been married have indeed "come a long way, baby' toward earnings equality with men.

MARKET IMPEDIMENTS

While for the most part wage differentials reflect attributes of employees other than sex, it is true that impediments to market operation may produce discrimination-like wage differentials. Impediments which have this effect include minimum wage laws and union entry restrictions. However, the most significant impediment to market response is that a large fraction of the labor force is employed by the public sector.

Public sector employers, unlike their private sector counterparts, have no financial incentive which inhibits them from discriminatory employment practices. The public sector bureaucrat neither gains nor loses financially as a result of his or her employment decisions, and is free therefore to engage in whatever form of discrimination suits him or her.

Even in this case, however, EPFEW laws and/or quotas may not be in the best interests of the oppressed, a question to which we now turn.

AFFIRMATIVE ACTION IN THE PUBLIC SECTOR

It is impossible to overestimate the importance of the distinction between discrimination in the private and public sectors. We have seen that in the former sphere, there exist market forces which continually erode the scope of prejudicial behavior. There is, unfortunately, no such tendency in government.

Given the great difficulties, social costs, and unintended negative consequences of proportional representation requirements, quotas, and other similar prescriptions based on retrospective results, and given the market's ability to reduce discriminatory behavior—in the absence of legislation which retards this process—a case is made, throughout this book, against the employment of affirmative action programs in the private sector.[24] We also noted above that the incentive system operating in the private sector may not work in the public sector. Accordingly, we must now assess the case for equal opportunity programs (based on quotas and proportional representation) in the field of public employment.

At the outset, this seems an attractive idea. There are thousands of minority group members, especially in the southeastern U.S., in the northern and western states, and in many of the Canadian provinces as well who have been victimized by discriminatory hiring practices on the part of public agencies. This has imposed real and lasting costs on the groups out of favor, whether based on race, sex, national origin, or some other criteria.

Discrimination in the public sector, moreover, is considered unjust and immoral by many. The funds which pay for government employment come from all citizens—including minority members. For anyone to be excluded from a public job because of race, sex, national origin, sexual preference, skin color, or any other such criteria,[25] after being forced to pay for this very same unemployment

---

[24] Some may argue that private discriminatory behavior is immoral and ought to be prohibited by force of law. Others may hold that, while discrimination is a negative characteristic, each individual is nevertheless entitled to make whatever decision suits his conscience—whether in commercial dealings, employment practices, housing decisions, or personal relations—provided only that he not commit fraud upon, or initiate aggression against, minority group members. Whatever the solution to this philosophical question, both sides may perhaps take comfort from one of the findings in Block and Walker, *Discrimination, Affirmative Action, and Equal Opportunity*: the tendency of the marketplace to financially penalize those who indulge in discriminatory practices, and thus to reduce, over time, the scope of this activity.

[25] There would appear to be numerous criteria upon which discrimination has, or is alleged to have, taken place, and upon which quotas, affirmative

through coercive taxes, is nothing more than a cleverly disguised, but particularly insidious, form of exploitation.[26]

---

action, or preferential treatment are now demanded. Some of the grounds include (1) obesity: see "Obese Are Victims of Bias: Professor," *Toronto Globe & Mail* (August 5, 1980), p. 13; (2) blindness: see "Group for Blind Suggests Job Quota," *Toronto Globe & Mail* (August 21, 1980), p. 1, and "Blind Woman and Guide Dog Win Rights Fight," *Vancouver Sun* (August 18, 1980), p. 8; (3) residence: see "Stop Provinces Reserving Jobs for Residents, Rights Chief Says," *Toronto Globe & Mail* (June 4, 1980), p. 10; (4) "reverse" discrimination: see "Barring White in Native Class Is Ruled Illegal," *Toronto Globe & Mail* (February 13, 1980), which tells of an Alberta Human Rights Commission finding against the University of Calgary for discriminating against a non-Indian woman by denying her admission to a special course specifically set up for native peoples; (5) ugliness: see "More to an Interview than Meets the Eye," *Toronto Globe & Mail* (July 19, 1980), p. F3, which shows that persons of "unattractive appearance" (and even sometimes persons of beauty) are discriminated against in hiring practices; (6) political beliefs: see "They're Biting the Hand that Won't Feed Them," *Toronto Globe & Mail* (August 9, 1980), p. 8, which tells of a Prince Edward Island Provincial Human Rights Commission finding that a public employee had been wrongfully dismissed for his political beliefs; (7) hirsuteness: see "Supreme Court Refuses a Motion to Force Grocery Clerk to Shave," *Toronto Globe & Mail* (February 10, 1980), which tells of a Winnipeg employer who could not legally compel his grocery clerk to either shave his beard, work nights "out of the sight of customers," or fire him.

[26] The situation with regard to discriminatory practices on the part of the government is a unique matter. It cannot be argued, as it could in the private case, that, no matter how morally reprehensible discrimination is, at least in the market sector it is done by an individual in his own name and with his own *money*.

When the government discriminates, it does so on *all* our behalf, and, adding insult to injury, with *all* our money, including that of the very persons who must bear the brunt of this practice. There can be few things more outrageous and galling than first forcing a minority group member to pay taxes for a public institution, and then allowing the public institution to turn around and refuse to hire or serve members of that very group.

In contrast, there is no such phenomenon in the private sector. If A discriminates against B in the marketplace, he at least does it with his own (A's) money; he does not first force B to contribute to his (A's) bank account and then turn

PUBLIC SECTOR QUOTAS?

Despite the superficial attractiveness of quotas for every conceivable minority group in the public sector, the case for such a program diminishes upon deeper analysis.

The difficulty is that quotas are unjust.[27] The beneficiaries (in those rare cases where someone actually benefits) are the *wrong* people: the 18- to 21-year-olds, applying for their first jobs,

---

around and use his money (B's) against him. It is even possible to make out a case for the non-criminal status—if not the outright morality—of private discrimination. Such behavior in the private sphere, it might be claimed, amounts to no more than a refusal to interact with another person. And the right to privacy would seem to justify the decision of one individual *not* to be involved with another. Such a case could hardly be made on behalf of government discrimination, however.

[27] Although many people interpret prejudice or discriminatory behavior as a willingness to engage in *physical aggression* against a despised person or group, this interpretation is about as far away as it is possible to get from a clear understanding. On the contrary, a sharp distinction must be made between *refusing to interact at all with a person*, and *threatening physical abuse against him*. The former is all that is done by a hermit, although on a larger scale; and if it is no crime to refuse to deal with *all* of humanity, then it might be argued that it can scarcely be a rights violation to avoid dealing with only *some* people.

Physical abuse, in contrast, is the act of a criminal; it is what murder, kidnapping, extortion, and assault and battery all have in common. It is altogether *different*, in this view, from a mere refusal to interact with (some of) humanity.

Exception must be taken, then, to William Johnson's claim of a "continuity between getting upset about French on corn flake boxes [objecting to a law which compels bilingualism on commercial products] and attacking innocent campers" (several young Francophones, from Quebec, working in British Columbia were viciously beaten by local hoodlums who uttered racist epithets). See *Toronto Globe & Mail* (July 15, 1980), p. 8. While some who engage in the former *may* engage in the latter as well, there is the world of difference between these two activities, and no necessary connection between them. " Getting upset," moreover, is a *right* of all citizens in a free country, while physically attacking innocent people is, and should always be, a crime, severely punishable to the full extent of the law.

who never bore the brunt of past employment discrimination, by definition. The real victims are those who would have liked to have been police officers, firefighters, letter carriers, and civil servants in the past but were not even considered, even though fully qualified, because of their race or sex. But these people, for the most part, are already either settled in their present jobs or retired from the labor force. If anything, monetary settlements might seem a preferable alternative.

Another problem is that quotas are based on the premise that in the absence of discrimination, each minority group would be proportionally represented in every job classification. But as Sowell and Williams make abundantly clear in their contributions to Block and Walker, *Discrimination, Affirmative Action, and Equal Opportunity*, not only is there no evidence for this conclusion, there is every reason to believe the exact opposite. Minority groups are heterogeneous, with different ages, educational levels, geographical locations, cultures, histories, and so on.

If quotas are not the ideal answer, what may be done instead to correct the obvious injustice of discrimination in the public sector?

A MODEST PROPOSAL

One suggestion is that laws prohibiting discrimination in the public sector be strengthened. This would include severe fines and loss of job penalties to the *individual* civil servants found guilty of such behavior. Fines leveled on government *per se* would do little good since they can be passed along to (innocent) citizens through higher taxes. People who feel victimized by discriminatory practices on the part of government would be able to sue for damages on this account, and freedom of information laws would be broadened so as to allow access to employment application test scores or other relevant documents upon which such a suit could be based. If such machinery is put into place, in this view, it will go a long way toward stopping public sector discrimination, *de facto* as well as *de jure*.

INSURANCE

Laws prohibiting discrimination also threaten to play havoc in several other fields. Insurance companies commonly "discriminate against" the elderly and the sickly; they either refuse to grant life insurance, or only do so at significantly higher premium rates, for example, to a 70-year-old man with a heart condition. Should such discrimination be permitted?

Insurance is an industry dedicated to pooling and spreading risk.[28] While health, injury, or sickness of any one person is beyond prediction, actuarial tables have been established for the probability of such occurrences in the aggregate. Because of this, insurance companies can charge premiums to large numbers of people and underwrite the costs of the unfortunate few; all customers pay a relatively small amount, in effect, for the security that should they be struck by calamity, they or their loved ones would be protected from great expenses, and thus would remain financially secure.

But if the system is to work well, the insurance company must make fine distinctions between people regarding the likelihood of catastrophe. It must base the payment of premiums on the degree of risk. (Indeed, its profits depend almost entirely on this ability.) Failure to make these distinctions (i.e., *discriminations*) based on riskiness, and to tailor premiums to the degree of risk, will lead to bankruptcy, for the low-risk customers will tend to migrate to other insurance firms, encouraged by the lower premiums there. The company which does not discriminate will therefore be left with high-risk patrons; it will either have to charge them more, thereby effectively discriminating (specializing in high-risk ventures) or face bankruptcy as the high payouts swamp the small premiums.

It might be argued that *all* insurance companies should be forced to adopt a non-discriminatory posture. In this way, it might be contended, none of them could gain a competitive advantage over any of the others.

---

[28] Ludwig von Mises, *Human Action*, p. 109.

A DIFFICULTY

The difficulty with this plan is related to a little known but highly important benefit conferred upon society by insurance. (The social good created by the insurance industry is as hard to overestimate as it is unknown by the general public.)

Let us suppose that overeating leads to heart disease, that houses built in geographical areas A, B, and C run greater risks of fire, storm, or flooding damage, and that high marks in high school driver education courses are associated with fewer automobile accidents. As a result, insurance companies, in their unending quest for profits, will charge lower premiums to people who alter their actions to conform to these discoveries (losing weight; not building in dry forests or near flooding rivers; enrolling in traffic safety courses).

People are thus led, as if "by an invisible hand" (but actually by the *insurance industry* and the price system) to try these different modes of behavior. Apart from the inalienable right of insurance companies, and everyone else, to practice this sort of discrimination, *this* is why it would be very unfortunate to prohibit all insurance companies from discriminating: there would be fewer economic incentives rewarding and encouraging such "safe" behavior.

PENSION PLANS AND SNOOPING

A case in point is the recent Canadian Human Rights Commission regulation[29] condemning discrimination between men and women with regard to pension plans. It is a plain actuarial fact—established through years of insurance experience—that women tend to live longer than men. With sexual discrimination prohibited, equal pension premiums would render men more profitable customers to insurance companies, as on average they will collect benefits for fewer years. The Canadian Human Rights Commission prohibition will therefore tend to result in (1) the encouragement of male over female labor (men will now be cheaper to employ); (2) the segregation of the labor

---

[29] *Toronto Globe & Mail* (April 14, 1980), p. 6. See also *Toronto Globe & Mail* (January 25, 1980).

force by sex (so that no one employer would have to make different contributions on this basis); (3) the withdrawal of employers, especially small ones, from pension plans altogether; and/or (4) the migration of companies to areas which do not prohibit discrimination in pension premium payments on the basis of sex. Needless to say, any of these eventualities would effectively discourage workers from pooling risks concerning retirement income.

Another case in point is the order of the Ontario Consumer and Commercial Relations Ministry to the Fireman's Fund Insurance Company. The ministry enjoined the insurance company from questioning its clients about their convictions on alcohol or sex-related offences, on whether they are usually restless, sad, or sweaty at night, and on other personal subjects.[30]

Frank Drea, the former Ontario Consumer Affairs Minister, objected to this practice on two grounds: first, he claimed it was an invasion of privacy; and, second, that it was compulsory, since the company offered a discount on its policies of up to 30 percent for those who filled in the questionnaires and demanded full price from those who refused.

CUSTOMER DISCOUNTS

There are some serious difficulties in this position. Scores of firms, representing dozens of industries, offer customers a discount if they, in turn, do something, otherwise onerous, desired by the company; and they refuse these special discounts to customers who will not so accommodate them. For example, many banks offer customers who maintain certain minimum ($500) balances free or reduced-price checking services, and refuse this to those whose deposits are not sustained at these levels. Mail order houses usually give special benefits to those who pay in advance.

Other firms commonly offer discounts only to those who will, for example, shop, demand service, purchase, or put in an appearance at a time convenient to the supplier, not necessarily to the customer, and

---

[30] See "Drea Tells Firm to Stop Questions" and the editorial "Wearing Nothing but a Seat Belt," both in *Toronto Globe & Mail* (July 31, 1980), pp. 5, 6.

refuse price reductions to those who insist on satisfying their own schedules. Department stores offer discounts at "January and August white sales" to people who defer their sheet and linen purchases until after the holiday and summer season; bowling alleys typically discount their admission prices to those who play from midnight to 4 a.m.; church dances usually reduce their ticket prices to patrons who show up "early" (i.e., "before 8:30 p.m."); theatre goers can often save money by attending matinees, not Saturday evening performances; airline travel costs less at night than during the daytime. Government rate-setting boards have even accorded permission to electric and telephone utilities to vary price in correlation with peak demands (long distance telephone calls cost more during business hours than in the wee hours of the morning).

CONSUMER TIPS

It is well known and has been for many years that those who buy "wholesale" or in bulk can usually save money compared to fellow shoppers at the retail level. But recently, special discounts have been offered by "no frills" grocery supermarkets, and by "self-service" gas stations—but only to customers willing to make the special efforts required on their behalf. Similarly, people are learning that giving advance notice to companies usually leads to special discounts. Examples include booking airline flights well ahead, purchasing a series of concert tickets for the whole season, subscribing to magazines for two or three years at a time, joining a book or record club, and committing oneself to a certain level of future purchases. Financially troubled municipalities such as New York City have even given special real estate tax breaks to property owners who pay in advance, while charging the same old (high) rates to those who pay on time.

Would anyone care to suggest that these and other similar commercial innovations amount to compulsion? To coercion? That these firms "have no right" to offer their customers discounts as a reward for behaving in a way that the firm wishes? Hardly. And since there is no difference in principle between an insurance firm offering discounts to customers who answer survey questionnaires and all these other cases,

Drea's charge of compulsion and harassment against the Fireman's Fund Insurance Company falls to the ground.

Nor is this practice an "invasion" of privacy. It is rather a voluntary confidence of a personal nature given by the client to the insurance company, in return for the 30 percent rate reduction. It is certainly no more an "invasion" of privacy than the voluntary confessions widely accorded to clergymen, lawyers, and psychiatrists in our society. To be consistent with its Fireman's Fund decision, the Ontario Consumer and Commercial Relations Ministry would have to ban personal declamations in these areas as well—ludicrous and manifest folly if ever there was one.

WHY THE QUESTIONNAIRES?

Having settled the legitimacy of these questionnaires, let us now inquire as to their social usefulness. The insurance company did not embark upon this project out of sheer cussedness, perversity, or morbid curiosity; it was rather an attempt to save money for its customers, and thereby earn greater profits for itself—something fully in keeping with its legitimate mission as a Canadian business firm.

How does this work? If Fireman's Fund could better discriminate on the basis of its questionnaire between high- and low-risk customers, it would be in a position to ask lower premiums of the latter group while still maintaining, or even increasing, its profit returns. And not only that. The company could then expand its base of operations with its new lower rates, attracting customers both from competitors and from the presently non-insured public. Conceivably, this greater volume might even allow the firm to pass some of these savings on to its original high-risk customers, thus benefiting both the high- and low-risk groups. If not, even the people in the high-risk group are still not made worse off by the questionnaire, as they are always free to patronize other insurance companies which do not make these fine distinctions.

Alternatively, the scheme might fail and may not reliably measure risk; it might be too costly to operate, even if it does. In this case, the company, and it alone, will be the loser. It would be unwise public policy to prohibit such experiments, even so; first, because we cannot tell in advance whether it will succeed or not; and, second, because this is precisely how commercial progress is gained—through trial and error.

"AGEISM"

There are also affirmative action guidelines approved by several U.S. Bank Regulatory agencies[31] prohibiting discrimination in borrowing. These bar credit application discrimination on the basis of race, color, religion, national origin, gender, marital status, age, and receipt of public assistance benefits. Let us take age as an example, and apply the analysis developed above.[32]

The abiding interest on the part of the lender, it can readily be imagined, is the likelihood that the principal, plus interest, will be repaid; and if not, that there will be enough collateral to make good on the loan. All else pales into relative insignificance compared to this main concern.

One obvious shortcoming with age non-discrimination is that persons under a certain age, usually 16, 18, or 21, depending on the jurisdiction, are not even legally obligated to pay their debts. Surely banks and other lenders could reasonably be expected to "discriminate" against such persons, under present legal codes. But even if these laws were rescinded, or if the affirmative action guidelines on age were reinterpreted so as not to apply to such young people, difficulties still remain.

An important determination in lending policy is the creditworthiness of an applicant: the likelihood that he will repay, on time, at no further cost or inconvenience to the financial institution. And young people, even if legally liable for their debts, are not widely perceived as

---

[31] These agencies include the Federal Reserve Board, the Comptroller of the Currency, the Federal Deposit Insurance Corp., the Federal Home Loan Bank Board, and the National Credit Union Administration.

[32] *Wall Street Journal* (June 22, 1978). On age bias, see also *Toronto Globe & Mail* (February 18, 1980), p. 5.

sufficiently creditworthy. Consider a person aged 22 who wants to borrow $4 million. He may have enough collateral such that, if he defaults, the lender would be able to recoup his losses. But this costs money, time, and aggravation. An older person with a longer track record may be more attractive, even if he has less collateral.

Forcing banks to ignore the age of the borrower would put them at a competitive disadvantage relative to other lending institutions. And if *all* lenders could somehow be prohibited from discriminating on the basis of age,[33] this would entail higher recovery costs for bad loans. Banks would thus be forced to offer lower interest payments on savings. This would reduce saving, investment, and lending, with negative repercussions on the economy.

SIZE DISCRIMINATION

Affirmative action has also been applied, all across Canada, to personal characteristics such as height. In Edmonton, for example, Tall Girls Shops Ltd., a family business with branches in 13 major cities,[34] was refused permission by the Alberta Human Rights Commission to advertise for tall (female) sales clerks. Mr. Gould, the general manager of the concern (which caters to women who average 5' 10" in height, and excludes women below 5' 7"), felt that tall sales clerks "could better understand the needs of their customers." But this line of reasoning was rejected at a Human Rights Commission meeting held in Calgary.

It is easy to see why the Alberta Commission withheld permission to advertise for tall sales clerks: discrimination is, after all, discrimination, and must be stamped out under the Human Rights Code. It is a little more difficult to discern why Tall Girls Shops Ltd. was allowed to continue discriminating against men in its quest for tall *female* clerks. The commission gave "for reasons of modesty" in

---

[33] They cannot. Loansharks, black marketeers, usurers, and underworld lenders have not been driven out of business. With age-affirmative action for legitimate concerns, these alternatives would be given a new lease on life.

[34] *Toronto Globe & Mail* (September 14, 1979).

explanation, but did not venture to show why mere "modesty" was placed before presumably more important "human rights."

Nor is it clear why this company was allowed to continue its discrimination against short *customers*, while being reprimanded for favorable treatment accorded tall *employees*. Surely the very name of the Tall Girls Shops Ltd. may be considered an affront to short women who want to purchase clothing. One cannot help wondering if the day will ever arrive when tailoring clothes for people in accordance with their height and girth will ever be considered discriminatory and therefore prohibited; such a practice must of necessity make (invidious) distinctions between individuals, and this is what the equalitarian philosophy would appear to deem improper.

HOW TALL IS TALL?

Similar analysis can be applied to the Toronto Towers Tall Club,[35] which limits membership to men above 6' 2" and women exceeding 5' 10". This organization puts on a beauty contest in order to pick a "Miss Tall Toronto"—an "unfair" contest if ever there was one, because it necessarily precludes short women from consideration. (We pass lightly over the question of whether beauty contests *per se*—and perhaps the institution of marriage, for that matter—improperly discriminate against ugly people.)

But these are matters of aesthetics, unworthy, perhaps, of the attention of dismal economists. More to their interest then will be a statistical study which concludes that 6' plus men in the United States earn 8 percent more than their shorter counterparts who are under 5' 6". This works out to a $500 annual pay hike for each additional inch of height. A Canadian survey shows similar results. Men who earned $25,000 per year or more were 3.7" taller, on the average, than those whose income fell into the $5,000–$10,000 bracket.[36]

SHORT POLICE

---

[35] *Toronto Globe & Mail* (July 1, 1980), p. 12.

[36] Ralph Keyes, *The Height of Your Life* (Boston: Little, Brown & Co., 1980). Also *Toronto Globe & Mail* (July 10, 1980), p. 15.

Another case of height discrimination took place in Toronto, where local police were criticized in the Clement Report, chaired by the former Attorney General of Ontario.[37] The finding was that the current minimum physical requirements of 5' 8" and 160 pounds for men are discriminatory.

In defense of these rules, Philip Givens, Chairman of the Metro Board of Police Commissioners, stated, "We don't want a 5' 5" karate expert; we want someone who will be able to put down a potentially volatile situation just by walking in." Mr. Clement rejected this reasoning and suggested instead the RCMP system, whereby potential recruits are awarded points for height, weight, strength, intelligence, education, etc., in competitive examinations.

But there are difficulties with this alternative as well. While a point system based on height may be more *flexible* than an outright prohibition, it is no less discriminatory. Short people are still placed at a disadvantage when awarded fewer points than their taller brethren. (The point system, moreover, discriminates against all people with low scores on the *other* criteria, such as weight, strength, intelligence.) Right now, the National Basketball Association practices outright discrimination against short people (other things equal— such as speed, endurance, intelligence—they prefer the seven footer to the five footer). Would anything essential change if the NBA were instead to adopt the RCMP method of allocating joint credits partially based on height? Hardly. Short people would still find it more difficult to find acceptance in this "world of the giants."

RENT CONTROL LEADS TO DISCRIMINATION

When rents are forcibly held below the point at which demand and supply can be equilibrated, the amount of residential housing space tenants *want* to occupy exceeds that which landlords are willing to make available. These extra rental units have to be rationed in *some*

---

[37] *Toronto Globe & Mail* (March 26, 1980), pp. 5, 8.

manner. With upward movements in rent levels precluded by law, other mechanisms play a greater part.

Nepotism, discrimination, favoritism are the answers; all play an increased role. The landlord cannot (legally) charge more rent; so he feels, with some reason, that he can pick and choose on whatever other basis suits him. If he is so disposed, for example, he can choose beautiful young women as tenants, or people without children, or, given the case we are considering, white persons.[38]

At one fell swoop, the least favored elements of society, the groups who otherwise would bear the brunt of discrimination (tenants with children, ugly women, older persons, homosexuals, blacks, native peoples, minority group members) will have lost the one thing that enables them to compete with more "attractive" individuals: the ability to pay for what they want. Prohibited by law from offering greater financial remuneration, they will be at the bottom of the list of tenants waiting for choice apartments.[39]

---

[38] True, laws can be passed prohibiting this latter alternative, but they are hard to police. Even if such a law decreases discriminatory activity on the basis of race, it is not likely to succeed. Government will have *first* unleashed a bout of discrimination upon the private sector, through its unwise rent control law, and only then have attempted to eradicate it. The net result will inevitably be an increase in discrimination compared to the situation in which government did not act at all. The government will, of course, take credit for its (secondary) efforts in "solving" the problem. It will be the rare individual who can follow the somewhat complex chain of reasoning necessary to see the government's true role. Anti-tenant-discrimination legislation, moreover, will have unintended negative consequences similar to those created by affirmative action programs.

[39] For an account of landlord discrimination, under rent control, against: (1) families with children, see "Choosey Landlords Targets of Council," *Vancouver Sun* (September 24, 1980), p. A8; (2) male college students, see "Report Biased Landlords, Male Students Are Urged," and "Preferred," *Toronto Globe & Mail* (August 18, 1980), p. 9, 6; (3) the handicapped, see "Landlords Won't Rent to Man in Wheelchair," *Vancouver Sun* (October 25, 1980), p. A3, and "Landlords Close Doors to Thalidomide Victim: Deformity Makes Her an Unwanted Tenant," *Vancouver Sun* (January 14, 1981), p. B1.

Usury

Usury prohibition is another law created with the best of intentions but which has unintended and negative side effects on the poor and racial minorities—the very people the enactment was (presumably) designed to protect. A law which places a ceiling on interest charges might seem to guarantee loans at lower rates than would otherwise have taken place. After all, if the law compels interest on loans lower than otherwise might have prevailed, it would seem to follow that people would be able to borrow money at improved terms, and that the poor and minority group members might be the beneficiaries of such a program.

In actual practice, however, nothing could be further from the truth.

What determines the interest premium people pay for loans is their *creditworthiness*, the likelihood that they will repay. Creditworthiness is not something granted to the borrower by the lender; on the contrary, the borrower has it, or fails to have it, when he makes the first approach. It is based on, among other things, reputation, reliability, "standing" in the community, collateral, hard work.

For reasons that need not concern us here, blacks and other minority group members are usually perceived to have less creditworthiness than other people. They are regarded as high risk borrowers. They do not pay the prime rate (the rate charged by banks to their most wealthy, reliable, and established customers); nor do they pay even the slightly higher rates usually accorded businesses and individuals with more modest financial accomplishments. When minority group people obtain loans at all from "legitimate" sources, they find they must pay additional premiums which defray the higher risks undertaken by those who agree to lend them money.

NO LOANS

But if legitimate lenders face an interest ceiling, they will not be able to recoup their losses on high risk loans with premium interest

---

Whether these landlords are allegedly discriminating on their own account, or in behalf of tenants, however, is by no means clear.

rates. Their natural inclination will be not to lend money at all to high-risk minorities.[40] Leon Louw says,

> In other words, the only way in which poor people can compete with rich people for the available credit or capital is to offset their disadvantage in terms of risk by offering a compensating difference in the form of higher interest. Usury laws limit the maximum permissible interest rate or terms of repayment to that level at which rich people or low-risk borrowers can obtain credit, but at which high-risk borrowers are priced out of the market. This means that the law paraded as being for the protection of the poor against exploitation, in fact discriminates against them and diverts credit and capital from the poor to the rich.[41]

Enter the "loan shark," or black market lender. Cut off from the normal source of loanable funds, the high risk minority borrower has no alternative but to turn to the underground or underworld economy. Here, such niceties as interest rate ceilings are ignored. The result is *much* higher interest costs than would otherwise prevail.[42] Nor is the lender hemmed in by time-consuming legalistic machinations; in case of default, he can quickly send in his goon squad with baseball bats and "cement shoes" to ensure loan repayment.

The prohibition of usury, then, has the exact opposite effect to its widely trumpeted intention. Instead of lowering interest charges for the poor and minority group members, it raises them. And instead of dealing with a bank or legitimate finance company, it forces the poor and minority group member into the clutches of people who will not hesitate to inflict serious physical sanctions in case of default.

---

[40] Laws which make it more difficult for legitimate lenders to legally repossess their funds upon default of the loan have a similar effect.

[41] Louw, "Free Enterprise and the South African Black," p. 3.

[42] According to anecdotal evidence, interest charges demanded (and received!) by loan sharks varies from 2 percent to 5 percent to 20 percent per *week*, depending on the time period of the loan, and the creditworthiness of the borrower. See in this regard "Joey," with Dave Fisher, *Killer: Autobiography of a Mafia Hit Man* (New York: Simon and Schuster, Pocket Book, 1974), p. 86.

ZONING

Zoning is another legislative enactment which, although it does not even mention specific racial or ethnic minority groups, nonetheless has the effect of discriminating against them.

How does this work?

Zoning was conceived in order to preclude the close location of "incompatible land uses," such as the proverbial glue factory and office tower.[43] But even this noble-sounding mission is fraught with danger for the poor and minority group peoples, for under the guise of eliminating such obvious nuisances, zoning has made it more difficult for *any* commercial enterprises to infiltrate into the poorer neighborhoods.

This zoning prescription appears as an obvious benefit to those fortunate enough to live in high-quality suburbs. They most often do not work where they live, and usually have automobile access to the business districts, recreational, and shopping areas of their cities. But for many of the poor, prohibiting commercial development in their neighborhoods has meant greater unemployment, or a longer journey to work, and greater difficulties and inconvenience in purchasing amenities.[44]

EXCLUSIONS

Less noble sounding are the aspects of the law which have come to be known as "exclusionary zoning." These are the clauses which specify minimum lot size of dwellings, which demand high quality structures, which, for example, disallow mobile and prefabricated homes. Although they also scrupulously avoid mention of the poor or minorities, it does not take a long chain of reasoning to see that these groups actually bear the brunt of this law. Leon Louw says in this regard:

---

[43] See Walter Block, ed., *Zoning: Its Costs and Relevance for the 1980s* (Vancouver, British Columbia: The Fraser Institute, 1980).

[44] The truth seems to be that the juxtaposition of many supposed "incompatible uses" is perceived by some as a benefit but by others as a harm. See Block, *Zoning*, pp. 35, 36.

Zoning laws usually limit the number of people who may occupy, or the amount of housing which may be built on, a given piece of land. The effect is that the poor, who could compete with the rich for prime land by pooling their money and living in higher densities, are precluded from doing so.[45]

Nor are the poor and minorities taken in by the siren song of zoning. An analysis of a straw vote which rejected legislation in Houston indicates that the poorer and more heavily weighted black areas tended to oppose zoning, while the more affluent, exclusionary, and caucasian districts tended to favour it. For example, in an area on the east side of Houston designated "Negro" by the *Houston Post*, comprising 2/3 tenants and with a 95.3 percent vote for the Democrat in the gubernatorial election, 72.3 percent of the voters rejected zoning. In Sharpstown, an affluent area designated "almost all white" with virtually no tenants, which voted by a 74.3 percent margin for the Republican gubernatorial candidate, only 31.7 percent of the people voted against zoning.[46] Reports Bernard H. Seigan:

> The predominant pattern of voting shows that high-income precincts (middle-middle to upper, inclusive) in the newer areas of the city generally supported zoning and that the lesser-income precincts (lower and lower-middle) in the older areas generally opposed it. In general, restricted areas wanted zoning, whereas unrestricted areas rejected it. ... There was an exceedingly high correlation between the voter's record in the straw vote and the voter's economic status as indicated by median value of home owned or average monthly rental.[47]

---

[45] Louw, "Free Enterprise and the South African Black," p. 3

[46] Bernard H. Seigan, *Land Use Without Zoning* (Toronto: Lexington Books, 1972), p. 29.

[47] Seigen, *Land Use Without Zoning*. This does not imply, of course, that each voter does an intensive cost-benefit analysis of the effect of such legislation on his or her pocketbook. But it does indicate a rough way that people correctly perceive their self-interest in zoning.

We must conclude, in the light of this evidence, that governments now enjoy an unmerited reputation for solving the problems of human rights and discrimination. On the contrary, affirmative action, EPFEW, and various anti-discrimination initiatives have backfired, harming the very minorities they were supposed to protect. Government programs such as minimum wage laws, anti-usury codes, rent controls, and zoning legislation have had unforeseen and negative consequences for the minority peoples, who have been among the greatest victims of discrimination.

19. DISCRIMINATION:
AN INTERDISCIPLINARY ANALYSIS

DISCRIMINATION HAS BEEN TREATED BY LARGE PARTS OF THE academic community as though it were not amenable to logical analysis, be it economic, ethical, or political; as though the very consideration of alternative viewpoints were somehow unsavory. The philosophy of "feminism," "human rights," "multiculturalism," and "political correctness" has so permeated intellectual discussion that criticisms of the mainstream view take on an aura of illegitimacy at the outset, even before arguments are heard in their behalf. This is highly unfortunate. If nothing else, John Stuart Mill's "On Liberty" should give us pause before closing our minds to alternative perspectives.

At one time in our recent history, the term "discriminating" had a positive value. It was a compliment. To say that a person was discriminating was to say that he was able to make fine distinctions. Today, of course, to say that someone is discriminating is to charge him with prejudice. This modern view is embodied in the so-called human rights codes of society, wherein it is illegal to discriminate against people on the basis of race, religion, sex, national origin, handicap, sexual preference, age, etc. Discrimination now carries a legal penalty—a fine, and even a jail sentence to back up the prohibition.

Journal of Business Ethics 11 (1992): 241–54. In-text references can be found in the bibliography section of this book.

CLASSICAL LIBERALISM

Let us then consider an alternative philosophical treatment of discrimination, sometimes known as classical liberalism.[1] It asks one and only one question: "When is the use of (state) force justified?" and gives one and only one answer: "Only in response to a prior rights violation." As such, this view must be sharply distinguished from theories of ethics. This is crucial, because there is all the difference in the world between claiming that a person should not be imprisoned or legally penalized for engaging in act X and claiming that act X is moral. It is no contradiction to oppose the criminalization of discrimination on the basis of race, sex, national origin, etc., while at the same time declaring that such behavior is immoral and unethical. And that, indeed, is the stance maintained in the present paper. Discrimination is defended, here, in the very limited sense that perpetrators should not be incarcerated, fined, or otherwise interfered with by governmental authorities. The present writer, however, finds such behavior odious, and morally repugnant in the extreme.

Classical liberalism is predicated on the premise that we each own our own persons; we are sovereign over ourselves. We have property rights over our own bodies, and in the things we purchase, or receive through any other legitimate mode, such as gifts, inheritance, gambling, etc. (Nozick 1974, pp. 149–182). Intrinsic to this way of looking at things is that there are boundaries. My fist ends here, your chin begins there. If the former touches the latter, without being invited to do so, I have invaded you. The essence of this philosophy is that any barrier invasions such as rape, murder, theft, trespass, or fraud are strictly prohibited.

Conversely, within one's own sphere, the individual is free to do anything he wishes, provided only that he does not violate

---

[1] This paper was written before the present author became aware of Narveson (1987). Although the two articles were written independently, there is a great deal of overlap between them—as is only to be expected when two reasonably competent analysts start out with virtually the same premises (classical liberal, in this case), and apply them to the same set of issues.

the rights or borders of others. Conceivably, people might be hurt deeply by friendship or patronage withheld, but it is the individual's right to withhold benefits of this sort, since such acts of omission cannot rationally be interpreted as a boundary crossing. As long as an individual's person or property is not invaded, no indictable offence has occurred and, accordingly, no penalty—no fine or jail sentence—should ensue.

From this philosophy is derived "the law of association," namely, that all interaction between free, sovereign, independent individuals should be voluntary and on the basis of mutual consent. On issues of pornography, prostitution, free speech, and drugs, the well-known phrase "anything between consenting adults should be allowed" demonstrates this philosophy. The classical liberal variant of this expression, in Robert Nozick's (1974) felicitous phraseology, is that "all capitalist acts between consenting adults" should likewise be allowed.

All acts, whether personal or commercial, should take place on the basis of mutuality. From this we derive that discrimination too is a right and, therefore, it should not be a criminal act to indulge—on whatever basis one chooses. But here it is important to emphasize that what is meant by "discriminate" is something very particular. It is to ignore, avoid, evade, have nothing to do with, another person. It most certainly does not imply the "right" to lynch or beat up or enslave or commit assault and battery upon someone from a despised group. If I don't like bald people with beards who wear glasses, for example, I don't have to have anything to do with them. I shouldn't be fined or jailed for refraining from dealing with them, according to this philosophy. On the other hand, I can't approach such people and punch them in the nose. I should be incarcerated if I indulge in any acts of this sort. In other words, I can do anything I wish to people against whom I hold prejudices—provided only that I do not engage in border crossings, or violation of their space (persons and property rights). I can "cut them dead" (socially and commercially), but I cannot commit even the slightest violence against them.

Is it "nice" to discriminate against people? Is it "reasonable" to prejudge an entire group or persons, based on negative experiences with a small sample? Certainly not.[2] In the popular belief, discriminators are hateful and wicked for not wanting to have anything to do with certain groups of people. As well, they are deemed illogical in that they over-generalize from a small sample to an entire population.[3] However, the issue presently facing us is not the moral or scientific status of discriminators. We are primarily concerned with whether the individual has a right to act in this way, and with the economic implications of this philosophy, not with whether or not it is nice or reasonable for him to do so.

---

[2] A very eloquent statement in behalf of this view was made by Booker T. Washington, on May 31, 1897, during the unveiling of sculptor Augustus Saint-Gaudens's monument to the 54th Regiment of Massachusetts Volunteer Infantry, the first black fighting unit to take part in the Civil War. It was made to commemorate its participation in the battle to capture Fort Wagner, during which campaign the regiment sustained heavy losses:

> The black man who cannot let love and sympathy go out to the white man is but half free. The white man who would close the shop or factory against a black man seeking an opportunity to earn an honest living is but half free. The white man who retards his own development by opposing a black man is but half free. The full measure of the fruit of Fort Wagner and all that this monument stands for will not be realized until every man covered by a black skin shall, by patience and natural effort, grow to the height in industry, property, intelligence and moral responsibility, where no man in our land will be tempted to degrade himself by withholding from his black brother any opportunity he himself would possess. (*Toronto Globe and Mail*, Dec. 15, 1989, p. A 16)

[3] If one considers the word "prejudice" etymologically, it means to pre-judge. That is, to make up one's mind about an issue before all the facts are in. But suppose you open up a door, go into a room, and close the door behind you, and then, lo and behold, you are confronted by a tiger sitting on a couch. Do you act empirically, in a non-prejudicial manner, and go up to the tiger to engage in a close examination, to see if this particular member of the species will act like most of its fellows, and begin to maul you? Or do you take one look, and then head quickly for the nearest exit, based on your general experience and knowledge of the breed, before you know the facts about this particular animal. Most people would act in a prejudiced manner in this regard, and would not apologize for it. (I owe this example to Walter Williams.)

HUMAN RIGHTS

Let us examine the "human rights" viewpoint in light of classical liberalism. Current "human rights" legislation only applies to commerce and sometimes to clubs, but not to personal interactions. This is puzzling because the advocates of such laws usually regard interpersonal relations as more important than commerce. Contemplate the fact that all heterosexuals discriminate against half the population in the choice of sexual partners. As do homosexuals. It is only bisexuals who are not guilty of this practice. (But most bisexuals presumably discriminate on other criteria: beauty, health, youth, wealth, honesty, sense of humor, common interests, personality, etc.) Therefore, if we consistently carry through on the anti-discrimination philosophy, we ought to punish everyone except bisexuals. Or consider marriage patterns. There is very little intermarriage, relative to the totals, across racial, ethnic, and religious categories. From this, one can deduce that racism in general, or discrimination in particular, plays a significant role in marriage choices. To be consistent with the underlying philosophy of "human rights" advocates, when people apply for marriage licenses they should be asked: "Have you dated people from other backgrounds; did you give them a fair chance?" If not, no marriage should be permitted. Certainly, friendship patterns are based on all sorts of discriminatory patterns. Is this wrong? Perhaps; it might well be. Should this be punished by law? Hardly.

Some people maintain that we should enforce anti-discrimination legislation in commerce but not in personal relations[4] because a

---

[4] There is a tradition among some civil libertarians (the British Columbia Civil Liberties Association is a strong case in point) that commercial liberties are very much inferior to personal ones. This sentiment finds expression, for example, in the denigration of commercial free speech rights (e.g., tobacco advertising) in contrast to the right to engage in free speech in the political or scientific arenas. One implication of this perspective, however, would be that the legal protections afforded the public policy statements "A subsidy for the XYZ cigarette company is in the public interest" or "Cigarette smoking is good for you" would be far stronger than those granted in behalf of the advertising statement "Buy XYZ cigarettes." In the classical liberal philosophy, in sharp contrast, no such distinction is maintained. On the contrary, liberty is

store, office, factory, or workplace is "open to the public," while no such stricture applies to friendship and other personal relationships. Such a claim is hard to defend, however. A store could conceivably be open only to the blond blue-eyed public—all others are advised go elsewhere—or to the left-handed redheaded public—or base its clientele on whatever criterion it wishes to employ. There is no logical reason why an offer to commercially interact with some people should be interpreted as an offer to business with all.

Second, "human rights" legislation is applied in a biased way. For example, with regard to considerations of national origin, many countries discriminate against foreign investment and treat the domestic variety more favorably. Tariffs discriminate against foreigners; so do immigration policies. University students from other nations commonly have to pay more for their education than citizens of the host country. These are all forms of discrimination based on national origin. And yet the response to these rights violations on the part of the human rights advocates and civil libertarians is curiously muted. This is difficult to reconcile with their position since, in other contexts, they single out discrimination in business for particular opprobrium.

Let us consider some other examples. Women's consciousness-raising groups are not open to men, while legal sanctions have been applied against men-only private clubs. Black Muslims do not allow white people to join them in prayer.[5] Similarly, Sikhs and Orthodox Jews, among many other religious groups, confine their prayer meetings to likeminded people. Boycotts of lettuce, grapes, and other such union-inspired activities certainly discriminate against people who are despised, at least within parts of the counterculture. The Brownies, Girl Guides, Boy Scouts, YMCA, YWCA, Young Men's

---

conceived of as a "seamless garment," and no aspect of it is denigrated in behalf of any other.

[5] In his most anti-white, racist days Malcolm X was once asked if any white man—living or dead—would have been allowed to join the Black Muslims. He replied that John Brown would have been acceptable (Breitman 1965, pp. 224–25).

Hebrew Association or Young Women's Hebrew Association all discriminate on the basis of gender.

While some of these examples may seem frivolous, there is an important point to be made. Non-discrimination is put forth as a basic human right. How, then, can there be exceptions? Surely, it is a basic human right not to be raped. Do we have exceptions incorporated into the law? No; the very idea is ludicrous. It is likewise a basic human right not to be murdered. Again, there are no exceptions. If it is a basic human right, we infer, exceptions are intolerable. The fact that exceptions to the laws prohibiting discrimination are not only not intolerable but are instead widely espoused, even by defenders of the philosophy, indicates that it is not at all a basic human right not to be "victimized" by discrimination.

As well, many of these distinctions have been made with a certain amount of hypocrisy. Women's consciousness-raising groups are widely considered to be properly closed to men, but male-only private clubs have been subjected to intensive governmental pressure to change their membership practices. In many cities, women are allowed to join the Young Men's Christian Association, but men are not allowed to enroll in the Young Women's Christian Association. On many university campuses, there is provision for blacks-only dormitories and cafeterias; providing the same amenities for whites would be widely seen as anathema. At one major Pacific coast university, the administration had organized a homosexual appreciation week; when students organized a heterosexual appreciation week, they were punished by university authorities. In the U.S. House of Representatives, there is a widely recognized Black Caucus; no such white counterpart can even be contemplated, given the likely outraged response. "Black is beautiful" is a respected rallying cry for a significant minority of the population; anyone attempting to promote the counterpart "white is beautiful" would be summarily dismissed as a racist.

A possible defense of this state of affairs is that it is justified for the downtrodden and denigrated minority to discriminate against the majority, but not for the latter to undertake such actions with regard to the former. There is one obvious difficulty with such a response: it cannot be made compatible with the view that non-discrimination is a basic human right. If it were so, then no one would have the right to discriminate against anyone at any time, for any reason.[6]

Another important point to consider is the backlash that special government treatment for minority groups has engendered. States Thomas Sowell (1990, p. 28): "One of the clearly undesired and uncontrolled consequences of preferential policies has been a backlash by non-preferred groups. This backlash has ranged from campus racial incidents in the United States to a bloody civil war in Sri Lanka." In Canada, Marc Lepine entered the engineering school of the University of Montreal, and at gunpoint forcibly separated the male and the female students, whereupon this person, who had previously complained about affirmative action benefits of women, cold bloodedly murdered over a dozen co-eds. Feminists in Canada and elsewhere have unsuccessfully attempted to deny any connection whatsoever between this brutal and dastardly act, on the one hand, and resentment against governmentally imposed preferential treatment for women on the other.

Why only include race, religion, sex, national origin, handicap, sexual preference, and age among the categories upon which it is illegitimate to discriminate? Why not also consider under this rubric people who are fat, drunk, stupid, smelly, ugly, short, bald, color blind, tone deaf, humorless? One response to this *reductio ad absurdum* might be that the presently legally protected categories are justified in terms of one's ability to change. If a person cannot alter his condition, it becomes impermissible to discriminate against him; if he can, it is permissible.

But there are difficulties with this rejoinder. First, why is it morally relevant? Even if an inveterate rapist for some reason could not change his desire to indulge in such activity, it would still be just to visit physically violent sanctions against him to make him cease and

---

[6] If we were to carry through fully and consistently on the logic of this premise, then blacks would have the right to rape and kill whites; Indians could legally steal from non-Indians; Jews could have "open season" on Germans.

desist. Second, this argument cannot possibly explain the present distinction between categories which are and which are not legally protected from discrimination. For example, changes in religion are relatively easy to incorporate, at least in comparison to an alteration in height. And yet discrimination on the basis of religious belief is commonly proscribed, but not that based on bodily size.

Another response might be that such categorization is made on the basis of the level of suffering undergone by the minority group. But those who are fat, drunk, stupid, smelly, ugly, short, bald are also denigrated. Surely these people suffer just as much if not more from discrimination as do some of those who are not legally recognized as "minorities."

Many so-called human rights advocates would happily add these additional categories to the list of people against whom it would be illegal to discriminate. While a short, fat, bald man with splotchy skin, glasses, and a squeaky voice can make an important contribution to society, he does not look the part, and is usually reimbursed and befriended accordingly. Maybe we should incorporate into the law a prohibition against discriminating against such persons. However, if we keep adding to the list, no one in our society will be able to interact with *anyone* on a truly voluntary basis.

HARM FROM DISCRIMINATION?

Why do the "human rights" advocates champion these ideas? One possibility may be that they identify with and want to protect the underdog against suffering. But there is a strong objection to this view: the underdog does not greatly suffer—at least in the economic sense—from private discrimination. To be sure, there is some harm which does befall a minority group which is the target of discriminatory behavior. Certainly, such groups of people are better off if the majority is favorable to them, or at least views them with indifference. But the injury is minimal. It could not be otherwise, given that Jews and Chinese have long been amongst the groups most highly discriminated against in our society, and yet have incomes far in excess of the average (Sowell 1981a; 1981b; 1983).

In order to see why this is so, it is incumbent upon us to briefly review the economics of boycotts, of which discrimination is only a particular case. The reason boycotts are almost always relatively unsuccessful (even when engaged in on the part of millions of people, over many years, such as in the case of South Africa) is because of the fail-safe mechanism which necessarily accompanies them (Abedian and Standish 1985; Hutt 1964). To the extent that a boycott is successful, it worsens the economic condition of the "victimized" group—at least initially. For example, if the boycott is through employment—the majority will not hire the minority—the wages of the minority decrease, and/or their unemployment rate increases. If the majority will not sell food to them, the price they become willing to pay for these items rises. As this process continues, their plight worsens. But, as their condition declines, it becomes more and more financially tempting on the part of both boycotters and non-boycotters to deal with these targets of the discriminatory behavior, in spite of the initial prejudice which led to the boycott in the first place. For example, if racial prejudice leads to whites refusing to hire blacks, thus lowering their wage levels, "this would mean an opportunity for some employers to reap unusually high profits by concentrating on hiring members of such low-wage groups. Even if employers of all other groups were too blinded by prejudice to seize this opportunity, it would leave a great opportunity for extra high profits by employers belonging to the same ethnic group" (Sowell 1975, p. 165). A successful boycott, in other words, carries within it the very seeds of its ultimate failure.[7]

---

[7] This accounts for the fact that the South African economy is doing quite well, despite a deep-seated, well-entrenched, long-standing boycott against it. When most civilized nations refuse to buy South African products, their prices fall, which makes it almost impossible for those interested in wealth maximization to continue to resist making purchases from that country. Similarly, when most civilized nations refuse to sell to South Africa, the prices obtainable rise, making it more and more costly to continue the boycott. The better organized the boycott, and the more people who take part in it, the more quickly its internal contradictions become apparent.

A similar economic analysis may be applied to the problems facing the authorities now engaged in the "war against drugs." The more opium producers killed, the more heroin captured, the more marijuana burned, the

But what of the plight of the minority during this process? Are they not grievously harmed in the interim? Not at all. So well does this "failsafe" mechanism operate that it is all but impossible to find evidence of the incidence of such boycotts. That is, it cannot be shown that there are greater profits to be earned in hiring such minority members, as there would be were they being victimized by discriminatory boycotts: "the experience of employers hiring members of an ethnic group that has lower earning and/or higher unemployment rates does not show remarkable success, and in many cases elaborate and costly programs have produced very meager results, even when subsidized by large government grants" (Sowell 1975, p. 165).

Abella (1984) claims to have shown harmful effects on the well-being of minority groups as a result of discrimination, but her methodology is questionable on several grounds (Block and Walker 1985). For example, she allocates the entire difference between black and white earnings (that cannot be statistically explained by quantifiable variables) to discrimination, thus ignoring other possible sociological and cultural differences which cannot be so easily quantified; to wit, she regards years of schooling as a homogeneous good, even though there are great disparities in the quality of schooling received across racial categories, even though the subject specializations are widely disparate—and correlated with income. That is to say, blacks are often concentrated in fields with lower average earnings.

Perhaps the best refutation of the methodology has been penned by Sowell (1990, p. 25), who states:

> When two groups differ in some way—in income for example—and 20% of that difference is eliminated by holding constant some factor X (years of education, for instance) then in a purely definitional sense statisticians say that factor X "explains" 20% of the difference between the groups. ...
>
> The potential for misleading explanations can be illustrated with a simple example. Shoe size undoubtedly correlates with test scores

---

more poppy fields sprayed with poison, the higher will be the prices of these illegal drugs, due to falling supply. But the higher the prices, the more the incentive which remains to create still other sources of supply.

on advanced mathematics examinations, in the sense that people with size-3 shoes probably cannot, on average, answer as many questions as correctly as people with size-12 shoes—the former being much more likely to be young children and the latter more likely to be older children or adults. Thus shoe size "explains" part of the math-score difference—in the special sense in which statisticians use the word. But nobody can expect to do better on a math test by wearing larger shoes on the day it is taken. In the real sense of the word, shoe size explains nothing.

When a statistician testifies in court that his data can "explain" only 40% of income disparities between groups by "controlling" for age education, urbanization, and whatever other variable may be cited, the judge and jury may not realize how little the words "explain" and "control" mean in this context. Judge and jury may conclude the other 60% must represent discrimination. But virtually no statistical study can control for all the relevant variables simultaneously, because the in-depth data, especially along qualitative dimensions, are often simply not available. By controlling for the available variables and implicitly assuming the unaccounted-for variables do not differ significantly between groups, one can generate considerable residual "unexplained" statistical disparity. It is arbitrary to call that residual "discrimination."

Looked at another way, groups with visible, quantifiable disadvantages often have other, not-so-visible, not-so-quantifiable disadvantages as well. If statistics manage to capture the effect of the first kinds of disadvantages, the effects of the second kind become part of an unexplained residual. It is equating that residual with discrimination that is the fatal leap in logic.

THE ECONOMICS OF THE "PAY GAP"

There is an objection often put forth against our claim that the people subjected to private discriminatory behavior are not harmed by it. Are not the wages, salaries, and incomes of women reduced because of economic discrimination against them? The so-called wage gap is offered as contrary evidence to our thesis. The fact is that at present the female/ male income ratio is about 0.65. This ratio has been rising very slightly for the last few years, but over the past few decades has shown a great stability (Block and Williams 1981; Block and Walker 1985; Paul 1989; Levin 1984; 1987). For every dollar the male earns, the female earns 65 cents. Isn't this evidence of actual harm not based on law or government or violence or coercion or boundary trespasses but rather on private discrimination? Paradoxically, the answer is No.

There are two reasons for taking this stance. First of all, there is the statistical explanation. Yes, the average wage of all females divided by the average wage of all males is 0.65—there is no dispute about that. But this gross statistic hides more than it reveals. As it turns out, the explanation for this state of affairs is not at all discrimination against women, but rather the asymmetrical effects of the institution of marriage on male and female incomes. Matrimony is strongly associated with increased male incomes and decreased female incomes. The so-called "pay gap" of 35 percent associated with the wage ratio of 0.65 is almost entirely due to the asymmetrical effects of marriage. The plain fact of the matter is that the division of housework, childcare, shopping, cooking, and other such activities is very unequal within most marriages. As well, married women's attachment to the labor force is vastly below that of men (Hoffmann and Reed 1982; Sowell 1984).

This can be shown in two ways. First, segregate the population by marital status, and derive a female/male income ratio for each sub-category. Block and Walker (1985a,b) divided their sample into the ever and the never married. (The former classification consists of married, divorced, separated, and widowed; the latter, as its name implies, is comprised only of those people who have never been married.) When calculated in this manner, the ratio for the ever-marrieds falls to below 0.40; that for the never-marrieds rises to unity. In other words, the "pay gap" increases from 35 percent for all females to a truly horrendous 60 percent for the ever-married females. By contrast, the pay gap for all females decreases from the 35 percent level to virtually zero for the never-married females. Does this mean that the employer has a particular hatred for married women? This is the only interpretation consistent with the "feminist" mythology. However, contradictorily, in this view, the prejudiced male is supposed to favor married women, given, of course, that they are "barefoot, pregnant and in the kitchen." He is presumed to hate single women—those who do not marry, presumably because they have no respect for men and patriarchical institutions. But the statistical findings indicate the very opposite. When the data are broken down by marital status, it is not the single women, the never-marrieds, who "suffer." Rather, it is the marrieds who do.

The ratio for full-time employed never-marrieds in Canada ranges between 82.9 and 109.8, depending upon date (1971 or 1981), and educational background (Block and Walker 1985 p. 51). For never-married persons aged 30 years old and above, Block and Walker (1982, p. 112) found a female/male income ratio of 0.992 for 1971; for comparable ever-marrieds, the ratio was 0.334. For U.S. data, Sowell (1984, p. 92) reports:

> Women who remain single earn 91% of the income of men who remain single, in the age bracket from 25 to 64 years old. Nor can the other 9% automatically be attributed to employer discrimination, since women are typically not educated as often in such highly paid fields as mathematics, science, and engineering, nor attracted to such physically taxing and well paid fields as construction work, lumberjacking, coal mining, and the like. Moreover, the rise of unwed motherhood means that even among women who never married, the economic constraints of motherhood have not been entirely eliminated.

As it happens, the wage ratio of non-married males to married males is about the same as between all females and all males. Namely, there is a "gap" of some 35 percent. Interestingly, there have been no analysts who have come forth with the claim that this is due to discrimination. Does this finding indicate that employers discriminate against bachelors? No. It is due to accounting practices which are not designed for economic analysis. The married male has an "assistant"— in effect—helping him to earn that income. It is true that only his name appears on the check, but she is earning it too. She might have helped put him through college. She engages in all sorts of ancillary activities which contribute to his success. However, in the statistical accounts, she is not credited with helping to earn this money. She spends this money in many cases, but governmental statistical agencies typically do not take cognizance of the fact that she has helped to earn it.

It is thus erroneous to deduce from these statistics that discrimination can account for the male-female wage disparity. The reason women on average only earn 65 percent as much as males is because their productivity is only 65 percent of their male counterparts. This is not necessarily due to any inherent economic weaknesses on their part, however. As we have seen, the explanation is marital status. According to the best statistical estimations, never-married women and never-married men have equal productivity, and thus equal salaries. Married women are only 65 percent as productive as men in the market on average because they specialize in raising children and taking care of the household. Even those women who have advanced degrees or training do not typically keep up with the latest developments in their professions; at least, they do not do so as assiduously as their married male counterparts.

Now let us consider the second reason in favor of the marriage asymmetry explanation of the wage "gap," *vis-à-vis* the discrimination or exploitation hypothesis. Notice the logical implications of the discrimination model. Assume that the productivity of males and females is exactly equal to each other. Assume the productivity of both to be at the level of $10 per hour.[8] Suppose further that the wage for males is $10 and for females it's $6.50 an hour, in order to maintain our ratio of 65 percent. Under these conditions, it would be as if the woman has a little sign on her lapel stating, "Hire me, and if you do I'll bring you an extra $3.50 an hour in pure profit." If the employer hires a woman, he can keep this $3.50, with no extra effort on his part. It goes without saying that all profit-maximizing employers would be vitally interested in discriminating in favor of additional returns. Without question, they would hire the women. But suppose that the employer is a sexist, who hires the man. If so,

---

[8] We focus on productivity—or more strictly marginal revenue product— because that is why employers pay wages—to obtain productivity from their employees. It is a well known axiom in economics that wages tend to reflect the level of productivity of the workers (Samuelson 1976, ch. 20).

he will tend to go broke. His competitors, the employers who hire females, will be able to undersell and drive him to the wall.

It is ludicrous, economically speaking, to suppose that anything like this could long endure: that employers could discriminate against equally productive women, and yet remain in business for any appreciable amount of time. Yet, this is precisely the scenario implied by the discrimination hypothesis. Similarly, it is also an implication of this discrimination theory that profits would be positively correlated with the proportion of female employees, both across firms and industries. That is to say, if employers can really exploit women by paying them less—due to rampant discrimination—then they would earn more profits, the more women they have on their payrolls. But this, too, bespeaks economic illiteracy. Profits tend to equalize, *ceteris paribus*. If 50 percent profits can be earned in industry A, and 1 percent in B, then investment will tend to leave the latter for the former. But as capital leaves B, this raises the profit level to be derived there; similarly, as money comes flooding in to the greener pastures of A, it lowers returns. What will be the effect of a law that compels employers to pay "equal pay for work of equal value?" Suppose the law requires employers to pay women $10 an hour when their productivity is really only worth $6.50, on average. An employer would be very reluctant to hire such people. If he does, he will lose money on each employee he takes on; eventually he will be forced into bankruptcy. As a result, the unemployment rate for women will be higher than it would otherwise have been, in the absence of such pernicious legislation. This is precisely the same effect as that of the minimum wage law. It functions so as to price women out of the labor market.

Consider the case of the ugly secretary and the beautiful secretary. In the real world, beautiful secretaries have an advantage over ugly ones. It may not be appropriate to discuss this economic phenomenon in certain circles; beauty may be strictly irrelevant to the job at hand; this phenomenon may be hurtful to non-attractive women, but that is the way the actual economy, and in general society, functions. One might ask, how is it that ugly secretaries ever get a job if just about everyone is prejudiced in favor of beauty? The answer is a phenomenon expressed in economic jargon as "compensating differentials." The market works in such a way that the salaries that less-fortunate women can attract decreases, making them a better bargain in the labor market. Comeliness is preferred, other things equal, but if other things are not equal, namely wages, then even those who discriminate in its favor may not choose to indulge their tastes in this way.

If the law mandates that all women be paid the same salaries, however, the underdog (the unattractive secretary) would be hurt the most. For under this condition it would be more difficult for those women to obtain jobs in the first place. Under the present system of free and flexible market wages, at least they can find employment. The same analysis applies to any despised group, whether discriminated against on the basis of gender, race, national origin, beauty, or age.

If a law is passed saying a young person cannot be paid less than an older one, that deprives the young person of his saving grace in the market, namely, the ability to work for slightly less money. In nature, weak animals have a compensating differential. The porcupine is otherwise frail, but it has quills; the skunk is powerless, but it uses odor as a defense; the deer is fragile, but it can run very fast. If these compensating differentials were somehow to be taken away, these animals would be well nigh doomed to extinction. In like manner, if the ability to work for less until they can gain experience is taken away from young people, their unemployment rate increases. This is precisely the scenario which obtains in the modern era, due to minimum wage legislation. Equal-pay legislation would do for women what the minimum wage has done for teenagers. All true feminists—those who espouse public policies which have the effect of benefiting women, as opposed to mouthing pious platitudes about their intentions to this end—must therefore oppose such wage controls.

RIGHTS AND DISCRIMINATION

If private discrimination is virtually powerless to harm its intended victims, government discrimination (Demsetz 1965; Higgs 1977; Lundahi and Wadensjo 1984; Stiglitz 1973) and state and private violence are entirely another matter (Kendall and Louw 1986; Williams 1989). The confusion between these two superficially similar phenomena[9] may account for the popularity of "human rights" legislation on the part of people who favor the downtrodden. In the 1940s and 1950s, blacks in the southeastern United States certainly did suffer from private violence. The Ku Klux Klan and others engaged in lynchings, cross burnings, and other terroristic activities. This is certainly an uninvited border crossing—the chins of these downtrodden groups were infringed upon by the fists of the aggressors. However, this is not at all what is meant by private discrimination.

Before proceeding further, therefore, a sharp distinction must be made between public and private discrimination. In the classical liberal world view, only private individuals have a right to discriminate. Government may not legitimately engage in such behavior. We all pay taxes in order to finance government services. If the state singles out one group, Catholics or Punjabis for instance, and either subsidizes or penalizes them, this is unfair and improper. Affirmative action is an instance of government discrimination. For devastating critiques of this program, see Levin (1987), Roberts (1979; 1982), Sowell (1982; 1990), and Williams (1982a).

There is a very important implication of this premise for public universities. To be admitted to state institutions of higher learning, entrance exams—usually based on intelligence and/or knowledge— have to be passed. In the terminology we are now using (Hagen 1977), the university discriminates on behalf of those who are thereby accepted as students. But other people were rejected; that is, they were discriminated against on the basis of their lack of knowledge or intelligence. This is improper and should not exist, in the philosophy under discussion. True, if public universities were to adopt a strict policy of non-discrimination on the basis of mental acuity, they would cease to exist as centers of higher learning; if

---

[9] There is all the world of difference between the invasive use of force, on the one hand, and the peaceful but assertive refusal to interact, on the other. Indeed, in the entire realm of political philosophy, there is scarcely a distinction more important to make, nor one easier to make. Nevertheless, for many people, the distinction between these two concepts is hard to discern. This is all the more reason to make it clearly and repetitively.

they wished to continue to discriminate on this ground, and to do so legitimately, they would have to be privatized.

Another very important distinction to be drawn in this regard is that between discrimination and the initiation of violence. The former is (relatively) benign, the latter malignant. Only the former is compatible with a regime which respects individual rights as adumbrated above; the latter certainly does not. However, it is also crucial to differentiate between private and public discrimination. It is vitally important to do so, because there is often a superficial resemblance between the two phenomena. Yet, as the latter but not the former also incorporates the initiation of violence, it and it alone is intractable from the point of view of the victims.

Consider in this regard that spate of infamous legislation known as Jim Crow (Williams 1982b).[10] Here, rights were violated on a massive scale, and great harm was perpetrated. Blacks had to sit at the back of the bus because of legal requirements. If they tried to take a seat anywhere else, they would be jailed. Similarly, they were legally restricted in terms of the washroom and drinking fountain facilities (Wharton 1947; Welch 1967).

Contrast this with a very different scenario. Instead of this back-of-the-bus practice being mandated by law, suppose that it were the result of merely private discrimination. We assume, then, that in the ex-Confederate states of Dixie, a view existed to the effect that the appropriate place for blacks was in the back of the bus, and that this was a widely upheld belief on the part of the majority white population, although not—and this is crucial—buttressed by supportive state intervention. In such a case, the typical entrepreneur would say to himself, "How can I maximize profits, given this situation?" On the assumption that blacks wanted to ride on the front of the bus, but were prevented from doing so by the owners of the extant bus firms, this entrepreneur would start another bus line, one on which blacks can ride anywhere they want—front or back—as long as they pay for this privilege.

---

[10] An economically similar system of law is the case of apartheid in South Africa (Williams 1989; Louw and Kendall 1986; Hutt 1964).

The problem in the Jim Crow South was that this would have been illegal. Entrepreneurs were required to obtain a permit or franchise in order to start up a competing bus line. But the same statist powers that forbade blacks the front of the bus also prohibited entrepreneurs from coming to the rescue of the minority group in this commercially competitive way. Operation permits to alternative bus firms were simply not granted (Wiprud 1945; Moore 1961; Eckert and Hilton 1972). In this instance, the underdog could not be helped by the market—not through any fault of private discrimination, but because of the far more deleterious public variety.[11]

In the event, to continue our historical exegesis, blacks had to wait decades until the political realities became such that a majority of the electorate finally repealed Jim Crow. Had the market been allowed to operate freely at the outset, the effects of this pernicious legislation could have been rendered ineffective in the short time that it would have taken an entrepreneur—black or white, it makes no difference—to set up a competing bus line. The market, in other words, is potentially the best friend of the downtrodden black minority group. Free enterprise is not the enemy. When it is obviated by state power, however, as occurred, unfortunately, in the case we are considering, this help remains only that—a potential.

"Human rights" advocates are so enthused about the so-called rights of people not to be discriminated against, that they neglect the real rights of people to engage in discrimination. Consider people forced to send their children to school where the teacher is gay. Parents resent this strongly, but are often unable to resist. Why not look at these people as underdogs and defend their rights? Surely, homosexuals have a right to practice the lifestyle of their choice. But

---

[11] If the majority refuses to sell food to the minority, other people will leap into the void, in order to "exploit" the relatively hungry minority. They will be lured by the prospect of being able to earn greater profits, but in so doing, they will drive down the food prices the minority will have to pay. It is only if the majority utilizes force or violence to keep such profit-maximizing good Samaritans away from the minority that this process will not work.

inflicting themselves upon unwilling recipients is hardly consonant with the law of free association.

There is also the case of Nova Scotia school board which ruled that a teacher who carried the AIDS antibody and thus might likely develop this dread disease was to be returned back into his sixth grade classroom. Imagine the agony of parents forced to send a child to a place where they think there might be a chance of his contracting a fatal disease.[12] A case could easily be made that these parents are the underdogs. Our failure to defend people in such a position stems from moral myopia—the rights of some people are more important than the rights of others.

Expressing it that way implies, however, that rights can conflict with one another.[13] Properly understood, however, this cannot occur. If there is a seeming contradiction between rights, one of them is not really a right. People do not have a right against other people that they have to interact with them whether they want to or not, as the so-called

---

[12] To be sure, scientific evidence indicates that AIDS cannot be disseminated by casual contact of the sort likely to be engaged in by school children in the classroom. But this is hardly relevant to the point at issue, namely the right of free association. People may wish to avoid contact with others for the most frivolous or scientifically erroneous of reasons. The question is, do they have a right to do so? And the answer is clear, at least for those who take individual liberty seriously.

[13] Suppose a white (black) female prostitute refuses to conduct her business with a black (white) male would-be customer. It might be argued, at least in jurisdictions where prostitution is not prohibited, that since she is engaged in a clearly commercial venture, and thus can be construed as being "open to the public," that she be legally forced to entertain all customers who can meet her price (and also that she not price discriminate on the basis of race). But if she is forced to do so, this is a violation of women's rights; if not, it constitutes racial discrimination, and thus a violation of the rights of minority group members.

This contradiction, of course, does not arise under classical liberalism, which countenances only negative rights; e.g., the right not to be murdered, raped, stolen from (Block 1986). Here, there can be no conflict in rights, for the woman is seen as the sole owner of her own body, with the right to dispose of it exactly as she wishes. And this includes the rights to engage in sexual relations with anyone she chooses, for any reason acceptable to her.

human rights philosophy would have it.[14] Rather, in the classical liberal philosophy, people should be free to do whatever they please as long as they don't violate the space of other people by invasion.

What are the free-speech implications of our analysis? Statements specifically discriminating against particular groups of people have a long pedigree in the civil liberties debate. They have been characterized as "hate literature." They are displeasing, even malevolent. But banning them is a clear violation of free speech rights.[15] Surely, any philosophy which takes seriously our rights of free expression would be exceedingly uncomfortable with a juridical proscription of "racist" statements.

---

[14] A similar analysis arises with regard to exceptions that are commonly made to the anti-discriminatory laws. For example, it is seen as illicit to discriminate between males and females, but there are separate (but equal?) washroom facilities assigned to men and to women. If this really were a matter of rights, such exceptions would not, could not, be tolerated. Similarly, discrimination between the sexes blatantly occurs in the field of sports, and is accepted by otherwise consistent adherents of the "human rights" philosophy: namely, there are separate divisions for males and females in university, Olympic, and professional sports. For example, male and female basketball, tennis, and volleyball players do not complete against each other: nor do track and field athletes. (Such an occurrence would hardly be allowed, in the case of race; could we countenance separate sports leagues for whites and blacks? for Jews and Gentiles? The very idea would be preposterous in the "human rights" world view, and yet, the very same principles apply to gender distinctions.) There is little doubt that were there only one athletic event, open to members of both sexes, that there would be virtually no female representatives who could successfully compete. Florence Griffith-Joiner, for instance, might hold the female world record for the 100 meter dash, but if she had to compete directly with males, she would not have even qualified to enter the Olympics.

[15] In classical liberalism, free-speech rights are interpreted as but an aspect of the more basic rights to private property. For example, if someone breaks into my house at 3:00 am., and starts reading in a loud voice the sonnets of Shakespeare, he may not properly object, if I toss him bodily out onto the street, that I have violated his rights of free speech. He has no rights of free speech—on my property. He has such rights only on his own property, or on that (a hall, auditorium, newspaper advertisement, etc.) which he has rented from someone else.

THE SOCIOBIOLOGY OF SEXISM

Now that we have established that private sexism, like racism, is impotent to greatly harm the economic well-being of the "victimized" group (in sharp contradistinction to sexist and racist policies pursued by government bodies, or the violence employed by states or individuals), we venture into an exploration of the question of why it is that sex discrimination exists in the first place. (What is meant by sexism in this account is first making distinctions between men and women, and then treating members of the two genders differently.) The most common explanation for this is that people are nasty, perverse, and misanthropic. The problem with this hypothesis, apart from being circular, is that it in no way comes to grips with why the nastiness and perversity which is undoubtedly part of the human condition is channeled into "anti-female" directions.

The sociobiological account of sexism does not fail on these grounds. Consider the following case: a ferry boat capsizes and there is only one lifeboat available. The common sexist order of preference is women (and children) first and only then men, a long way second. Why is it that we have this deeply embedded sexist idea that women are to be placed on a pedestal in this way? Why not let women take their chances along with men in the mad dash for the lifeboat? In the widely popular "feminist" analysis, this is because men regard women as little better than children in terms of intelligence, physical strength, and maturity, and if children should be saved first because of their relative weakness, then so should women.

The sociobiological explanation of this event provides a sharp contrast (Wilson 1975). In this view, the women-and-children-first rule came about because it ensured the survival of our species. Women are biologically far more precious than men, and any species that does not base its actions on this rule is thus far less likely to survive than one that does. This is why the chivalrous notions are so deeply embedded in our psyches: the human race has been acting on these principles for eons of time. Those parts of the race which did not have long ago died out.

Consider Germany, Poland, and the Soviet Union after World War II; practically an entire generation of men in these countries were killed; the lives of the women were, by and large, spared, at least relatively speaking. A gigantic proportion of men in each military age cohort were wiped out: women of child bearing age tended to survive. Is this even noticed by the Germans, Poles, and Soviets very much in the modern day, in terms of demographic implications? No. The next generation is just as large and just as well educated. It was almost as if this tragic loss had simply not occurred. Compare that scenario to the following hypothetical case. Suppose three-quarters of the women of the Soviet Union of childbearing age were killed, but hardly any of the men, the exact reverse of what actually occurred. What would be the demographic results in such a case? They would be no less than catastrophic. Not only would there be great danger for the next generation in these countries: the real question would be whether there would be *any* next generation or not!

Suppose that there were two races of apes, otherwise equally fit to survive, which had different customs regarding warfare. One group of apes (call them the human apes) did not allow their females to fight: instead, they tried to protect them as much as possible. When fighting took place, it was with the expendable males in the front lines. The other group of apes (call them extinct) either pushed the women forward to front lines of battle or were egalitarian—no "spurious" distinctions were made between the males and the females, they all went out and fought on an equal basis. Which group would survive? Obviously, the first group, the "human" apes, because, like it or not, women are more precious when it comes to survival of the species. This is so because one male and 25 females can leave as much progeny as 25 males and 25 females are capable of producing. That is, 24 of the males are all but extraneous to the process. It may be nice to have them around—at the very least they can furnish added protection—but biologically speaking their roles are as necessary for the survival of the human species as are drones for the survival of bees. That is why farmers commonly keep one bull for 25 cows—and not the other way around. However incompatible with the "feminist" view of the world, this biological fact simply cannot be denied.

This is a very powerful explanation of why women are dealt with as if they are much more precious than men. Because they *are*. Some people don't care about the survival of the human race, but this is irrelevant. We are now trying to understand why discrimination between men and women is so deeply imbedded in the human psyche, and in the sociobiological analysis we have found a logical explanation. This is a positive enterprise, to which truth and falsity apply, not a normative one, which pertains to the categories of good and bad, like and dislike. In other words, this perspective may be incompatible with the world view of the "feminists," but the evidence in its behalf is overwhelming nonetheless.

Conclusion

Our interdisciplinary account of the discrimination—utilizing insights from economics, politics, philosophy, sociology, biology, statistics, and history lends credence to our public policy recommendation: that this behavior, although immoral in many cases, should not be prohibited by law. Many of the goals of people of good will—for peace, prosperity, and tolerance—will, paradoxically, be more likely of attainment under a legal regime which allows for the free association of individuals on a strictly voluntary basis, rather than under one which compels such interaction. The latter can often backfire, as racial violence on university campuses, following affirmative action and mandatory "politically correct" thought, eloquently attests. So far has our present society lost sight of its classical liberal historical roots that the case for liberty in human relationships may seem to some to be vaguely racist, sexist, or otherwise morally objectionable.

20. Affirmative Action: Institutionalized Inequality

In 1961, President John F. Kennedy established a program of "affirmative action" with the declaration of Executive Order 10925. He defined the initiative as "public and private programs designed to equalize hiring and admission opportunities for historically disadvantaged groups by taking into consideration those very characteristics which have been used to deny them equal treatment."[1]

Upon first glance, this policy seems like a well-intentioned, well-deserved method of reparation. Affirmative action programs do indeed intend to set things right. However, implementation poses a clear and puzzling contradiction. In order to repay one group, the government proposes to take away the freedom of others. This includes, but is not limited to, infringing upon the right of employers to hire whomever they choose. It also discriminates against prospective applicants for jobs or to schools who are immediately put at a mandated disadvantage simply because of their race or gender.

Discrimination against minorities based solely on skin color or ethnic origin is an ignorant and unfortunate practice. However, it is our right as free individuals with personal liberty to hold whatever

---

Walter Block and Timothy Mulcahy, *The Freeman: Ideas on Liberty* (October 1997).

[1] Donald Altschiller, ed., *Affirmative Action* (New York: The H.W. Wilson Company, 1991), p. 5.

opinions or prejudices we choose. If we are to be logically consistent, this right must be carried over to the employer to hire people based on whichever characteristics he chooses. If an employer had a deep aversion to people with brown eyes and hired people accordingly, it would be a violation of his rights to force him to hire brown-eyed people. Then there is nepotism: a private bank owner who hires his cousin rather than another, more highly qualified applicant who is not a member of his family.[2] Should this man be punished by law? Clearly the answer is no. Certainly not if we value the right of free association. Laws prohibiting people from interacting with others, whomever they choose, for whatever reason, are a violation of their freedom to associate. We hold this right well-nigh sacred in some arenas: dating, friendship, marriage. No one has a legal obligation, say, to be colorblind (or gender blind) in his choice of a marriage partner. If affirmative action is such a moral, appropriate policy, why do not even its most fervent advocates counsel its use in such personal arenas?

THE PRICE OF DISCRIMINATION

As it happens, the market serves to eliminate discrimination, its legal, moral, and logical status notwithstanding. In a free market, employee compensation can only be truly successful if skill and productivity serve as the only basis for choice. According to economist Thomas Sowell, "The competitiveness of the market puts a price on discrimination, thereby reducing it but not necessarily eliminating it."[3]

By this, Sowell means that, in a competitive market, the person being discriminated against is not the only one who is penalized. If an employer refuses to hire all blacks based solely on their skin color, and in the process hires less-qualified whites, a competitor who chooses employees based on productivity will end up with the cheaper, more highly skilled work force and outperform the racist.

---

[2] Steven M. Cahn, ed., *The Affirmative Action Debate* (New York: Routledge, 1995), p. 39.

[3] Thomas Sowell, *Markets and Minorities* (New York: Basic Books, 1981), p. 40.

Eventually, enough other firms will realize they can outperform their racist counterpart by hiring based on productivity, and he will tend to be pushed out of the industry when his business fails. In this manner, the free market provides a clear incentive not to discriminate according to race.

A classic example of this is the signing of Jackie Robinson by the Brooklyn Dodgers in 1947. By voluntarily excluding blacks from baseball, the owners had, in fact, neglected a large pool of talented athletes. When the Dodgers turned to this sector of the labor market, "they acquired a competitive advantage which other teams could not allow to continue indefinitely."[4] If the other teams had continued to discriminate against blacks, eventually they would have lost more and more games, and like a firm in any other industry, would have faced failure.

Consider how an affirmative action policy would affect the National Basketball Association.[5] Today, in a free market for basketball players, the majority of players in the NBA are black. Were we to apply affirmative action here, the law would require fair representation of whites, Hispanics, and Asians. That even the most radical advocates of this policy never so much as contemplate such a course of action constitutes further indication of its intellectual bankruptcy.

If the government mandated that white players be given preferential treatment because they are underrepresented in the NBA, the overall quality of the game would suffer, as lesser-qualified whites took the place of more highly qualified blacks, simply because of their skin color. The fan would most likely not be pleased with the fact that he would be receiving less for his ticket dollar than in a free market, where the most productive, most qualified players were on the floor. This watered-down product would ultimately lead to

---

[4] Ibid.

[5] Following the same train of thought as in previously mentioned examples, if a team in a free market discriminated using something other than productivity, it would lose both games and money.

reduced ticket sales and the turning to substitute goods, namely, other forms of entertainment.

Affirmative action should be rejected by Americans of all races. It unfairly places whites at a disadvantage by limiting choice. For non-whites, it is a slap in the face: there is an institutionalized implication that they need government aid. It tends to exacerbate existing stereotypes and deepen racial rifts. It breeds contempt in the workplace, placing doubt in the minds of some whether their co-workers received the job based upon merit. It is a direct assault on the pride of the minority worker who has worked hard to improve himself, and has earned his position honestly.[6] It is also a disincentive for others to invest time in education and self-improvement.

Affirmative action is an immoral policy that must be ended. Instead, we must legalize a situation where everyone is viewed without color. In this "colorblind" society the free market would ensure equality in the sense that people would be judged according to their ability and qualifications, rather than by irrelevant, artificially imposed qualities.[7] In this sense, while every member of society may not succeed equally in a market, they will sink or swim based on their personal merit and be ensured an equal opportunity in the purest sense. Of course, if private people, groups, or individuals, wish to pursue affirmative action, reverse discrimination, or even the other variety against which our "civil rights" legislation was created to combat, the law of free association gives them the right to do just that.[8] In this paper, we were mainly concerned to *reduce* government discrimination, surely a very different matter.

---

[6] Walter Block and Michael Walker, *Discrimination, Affirmative Action, and Equal Opportunity* (Vancouver, British Columbia: The Fraser Institute, 1982).

[7] Terry Eastland, *Ending Affirmative Action: The Case for Colorblind Justice* (New York: Basic Books, 1996).

[8] Walter Block, "The Economics of Discrimination," *Business Ethics* 11, (1992): 241–54.

21. BANKS, INSURANCE COMPANIES, AND DISCRIMINATION

WHY MIGHT INSURANCE COMPANIES CHARGE HIGHER RATES TO urban residents? Why might city dwellers be less likely to receive loans than their suburban counterparts? Cities are often populated with a higher percentage of minorities, so one hypothesis is that bankers and insurers are engaging in discrimination. Another hypothesis, however, is that insurers and lenders make business decisions based on the drive for profits, rather than discrimination. If the latter hypothesis is correct, many of the government interventions may actually lead to the unintended consequence of precluding city dwellers and minorities from the market. Since the goal of policy is to give access to financial services to more individuals, not fewer, an economic analysis of the public policy prescriptions will be useful. We seek to determine whether government intervention in the insurance and loan markets is an effective way of assisting urban consumers.

First, let us ask why insurance companies might charge higher rates to urban consumers. Do they discriminate because they only want to do business with their suburban brethren? Do they do it so they can exploit minorities into paying higher premiums? Is there a collective agreement among non-minority-run businesses?

Walter Block, Nicholas Snow, and Edward Stringham, *Business and Society Review* 113, no. 3 (2008): 403–19. In-text references can be found in the bibliography section of this book.

Let us assume, for the moment, that the answers to these questions are yes, that the individuals at banks and insurance companies are discriminatory. If all of these suppositions are true, what will the pricing structure of the discriminatory companies look like? Let us say that home insurance at market rates is $2,000, but urban minorities are overcharged. Just because of their demographics, they have to pay $3,000. By simply discriminating, these insurance companies have enabled themselves to make an extra $1,000 profit on every minority person they insure.

This would be awful, but is it really possible? In this case, insurance companies would try to insure as many minority customers as possible. The more minority customers they sign up, the higher their profits. No profit-driven company would pass up the opportunity to make so much extra money, so they want to attract even more minority customers. Indeed, why would the company bother with non-minority customers at all? With so many profitable minority customers to insure, non-minority customers would be shown the door.

But this institution cannot last for long. Other companies alert to profit opportunities would catch on and undercut their competitors by offering insurance for slightly less. This would attract further business from the minority community, so instead of making $1000 profit on a handful of downtrodden, it could make, say, $900 profit on hordes of people. The latter position would yield enormous profits. Would this be the final outcome? Would minority customers now be exploited, only this time to the tune of $2,900 at the hands of a new competitor?

The answer is no. Retaliation would ensue, and others would charge less, to increase profits in the same fashion. In this case, companies charging $2,900 would lose customers and have to lower their price as well. This process would continue until the price paid by the customer roughly equaled the marginal cost to the company, $2,000. With competition, no firm would be able to exploit minorities by charging them $3,000 for $2,000 insurance. In the long run, if the price of the insurance to a customer stays at $3,000, then that must be its market value.

So why do disparities between insurance rates persist in the absence of laws forcing them to conform? Simple: many insurable risks are higher in the inner city where the minority population is proportionately higher. Through no fault of their own, city dwellers are often faced with higher rates of crimes against their property.

If property is more often the target of burglary, the inner-city insurance customer would need to be reimbursed more often than his suburban counterpart, and this translates to higher premiums. It is totally unrelated to racial discrimination (Williams 1982). All of the additional costs to the insurance company require higher premiums if bankruptcy is not to ensue. The fact that city residents face a higher risk of infringements on their property is unfortunate, but insurance companies set their rates based on actuarial tables, not personal worldviews. If they did, it would create profit opportunities for companies that were more sensible.

Should the owner of a house in a flood plain assume that he should pay the same rate as someone out of harm's way? Of course not. The property has higher risks, and will have higher premiums. There is no discrimination operating here. To the extent that irrational discrimination exists, it would get penalized by the market process.

Yet, some people argue that it is unfair that people should be penalized merely for living in a high-crime neighborhood. The theory is that they have a hard enough time as it is. Insurers should not add to the burden by tacking on penalties for poor living conditions that residents would change if they could. For this reason, many state governments, most famously Massachusetts, have set maximum price ceilings on insurance premiums.

The question becomes whether government intervention in the insurance market is the most effective way to benefit the down-trodden. Unfortunately, government intervention with insurance rates has the unintended consequence of preventing many people from finding insurance. Let us say a company is legally forbidden from charging anything above the going rate for insurance in the suburbs, $2,000. What customers will insurers tend to want to insure? With a price ceiling imposed, the insurance corporations will do everything they can to not insure any inner city residents. The inner city residents will be discriminated against in a real sense, but in this sense the problem is not inherent in the market, the problem stems from price controls. The companies are not being racist; they are simply responding to perverse incentives created by bad policies. The government has moved us from a situation where there had been no shortage of insurance for people in the inner city to one where it is virtually unavailable.

Another tactic is to impose anti-discrimination laws that impose penalties if government notices any systematic disparities in the pricing structure for insurance between racial groups. The company will still face the reality that risk pools are not equal for all people. The companies have to be more subtle about it, but they will do what they can to avoid high-risk areas. In this way, anti-discrimination law works like a price control. It distorts the availability of insurance, raises premiums for everyone, restricts innovation, and dampens competitive bidding among suppliers.

Nowhere is this more obvious than in auto insurance, where states like Massachusetts and New Jersey both mandate insurance and prohibit discrimination. The result has been a financial disaster for consumers. As Kurkjiin (1995a) reports, "Massachusetts is one of few states that prohibits [insurance companies from writing policies that insure homes at their fair market value, instead of their replacement cost], and the financial impact is particularly tough in poorer neighborhoods." The unwillingness of the insurance industry to provide coverage to inner city residents has not stemmed from inherent racism. Rather, it stems from the fact that they are unable to charge prices that cover the costs involved—let alone prices that allow for profit.

Similar problems exist with bank lending to urban minority clients. Many people believe that banks make their decisions based on race rather than on profits, and that the government must step in. If all demographic groups had the same credentials and banks bypassed minority borrowers, there would be a clear case of unfair discrimination. Let us say that most banks are guilty of such prejudice and are unaware about the good risks that certain demographics represent.

If a group of minority borrowers could not receive loans because of unfair discrimination, they would do whatever possible to receive a loan. Such individuals would be so desperate that they would be willing to pay higher than the market interest rate. With a large group of otherwise qualified people willing to pay higher rates, any bank would be foolish not to lend to this group. The first bank to notice the situation could enhance profits by charging these qualified people higher rates. The bank could be run by one entrepreneur who cares more about profits than about discrimination.

The company that discovers this market opportunity would earn above-normal profits by catering to minority borrowers, and discriminating against non-minority borrowers. But this situation could not long endure. Just as in the insurance example above, the banks would compete until long-run profits were zero (Block 1992). Banks would keep undercutting each other's prices in order to attract profitable customers. This process would continue until the point where these qualified minority borrowers would be paying the same rates as their non-minority counterparts. Eventually, all others catch on, and lending rates to the two groups will be the same, all else equal.

In the current world, all else is not equal, so lending rates may differ between demographic groups. Even though every individual has different credentials, government believes that there should be no disparities between groups such as race. Unfortunately, certain minority groups do, in fact, receive a disproportionately lower percentage of loans. But this reflects not personal preferences of bankers but differences in applicants' income, credit ratings, default risk, and assets. Because each individual is different, we should not expect to see averages across groups to always be the same.

Interestingly, when looking at the data, adjusted for all of these factors, we find that some minority groups receive a higher proportion of loans than their credit would suggest. Jacoby (1995) reports that Federal Reserve economists tracked 220,000 federally insured loans and discovered "a higher likelihood of default on the part of black borrowers compared with white households." This finding brings doubt to the hypothesis that current lenders discriminate *against* minorities. If banks were indeed rejecting qualified minorities, then the minorities who did receive loans must have been extra-qualified and would have lower default rates.

Lending to borrowers who are more likely to default is likely a consequence of non-discrimination law, which has used ends determined by politics and pressure groups. For example, regulators need only have a reason to believe that discrimination has taken place before fining banks, blocking mergers, or stopping other kinds of regulatory applications that banks may be working on. Moreover, regulators look for three types of supposed evil: "blatant discrimination," "different-treatment discrimination," or "adverse-impact discrimination." The burden of proof is generally on the accused.

With advances in banking, neighborhood-based banking is in decline, but still there are claims that banks "red line" certain areas out of the lending market, a charge which banks have denied for decades. But there would be little negative effects of red lining, even if done conspicuously. If anything, it alerts competitors that a bank is writing off whole sections of the city where there might be profits to be had.

Again, even if bankers are inherently discriminatory, unless they are willing to forgo profits, their criterion for making loans will be expected monetary returns. If a lender finds few residents in a specific neighborhood qualified for loans, he will take his business elsewhere. Banks look at a potential borrower's likelihood of paying back a loan and these factors of course differ from person to person. But it may be the case that neighborhoods consisting of rental housing have fewer good candidates for home mortgage loans.

To determine whether red-lining should be prohibited requires deciding whether loan decisions should be made by people putting their money on the line or by political agents. Should lending institutions be compelled to make loans against their better judgment? According to many, the answer is yes. For example, the number of hurdles that Fleet Financial Group had to pass when it purchased

Shawmut National Corporation demonstrates this well. Unless the newly formed company promised to make large amounts of loans to the disadvantaged, Massachusetts regulators would not approve the merger. As Reidy (1995) detailed:

> [The most recent commitments] bring to more than $600 million Fleet's commitments in recent months to affordable housing, mortgages, and small business loans. The programs, analysts said, are part of Fleet's efforts to mute opposition from community groups and state agencies as it seeks the approval of federal regulators to purchase Shawmut.

Eventually, the merger was approved, but the politicians imposed significant costs. This is just one of the many examples of how financial decisions have become more and more influenced by the political process.

The insurance market faces its share of government involvement as well. As principles of economics demonstrate, price restrictions prevent supply and demand from equilibrating, creating shortages or surpluses. Because of various price restrictions and regulations, insurers have simply chosen not to underwrite large classes of goods. To fill this void, government is put in the odd position of either mandating private provision or providing financial services itself.

Both controlling private firms and creating state-run enterprises can create perverse incentives. Invariably, this leads to more government involvement (Mises 1992). A state-sponsored insurance company crowds out private firms, because they now have a competitor that can charge less and take tremendous losses without going out of business. The Massachusetts state-sponsored *Fair Plan* provides insurance to people who cannot obtain the private variety. In Roxbury, northern Mattapan, and southwest Dorchester, where a higher percentage of minorities live, over three-quarters of the insured homes are covered by the *Fair Plan*. This compares to half a percent of all homes in Newton, a town with a lower percentage of minorities (Blanton 1995). But the costs of government policies are often ignored. Just because government provides a service does not mean it is free to society. When a state enterprise's expenses exceed its revenue, taxpayers end up footing the bill.

Government regulation is usually promoted as a measure to benefit consumers, while in actuality it can have the opposite effect. It is quite possible that when increased regulation raises costs to producers, they will pass those on to consumers. What has been the result of the regulations and more involvement in Massachusetts? Have they really helped citizens against high insurance costs? The answer is pretty clear: "On average, Massachusetts drivers pay the third-highest auto insurance bills in the country. With rates set by law every year, there has been little opportunity for competition" (Kurkjiian 1995b). With all of its interference in the market, government does not seem to be an effective tool for increasing choices for consumers.

This leads to the question of what is government's proper role in a market economy. Should government be providing banking and insurance to all comers? If the answer is yes, then what makes the insurance industry unique? Consider a contrived example to demonstrate the effects of government interference in these markets. In an effort to make refrigerators more affordable, the state could impose restrictions on that industry. Supposing Frigidaire would charge five hundred dollars for its product, should the government prohibit any price over one hundred dollars? Then, once companies stopped selling as many refrigerators as before, should the bureaucrats mandate that they sell more? Now, Frigidaire would be less likely to sell their refrigerators anywhere, but especially in inner cities. Would they be discriminating by not selling as much? Should the state step in and force them to sell more refrigerators to inner cities, or would Frigidaire not be able to satisfy the need? Should the government then provide affordable refrigerators to the people? This whole scenario is folly. Right now, there simply is no refrigerator "crisis." The U.S. has no "refrigerator policy."[1]

But how different is that imaginary case from what the government is doing to financial services? If the insurance and banking industries

---

[1] That, undoubtedly, is why there is no problem.

were able to operate freely,[2] everybody who could afford and wanted services could get them.[3] There would be no shortages and no need for state-provided services. With fewer restrictions, the quality of services would also increase.

Economic logic forces banks and insurers to be driven not by considerations of discrimination but by the promises of profits. Like the refrigerator industry, anyone who is willing to pay for a good would be able to obtain what they want. Should we allow companies to charge more and allow people to pay more if that is what both parties prefer? Higher insurance rates and higher loan-rejection rates all occur because of higher inner-city costs and higher default risks. As we have seen, discrimination does not cause the higher prices; it is, rather, higher costs that cause higher prices. In an unregulated market, would there be equal insurance rates and bank loans to all people? Any differences among groups, just as differences among individuals, would be reflected in market phenomena. Unfortunately, in the current market, government policies have made it more difficult for city residents to purchase the financial services they demand.

---

[2] Nothing here should be taken to imply that the present authors believe these to be completely free. On the contrary, both depend on restrictions on entry and other illegitimate government interventions. For more on this, see Rothbard (1983, 1994).

[3] It is even less clear why those who advocate policies to help the poor do not request that the poor be given cash transfers to purchase insurance. Perhaps there is an ulterior motive for supporting regulation (Stigler 1971).

PART THREE
MALE-FEMALE EARNINGS AND EQUAL PAY LEGISLATION

IT SEEMS AS THOUGH EVERYONE KNOWS THAT WOMEN GET PAID less than men. However, as this section shows, it's only true that *some* women get paid less than men. It is important to understand which women get paid less, and why. As it turns out, there are good reasons for the difference.

Once these reasons are identified, the problems with so-called "equal pay" legislation can be understood. Whenever legislators pass measures that distort market incentives, there will be unintended consequences. Such consequences are often the exact opposite of the desires of the proponents.

This section includes two speeches and several newspaper articles, including a brief exchange with a critic who favors such legislation and objects to the interpretation offered here.

22. SEMINAR ON RACISM AND SEXISM

WELCOME TO THE SEMINAR ON RACISM AND SEXISM. (LAUGHTER). I'm not kidding. That is the title of the seminar, and it is an accurate one. It might sound funny but it is really very serious. This is because the critics of capitalism accuse the market of being in bed with or intimately connected to racism and sexism. They think that deep within the bowels of free-market economics is prejudice against blacks, women, homosexuals, whomever. This charge needs to be considered very carefully, to be dealt with, because it is very serious. In a sense, the entire free-enterprise edifice is at stake here.

WAGES AND MARGINAL REVENUE PRODUCT

Let us start off by just reviewing the economic concept of marginal revenue product. Sorry to have to bore you with such technical economic considerations, but they are crucial to understanding this issue. Marginal product is the change in total production when one more worker is hired. The marginal revenue product of the Xth worker is the total revenue product of X employees minus the total revenue product of X - 1 of them. Or, to put this in English, to arrive at the marginal revenue product of the 101st worker, you subtract the total revenue product of 100 workers from the total revenue product of 101 workers. What is left is the marginal contribution of the 101st employee.

This is excerpted from a speech given by Walter Block at Mises University, Auburn, Alabama in the summer of 2005.

Assume that a bunch of workers produced $10,000 in an hour. Then we hired one more, and the total revenue of the firm went up to $10,005. I attribute the change to the 101st worker and say that this additional $5 is the 101st worker's marginal revenue product or productivity per hour.

Now, there are three possibilities with regard to wages and marginal revenue productivity on the market. One is that the wage will be higher than the marginal productivity, for example, it will be $7, while the productivity of the worker is $5. However, any company paying its workers more than it gets from them is going to go broke. The second option, if the firm pays its workers below what their productivity is, they will quit and look for other jobs where they can get more money. If, somehow, an employer succeeds in paying a worker $2 for a contribution of $5, some other employer will bid it up to $2.01 or $2.02 or $2.03 and eventually it will get up toward $5, so the third option is that employees will be paid according to their marginal revenue product.

So we economists, and this isn't just Austrians but pretty much all economists except the Marxists (and I'm not sure they are really economists), adhere to the marginal revenue product theory of wage determination: wages are dependent upon productivity.

What, in turn, determines productivity? Well, how hard the employees work, how smart they are, how much training they have, how much capital equipment they can call upon. All of this, in turn, depends upon economic freedom. The more economic freedom, the more of all these things you'll have, and hence the more productivity.

RACISM

Okay, so much for a brief overview. Let me now introduce racism and I'll focus most of the time on sexism or prejudice against females, but I want to first talk a little bit about racism.

There are two kinds of things that go under the general heading of racism. One of them consists of broad empirical generalizations that happen to be true. For example, Walter Williams, a very famous black economist, poses the following problem: Suppose you go to a place like Auburn University. I will give you $500 if you can find someone who can (1) dunk a basketball and (2) solve a quadratic equation. You can offer them $100 to perform these tasks. But you can't ask them anything. All you can do is pick one person out of the masses of Auburn students. Walter Williams said, well, if you use broad empirical generalizations or induction, you'd be very wise to go to a black male and say "I'll give you $100 if you can dunk a basketball." On the other hand, you would be very wise to go to some sort of nerdy-looking, maybe Oriental, kid with a pocket protector and big glasses and say "I'll give you $100 if you can solve the quadratic equation."

But suppose you do it the other way around. That is, ask the geek to dunk, and the brother to solve the math problem. Walter Williams says that you're probably not going to win the $500 reward, based on broad empirical generalizations. And indeed, there's nothing wrong with saying this; it is true. It is just a matter of using common sense, or pre-*judice*, sometimes called prejudice. This just means pre-judging based on past history. It is eminently reasonable to bet that some black kid can dunk the basketball and some Oriental kid with thick glasses can solve the quadratic equation. If this be racism, well, so much the worse for me; it is just common sense applied to a sensitive issue.

Here is another example Walter Williams offers. Suppose you go into a room and you see a tiger sitting on a couch. What do you do? You have two courses of action. One, you could be prejudiced against tigers and close the door (laughter) and sort of hold the door there and call the cops or the animal control people. Or you can be unprejudiced, don't pre-judge tigers, don't profile this tiger on the basis of previous tiger behavior. Here, you go up to the tiger, and say "Hey, what's happenin' tiger?" (laughter) "How's it shakin'?" and you try to give him a high-five. Or, you ask him "Are you vicious?" You are open-minded: just because every other tiger you've ever met will bite, you stay open to the possibility that maybe this tiger won't. If this is racism (or species-ism), make the most of it. This sort of thinking is just behaving on the basis of empirical evidence.

Or, to get back to what I was talking about, the same applies to making the claim that blacks have a lower productivity than whites, on average. There are various theories as to why this should be. People on the left say, This is due to racism, or a vestige of slavery. In the view of Richard Herrnstein and Charles Murray, it is based on IQ.

But I am not interested in *why* this is the case. I am only interested in the conclusion: on average, blacks have lower productivity. That's why they have lower wages, not because of prejudice and discrimination.

FIGURE 1

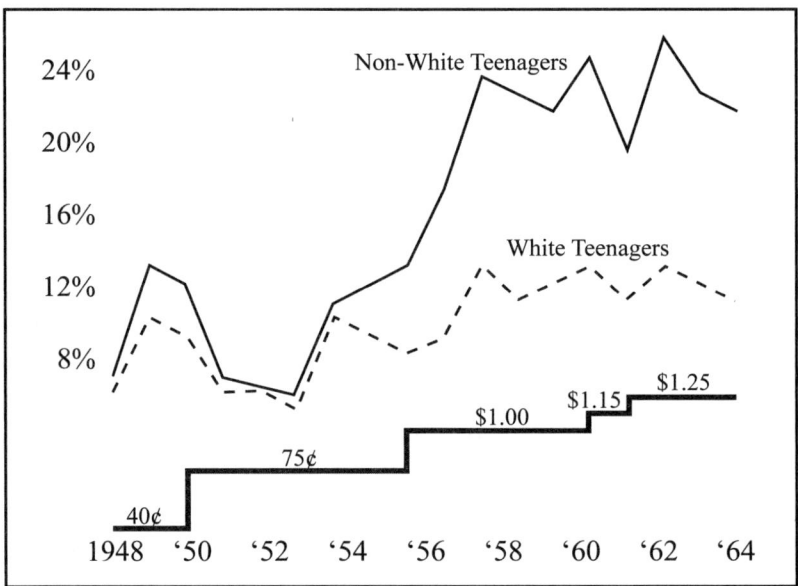

Consider the effects of the minimum wage law, which rises in a stepwise function, on the unemployment rates of white and non-white teenagers. As you can see in Figure 1, the latter is very much higher than the former. And the question is "Why should this be?" The reason is that if you have a minimum wage above productivity levels, you'll have unemployment.

If a person has a $5 an hour productivity level and the minimum wage is $7 an hour, you lose $2 an hour if you hire such a person. There is a higher unemployment rate for blacks than whites because white kids have a higher productivity level than black kids.

Now consider real racism, or real preferences. Again Walter Williams: "When I decided to get married, I immediately eliminated half the human race as a possible marriage partner." He was heterosexual so he didn't want to marry any man (laughter), so immediately he reduced his candidates by half. Three billion members of the human race would not even be considered. What a horrible person he is. A racist, he wanted to marry a black girl, so he engaged in his preference for black women, and he immediately put to the side all white women and oriental women and all other women. Here, he was engaging in racial pre-judice, namely, selecting a mate on this basis.

Of course, he has other preferences besides sex and race, namely, he wanted an attractive woman who had a sense of humor, who was bright. So the man is not only a racist and a sexist but a lookist and a smartist; he is really a bad guy. We ought to put him in jail. Of course, I'm kidding.

Most people, when they think of racial prejudice, picture hanging black people. Now, that is obviously a different kind of racism than making an empirical generalization on one hand or engaging in preferences on the other. Using violence on racial minorities is so different than those two things that we really need a different language to distinguish coercive racism from the non-coercive variety.

EMPLOYER DISCRIMINATION

In nature, the skunk is a very weak animal, and if it didn't have its special smell, it would probably go extinct. Similarly, the porcupine, if it didn't have its quills—think of two porcupines mating, they're gonna be very careful as to how they get together—but if it weren't for those quills, the porcupine would also go extinct. Similarly, the deer is a very weak animal except that it is fleet of foot. Each of these members of the animal kingdom has some sort of compensating differential it can use to overcome what would otherwise be considered a very serious weakness.

So is it in economics. This applies to racial prejudice of the preference type, to the employer who doesn't want to hire blacks. He isn't hanging them, he is only engaging in a certain taste: he prefers whites to blacks as his employees.

Well, blacks have a compensating differential just like the skunk, porcupine, and deer. And what is it? The ability to work for lower wages. Assume that at least some employers were racist and wanted to indulge their preference against blacks. This would imply a lower wage for this group, below what their marginal revenue productivity would otherwise imply.

But this means that if you hired a black, you would make more profits on him than if you hired a white, because the wage of the former was driven down for reasons having nothing to do with productivity—do you get it? do you see the compensating differential at work?—and then you would be able to drive out of business your competitors who were prejudiced against blacks. This is why I say that, under free enterprise, you don't tend to have any racial preferences being indulged in because they continually get driven out of the market. Those who engage in it, whether against women or blacks, it doesn't matter, pay more for workers than those who only are prejudiced in favor of green, as in money. Why, then, are black wages below those of whites? Because their productivity is lower. What in turn, accounts for this? A full exploration here would take us too far afield. Suffice it to say that there are two main theories. First, vestiges of slavery and Jim Crow legislation. Second, lower IQs.

If you have a white and a black kid and they have equal productivity, and the wage of the black is $3 an hour and the wage of the white is $4 an hour, if you hire only whites you pay your labor force $4 an hour, your competitor pays only $3 an hour, he'll be able to underprice you and drive you out of the market. As a result, racial or sexual or any kind of discrimination does not long endure under a regime of economic freedom.

So far, I am only talking about discrimination on the part of employers. There are three sorts of racial or sexual discrimination that are possible in the labor market. One is on the part of the employer, and I hope I've convinced you that any incipient tendency for employer discrimination will vanish *unless* there is a minimum wage law, or something of the sort.

Why? If there is a minimum wage law, then you have discrimination on the cheap. Then there are no penalties. In other words, if you have to pay more than a certain amount, what you do is you take away the smell of the skunk or the quills of the porcupine or the fleetness of the deer or the ability of black teenagers to work for a lower wage, *then* it doesn't work. So it is only on the free enterprise system that discrimination of this sort tends to be eradicated.

EMPLOYEE DISCRIMINATION

Okay, so much for employ*er* discrimination. Employ*ee* discrimination occurs when one group of employees hates the other group of employees, say, whites and Orientals revile each other, or blacks and whites, or Orientals and blacks, whatever. The result in this case is not unemployment or wage differentials; rather, it is segregation in the labor force.

For example, I'm an employer, and I have whites and Orientals on my staff who hate each other; when they get near each other they fight, which reduces their productivity. What I do is I keep them separate. Let's say I'm building houses, so in this development, the one group builds the houses in this section and the other builds houses far away from them. If I have a factory, I keep them in separate parts of it.

CUSTOMER DISCRIMINATION

The third type is *customer* discrimination. That is where this idea of Walter Williams being the customer and trying to find a wife in the marriage market comes in. That is harder to dissipate; it can last longer in that there are no strong market sanctions in operation, in contrast to the employer case. However, even here, there are penalties: consumers with a taste for discrimination will have to pay more than those who are color blind. In the market, you might have different groups of people being voluntarily segregated from one another.

Minorities need not fear the market. There are sources that will come to their rescue as long as you don't have things like minimum wage laws to interfere with this process.

SEXISM

Okay, that is all I'm going to say about racism. Let me now talk a little bit about sexism. Here, I am going to deal with two issues. One, is there a male-female wage gap attributed to prejudice against women and capitalists being evil? And then also, second, I'll talk about the glass ceiling. Why is it that there are so few women in top CEO positions or top politicians or leading scholars in physics or math? The latter is the issue over which Larry Summers, the president of Harvard, got in trouble for daring to discuss. I'll be more than merely discussing this.

MALE-FEMALE WAGE GAP

Here are some cartoons that illustrate the left-feminist, view on discrimination. (Laughter). The first shows a boy baby and a girl baby. They are looking into their diapers, and the caption says "Oh … that explains the difference in our salaries!" This is a socialist feminist cartoon indicating that the reason females are paid less is that the market or employers hate women or deprecate their contributions or diminish them.

This is puzzling because the idea is that most employers are white and male, and somehow they hate females. I mean, the males I know don't hate females. (Laughter). If anything, the very opposite is the case.

Here is another cartoon in this genre. A businessman who has obviously had a bad day is having a beer, and he says to the bartender, "I feel like a man trapped in a woman's salary." The idea here is that there is something endemic in markets that lowers female wages and this guy just is getting in touch with his feminist side.

There are two theories as to why females earn less than males. Before I get into them, let me start off by agreeing with the claim that, indeed, females do make less than males on the market. I do not at all deny that.

The mainstream economic analysis of this situation can be depicted in the supply and demand curves of Figure 2. Whether for whites *vis-à-vis* blacks (left panel), or women vs. men (right panel), in each case there is an original supply and demand curve for labor. Then, we introduced racial (or sexual) discrimination against both supposedly downtrodden groups. When we do, the demand curve for labor in each case, originally based upon marginal revenue product, or productivity for short, now incorporates, also, discrimination, and shifts to the left.

FIGURE 2

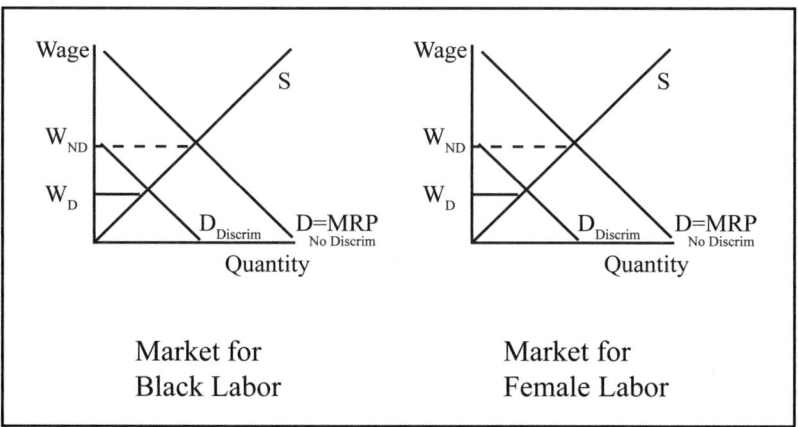

Market for
Black Labor

Market for
Female Labor

Since employers are discriminating against black laborers, their wages fall, and fewer of them are hired. It is the same things for males and females. The demand curve based on non-discrimination or marginal revenue product is only a first approximation. You then add discrimination to the mix to explain why blacks and females get less money than their white and male counterparts.

Let me offer some quotes in support of this mainstream contention. Here's a quote from a feminist: "Jobs held by women are valued less than those held by men, which accounts for the wage gap." A typical sort of claim. And then, they will give you all sorts of statistics to buttress this: "Women with a university degree earn just $1600 a year more than men with a high school education." "Working women who graduated from a university earn just $4,000 more than men with less than grade 9 schooling." These statistics go on and on, explaining that female contributions to the economy are valued less than male contributions.

As I said, I agree that women do earn less than men. Looking at data from the statistical abstract in the 1980s and early 1990s, median weekly earnings for full-time workers, female wages as a percentage of males starts in the 60 percent level and then it gets up to about 75 percent. For the black-white comparison, it's about the same, only it's more stable, staying around 75 percent, 78 percent.

There is a wage gap of some 25 percent, depending upon the year and depending upon whatever else you hold constant. The shift in the demand curve is the theoretical way to explain it and the statistics do bear it out that women earn less than men and blacks earn less than whites.

According to the mainstream, the explanation is racial or sexual discrimination. The other theory, the one that I espouse, is that rather, differences in marginal revenue product account for the earnings gaps. Remember, we started off the hour by saying that marginal revenue product is what determines wage rates. So, if blacks have lower productivity than whites, or if females have lower productivity than males, well, that would account for the wage gap without any discrimination needed.

MARITAL ASYMMETRY HYPOTHESIS

I want to now offer you reasons for thinking that females on average have lower productivities than men. Why is it? Are women inferior?

Well, in the 19th century, they probably were inferior in terms of productivity, because men are stronger than women, have more upper body strength, stronger legs, and when a lot of jobs were in the mines and in the factories and cutting down trees and pushing horses around, it doesn't take any great leap of insight to think that men would be more productive. After all, and this is not contentious, men are bigger and stronger and meaner and they can push horses and cows and trees around better than women can, and men can dig with shovels more effectively.

So in the 19th century, we would expect, even without any discrimination, for there to be some wage gap indicated by the productivity differential. But now in the 21st century, where most of these jobs are done by a button or a lever or from the cab of a truck or a combine, and many, many more jobs are brain jobs and not brawn jobs, the productivity differential would just about disappear. I would expect that, on average, men and women would be equally productive, and, thus, that in a full free-market system, their wages would be equal.

How, then, do I explain this wage gap that persists even to the 20th and 21st century? I entirely reject that supply and demand analysis. Or, rather, I see it as the barest of starting points of the analysis, not the completion. Let me explain by picking on a student, as is my wont. What's your name?

[Student]: Jay

Jay. Suppose Jay and I have the same time for the quarter mile. We can each run it in 52 seconds. That is pretty good time for high school runners; well, at least it was when I was in high school. It is not a good time for the Olympics. You have to go in about 45 seconds to be competitive there.

So Jay and I line up at the starting gate, and just as the gun is ready to go off, I put a 50-pound sack on his back. Who is going to win the race, given that we are otherwise evenly matched? I am going to kill him! Right? Because I'll run the distance in my usual 52 seconds and he'll chug around with a 50-pound sack on his back. If he can finish in under 5 minutes, he is doing pretty well.

My claim is that most women have, in effect, a 50-pound sack on their back, and that is why, on average, their productivity is lower than that of men. And what does this 50-pound sack consist of? It consists of marriage. This is the "Marriage Asymmetry Hypothesis"—the assertion that marriage enhances male productivity in the market and reduces female productivity.

Now let me take a little survey. If you're married, answer me on the basis of your own marriage. If you're not married, respond on the basis of the marriage with which you're most familiar, probably your parents' marriage.

Here are three choices with regard to housework, child rearing, doing errands, shopping, gardening, getting up in the middle of the night to take care of the kids, cooking, cleaning, doing laundry, doing the dishes, all those tasks.

The first choice is that this is done equally between husband and wife. Raise your hands. How many say that that is true of the marriage that they're now thinking about? I've got one liar there, two, three liars. (Laughter).

How many say that the husband does more than the wife? Zero.

And how many say that the wife does more than the husband? Obviously. (Almost the entire group raises their hands). Truth-tellers here. (Laughter). And these two are married and they are still lying through their teeth. (Laughter) I know why he's raising his hand (Laughter). He doesn't want to get in trouble with his wife.

You don't have kids yet?

[Student]: No, we don't.

Just wait. (Laughter). Just wait and see who gets up at 3 in the morning, when the baby cries. I'm not talking about just breast feeding which obviously only one of you can do. I'm talking about everything else involved in child rearing.

When my wife and I had our first kid, she hardly let me near the baby! The same with the second one. I mean, her instinctual attachment or attraction to the baby was amazing. I love my kids, I hugged them and kissed them all the time, well, at least when they were a bit younger. But her attachment to our children was vastly superior to mine. My wife practically shunted me aside when it came to bringing up our children.

I am making a point about opportunity cost. This is a basic element of Austrian economics. It should be of all economics, but the neoclassicals only pay lip service to this concept. But opportunity or alternative costs is a basic element of Austrian economics. If you want to be a concert violinist, what do you have to do? You have to practice all day. You know that joke: "How do you get to Carnegie Hall? Practice." (Laughter.)

(In response to a puzzled student's facial expression:) Look, if I have to explain the joke we're in trouble. (Laughter.)

Well, if you want to give concerts, you are going to have to practice the violin, 6, 8, 10 hours a day. But if you do so, are you going to be a good heart surgeon? No, because a heart surgeon, too, has to take care of business for many hours of the day.

There are opportunity costs. If you have your heart and mind and soul on the home, and child rearing, if you are doing a vastly disproportionate amount of home work, well then it should be no accident that your productivity in the market, which is a very different thing, should be lower. It's as if you have the 50-pound sack on your back during the race. Of course you'll have lower productivity.

Here's another joke. The husband and the wife are both chemists; they both work in the pharmacy, pharmaceutical company, lab, whatever, all day. They come home at night together at 8 o'clock. What does the husband say to the wife? "What's for dinner?" This occurs because he is not as good a cook as she is for various cultural, or rather biological, reasons, but we'll get to that in a bit.

Another story. The husband and wife both have a job in Auburn, and one of them gets a great job offer in San Francisco; the other will just have to take what he or she can get when they both arrive. Under what conditions are they more likely to move? To enhance the husband's income or the wife's income? Obviously, the husband's income. This is because the couple acts as if they're a profit-maximizing or wage-maximizing firm. If they expect to have say, three babies, each three years apart, starting in three years, by the time the youngest one is in kindergarten and the wife can then go back into full-time work, 15 years will have passed.. So isn't it silly to move where the wife gets a job and the husband has to take whatever he can get: drive a cab or be a waiter? Do you get the point?

So the couple is acting, even if they have equal abilities, and even if they have equal attachment to the home, so as to maximize his income. Is it any wonder that his income and productivity is higher than hers? That is the marital asymmetry explanation.

Here's a quote with regard to housework, about two sociologists (from *Newsweek*):

> To their surprise, the sociologists discovered that the social and economic gains won by so many American women during the past decade have had remarkably little impact on the traditional gender roles assumed by the more than 3600 married couples in their study. Although 60% of the wives had jobs, only about 30% of the husbands believed that both spouses should work, and only 39% of the wives thought so. No matter how large their paycheck, the working wives were still almost entirely responsible for the couple's housework. Husbands so hated housework, the researchers found, that wives who asked them to help out could sometimes sour the marriage.

We just took an informal survey here. It showed that the overwhelming number of people, based on the marriage with which they are most familiar, the wife does the lion's share of the housework. The husband hardly does anything.

LOGICAL PROOFS

I have two sets of proofs for this contention, namely, that it is the marital asymmetry hypothesis and differential productivity of husbands and wives that accounts for the pay gap and not prejudice on the part of employers. The first set of proofs is logical. The second set is empirical.

First, let us consider the logic of the matter as shown in Figure 3. What the left-wing feminists are asking us to believe is that the productivity of male and female is the same, and I'm assuming that the productivity is $10 an hour, and that the wage of the male is $10 and the wage of the female is $7.50 which would give roughly the 25 percent wage gap that we're talking about.

FIGURE 3

	Male	Female
Wage	$10	$7.50
Productivity	$10	$10

Profit = Productivity - Wage
Male: 10 -10 = 0
Female: 10 - 7.50 = 2.50

They are asking you to believe that this is an equilibrium situation. Let us do a profit analysis on this hypothetical data. Now suppose you are an employer, and as you know, the profit earned off of workers is based on their productivity minus the wage you pay them. It is clear that the profit earned by your firm from the male is $10 productivity minus $10 wage or zero, which is fine; in equilibrium there are no profits. But what is the profit from the female? Well, the woman is equally productive at $10 an hour and you are paying her $7.50, so you, as her employer, make $2.50 an hour off of her. It is as if she has a little sign on her lapel, saying, "If you hire me, you make an extra $2.50 over and above what you could by hiring a man." You see the point? This could never ever last.

A foolish "sexist pig" might say, "No, no, no, women belong barefoot, pregnant, in the kitchen, I am never going to hire one, ever, because they are evil, or inferior, or whatever. I'm only hiring men. And I'm paying them $10-an-hour." Remember, in our example, the women are just as good as the men, in terms of productivity, but you can have them for a mere $7.50. Well, you make an extra $2.50 off of each one of them. You'll be able to underbid the counterpart, male, chauvinist pig employer and drive him out of business.

Another implication of this is that in industries that are even nowadays mainly dominated by men, forestry, mining, cement works, they would make less profit than in industries where they could exploit women, such as secretaries or librarians or teachers. But we know that profits in all industries have to be the same (abstracting from risk). Otherwise, there would be a movement of investment money to bring them toward equality. If the profits in copper are higher than in steel, people will get into copper lowering the profits there and get out of steel raising those profits until there is some sort of equilibrium at least approached; at least, there is a continuing, ongoing tendency in this direction.

So this story is just nonsense on stilts. It is just plain crazy. It's lunacy. It's illogical. Who is that guy with the pointy ears? In Star Trek? Yes, Spock! Thanks. He'd say "This is illogical." This can't be.

The do-gooders say, "Let's have a legal minimum wage for men and women." This is called equal pay for equal work. If we did that, then we would pay men and women $10. In this case assume the male productivity is also $10, but now, the female productivity is realistically $7.50, as shown in Figure 4.

FIGURE 4

	Male	Female
Min. Wage	$10	$10
Productivity	$10	$7.50

Again, this is not because women are inferior, but because they have something else on their minds, they have a 50-pound sack on their back when it comes to working in the market. There is no biological inferiority, certainly not in the 20th or the 21st centuries, although there might have been one in the 18th or 19th centuries because of this upper-body-strength business. But if you do the profit analysis, the firm will now lose money on women if you have to pay them $10 and they are only worth $7.50. Then adult women will be unemployed, the fate now suffered by teenagers.

Regarding equal-pay-for-equal-work legislation, you already *get* equal pay for equal work in the market. It doesn't seem that this is the case, since females earn less than males, and are supposedly equally productive. But they are not. Women who would otherwise have equal productivity with men, instead have less, because of their intensive home and baby interests. If you demand that the two genders be paid the same amount even though females are worth less on the market, they will become unemployed. Then, firms will lose money if they hire a woman (at a wage higher than her real productivity level). Right now, the male and female unemployment rates are about the same. But if this stupid and evil law were enacted, that would no longer hold.

So much for the pure logic of the matter.

EMPIRICAL PROOFS

Now for the empirical side. Remember, what I just said is that marriage enhances male incomes and lowers female incomes.

Well, what about people that have never been married? Not widowed people who have been touched by the institution of marriage, not divorced people, not separated people who have also been touched by the institution of marriage, but people who have never been married. At all. Not widowed, not separated, not divorced, not nothing. Just never married. The implication of what I'm saying is that here, the wage gap should be zero. Right? Because I'm tying this whole thing on marriage, so therefore, if we abstract from marriage, and there are people that have never been married, the wage gap ought to go away. Entirely.

Let us look at the statistics in Table 1. Female-to-male earnings in percentage terms. Total (all people, whether ever married or not): 37 percent. Ever married: 33 percent. Never married: 99 percent.[1]

---

[1] Walter Block, "Economic Intervention, Discrimination, and Unforeseen Consequences," in *Discrimination, Affirmative, Action and Equal Opportunity*, Walter Block and Michael A. Walker, eds., Vancouver: The Fraser Institute, 1982), pp. 101–25.

Table 1 | Female / Male Earnings in % Terms

	Total	Ever Married	Never Married
Canada 1971, aged 30+	37.4	33.2	99.2
Canada 1971, university degree	61.2	56.8	109.8
Canada 1982, HS diploma	67.4	63.8	93.4
	All	25+	16–24
U.S. 1983, all workers	76.8	74.4	94.8

Just look at the top line here. This is a smoking gun for the marital asymmetry hypothesis. It says that men and women who have never been married earn about the same amount of money. I got these statistics when I was working at the Fraser Institute in Canada. Statistics Canada, which is the equivalent of the Bureau of Labor Statistics in the U.S., didn't even calculate this material. We had to pay them tens of thousands of dollars to make a special calculation for us. And when they saw that, they didn't believe it and they didn't like it, but they gave it to us because we had paid them for it.

This is proof positive, if you believe in empirical proofs. I don't, I don't trust their statistics any more than I can throw them; I rely more on what I said was the logic of it, but it is nice to have the empirical evidence illustrate the point. Not prove it, but illustrate it.

You see, the prejudice or discriminatory hypothesis doesn't make sense. It is dead from the neck up. Here I am, I'm a male chauvinist pig, I hate all women, I want to deprecate them, I don't distinguish between married and unmarried women, between widowed, separated, and divorced women, they're all women, and to hell with them! Right? That's my attitude! Well then why am I discriminating against ever-married women and not never-married women? The facts are simply incompatible with this interpretation of the average employer.

Here are some more statistics. Consider the female/male earnings ratio for Canada 1971 for those with a university degree, for all, ever-married, and never-married. Notice the gigantic difference in the last figure: females actually earned 9.8 percent more than males. For a while, I was competing with Walter Williams and Thomas Sowell to see who could get the highest female-to-male ratio for never-marrieds. They were working on U.S. data, me on Canadian. I forget who won this battle, but 9.8 percent is pretty significant.

Consider again the fact that never-married females earn "only" 99.2 percent of what their male counterparts do. Is this incompatible with the marital asymmetry explanation? Not at all. When you're dealing with statistics, you don't ever get full clarity. You are not going to get 100 percent. The statistics are always going to diverge a little bit from that "ideal." Sometimes the data are wrong, sometimes, surveyors make mistakes. And, who says that male and female productivity is *exactly* equal? The figure 99.2 percent is as close as you are going to get to support a hypothesis in the real world of statistical data.

And the same applies to the figure 93.4 percent, where the wage gap is about 6 percent. But when you get a wage gap of 6 percent as opposed to 30 percent, that's no gap at all. What I am trying to say is that you cannot expect full support of any hypothesis, such as the marital asymmetry explanation of the male female income gap. The figures vary around 100 percent, some higher, some lower.

Now take the last line of table 1. Here, what we did, instead of comparing male and female based on marital status, we took a proxy variable for ever-married and never-married. What we said is people who are 16–24 are in effect never married (of course there are some exceptions) and compared them to people who are 25 and above, and posited that this latter group is a proxy for the ever marrieds (again, of course, there are exceptions). Look at the resulting female-male ratio, at the gigantic difference there, between all, and the other two groupings. The idea here is that being 25 and above is a proxy variable for being ever-married, because more people who are 25 and above have ever been married, whereas people 16–24, some of them have been married, but fewer, so we're saying that a proxy variable for never-married is being younger. Look at the gigantic difference in the wage gap. So it's just another way of indicating what's going on here. Namely, among the "ever marrieds" here, now shown by age 25+, the wage gap between female and male is about 25 percent. In contrast, amongst those aged 16–24, the gap falls to about 5 percent. Again, why would supposedly male, chauvinistic employers discriminate against women in such different ways, based solely upon their age, of all things?

Let us now summarize this part of the talk. There is a wage gap. The reason that we have a wage gap has got nothing to do with prejudice or discrimination of any kind on the part of the business firm. The reason is different productivity levels. If it weren't different productivity levels, if they had the same productivity, anyone engaging in discrimination would lose money and tend to go broke. So in the long run, in the marketplace, discrimination would be continually eroded and weeded out; presumably, at any given time, it would be gone.

GLASS CEILINGS

Okay, I'm going to get into the really radical stuff—the glass ceiling. That is, why are there so many men, and so few women, at the very, very top of virtually all professions, from business to the arts to athletics, to politics to, well, just about everything else? Why is it that women can only rise so high, and no higher? Why do we have a glass ceiling? When Larry Summers asked this, and he said that it is possible that the explanation is that male and female brains are different, he practically got fired as president of Harvard. Well I'm going to go further than him, way further—happily, I won't get fired as president of Harvard, because I'm not—but I'll go further than him and say it's not a possibility, this is a really good explanation for the glass ceiling: biology. That is, women and men are very different biologically, and this alone explains the glass ceiling phenomenon.

How are they different biologically? Well, before I give you my analytic device, let me buttress the case that they are very different. First of all, let's take prisons. What percentage of men and women are in prisons? Around 95 percent of all prisoners are men, and around 5 percent are women.[2] What percent of males and females are in mental institutions? Again, the same sort of statistic arises: around 95 percent of inmates in mental institutions are men, and around 5 percent are women.

What percent of people are in cemeteries before their time? Obviously, at the end of the day, all men and all women end up in cemeteries. None of us escapes life alive. By "before their time" I mean that if you were to look at 25–50-year-olds who are already in cemeteries, whom would we find? Again, you get the same 95 percent – 5 percent split as before. Whether this results from war, or fighting, or gangs, or mayhem, or robberies gone bad, men are vastly overrepresented in this statistic.

This is part and parcel of the glass ceiling, the left tail of the explanation, so to speak. Look at figure 5. What we have here is a frequency distribution; on the x or horizontal axis there is something like I.Q. or ability, however measured. So far I have been describing points A and B. A is on the male curve at the top of the diagram, and B is on the female curve, which juts up in the very middle of the distribution, but otherwise lies below the male curve. If you look at places over here on the far left of the distribution, that is where prisons, cemeteries for people before their age, mental institutions, we find virtually all men and no women. A is in effect the 95 percent I have been talking about, and B is the 5 percent.

---

[2] Editor's Note: "By yearend 2002, women accounted for 6.8 percent of all prisoners, up from 6.1 percent in 1995. Relative to their number in the U.S. resident population, men were about 15 times more likely than women to be in a State or Federal prison. At yearend 2002, there were 60 sentenced female inmates per 100,000 women, compared to 906 sentenced male inmates per 100,000 men." Paige M. Harrison and Allen J. Beck, Ph.D., "Prisoners in 2002," *Bureau of Justice Statistics Bulletin* (July 2003), http://www.ojp.usdoj.gov/bjs/pub/pdf/p02.pdf.

FIGURE 5

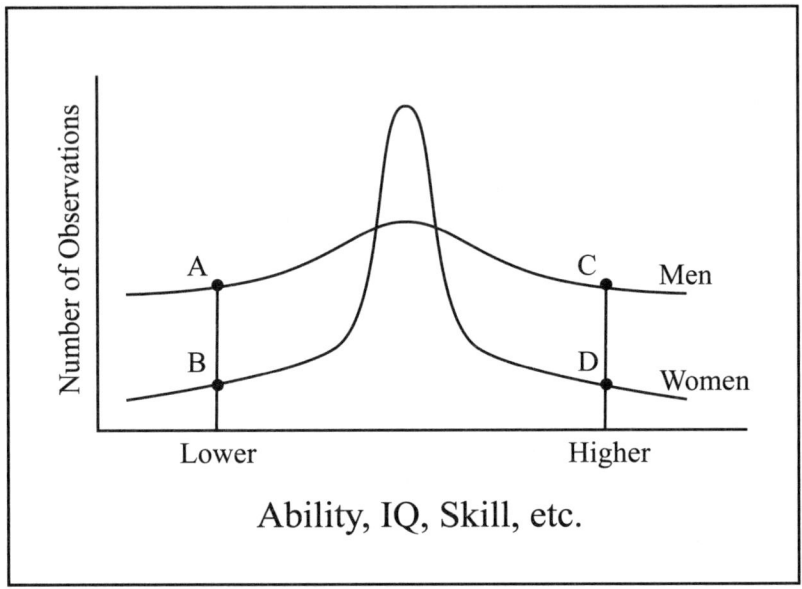

Now let us look at the far right side of the distribution. What's going on here? Well, let's take grandmasters in chess. It used to be, before the Polgar sisters—anyone into chess here? no—before the Polgar sisters, three Hungarian sisters, the best grandmaster (they have ranking of chess grandmasters), the highest-ranked woman grandmaster was around 450th. Then the Polgar sisters came bursting into the chess world in the last 10, 20 years. They are amazing. The worst of them is around 300th. The second best of the Polgar sisters was roughly the 200th ranked grandmaster. And the best of them I think was ranked 20th. Some ungodly high ranking; the best in all of chess history. Namely, in chess grandmasterships, the men are the 99 percent level and the women are at the 1 percent level.[3]

---

[3] Editor's note: As of October 2006, Judit Polgar is the #1 ranked woman in the world, and #16 overall. Zsuzsa (Susan) Polgar has been ranked as high as the #1 woman in the world, but she has not made the Top 100 overall. The third sister, Sofia, is an International Master, but not a Grandmaster. There are

Let's take Nobel prizes. And I'm not talking about wishy-washy, wussy fields like Literature, where they give it to females to even things out. I'm talking about physics, and chemistry, and even economics. In economics, there is but one female Nobel prize winner: Elinor Ostrom in 2009. To the best of my knowledge Madame Curie is the only one who won in physics, or any of the hard sciences.[4]

In math, they don't have any Nobel prize, but there is the Fields medal; so far, only men have won. Now let us consider CEOs of companies and presidents of countries. There was Indira Gandhi, Golda Meir, there was Margaret Thatcher, and there was this gal in the Philippines, I forget her name, and that's about it. Uh, Gloria Arroyo. You know, four that I could name, and that probably exhausts all the ones unless I'm missing Lichtenstein or something like that. We are now talking points C for the men and D for the women.[5]

---

nearly 1000 grandmasters, so she is not in the top 1000 overall. Thus, there is exactly 1 woman in the top 100 chess players, or 1 percent. For the ratings by the Federation Internationale des Eches (World Chess Federation), see: www.fide.com/ratings/toplist.phtml

See also: http://en.wikipedia.org/wiki/Judit_Polgar.

[4] Editor's note: "Female Nobel Prize laureates accounted for 34 out of a total of 723 prizes awarded as of 2005. Marie Curie is not only the first woman to be awarded a Nobel Prize, but also one of four persons to have been awarded the Nobel Prize twice," according to: http://en.wikipedia.org/wiki/Female_Nobel_Prize_laureates.

There have been 11 women who won the Nobel in hard sciences: 3 in chemistry (out of 148), 2 in physics (out of 176), and 7 in physiology/medicine (out of 183). Even Literature has had only 10, compared to 102 men. The Peace Prize has had 2 women, compared to 114 men. In Literature, women won 10 times (out of 102), including 1991, 1993, 1996, and 2004, so even in our P.C. era, women aren't winning this award all that frequently.

[5] Editor's Note: http://en.wikipedia.org/wiki/List_of_Female_Presidents shows 39 women presidents between 1953 and 2006. Wikipedia lists 98 countries with presidents at http://en.wikipedia.org/wiki/Category:Presidents, but of these, it lists only 7 current female heads of government: Gloria Macapagal-Arroyo is President of the Phillippines, Helen Clark is Prime Minister of New Zealand, Luisa Diogo is Prime Minister of Mozambique, Ellen Johnson-Sirleaf is President of Liberia, Angela Merkel is Chancellor of Germany, Maria do

Virtually all the leaders, the CEOs, the math, the physics, the chess, are males. It is almost as if males are God's or nature's crap shoot, and females are nature's or God's insurance policy. Females are all clustered toward the middle. Right? There are very few females out on these tails, whereas men are all over the lot.

I am drawing these frequency distributions to accentuate the point I am trying to make. They are not derived from any official statistics. I am drawing the curves in the way I have so as to make my point clearer. Namely, the variance of women is very low. The standard deviation of women's abilities is narrow. They are virtually all clustered toward the middle; there are very few outliers. Yes, every once in a while there's Lizzie Borden who kills someone, but this is very, very rare.

Women are clustered in the middle. That is why we have a glass ceiling. Not because of prejudice, or discrimination, or capitalism being evil, or anything like that. It's because women are God's or nature's insurance policy and men are His crap shoot. And in the crap shoot, some men get very, very good genes, and other men get very bad genes and end up in a bad way.

The question to which I now want to address myself is "Why is it that this is so?" I hope I've convinced you that it *is* so.

Yes?

[Student question.[6]]

Well, this means that there are a lot of women in the middle, in other words, who have average IQs or average abilities.

Yes, you understand me. These women over here at D are better than these men at A. So "better" means further along to the right on the X axis. It's IQ or some sort of generalized ability, the kind that gets you Nobel prizes, chess grandmasterships, CEO status, etc.

Carmo Silveira is Prime Minister of the Democratic Republic of São Tomé and Príncipe, and Khaleda Zia is Prime Minister of Bangladesh. Given the roughly two hundred countries currently in existence, the 7 women heads of government amount to approximately 3–4 percent.

[6] The student question was not clear on the tape recording, but the meaning can be inferred from the answer.

SOCIOBIOLOGY

Let us discuss sociobiology in this regard. Sometimes known as evolutionary psychology by people who want to be politically correct, the theory is that we are the way we are now because of what it took to survive a million or so years ago. We are descended from people who liked babies, who were unhappy with crying babies, and took pleasure from happy babies. Imagine another tribe just like us with the same abilities, the same opposable thumb, the same IQ, only they didn't care about babies. What would have happened to them? They would not have survived.

Similarly with aggression. Males are much more aggressive than females. Any society composed of, who are those women warriors, what are they called? Amazons. Any Amazon society would not have outcompeted our own. We come from a patriarchal society. An Amazon society that sent the women out to fight and allowed the women to serve as cannon fodder, undertaking dangerous hunting and fighting, would go extinct. Look, the reason the farmer keeps 50 cows and 1 bull and not 50 bulls and 1 cow is because additional males are superfluous. Right? You don't need that many men to impregnate all the females. But every time you lose a female, you lose population, and if you're having a competition between our patriarchal society and these other matriarchal societies (if they ever existed in the first place), we whip them because we use the extraneous men, not the precious women, as cannon fodder. Correctly so, from a biological point of view.

Germany and Russia had a fight with each other in World War II, where they kicked the crap out of each other. At the end of that war, there was hardly a man left standing between the ages of 20 and 50; certainly, there were relatively few of this age cohort who were able-bodied. There were a few around. But they were enough, more than enough, to impregnate any woman that wanted to get impregnated. (Laughter) They must have had a grand time; this just shows how generous men are with their sperm. But, the societies lasted. Both Germany and Russia survived.

Now suppose that the war between the Nazis and the commies had been conducted by women, where men were mainly the bystanders, such that there were hardly a woman between 18 and 40 who was alive. There would have *been* no next generation. You see why it is that women are much more important, biologically, than men are.

Okay, now, here is our own society. I say our society is this way, patriarchal, not matriarchal. One way to prove this to take the opposite scenario, and show why that couldn't exist. This is an economic way of arguing. You want to prove something? Take its opposite and show why that's ridiculous.

So, let's suppose that on figure 5, the curve AC now depicts females, and BD indicates males. The very opposite of our previous, correct assumption. Let's suppose that there was this other society a million years ago that was just as good as our society in terms of ability, in terms of inventing the wheel, using tools, and just as strong and smart as us, only there, the men were the insurance policy BD—this is now the men, right?—and the females are this group, AC.

Why are we whipping them demographically? First of all, all these females over here at A are going into early graves, they're going into the caveman version of mental institutions and jails. Right? None of these women are now available for child creation.

So how can this matriarchal society outcompete us when a very high proportion of their women can't have babies? Or if they have babies, they kill them, or at best mistreat them. Remember, there are now lots of women out there at point A, who are incompetent idiots. Their incompetence places them at the left tail of the distribution. You see that?

On the other hand, these women at C, the ones who were inventing the wheel and better spears and stuff, they're out hunting wild animals and they are getting decimated. Do you see why a society that's constituted that way would not compete with ours?

Now look, I have a daughter. I don't much like this sociobiological analysis because I want her to win a Nobel prize in something or other.

She's a very bright girl. When she was in high school, she used to beat the nerd boys in math and physics. In college, she got great marks. She's now taking a Ph.D. in neuroscience at Johns Hopkins which is one of the best places in that field. A very bright girl. Very, very bright. She explains to me what she's doing and I don't know what the hell she's talking about. (Laughter) Very bright girl. I'd love for her to be at the top of her profession; break right through the glass ceiling. And she has a chance, just a very small chance, for there are very few girls that are that bright. She is located at point D in figure 8.

I'm not saying to the females in the audience, "Don't try. Don't strive. Don't become a great Austrian economist or a great libertarian." I'm just saying the odds of a girl being the next Murray Rothbard are much less than a guy being the next Murray Rothbard. Because there are just so few people, so few females out there in the IQ of 180 or 200 or something like that. Very, very few. Males greatly exceed them. C is far greater than D, and remember, we are getting back to reality, C is where leading males are located and D is for their counterpart females.

I don't much like it. It would be nicer in some way if reality weren't that way. I take the position I do, however, because I am trying to explain why we have a glass ceiling. And this seems to be the best explanation for that phenomenon.

And with that I stop and now call for questions.

QUESTIONS AND ANSWERS[7]

ANSWER 1

Let me make two comments in response. First of all, you don't have to be respectful. I mean, as long as you don't come up to the stage and punch me out (laughter), I'm ok with you raising your point. You're bigger than I am, and as long as you're not nasty, I

---

[7] Editor's note: The student questions were unintelligible on the tape. What follows are the answers, alone. Hopefully, the intelligibility will be attained through the context.

encourage people to ask sharp, acerbic questions. I'm putting forth very controversial views. It would be churlish of me to say "No, you have to treat me with kid gloves." What I want you to do is to take your best shot, intellectually, as you have been doing, so don't be apologetic, and say, "Oh, you know, I, I'm trying to be easy on you," or something like that.

Now, my claim is that there *never was* any of this discrimination. There *never was* any of this stuff that critics of the market are alleging. Racism or sexism, or any form of discrimination on the part of the employer do not account for wage differentials, nor did they ever. If there was any of this sort of thing in operation, the market would have eradicated it. Could there be some vestiges of it? Sure. The market is not perfect, but the market keeps grinding away at people who pay women lower than their productivity levels.

On the other hand, do not forget, there is such a thing as consumer discrimination. If whites in the south in past decades did not want to sit at the same lunch counters with blacks, and the employer banned blacks outright, or arranged to have them sit at a different part of the restaurant, that counts as consumer, not firm, discrimination.

So there were never any restrictions on entry or any of that stuff. Women, for many years, could go to law school or whatever, or become a doctor. There were very few of them that wanted to be, so that would be my rough answer to the question.

ANSWER 2

I'm not assuming that the market is perfectly competitive. It would take me too far afield to give the Austrian critique of this concept. Suffice it to say that I am assuming rivalrous competition; in effect, that there are no barriers to entry. If profits rise in an industry, no law bars newcomers. Based on this, there is a tendency in this direction of equating wages and productivity levels. The real reason women were not or are not doing as well as men in terms of wages was because of productivity differences, not employer discrimination. Not because of culture, because culture emanates from biology, and biology plays a great role in male-female differences.

ANSWER 3

Yes, there is discrimination on the part of consumers. When you go to a Chinese restaurant, most consumers want to have a Chinese waiter, even though you don't really need one, nor do you really need a Chinese chef, because surely Westerners can cook just as well as the Chinese if they just learn how to do it. It's just that consumers want this.

Similarly, with airplanes, it used to be that the stewardesses all had mini-skirts, because the airlines couldn't compete on the basis of price, so they started competing in terms of shortness of skirts, youth and beauty of the women. And most men want to see young scantily clad women. There are sociobiological reasons for this too. Suppose a different culture had as its male ideal women between the ages of, say, 50–70; while ours focused on females between the ages of, oh, 18–35. Those guys salivated over older women, and pretty much ignored younger ones as sex objects, the opposite of typical male reaction in our own society. Who would win the biological competition? Obviously, we would out-compete them. In the extreme, if none of their males coupled with young women, but only much older ones, they would die out in just one generation. Actresses of a certain age complain they can no longer get leading roles. This is why.

It is only because of affirmative action that you have male stewardesses, what do you call them? Flight attendants. If not for that, they'd all be female and they'd be young and pretty. In the free society, there would be ageist discrimination like it used to be decades ago. Firms would fire a stewardess after she got to be 30 or so, so there would always be young ones, because men want young women for sociobiological reasons.

Let me take another hack at this. Imagine there was a society where when the males saw a woman in her 60s they said, "Whoop dee do. Let me at her." And when they saw a woman of about 25, they said, "Nnnn, not ripe yet." How many babies would that society have? Not too many. The reason our males find a 25-year-old woman more attractive than a 65-year-old woman, despite the fact that there are some 65-year-old women who are very attractive, but men gravitate toward the 25-year-old is because we descend from a tribe that liked 25-year-olds because if they liked 65-year-olds, we would no longer be around because you can't have babies with them.

ANSWER 4

There was this MIT case, where the women in the physics department were moaning that their offices were smaller and the male physicists had more staff and higher salary. But if you look at their publications, and their publications are supposed to be double-blind refereed so you don't know who the sex of the author is, I would imagine, I haven't discovered this or haven't examined this because there had been no statistics forthcoming, but I would imagine that all the female ones that were married had way fewer publications and lower-quality publications than the males, because of this interest in the home and all. It is more than passing curious that information of this sort was never forthcoming in this imbroglio.

I suspect that most of the females in physics and math are there in the first place due to some sort of affirmative action. When Harvard President Larry Summers was apologizing for daring to discuss these issues, he promised a new $50 million program to hire female scientists. Well, when he uses $50 million to hire female scientists, the money will not go to the best scientists, who are male. Rather, this is an affirmative action for female scientists, not the first one either.

ANSWER 5

All I can say is that if women or blacks are more productive, they will be paid more. Oprah Winfrey is a black woman and she is paid very well, she is probably in the highest one-tenth of one percent of all wage earners. And the reason is she can put people in the stands and she interests them and they buy products that she endorses.

Suppose I said, "Well, she's a black and a woman and therefore I'm not going to hire her for any amount of money." I wouldn't be making much profit. The guy who did hire her would make more than I, and be able to drive me out of business. And what about all those black rap stars, athletes, musicians, actors? It is the same with female actresses, movie stars, popular singers. The ones who sell lots of tickets, who attract avid customers, are compensated very well.

Of course, these are exceptions. Most women are clustered in the middle of the distribution and are paid accordingly.

ANSWER 6

I agree with you. When we have things like the minimum wage law, it exacerbates these problems.

Thanks for your attention.

23. Directions for Future Research in Equal Pay Legislation

There are many Canadians who now support equal-pay legislation.[1] As one indication of the popularity of this idea, the three major political parties in this nation seem to have adopted for themselves several of the major planks of this program.[2]

But there are problems. If legislation incorporating equal pay for equal work and equal pay for work of equal value is enacted, the present (mainly) marketplace determination of wages will inevitably tend to be replaced by the arbitrary edicts of civil servants, bureaucrats, consultants, judges, and/or human rights boards.[3] In contrast, one of the important functions of wages in the market system is to allocate

---

Originally appeared in *Toward Equity: Proceedings of a Colloquium on the Economic Status of Women in the Labor Market*, Muriel Armstrong ed., Ottawa: The Economic Council, pp. 119–21, 179–82.

[1] There are two major variants: equal pay for equal work and equal pay for work of equal value.

[2] The debate between Brian Mulroney, John Turner, and Ed Broadbent on Women's Issues, August 15, 1984. See *The Globe and Mail* and *The Vancouver Sun*, August 16, 1984. This is also the subject of bipartisan agreement in the United States, as the "comparable work" bill H.R. 5680 passed by a vote of 413 to 6 (on June 20, 1984).

[3] See National Academy of Sciences, *Women, Work, and Wages* (Washington, D.C.: 1981). In this system, the "value" of jobs is determined by arbitrarily assigning points, or scores, to the standard elements of jobs such as skill, effort, responsibility, and working conditions.

labor to its most needed and productive locations. If this process is short-circuited by equal-pay-for-equal-work (EPFEW) and equal-pay-for-work-of-equal-value (EPFWEV) legislation, then labor mobility to that extent will be reduced.[4] But it is important that workers locate themselves in accord with changing consumer demands. Unless they can be induced to act in this manner by market signals in the form of wage changes, the flexibility of the economy will be diminished.[5] As well, equal-pay enactments function so as to "protect male jobs from low-wage female competition."[6]

Things would be bad enough if EPFEW and EPFWEV were required to right wrongs now existing in the labor market. Then, we would have to face a tradeoff between the injustice of discriminatory

---

[4] Without wage differentials to lead workers around "as if by an invisible hand" (said Adam Smith), the only remaining market signal will be the varying unemployment rates in several industries. (Workers will shift from high-unemployment sectors to low-unemployment ones.) However, labor mobility will still be reduced, with only one effect, not two, working on its behalf. As well, there is a tendency for our present unemployment insurance program to enhance unemployment and to decrease labor mobility. See Herbert C. Grubel and Michael A. Walker (eds.), *Unemployment Insurance* (Vancouver: The Fraser Institute, 1978). It is thus difficult to see how the Canadian labor force can be successfully induced to organize itself in accordance with the ever-changing desires of Canadian consumers under a regime of relatively fixed wages.

[5] It is clear that equal-pay enactments are but yet another version of wage controls. Yet, the experience of centuries of wage controls has shown that they misallocate labor, harm the best interests of most employees, and reduce economic efficiency. See Michael Walker, ed., *The Illusion of Wage and Price Controls* (Vancouver: The Fraser Institute, 1976).

[6] Morley Gunderson, "Factors Influencing Male-Female Wage Differences in Ontario," (Toronto: Research Branch, Ontario Ministry of Labour), p. 103. Similarly, in the Republic of South Africa, the white-racist unions advocate equal pay for equal work as a better means than job reservation laws of protecting their jobs against the competition of lower-paid black workers. See Leon Louw, "Free Enterprise and the South African Black," Address to Barclay's Executive Women's Club, Johannesburg, South Africa, July 31, 1980, p. 4. This is a paradox. In South Africa, equal pay for equal work is advocated as a means of protecting a favored group (white unionists), while in Canada it is urged as a way of helping an unfavored group (females).

behavior imposed on women by employers and the risks of economic inefficiency. But a drawback of equal-pay legislation is that women are not being victimized in the labor market by the discriminatory practices of employers. Thus, such legislation will not be effective in its main object: it is a cure for which there is no disease.

According to the most recent statistics available, the ratio of female to male earnings in Canada is .64.[7] At first glance, this might appear as *prima facie* evidence of the existence of employer discrimination against women. But, while superficially plausible, such an explanation is highly untenable. In order to see this, let us assume that male and female productivity in the marketplace is exactly equal. If so, successful discriminatory employer behavior would entail that women, not men, were being paid far less than their marginal productivity levels. Should this state of affairs ever occur in the first place, it would be very unstable. For large profit opportunities could be gained by those willing to employ women. Sex-neutral entrepreneurs could drive to the wall those who insisted upon indulging in their "male chauvinistic" tastes for discrimination.[8] And in the process of

---

[7] This data is for 1982 and applies to full-time employees. See Statistics Canada, *Earnings of Men and Women, 1981 and 1982*, Cat. 31-577, 1984.

[8] Profit incentives, unfortunately, do not apply to the public sector. Bureaucrats who discriminate against women will thus run costlier operations, but they need not fear losing out to competitors and eventual bankruptcy. As a result, it would be plausible to expect a far greater rate of discrimination in government service than in the marketplace. Unfortunately, it is very difficult to make an empirical test of this proposition. This is because discrimination against women means paying them less than their marginal productivity, while paying men an amount equal to productivity or at least a wage rate closer to their productivity levels. The difficulty is that, in the public sector, there can be no independent measure of productivity. In the private marketplace, a wage rate indicates, at least in the *ex ante* sense, that the employer directly, and the consumer indirectly, values the contribution of the worker (productivity) more highly than the amount paid. In government service, in contrast, we are not even entitled to assume that marginal productivity always takes on a positive value. This is why in GNP accounts, government services are valued at cost; there are no independent measures of consumer valuation or productivity. A second problem is that it is by no means clear that only discrimination against women will take place in the public sector, nor even that discrimination against women will predominate over discrimination against men. Given the popularity of the idea of "reverse

"exploiting" the poorly paid women (by hiring them and bidding up their wages), these profit-oriented businessmen would act so as to equate male and female incomes.[9]

But the facts are clear. Women do earn far less than men. If this is not due to employer discrimination,[10] how then can we account for

---

discrimination" among civil servants, it would be a heroic assumption to take for granted the direction of any discrimination that occurs.

Because the profit-and-loss system discourages discrimination in the marketplace but not in the public sector, The Fraser Institute recommended that "government efforts ... ought to be directed primarily towards ensuring that discrimination does not occur in the public sector." See Walter Block and Michael Walker, eds., "Preface," *Discrimination, Affirmative Action, and Equal Opportunity* (Vancouver: The Fraser Institute, 1982), p. xvi. This recommendation has been challenged on the ground that female/male earnings ratios were actually higher in the public sector than in the private sector. See Margaret A. Denton and Alfred A. Hunter, *Equality in the Workplace, Economic Sectors, and Gender Discrimination in Canada: A Critique and Test of Block and Walker ... and Some New Evidence*, Women's Bureau, Discussion Paper Series A, No. 6: Equality in the Workplace (Ottawa: Labor Canada, 1982), pp. 12 and 34–40. But as we have seen, this finding is not incompatible with greater discriminatory behavior in the public sector—in this case against men and in favor of women. We know there will be more discrimination in the public sector than in the private sector. But we don't know whether it will be against women, or men, or both. Thus, the only empirical implication of this hypothesis is a greater variance in wage rates (other things held constant), not a higher or lower female/male earnings ratio. But this test has yet to be made.

[9] Just as nature abhors a vacuum, economics abhors an unexploited profit opportunity. And the existence of "exploited" labor—that is, employees paid a wage below their productivity levels—is just such a profit opportunity. If men and women have equal productivity, say, $10 per hour, and men are paid $10 while women are paid $6.40, then the sex-neutral firm could hire all the women it wanted at, say, $7.00, and severely undercut its competition. But if there were competition between such sex-neutral employers, women's wages would tend to be bid up to the $10 level. To illustrate just how powerfully business abhors a profit opportunity, consider the international mobility of multinational corporations. A large part of the motivation for the locational decisions of transnational enterprises is to "take advantage' ' of low-paid labor. They do so, of course, by moving in, opening a plant, and bidding wages up toward productivity levels.

[10] Even Jane Fonda, whose radical feminist credentials need take a back seat to no one else's, has run afoul of the equal-pay movement. Jane Fonda's Workout

it? There are several alternative explanations. The first and most basic is that the supposed male/female income gap is really nothing more than a statistical artifact. Consider married women first. One problem is that a "family's income is recorded in the official statistics under the husband's name"[11] alone. But most marriages, at least in their economic aspects, are like a business partnership. The husband may earn all or most of the income in a superficial legalistic or accounting sense, but it is due, in great part, to the wife's efforts that his salary is as high as it is. It is therefore highly misleading to credit the husband with all or most of his "own" income. It would be much more accurate to divide total family earnings by two and credit each marriage partner with a full-half share.

Suppose there were two attorneys in a partnership who agreed to split the proceeds of the firm equally. A, the "outside" partner, deals with clients, conducts the trials, and brings in new business. B, the "inside" partner, looks up the precedents, does the research, and manages the office. To credit A with all or most of the profits, a ludicrous supposition, makes exactly as much sense as assuming, as does Statistics Canada, that the typical Canadian husband really earns all or most of his "own" income.

In point of fact, husband and wife act in many ways to enhance the registered income of the former and reduce the registered income of the latter. This is done in order to maximize family earnings, given other family desires, such as raising children. Examples of such behavior are numerous. While this may be changing slowly, at present a married couple will typically choose a geographical location to enhance his earnings, despite what it does to hers.[12] As well, there

---

is currently being sued for $3 million by three former female instructors on grounds of discrimination in pay compared with male employees who do essentially the same work. Ms. Fonda's lawyer replies that the men were paid more because they were more productive in running clients through the exercise machines. See *The Vancouver Sun*, March 31, 1983, p. D8.

[11] Thomas Sowell, *Civil Rights: Rhetoric or Reality?* (New York: William Morrow and Company, 1984), p. 97.

[12] Barbara B. Reagan, "Two Supply Curves for Economists? Mobility and Career Attachment of Women," *American Economic Review* 65, no. 2 (1975): 102.

is almost always an unequal division of child care and housework responsibilities.[13] There are differing labor force participation rates,[14] education and training,[15] and advanced degrees.[16] One indication of the strong asymmetrical effects of marriage on registered earnings[17] (increasing the male's, reducing the female's)[18] is that the female/

---

[13] Martin Meissner, "Sexual Division of Labor and Inequality: Labor and Leisure," in Marylee Stephenson, ed., *Women in Canada* (Don Mills: General Publishing, 1977), pp. 166–74.

[14] Sylvia Ostry, "Labor Force Participation and Child bearing Status," *Demography and Educational Planning* (Toronto: Ontario Institute for Studies in Education, 1970), pp. 143–56.

[15] Alan F. Bayer, "Marriage Plans and Educational Aspirations," *American Journal of Sociology* 75 (1969): 239–44.

[16] Single female academics who received their Ph.D.s in the 1930s outperformed their male counterparts by becoming full professors in the 1950s to a slightly greater extent, even though all women in academia fell far behind their male colleagues on a variety of indices. See Helen S. Astin, "Career Profiles of Women," in Alice S. Rossi and Ann Calderwood, eds., *Academic Women on the Move* (New York: Russell Sage Foundation, 1973), p. 153 (cited in Thomas Sowell, "Weber and Bakke, and the Presuppositions of 'Affirmative Action'," in Block and Walker, eds., *Discrimination*).

[17] According to Sowell, as of 1971, never-married females aged 30–39 earned more than never-married males of that age, even though all women as a group earned less than half of all men as a group. Could this be due to anti-male employer discrimination? See Thomas Sowell, *Affirmative Action Reconsidered* (Washington, D.C.: American Enterprise Institute, 1975), p. 28.

[18] In the view of Denton and Hunter, in *Equality in the Workplace*, pp. 23–34, this effect of marriage on incomes cannot be substantiated empirically. However, their analysis is marred by a number of flaws.

First, they explicitly eschew our "narrow focus" on comparing never-married men and women; instead, they opt for a study of "all women in paid labor" (p. 24). But this leads to a poor test of our hypothesis. In our view, the best way to determine if there is any anti-female market discrimination is by considering only those who have never been touched by the institution of marriage: the never-married. A methodology that includes the ever-married (married, separated, divorced, widowed) cannot fully rule out the possibility of the asymmetric effects of marriage on male and female incomes. A better approach would have been to consider only the never-married category

male earnings ratio for those who have never been married is a startling .992.[19]

---

and to incorporate such independent variables of theirs as age, education, unionization, work interruptions, part-time and part-year work, and so on.

Second, they interpret discrimination as a residual; that is, they allot whatever earnings gap that cannot be explained by their other variables to discrimination. It is no more sensible to ascribe the pay differential between men and women to discrimination than it is to claim that the equally great or even greater income disparity between married and unmarried men is due to this source. Moreover, what of the possibility that this residual is due to other kinds of discrimination, apart from employer discrimination, such as discrimination against women on the part of consumers, fellow employees? Even if it made sense to interpret this residual as discrimination, it by no means logically follows that employer discrimination is necessarily responsible.

Third, even their own findings, improperly designed as they are, offer limited support to the marital-status hypothesis. Their Table 3 (p. 33) indicates that the "married" and "separated" categories are statistically significant at the .001 level. But why distinguish between "married," "separated," "divorced," and "widowed?" A proper test of the marital-status hypothesis would make no such distinction; rather it would combine all these categories together into "ever-married" status.

Fourth, and even more problematical, the authors' other independent variables serve as rough proxies for marital status (i.e., women with greater career interruptions are more likely to be married). Utilizing these, and then adding marital status, they find that these latter marriage categories add little or no explanatory power to the regression equations. But surely this is fallacious. For it was never contended that marital status makes a significant contribution to female/male income ratios over and above a whole host of variables that are correlated with marital status. This method of proceeding is almost guaranteed to invite problems of multicollinearity.

[19] See Walter Block, "Economic Intervention," in Block and Walker, eds., *Discrimination*, pp. 107–12. Alexander objects to this finding on the ground that the never-married "single women are ... older than single men" and that age is related to productivity. See Judith A. Alexander, "Equal-Pay-for-Equal-Work Legislation in Canada," Economic Council of Canada, Discussion Paper 252, (Ottawa: Economic Council of Canada, 1984), p. 27. But it is by no means clear that age is always positively related to productivity. On the contrary, it peaks in the mid-years; age is positively correlated with productivity before, negatively afterwards. In any case, the

A third explanation for the female/male wage gap is occupational choice: women tend to enter lower-paying occupations than men tend to enter.[20] Here, human capital obsolescence—because of time off for childrearing—will not occur to as great a degree[21] and will not penalize part-time work as stiffly.[22] Occupational choices toward low-income careers ("pink-collar ghettos") are also made

---

age difference in the sample was only 2.5 years, hardly enough to call into question an increase in the female/male income ratio of .374 for the total sample to .992 for the never-married. In this regard, perhaps their remark on p. 30 becomes more comprehensible: "It is impossible to refute Block's arguments, although I do not find them convincing." (Also, as reported in the original research, never-married females have 1.6 years more schooling than never-married males, work 3.3 more weeks in a year, and work on a part-time basis to a lesser degree, by 1.2 percent. However, since "living together" or "cohabitation" might be expected to have similar effects on male and female incomes as does marriage, and this phenomenon is not captured by official statistics on marital status, the ratio .992 may be an underestimation. Conceivably, the two biases might cancel each other out.)

[20] So important is occupational segregation as an explanation of the female/male wage gap that it all but disappears when "productivity-adjusted comparisons are made within the same narrowly defined occupations within the same establishment—the wage gap that is most relevant for equal-pay legislation." When this is done, the female/male adjusted earnings ratio "tends to be in the range of .90–.95." See Morley Gunderson, *The Female-Male Earnings Gap in Ontario: A Summary*, Employment Information Series, no. 22 (Toronto: Ontario Ministry of Labor, February 1982), p. 17. Also, on the basis of occupational segregation, Walter Williams rejects the discrimination hypothesis as an explanation for the fact that black/white female income ratios (1.0225 in 1970) are much higher than black/white male income ratios (.6925 in 1970). See Walter Williams, "On Discrimination and Affirmative Action," in Block and Walker, eds., *Discrimination*.

[21] Sowell, in Civil Rights, p. 94, notes that "women have historically specialized in fields (such as editor, teacher, librarian) that they could leave and re-enter some years later, without large losses from obsolescence (as would occur as a tax attorney, aeronautical engineer, medical researcher)."

[22] John M. McDowell, "Obsolescence of Knowledge and Career Publication Profiles: Some Evidence of Differences among Fields in Costs of Interrupted Careers," *American Economic Review* 72, no. 4 (September 1982): 761.

by unmarried women. Partially, this may reflect anticipated married status in the future. According to some analysts,[23] this choice may be due to women's lower self-esteem, or self-image, or fear of success. In their view, young girls are socialized into believing that they are inferior to boys, and that they must at all costs avoid competing with males. If true, this phenomenon could account for lower expectations and ambitions. On this basis, wives might reject raises or promotions and avoid entering higher-paying occupations in the first place,[24] for fear of making themselves unattractive to their husbands, present or future. To the degree that such behavior occurs, it is a personal tragedy for the women involved—psychologically, socially, and personally—in terms of the human potential destroyed. But the explanation for this must be complex and deep-seated: it can hardly be blamed on employer discrimination in the labor market.

There is a reason why the phenomenon of unequal wages between males and females seems to be in need of explanation. It is because of a basic assumption that, in the absence of discrimination, male and female earnings would be equal. And underlying this is the view that men and women have equal productivity in the labor market. (With unequal economic productivity, unequal wages would not be in need of any explanation.) But this is more of a pious hope than it is a conclusion based on evidence. That it should be taken as an article of faith that male and female productivities must always and ever be equal has more to do with political ideology than with the realm of economic reality.

So deeply entrenched is this view that it even spills over into methodology. In many econometric and empirical works, any male/ female income differential that cannot be accounted for on the basis

---

[23] Many feminist writers have claimed such phenomena do exist. See Meredith M. Kimball, "Women and Success: A Basic Conflict?" in Marylee Stephenson, ed., *Women in Canada* (Don Mills, Ont.: General Publishing, 1977), p. 85. For a more recent example of such commentary, see Judith Finlayson, "Any Way You Want Me," *Toronto Globe and Mail*, October 12, 1984, p. 11.

[24] C. Hoffman and J. Reed, "Imbalance Not Discrimination," in Block and Walker, eds., *Discrimination*.

of variables such as age, education, labor force participation, and so on, is assumed to be the result of employer discrimination. Discrimination, that is, is seen to be a "residual": if gender differentials cannot be explained any other way, they are accounted for on an *a priori* basis by discrimination.

But there are grave problems with such a view. First, "it would seem evident that the failure to explain the wage gap by a given set of variables is consistent with the operation of undiscovered variables having nothing to do with discrimination."[25] Second, the "human capital" variables employed in most regression analyses[26] of this type are only highly imperfect approximations of what really accounts for productivity. Years of schooling, for example, admit of great differences in quality. Their correlation with productivity is far less than exact. Third, this imparts a bias toward that which can be quantified as an explanation of the gender pay gap. Ruled out of court as unquantifiable are such things as ambition, perseverance, motivation, pride in being a breadwinner, reliability, competitiveness, attitude towards risk,[27] and, dare we suggest it, possible innate, biological, sex-linked differences.

Let us now return to equal pay for equal work and equal pay for work of equal value. We have already seen that one drawback of such

---

[25] Michael Levin, "Comparable Worth: The Feminist Road to Socialism," *Commentary* 78, no. 3 (September 1984): 15.

[26] See, for example, Morley Gunderson, "Decomposition of the Male/Female Earnings Differential: Canada, 1970," *The Canadian Journal of Economics* 12, no. 3 (August 1979): 479–85. See also Roberta Edgecombe Robb, "Earnings Differentials between Males and Females in Ontario, 1971," *The Canadian Journal of Economics* 11, no. 2 (1978). For a reply to the latter, see Walter Block and Walter Williams, "Male-Female Earnings Differentials: A Critical Reappraisal," *The Journal of Labor Research* 2, no. 2 (Fall 1981).

[27] Sowell, in *Civil Rights*, pp. 46–47, says that:

One of the most important causes of differences in income and employment is the way people work—some diligently, carefully, persistently, cooperatively, and without requiring much supervision or warnings about absenteeism, tardiness, or drinking, and others requiring much concern over such matters. Not only are such things inherently difficult to quantify; any suggestion that such differences even exist is sure to

enactments, as with all legislation interfering with the market process, is the tendency to retard the ability of the economic system to allocate labor to its (continually changing) most optimal employments. In the case of equal pay for work of equal value, third-party "experts" will be called upon to determine whether mainly male occupations, such as that of truck driver, are "really" of equal value to jobs held mostly by females, such as secretary. A spurious scientific objectivity will be imparted by numerically rating such aspects of these callings as training, responsibility, working conditions, education, and so on, and then adding them together to derive a total point score. Say what you will about such a scheme, at least it has one undoubted advantage; it will serve as a full-employment measure for lawyers, for the values assigned to each dimension can only be arbitrary. The procedure will thus open up society to a spate of contentious lawsuits, as the various newly created pressure groups endlessly strive for more favorable ratings.

The point is that there is no such thing as an intrinsic or objective "worth"[28] of a job (nor of goods and services such as paper clips, music lessons, and so on). On the market, crucial in the evaluation of employment slots are the subjective rank orderings of the consumers—the willingness of people to pay for things. The job of whip-maker, horse-trainer, or carriage-wright might have required

---

bring forth a storm of condemnation. In short, the civil rights vision has been hermetically sealed off from any such evidence. Both historical and contemporary observations on inter-group differences in work habits, discipline, reliability, sobriety, cleanliness, or cooperative attitude— anywhere in the world—are automatically dismissed as evidence only of the bias or bigotry of the observers. "Stereotypes" is the magic word that makes thinking about such things unnecessary. Yet, despite this closed circle of reasoning that surrounds the civil rights vision, there is ... evidence that cannot be disposed of in that way.

[28] All attempts to discern objective values—whether for employment, goods, services, whatever—have failed, and have failed miserably. For critiques of the medieval theory of "just price," and the Marxian attempt to establish "socially useful labor" as the objective measure of the value of goods and services, see Eugen von Böhm-Bawerk, "Value and Price," *Capital and Interest*, book 3, vol. 2 (South Holland, Ill.: Libertarian Press, 1959).

tremendous investments in skill and great responsibility. But with the invention of the horseless carriage and fickle consumer preferences, all this goes for naught. Were there such, the expert job evaluators at the turn of the century might have given these tasks high point totals. But on the market—that is, in reality—these jobs were suddenly rendered obsolete and valueless.

Presently, the jobs of dentists, dental hygienists, and teeth x-ray technicians all require much intelligence, years of intensive training, great diagnostic skills, and a high level of professionalism. Were the evaluators unleashed upon these jobs to work their magic, there is no doubt at all that a high point total would ensue. But if and when a cure for tooth decay is found, these skills will go the way of the dodo bird, as far as value is concerned. Consumers will no longer be willing to purchase their services, and the returns to human capital invested in these lines will fall precipitously.

Let us consider one more example. Suppose that female prison guards do exactly the same quality and kind of work as that done by male prison guards. We assume, in other words, that male and female prison guards do "equal work." But let us suppose that, for some reason, women are far more reluctant to enter this profession than are men.[29] Under such conditions, in the marketplace, female prison guards will receive higher salaries than their male colleagues. This, according to the logic of the equal-pay-for-equal-work philosophy, is obviously "unfair."

What can be done? If the female wage rate is lowered to that of the male, there will not be an adequate supply of women prison guards to satisfy the demand. If the male wage rate is increased to match that of the female,[30] there will be an oversupply of male prison guards.

---

[29] We also assume, for the sake of argument, a necessarily segmented labor force; males cannot be hired to guard female prisoners, and females cannot be hired to guard male prisoners.

[30] It by no means follows from the logic of the forced egalitarian philosophy that the lower wage of two occupations judged to be equal should be raised to match the higher one. It would be just as "equitable" to do the reverse. But most equal-pay legislation mandates raising the lower wage to the higher level. This creates unemployment. For in reality, if the marketplace wages

If the wage rate of both is set at some intermediate point, there will be an excess supply of men prison guards and a shortage of women prison guards.

If the expert evaluators also take into account this phenomenon in their evaluations of male and female prison guard jobs (as well as all other unquantifiable factors that determine wage rates), they will escape the quandary of creating either a shortage and/or surplus of prison guards, but two anomalies will be created. First, the results will be incompatible with equal-pay notions of fairness. If the unequal reluctance of males and females to enter this profession is considered by the evaluators, they will have to award more points to the female guards, since by stipulation they do the "same work"—this would be "unfair."

Second, and more basically, if the evaluators take into account all phenomena that determine wages in the economy, of what possible use can they be? At best, they will no more than replicate the pattern of wages established on the marketplace. More likely, they will only imperfectly succeed in achieving this goal. After all, entrepreneurs succeed or fail in business to a great degree based on how closely they can tailor wage rates to productivity levels. The compensation of the "experts," in contrast, will depend more on how well they satisfy their political constituencies. If there is, at best, only imperfect success in duplicating the market pattern of wages, this process will misallocate labor throughout the economy.

The implications for future research are clear. More attention should be paid to marital status as an explanation of female/male income differentials. Statistics should be published in a manner that more easily facilitates such research. Attempts should be made at an independent

---

of two groups are unequal, this tends to be based on unequal productivity levels. If the lower one is raised, elementary economic analysis indicates that unemployment will occur. See Walter Block, *Focus on Economics and the Canadian Bishops* (Vancouver, British Columbia: The Fraser Institute, 1983), pp. 45–55; and E.G. West and M. McKee, *Minimum Wages: The New Issues in Theory, Evidence, Policy, and Politics*, Economic Council of Canada (Ottawa: Supply and Services Canada, 1980).

definition and measurement of discrimination. The residual method—especially in the face of non-employer discrimination—should be rejected. In comparing private- and public-sector discrimination, wage variances—not wage rates should be considered.

24. Single Women Have Better Chance to Earn Equal Salary

Toronto (CP) Women who want to earn as much as men should stay single, says a new study released by the Vancouver-based Fraser Institute.

Single working women in Canada are paid, on the average, 99.2 percent of the salaries of their unmarried male counterparts, says the study released this week from the institute, a research organization that promotes the idea that the market should function freely.

Michael Walker, director of the institute, said "marital status is perhaps the most important explanation of male-female income differential."

"The salaries of never-married people are identical, regardless of sex," he said. This led the Institute to the conclusion that affirmative-action programs are misguided. In fact, the Institute says, laws and regulations designed to protect minority groups and women from discrimination actually hurt more than they help.

"Affirmative action programs harm highly competent minority persons by making it appear that their accomplishments are not due to their own efforts but to government largesse," the study says.

"They harm unqualified minority persons by placing them in positions that expose their incompetence, they harm minority persons excluded by increasing their frustration and lowering their motivation

Brockville Recorder and Times (Brockville, Ontario), January 30, 1982.

to attain job qualifications on their own. In addition affirmative action exacerbates racial and other inter-minority group animosity."

Walter Block, senior economist of the Institute who wrote the chapter on working women, said "Canadian women who have never been married have indeed 'come a long way baby' toward earnings equality with men."

Block said his research results "are truly staggering." "Never-married females in Canada earned $4,169.72 in 1971, while their male counterparts registered earnings of $4,201.24. The differential by sex for those who have never been married amounted to only $31.52 for an entire year—this translates into a female-to-male ratio of 99.2 percent."

Block said "we will have to wait several years for the results of the 1981 census to see whether or not this tendency persists."

25. Debunking the Mythical Gap

The Feminist move for equal pay is dead from the neck up. To be sure, legislatures are even now enacting this idea into law. But as the evidence continues to pile up, its intellectual foundation is crumbling.

The first nail in the coffin is that there is no wage gap between males and females. That ballyhooed statistic that says women's pay is only 64 percent of men's stems almost entirely from the asymmetrical effects of marital status. Marriage enhances the husband's income and reduces that of the wife.

When the incomes of people who have never been married are compared, the gap disappears. Fraser Institute research, based on StatsCan data, shows that at the last Canadian census, the earnings of never-married women were 93.4 percent of never-married men.

In the previous census, the female-male income ratio for 30-and-over never-marrieds was 99.2 percent; and in that year, the ratio rose to 109.8 percent for those with a university degree who were never married. That is, the average salary of females was 9.8 percentage points more than that of males.

The second nail emerges when we consider the exotic implications of the employer discrimination hypothesis of the pay gap. If this analysis were true, one would expect to find a systematic and positive

The Financial Post (Ontario, Canada), Thursday, March 9, 1989.

relationship between profit levels and the number of women in the firm or industry.

MARKET JUSTICE

The mythical "sexist pig" employer would soon go the way of the dodo, courtesy of market forces. If he were stupid enough to hire a male when he could have employed an equally productive female for less money (because of the pay "gap"), his gender-blind competitors would hire her, and price him out of business.

If market justice compels equal pay for equally productive workers in any case, what, then, is the effect of mandating this situation by law? The answer, in a word, is chaos.

Feminists are urging a wage-control system upon us that will award points—and thus higher salaries—to skill, effort, responsibility and working conditions.

These are all supply-side considerations. But the crucial determinant of the value of labor is demand for the product. The skill, effort, responsibility, and working conditions of the horse breaker changed not one whit when Henry Ford brought his "horseless carriage" to market. But because people demanded cars instead of horses, the salary of the horse trainer plummeted. According to feminist proposals, his compensation would have remained the same.

When programs incorporating these criteria have been implemented, the results have proved embarrassing. In Minnesota, a chemist, social worker, and nurse are all rated equally at 238 points, but in Iowa, the nurse is elevated to 248, the social worker falls to 192, and the chemist plummets to 173.

Instead of barking up the wrong tree with equal pay, feminists should be using their power and prestige to address our inequitable divorce laws. According to Lenore Weitzman, author of *The Divorce Revolution*, divorced women and their children suffer a 73 percent decrease in their standard of living, while their ex-husbands register a 42 percent increase in theirs. Female poverty is to a great degree a function of single motherhood.

26. Insight: Pay Equity Won't Close Wage Gap

In my *Commentary* article, "Debunking the mythical gap" (The Financial Post, March 9), I criticized the much-publicized feminist claim that the female-male earnings ratio of 64 percent stems from male, employer, and/or sexist discrimination.

I gave theoretical economic reasons and statistical evidence in support of an alternative hypothesis: namely, that this shortfall is almost entirely the result of the asymmetric effects of marriage on male and female incomes.

I claimed that marriage, with its vastly unequal division of housekeeping and childrearing responsibilities, and the differential attachment to the labor force it engenders, enhances the take-home pay of the husband, and reduces that of the wife.

In his column of March 15, "On Earnings Differentials: We must address the male/female wage gap," *Financial Post* contributing editor Arthur Drache took issue with my analysis. I thank him for this opportunity to further discuss the points he raised, which my 700-word format did not allow me to elaborate upon.

Let me begin by stating that all of the statistics published by the Fraser Institute on this topic are reported directly from Statistics Canada, or based on citations from studies of StatCan material. Not a single number in our two books, *Discrimination, Affirmative Action, and Equal*

The Financial Post (Ontario, Canada), March 28, 1991.

Opportunity, and *Focus on Pay Equity: A Critique of the Abella Royal Commission Report*, is "massaged," as contended by Mr. Drache.

NOT PUBLISHED

True, much of this information was not published by StatCan, especially the data on never-married status; rather, it was generated from StatCan computers, on a very expensive, cost-recoverable basis. But this is, perhaps, because StatCan is not aware of the marriage asymmetry hypothesis, or does not think enough of it to publish material that would allow the independent analyst to address it.

Drache expresses himself as "rather unimpressed" by the fact that never-married women over 30 with university degrees had an earnings ratio *vis-à-vis* men of 109.8 percent, because they "do not constitute a significant portion of the female work force."

In this, he exhibits a lack of appreciation for economic methodology. The difficulty we face is that there are no controlled experiments in nature, at least not very often. We cannot randomly assign some people to be married, and others not, and then study their income differences.

If we want to analyze the effect of marital status on income, we must compare the earnings of those who have been married with those who have never had this status. Beggars cannot be choosers; we cannot then insist that there be any particular number of ever- or never-marrieds—as long as their number is statistically significant, and StatCan never calculates any number that is not.

Let me emphasize, further, that the comparison being made here is not between these highly educated women in their high-earning years and all men, but rather between them and their male counterparts, namely, those of similar age and education. How does one account for the finding that such women earned 9.8 percent more than men on the anti-female discrimination hypothesis?

SHOULDER THE COSTS

In any case, if Drache is impressed by sheer numbers, what does he make of the fact, as I reported in my original column, that the earnings of all never-married women were 93.4 percent of all never-married men, and that the women in this category numbered 1,535,000, fully 26.2 percent of the total female labor force?

Drache then takes issue with the fact that our society in effect forces women alone to shoulder the costs of child-rearing and marriage.

In one sense this is simply untrue. Most women with children in Canada are supported by their live-in husbands (79.4 percent in 1988). In another sense, however, it is correct: women's earnings are lower than men's because of their family attachments. But this is only part and parcel of the fact that nothing in life is free; goods are scarce, and thus everything has a cost.

This situation is no less fair than that a person who devotes a large part of his life to any one task will be able to accomplish less in alternative pursuits than otherwise. Why Drache would expect this to be different for child-rearing is beyond me.

Note, further, that this objection is based not on the feminist discrimination hypothesis, but on the more correct notion that female wage rates are reduced by family responsibilities. In the very making of this point, Drache undercuts his earlier doubts about the veracity of the statistics.

The real problem for women, as I mentioned, is with our inequitable divorce laws. The courts do not take full cognizance of a wife's contribution to the marriage, which is often embodied in the husband's "human capital"; they treat the father's failure to honor even his inappropriately low child support payments far too leniently. This is not a part of our free-enterprise system, but rather an aspect of government failure.

The bottom line is that women's financial plight cannot be effectively addressed by a policy predicated on an erroneous explanation of the cause of the pay gap.

If pay "equity" succeeds in driving wages above market productivity levels, it will only exacerbate female unemployment rates—in the same way that, as the Economic Council of Canada and others have noted, minimum wage laws have already created joblessness for teenagers and unskilled workers.

Government-organized day care is a red herring in this discussion, having nothing to do with the real cause of the wage "gap." But since Drache raises the issue, let me say that I am all in favor of the care of children, but that I regard the parent and the family, not the state, as the best caretaker.

ATROPHIED

At one time in Canadian history, the family had no trouble taking care of its young, but this was before unwise tax, education, and welfare policies atrophied this form of organization, replacing individual and family reliance with dependency upon the state.

The best way to promote the family is not by further attacks on it, such as substituting state caretakers for parents, but by rescinding those policies which have brought this institution to its present disarray.

27. ON PAY EQUITY: MAKING THE NUMBERS SAY WHAT YOU WANT

AT THE RISK OF BECOMING TIRESOME, I SIMPLY HAVE TO RESPOND once more to Walter Block. To recap for those who are not regular readers, Block wrote a piece in *The Financial Post* on March 9, in which he stated that the wage gap between men and women, most often described by saying that women earn only 64 percent of what men earn, is a myth.

I wrote in response on March 15, that the gap was no myth and that I was unimpressed by Block's statistics. I further suggested that there was a significant economic penalty incurred by women who marry and become charged with primary family responsibility for child raising.

One possible (and only partial) solution to the problem would be freely accessibly day care for women who choose to (or must) work where the man of the family (if any) is unwilling to shoulder an equal part of the child-rearing burden. Indeed, Block seemed to suggest that child rearing is an "alternative pursuit," perhaps akin to golfing seven days a week.

Block then offered a rebuttal argument on March 28. (I would have responded to him earlier but I was enjoying the pleasures of Venice and conducting my semiannual survey of London casinos. It

Arthur Drache, *The Financial Post* (Ontario, Canada), April 11, 1989.

remains easier to win in London than in Las Vegas, but Block would undoubtedly challenge my "economic methodology.")

Block offered two sets of numbers.

He stated that in at least one set of statistics, it has been shown that never-married women over 30 with university degrees had an earnings ratio *vis-à-vis* men of 109.8 percent. He does not seriously attempt to refute my original assertion that this figure is not significant because the group is so insignificant in terms of the entire work force.

ECONOMIC IMPACT

Block seemed to rely on a second statistic, namely that never-married women earn 93.4 percent of the wages of never-married men and the women in this category are 26.2 percent of the female work force. I wonder how many men would be prepared to work for 93.4 percent of what their peers earn?

But given that Block and I agree that the main problem stems from the economic impact of marriage on women, I find it passing strange that he doesn't give any statistics on the wage gap between married women (presumably 73.8 percent of the women in the work force) and married men. I suspect that the reason is that if he gave these statistics, the wage gap would be 64 percent. And in my book, this makes the statistic far from mythical.

If I read Block correctly, he accepted that the gap is real, not mythical. But he offered only negatives in terms of solutions. He rejected pay equity. He rejected improved public child care facilities. And he rejected the new trend in divorce laws and property settlements.

He blamed instead "unwise tax, education, and welfare policies," and would improve the situation by "rescinding" them. What (if anything) they would be replaced by he didn't say. Perhaps he would ban marriage and child rearing, since these seem to be the root of the wage gap.

Or he might just want to be a little more up front and say that he believes that married women should not work outside the home. After all, if we passed a law excluding them from the work force, the wage gap would be decidedly narrowed and the unemployment rate would presumably plummet—providing you could get men to take on the low-paying jobs women now tend to hold.

There's an old adage that suggests that if something isn't broken, don't fix it. But insofar as economic equality for (at least) married women is concerned, something certainly is broken. Maybe pay equity and increased public facilities for child care won't solve the problem. But Block's statistics demonstrate that there is a problem and it is not mythical.

Almost every working woman in the country is aware that they are second-class citizens when it comes to lifetime's economic endeavors, even if it is (as Block would probably say) because they devote too much time to home and family and don't have the single-mindedness of males who can't get pregnant and who generally reject the role of even part-time "house husband," a pejorative term if ever I heard one.

There is a gap and an inequality here. Working women know it even if working economists do not. The challenge is to do something about it.

28. Commentary: "Pay Equity" Undermines Marketplace

Everywhere, people are waking up to the idea that social engineering, central planning, and socialist measures in general are bad ideas. The best means to achieve peace, prosperity, and economic progress is a greater reliance on the price and profit system.

But there is still some of this socialist philosophy underlying Arthur Drache's recent *Financial Post* columns (March 15, April 11). These essays, which call for government pay boards, have attempted to undermine the marketplace at its most vulnerable point—its system of free and flexible wages and prices. He has done so in criticism of my own attempts to explicate and defend the price mechanism (*Commentary*, March 9 and 28) from those who urge wage controls under the guise of "pay equity."

Let us make no mistake about it: without market-generated wages and prices, there can be no free enterprise system.

By subjecting wages to centralized control to promote pay "equity," all prices would be grievously affected. But prices have a crucial role to play in the economy. The price system is the means through which the market does its planning. In the absence of central direction of the economy, uncontrolled prices provide information about shortages and surpluses. Only free prices can impart incentives to market participants to cure these misallocations.

The Financial Post (Ontario, Canada), April 26, 1989.

It would be bad enough were Drache to advocate increased government ownership of Crown corporations, rent controls, marketing boards, and tariffs, which are each limited to specific sectors of the economy. Legislation mandating equal pay for equal or equivalent work, in contrast, reaches into every nook and cranny of commercial life.

DEATH OF THE ECONOMY

Such legislation could only be approached by a full-blown and permanent program of wage and price controls, which could spell the death of the economy.

It would be bad enough if there were a case for intervention on the basis of principles of justice. But the gap between male and female rates of pay is not caused by employer discrimination. On the contrary, the cause of this gap is the unequal attachment to the labor force of husbands and wives.

Fraser Institute research based on data compiled by StatsCan shows that the earnings of males and females who have never been married are indistinguishable.

Nor will his penchant for throwing money at problems without understanding them suffice. Public day care, another of Drache's pet projects, will only further erode the institution of the family. In any case, this program can hardly buttress the income of women without children.

As for reform of divorce laws and property settlements, this is long overdue. But the injustice here results from government failure, not to any problem with markets.

Fortunately, there are feminist groups in Canada which have not jumped on the equal pay bandwagon, and are, instead, attempting to reform divorce law, and to deal with the problem of the father who runs out on his child support payments. They are Real Women, Family Forum, and the Society for Children's Rights to Adequate Parental Support.

29. COMMENTARY: EQUAL PAY LAWS SPELL DISASTER

THE ADVOCATES OF EQUAL PAY FOR WORK OF EQUAL VALUE castigate the market for its inherent unfairness. Instead of the "anarchy" of free enterprise, they propose that all wages be set on the basis of skill, effort, responsibility, and working conditions.

These would be determined by boards of "experts," and tribunals of bureaucrats and civil servants, who substitute their "objective" assessments for the chaotic judgment of a system of competitive labor markets.

There are many and serious objections which can be leveled against such a system. Perhaps most important, the entire proposal is predicated upon a male-female wage "gap" resulting from employer discrimination. But as Fraser Institute research has shown, no such phenomenon actually exists.

OBJECTIVE MEASUREMENT

As well, contrary to the self-styled feminists, there is nothing intrinsic in a job that makes it worthy of compensation. Crucial in any determination of wage rates is the demand on the part of consumers for the service supplied.

Right now, for example, the skill, effort, responsibility, and working conditions of dentists are such that they receive high compensation.

The Financial Post (Ontario, Canada), Thursday May 5, 1988.

But were a cure for tooth decay to be uncovered tomorrow, their wages would plummet without any discrimination whatsoever in these objective measurements of the performance of dentists.

Further, any proposal that artificially raises the salaries of a given calling beyond its productivity level threatens it with unemployment. But equal pay enactments are always couched in terms of raising female incomes, never reducing those of males.

As such, they threaten to price women out of the market, in a manner similar to what has already happened to young people, who have been rendered less employable by minimum wage laws.

There is also the embarrassment that when boards or tribunals in the different jurisdictions have attempted to "objectively" set the value of a job, the results have varied widely. When entrepreneurs poorly estimate the worth of a job, they are automatically penalized. If they set wages too high, they risk bankruptcy; too low and they are likely to suffer severe quit rates.

Unfortunately, no such automatic reward and penalty device can operate in the public sector.

Equal pay legislation is a form of wage/price control. As such, wages are frozen in place, despite changing market conditions. For example, if there is a sudden need for more nurses, and fewer firemen, an inflexible wage system will be unable to encourage the former, and discourage the latter.

A decade ago, Canada rashly experimented with wage/price controls. It was a disaster. That we are seriously flirting with this unsavory idea so soon after underscores the point that those who are ignorant of history are doomed to repeat the mistakes of the past.

30. MALE-FEMALE EARNINGS DIFFERENTIALS: A CRITICAL REAPPRAISAL

IN THE MAY 1978 ISSUE OF *THE CANADIAN JOURNAL OF ECONOMICS*, Roberta Robb attributed between 58.9 percent (standardized for occupation and industry) and 75.4 percent (not standardized) of the male-female Ontario earnings differential in 1971 to sexual discrimination. We should like to point out several flaws in the analysis.

First, Robb seems to miss the point of the alternative hypothesis to sexual discrimination. That hypothesis is that marriage—and its asymmetrical effects on male and female career efforts, due to asymmetrical domestic responsibilities and commitments—means qualitatively different performance levels by men and women who are married, or have been married. Never-married women should be compared to never-married men, not all men (See Robb 1978, p. 357, tables 3 and 4). Age, even if it quantitatively captures work experience, does not get at this qualitative point. These are more than quibbles; they make an empirical difference in the results. Data cited by Sowell (1975) in *Affirmative Action Reconsidered* showed that "never-married" academic women receive higher pay than "never-married" academic men. Other studies cited there also detail the asymmetry of domestic responsibilities and the greater frequency of female subordination of individual career goals to that of the husband's

Walter Block and Walter Williams, *The Journal of Labor Research* 2, no. 2 (Fall 1981): 385–88. In-text references can be found in the bibliography section of this book.

career—notably in locating where he has the best opportunity, even if that is not where her best opportunities exist. In short, the effect of marriage on a woman is much more than a difference in labor force participation rates or continuity of employment. Comparing all men to never-married women seems to be an incredible procedure—however widespread—when marriage has opposite effects on the quality of inputs into a career, freeing the man's time and absorbing the woman's. Surveys show men and women themselves saying this, and we know of no serious reason to doubt it.

Second, Robb's estimates are not a reliable measure of the presence or absence of tastes that may influence practices, for while the experimenter may have reliable information on the productivity of a particular employee, there is no reason at all to believe that the employer is similarly blessed. Even if all the applicants have identical credentials, we cannot expect employers to perceive these credentials as equally creditable, even in a non-sexist world.[1]

Different people for different decisions choose to acquire different amounts of information prior to acting. There is a criterion used to determine the amount of information an individual will rationally invest in prior to making a decision: people search for information up to the point where the added cost of another unit of knowledge is just offset by the expected benefits that will be derived from that additional unit.

It is crucial to understand that both costs and benefits from an additional unit of information vary from individual to individual. On the cost side, economic actors differ in their ability or efficacy in the collection and processing of information. On the benefit side, people differ in their risk aversion and in their subjective evaluation of an additional unit of information, i.e., the marginal rate of substitution between the product of information (increased

---

[1] A similar argument can be made about the analysis of racial differences in other areas of economic life. In the poor-pay-more issue of the 1960s, experimentors conducted tests to determine whether there was racial discrimination in the sale of customer durables and credit terms by having couples shop for credit who differed only by race. See Williams (1973).

probability of making the "correct" decision) and all other goods is not the same for all individuals.[2]

Therefore, the conceptual experiment suggested by Robb cannot be viewed as a reliable measure of the absence or presence of sexist tastes. In such an experiment, it is important for the experimentor to recognize that while she may have reliable information that workers are undifferentiated except by sex, the employer may not. Even employers with sex-neutral tastes have to perceive that certain skills are distributed randomly if they are to select employees randomly. To the extent that skills are not distributed randomly, sexual attributes may be employed with some success as an indicator of the productivity level sought by the firm. Using sex as a "proxy" for some other characteristic is consistent with preferences that are malevolent, benevolent, or indifferent toward a particular sex.

The suggestion that sexual attributes will be used in worker selection or payment implies nothing about employer sexual tastes. It does imply scarcity. Employers cannot be sure of the productivity of a worker before he is hired; moreover, the worker's productivity may not be readily discernible after he is hired. The process of hiring uses resources. In addition, the trial period is costly; it, too, uses the resources of the firm in the form of added supervision, monitoring, and materials. Employers have incentive to economize on all of these costs.

A third difficulty is that Robb attributes to sexual discrimination all the male-female earnings differentiation that cannot be accounted for by her other independent variables (age, education, occupation, industry, hours worked, weeks worked, training, marital status) but these by no means exhaust the explanatory possibilities. Other phenomena which might possibly account for the male-female

---

[2] Given this line of reasoning, prejudiced behavior cannot have normative content. Most often in the discrimination literature, "prejudiced behavior" is used pejoratively in reference to individuals whose optimal amount of information is relatively small (in the opinion of the author). But we have seen that the quantity decision is individual, thus, there can be no meaning attached to "socially" optimal quantities of information for a decision.

earnings differential would include intelligence, motivation, determination, cheerfulness, ability to work well with others, etc. True, these are hardly amenable to statistical manipulation. But the time is long past when an analysis can be considered methodologically sound that considers only what can be (easily) measured, and attributes the remaining differential to one such variable: discrimination. At the very best, Robb's conclusion must be modified so as to attribute the male-female earnings differential left unexplained by her other independent variables to discrimination as well as these other "non-measurable" phenomena.

But let us make the heroic *ceteris paribus* assumption that males and females do not differ with regard to any conditions such as intelligence, motivation, etc. Let us further assume that no tastes whatsoever for sexual discrimination exist in the society. Would Robb's independent variables fully explain the Ontario male-female earnings differentials of 1971 even then? They would only do so under conditions of full and perfect general equilibrium in the economy.

The fourth difficulty with the Robb thesis, then, is that it implicitly assumes the existence of equilibrium. But the cessation of the market process is only an ideal construct, a heuristic device. Unless Robb believes that this can apply in the real world,[3] she cannot unambiguously attribute any unexplained differential to sexual discrimination. Some of it at least, must be blamed on the fact that the economy of Ontario in 1971 was in disequilibrium.

---

[3] Among the paradoxical implications of full equilibrium is that money could not exist (see Mises 1966, p. 417), nor could profits (see Kirzner 1973, pp. 1, 4, 13).

FEMINISM, SEX DIFFERENCES, AND SEX DISCRIMINATION

LEFT-WING FEMINISM DENIES DIFFERENCES BETWEEN MEN AND women. As a result, advocates of this position call for a change in societal approaches to gender-based issues. This, in turn, leads to a call for a change in public policies.

However, the failure to acknowledge differences is very different from the actual elimination of such differences. An exploration of the intersection of feminism and public policy provides an effective demonstration of some of their effects.

This section of the book includes two co-authored journal articles, as well as two reviews of an interesting book on the subject.

31. GENDER EQUITY IN ATHLETICS: SHOULD WE ADOPT A NON-DISCRIMINATORY MODEL?

FOR YEARS, INTERCOLLEGIATE ATHLETICS HAS OFFERED interested and able students opportunities to experience the lessons of competition, develop physical and leadership skills, be a part of a team, and perhaps most important, enjoy themselves. Good intercollegiate athletics programs require competitive parity, universal and consistently applied rules, and an opportunity to participate according to one's interest and ability. The majority of NCAA members have sought to assure the foregoing conditions, but there is considerable evidence that they have not fully succeeded with regard to women.

Because there was no assurance of equal opportunity in the range of components of education, Congress enacted Title IX of the Educational Amendments of 1972.[1] The federal law stipulates that

> No person in the United States shall, on the basis of sex, be excluded from participation in, be denied the benefits of, or be subjected to discrimination under any education program or activity receiving federal financial assistance.[2]

Roy Whitehead, Walter Block, and Lu Hardin, *University of Toledo Law Review* 30, no. 2 (Winter 1999): 223–69.

[1] Title IX of the Education Amendments of 1972, 20 U.S.C. §§ 1681–1688 (1972).

[2] 20 U.S.C. § 1681(a).

Interestingly, an often-ignored subsection of the statute, often quoted by football coaches, provides:

> Nothing contained in subsection (a) ... shall be interpreted to require any educational institution to grant preferential or disparate treatment to the members of one sex on account of an imbalance that may exist with respect to the total number or percentage of persons of that sex participating in or receiving the benefits of any federally supported program or activity, in comparison with the total number or percentage of persons of that sex in any community, State, section or other area.[3]

In 1991, the NCAA surveyed its members' expenditures for women's and men's athletics programs. The survey revealed that undergraduate enrollment was roughly equally divided by sex, but men constituted 69.5 percent of the participants in intercollegiate athletics and their programs received approximately 70 percent of the athletics scholarship funds, 77 percent of operating budgets, and 83 percent of recruiting money.[4]

In response to the study, the NCAA appointed a Gender Equity Task Force that submitted its report during July 1993. In its report, the Task Force defined gender equity as follows: "An athletics program can be gender equitable when the participants in both men's and women's sports programs would accept as fair and equitable the overall program of the other gender."[5] The report also defined the ultimate goal of gender equity as: "The ultimate goal of each institution should be that the numbers of male and female athletes are substantially proportionate to their numbers in the institution's undergraduate population."[6]

In January 1994, the NCAA members gave a lukewarm endorsement of gender equity by voting to encourage member institutions to

---

[3] *Id.* § 1681(b).

[4] National Collegiate Athlethic Association, *Final Report of the NCAA Gender-Equity Task Force I* (1993) hereinafter "*The Report*."

[5] *The Report*, p. 2.

[6] *Id.* at 3.

follow the "law" concerning gender equity.[7] One purpose of this article is to review the guiding regulations and cases that interpret the "law" for the benefit of those who are interested in effectively accommodating the interest and abilities of women athletes. We are concerned that the federal court decisions that have dealt specifically with Title IX and "gender equity" have generally failed to focus on the real meaning of Title IX, "fully and effectively accommodating the interests and abilities of women athletes."[8] This is due to a misguided focus almost solely on proportionality in numbers rather than on a real accommodation of athletic abilities.

Another goal of this article is to philosophically and legally examine the underlying principles of gender equity in athletics. To this end, we will criticize this "law" from a perspective based on property rights and economic freedom.

THE LEGAL AND REGULATORY REQUIREMENTS

The primary sources of gender equity responsibilities are found in Title IX, the implementing regulations,[9] and, perhaps more important, the Title IX Athletics Investigators Manual used by the Department of Education, Office of Civil Rights (OCR).[10] Judges who are involved in Title IX cases frequently cite the OCR Manual as authority. The OCR takes several major factors into account in determining whether intercollegiate athletic programs are gender equitable. The program components are accommodation of athletic interests and abilities; equipment and supplies; scheduling of games and practice times; travel *per diem* allowance; opportunity to receive coaching and academic tutoring; assignment and compensation of coaches and tutors; locker rooms, practice and competitive facilities;

---

[7] Amendment No. 2-1, Principle of Gender Equity, NCAA Convention, January 1994.

[8] 34 C.F.R. § 106.41(c) (1992).

[9] 34 C.F.R. § 106, effective July 21, 1975.

[10] Valerie M. Bonnette and Lamar Daniel, *Title IX Athletics Investigator's Manual* (Washington, D.C.: U.S. Department of Education, 1990), hereinafter "*The Manual*."

medical and training facilities and services; housing and dining facilities and services; publicity; and athletic scholarships.[11]

Although all the program components are considered important, perhaps the most relevant issue is whether the university is providing an effective accommodation of student interests and abilities. The regulations require institutions that offer athletic programs to accommodate effectively the interests and abilities of students of both genders to the extent necessary to provide equal opportunity in selection of sports and levels of competition.[12] The OCR uses three factors to assess the opportunity for individuals of both genders to compete in intercollegiate programs:

1. Whether intercollegiate level participation opportunities for male and female students are provided in numbers substantially proportionate to the respective enrollments;

2. Where members of one sex have been and are under-represented among intercollegiate athletics, whether the institution can show a history and continuing practice of program expansion which is demonstrably responsive to the developing interests and abilities to that sex; and,

3. Where members of one sex are underrepresented among intercollegiate athletics, and the institution cannot show a continuing practice of program expansion such as that cited above, whether it can show that the interests and abilities of the members of that sex have been fully and effectively accommodated by the present program.[13]

Unfortunately, very few institutions, especially those with football programs, are able to meet the first test, proportionality. Additionally, a training session with an author of the OCR Investigators Manual reveals that no institution, to his knowledge, has ever met the second

---

[11] 34 C.F.R. § 106.41; 34 C.F.R. § 106.37.

[12] 34 C.F.R. § 106.41(c)(1).

[13] *Id.*

test consisting of a history and practice of program expansion responsive to the interests and abilities of women.[14]

Given that few institutions can meet parts one and two of the test, we must focus on whether the institution is effectively accommodating the interests and abilities of the underrepresented sex.

Recall that the NCAA Gender Equity Task Force defined gender equity as having the same proportion of female and male athletes as in the undergraduate student body.[15] Much to the dismay of some interest groups, OCR has ruled that the third part of the test may be satisfied by the institution showing it has accommodated the interest and abilities of its female students although there may be a substantial disproportionateness of numbers between male and female athletes. According to the OCR, this may be demonstrated by showing that the opportunity to participate in intercollegiate athletics is consistent with the interests of enrolled women undergraduates who have the ability to play college sports, which can be determined by an external survey of the university's recruiting area, including high school and junior college competition, summer league competition, and sanctioned state sports. The university need only accommodate women who have the ability to play at the intercollegiate level.[16]

The OCR does not generally interview undergraduates who cannot play at the intercollegiate skill level. It is clear, however, that if the undergraduate survey, or external survey of the recruiting area, suggests that potential female students who possess the required interest and ability are present, and there is a reasonable availability of competition for a team, they must be accommodated. If the conference, for example, has women's softball, and softball interests and abilities are discovered in the undergraduate population and the recruiting area, the university must accommodate this by inaugurating a women's softball team.

---

[14] Lamar Daniel, Office of Civil Rights, (remarks to the Gulf South Conference Meeting, Birmingham, Ala., Jan. 26, 1994).

[15] See text accompanying note 6.

[16] *The Manual* at 21–28. See also 34 C.F.R. § 106.41(c)(1) (1992).

Second, there is perhaps the most misunderstood area of gender equity compliance: athletic financial assistance. OCR's manual provides that "institutions must provide reasonable opportunities for athletic scholarships awards for members of each sex in proportion to the number of students of each sex participating in ... intercollegiate athletics."[17]

OCR will determine compliance with this provision of the regulation primarily by means of a financial comparison. The requirement is that proportionately equal amounts of financial assistance (scholarship aid) are available to men's and women's athletics programs. This rule is often misinterpreted as mandating that the amount of financial assistance to male and female athletes be proportionate to their undergraduate enrollments. For example, if a university is 60 percent female and 40 percent male, 60 percent of the financial assistance would have to go to female athletes. Fortunately, or unfortunately, depending on one's point of view, the foregoing is not the test for compliance.

OCR measures compliance with the athletic financial assistance standard by dividing the amounts of aid available for members of each sex by the numbers of male or female participants in the athletic program and tabulating the results. Institutions may be found in compliance if this comparison results in substantially equal amounts (plus or minus two to four percent) or if a resulting disparity can be explained by adjustments that take into account a legitimate, nondiscriminatory factor.[18] Because of this interpretation, the institution described above with an undergraduate enrollment of 60 percent female and 40 percent male may be in compliance if it spends equal amounts on each male and female athlete even if there are more male than female athletes. For example, if an institution has an athletic financial assistance budget of $1 million and spends $700,000 of that on 70 male athletes and $300,000 on 30 female athletes, it has complied with OCR's requirements. Note that if 60

---

[17] *The Manual* at 14.

[18] *Id*. at 14–20.

percent of the participants in athletics programs are men, then male athletes should receive about 60 percent of the available athletic financial assistance even if the undergraduate female enrollment exceeds the male undergraduate enrollment.

If the financial assistance provided is not substantially equal, the OCR will determine whether there is a legitimate nondiscriminatory factor to explain the difference.[19] For example, the institution can justify the differences in awards by noting the higher tuition costs for out-of-state students that, in some years, may be unevenly distributed between men's and women's programs. These differences are nondiscriminatory if they are not the result of policies or practices that limit the availability of out-of-state scholarships to either men or women. Further, an institution may decide the awards most appropriate for program development. Often this practice may initially require the spreading of scholarships over as much as four years for developing programs, resulting in fewer scholarships in the first few years than would be necessary to create equality between male and female athletes. The OCR Investigators Manual, however, directs investigators to investigate carefully "reasonable professional decisions" when there is a negative effect on the under-represented sex.[20]

The regulations require "equitable" treatment for female athletes in the provision of equipment and supplies.[21] The OCR defines equipment and supplies as uniforms, other apparel, sports-specific equipment and supplies, instructional devices, and conditioning and weight training equipment. In assessing compliance the OCR takes a careful look at the quality, amount, suitability, maintenance and replacement, and availability of equipment and supplies to both male and female athletes. If there is a disparity, the university is in violation. The OCR permits nondiscriminatory differences based on the unique aspects of particular sports, and the regulations do not require equal expenditures for each program. For example, the

---

[19] *Id.* at 19.

[20] *Id.* at 20.

[21] 34 C.F.R. § 106.41(c)(2) (1992).

equipment for the (male) football team may be more expensive than the equipment for the women's volleyball team.[22]

The regulations also require equality in the scheduling of games and practice time.[23] OCR accesses five factors in determining compliance: (1) number of competitive events per sport; (2) number and length of practice opportunities; (3) time of day competitive events are scheduled; (4) time of day practice opportunities are scheduled; and (5) opportunities to engage in preseason and post-season competition.[24]

Considerable emphasis is placed on practice and game time. It is usual for women's practice to be scheduled immediately before or immediately after men's. As a result, female athletes may have to skip lunch or dinner or eat a very light lunch or dinner to effectively participate. Additionally, it is common to schedule women's games before men's games, starting them at about 5:30 p.m. This results in denying female athletes the opportunity to have their parents, friends, and acquaintances present at the event unless they live nearby or can get off work early. To be in compliance some programs have adopted a rotating schedule for practice and/or games. For example, every other women's game would start at 7:30 rather than 5:30 p.m. The men's team would alternate correspondingly.

The regulations require an assessment to decide whether the athletic program meets the travel and *per diem* allowances requirement.[25] OCR assesses the following factors in deciding compliance: modes of transportation; housing furnished during travel; length of the stay before and after competitive events; *per diem* allowance; and dining arrangements.[26]

The easy way for an athletic program to ensure compliance is to treat male and female teams alike. If male athletes stay two to a room,

---

[22] *The Manual* at 29.

[23] 34 C.F.R. § 106.4 1(c)(3).

[24] *The Manual* at 35–42.

[25] 34 C.F.R. § 106.41(c)(4).

[26] *The Manual* at 43–48.

they should house female athletes in the same manner. If the male team travels by airplane, the comparable female team should similarly travel. If they provide the male team a catered meal before the event, this arrangement should apply to the female team as well.

The regulations also require equality in the opportunity to receive academic tutoring, and assignment and compensation of tutors.[27] OCR looks for the academic qualifications, training, experience, and compensation of tutors. If there is any disparity in these opportunities, the university is violating Title IX.[28]

The regulations require equality in the opportunity to receive coaching and assignment and compensation of coaches.[29] The OCR looks at three factors in this regard: (1) relative availability of full-time coaches; (2) relative availability of part-time and assistant coaches; and (3) relative availability of graduate assistants.[30]

The OCR lists two factors to be assessed in determining compliance in assignment of coaches: (1) training, experience, and other professional qualifications; and (2) professional standing.[31] The policy interpretation lists seven factors in determining compliance in compensation of coaches: (1) rate of compensation; (2) duration of contract; (3) conditions relating to contract renewal; (4) experience; (5) nature of coaching duties performed; (6) working conditions; and (7) other terms and conditions of employment.[32]

It has been difficult to determine whether opportunity to receive coaching assignments and compensation of coaches is "equitable" because of the subjectivity involved in assessing the training, experience, and professional qualifications of coaches assigned to men's and women's programs. Although the OCR seems to limit its

---

[27] 34 C.F.R. § 106.41(c)(5) (1991).

[28] *The Manual* at 49–50.

[29] 34 C.F.R. § 106.41(c)(5)–(6).

[30] *The Manual* at 55.

[31] *Id.*

[32] *Id.*

investigation to the experience and qualifications of the coaches, at least one case seems to suggest that another factor—the size of the crowds and the ability to attract boosters—may be a factor in compensation.[33] The regulation's intent is that equal athletic opportunity be provided to participants, not coaches. When a coach's compensation is based on seniority or longevity, a recognized method of paying employees, alleging that a female team coach with five years experience is somehow being discriminated against because he or she receives less than a coach with fifteen years experience is difficult to prove. This situation brings up an interesting point because it is possible for a male coach of a female team to be protected under this provision because the intent of the Act is to provide effective coaching to females.

Perhaps the most important regulation from the health and safety aspect of athletics is the regulation that requires equal medical and training facilities and services.[34] In the recent past, and perhaps in some institutions today, female athletes only have access to trainers after male athletes, or access to only assistant trainers or graduate assistants. It is not unusual for the head trainer to travel with the men's teams and a graduate assistant or an assistant trainer to travel with the women's teams. One can be assured that the discovery of such information during the compliance review will result in a finding of discrimination in violation of Title IX. Schools must either hire a trainer for the women's programs who possesses the same qualifications as the counterpart for the men's programs, or have them travel with the teams on a rotating basis. There can also be other considerations; for example, some women's team coaches prefer a

---

[33] In the case of *Stanley v. University of Southern California*, the court found that evidence of the male coach's greater responsibility in raising funds and level of responsibility justified the disparity in salary. See *Stanley v. University of Southern California*, 13 F.3d 1313 (9th Cir. 1994). The court said that the men's team "generated greater attendance, more media interest, and larger donations" and that the men's coach, George Raveling, has fund raising duties not required of the women's coach (*id.* at 1322). The court found that the university was not responsible for "societal discrimination in preferring to witness men's sports in greater numbers" (*id.* at 1323).

[34] 34 C.F.R. § 106.41(8) (1992).

female trainer because she can room with the female players and reduce expenses.

To assess compliance and provision of medical training facilities, OCR investigates five areas: (1) availability of medical personnel and assistants; (2) health, accident, and injury insurance coverage; (3) availability and quality of weight and training facilities; (4) availability and quality of conditioning facilities; and (5) availability and qualification of athletic trainers.[35] The regulations specifically require gynecological care where such health problems are a result of participation in the athletics program.[36]

To achieve substantial proportionality in accommodating interests and abilities of both male and female athletes, it is clear that OCR will carefully review the recruitment of student athletes.[37] OCR looks at three factors in assessing compliance: (1) whether coaches or other professional athletic personnel in the program serving male and female athletes are provided with substantially equal opportunities to recruit; (2) whether financial and other resources made available for recruitment in male and female athletic programs are equivalently adequate to meet the needs of each program; and (3) whether differences in benefits, opportunities, and treatment afforded prospective student athletes of each sex have a disproportionately limiting effect on the recruitment of students.[38]

OCR carefully checks the recruitment funds allotted to each team and compares the proportionate recruitment funds with the proportion of male and female athletes in the athletics program. In judging whether the resources are equivalently adequate to meet the needs of each program, the OCR determines the availability of recruitment resources to both men's and women's programs, including access to telephones, recruitment brochures, mailing costs, and travel.[39]

---

[35] *The Manual* at 72–80.

[36] 34 C.F.R. § 106.39.

[37] 34 C.F.R. § 106.41; *The Manual* at 97–101.

[38] *The Manual* at 97.

[39] *Id.* at 99.

The rules allow nondiscriminatory differences in some cases. For example, the recruiting budget for a particular team—either male or female—may be increased because of a disproportionate number of student athletes who either graduated or dropped out of the program in a particular year, thereby requiring extra effort to replace them.[40]

WHAT IS COMPLIANCE?

In at least three instances, the federal courts have appeared to impose a more stringent accommodation test than the OCR.[41] Recall that the regulations state an institution is in compliance if it can show that it "fully and effectively accommodates the interests and abilities of female students who have the ability to participate in intercollegiate sports."[42] Most federal court cases stress that the percentage of accommodated female athletes has to be proportionate to the total female undergraduate enrollment rather than relate solely to those women who have the interests and abilities to participate.

For example, in a case involving Colorado State University, the court found that there was a 10.5 percent disparity in the percentage of women athletes and undergraduate women students.[43] It determined that the female participation in intercollegiate sports was not substantially proportionate to female enrollment and ordered the university to reinstate a women's softball team, hire a coach, and maintain a competitive schedule.[44]

In an ongoing case involving Brown University, the court ordered reinstatement of female teams when there was about a 13 percent

---

[40] *Id.* at 100.

[41] See generally *Cohen v. Brown University*, 991 F.2d 888 (1st Cir. 1993); *Cohen v. Brown University*, 879 F. Supp. 185 (D.R.I. 1995); *Roberts v. Colorado State Board of Agriculture*, 998 F.2d 824 (10th Cir. 1993); *Favia v. Indiana University of Pennsylvania*, 812 F. Supp. 578 (W.D. Pa. 1993), aff'd, 7 F.3d 322 (3d Cir. 1993).

[42] 34 C.F.R. § 106.41(c)(1) (1992); *The Manual* at 21.

[43] *Roberts v. Colorado State Board of Agriculture*, 998 F.2d at 830.

[44] *Id.* at 834.

disparity between the percentage of female athletes and the percentage of females in undergraduate enrollment.[45] Both the Colorado State and Brown University cases are difficult to square with Title IX because the opinions appear to rely solely on the proportionality test and to deemphasize the "interest and abilities test." This strong reliance on proportionality is contrary to the OCR regulations that tend to treat the prongs of the three-part test equally.[46]

The statute also prohibits reliance solely on proportionality by providing that

> [n]othing contained in subsection (a) ... shall be interpreted to require any educational institution to grant preferential or disparate treatment to the members of one sex on account of an imbalance which may exist with respect to the total number or percentage of persons of that sex participating in or receiving the benefits of any federally supported program or activity, in comparison with the total number or percentage of persons of that sex in any community, State, section or other area.[47]

The question posed is whether the strong emphasis on proportionality in the Colorado State and Brown University cases is, or should be, the trend in the law. Unfortunately for this determination, the U.S. Supreme Court denied *certiorari* in both cases.[48] To provide appropriate guidance, the question we must answer is: How will other circuit courts of appeals deal with the regulatory three-prong test, and, ultimately, what will the U.S. Supreme Court do when they eventually grant *certiorari*?

To answer the question, the remainder of part II of this article deals with the merits and appeals in the four separate decisions involving

---

[45] See generally *Cohen v. Brown University*, 809 F. Supp. 978 (D.R.I. 1992) (*Brown University I*), *aff'd*, 991 F.2d 888 (1st Cir. 1993) (*Brown University II*).

[46] 34 C.F.R. § 106.41(c)(1) (1992).

[47] 20 U.S.C. § 1681(b) (1972).

[48] See generally *Roberts v. Colorado State Board of Agriculture*, 998 F.2d 824 (10th Cir. 1993), *cert. denied*, 510 U.S. 1004 (1993); *Cohen v. Brown University*, 101 F.3d 155 (1st Cir. 1996), *cert. denied*, 520 U.S. 1186 (1997).

Cohen v. Brown University,[49] the district court decision in *Pederson v. Louisiana State University*,[50] and the recent "Clarification of Intercollegiate Athletics Policy Guidance: The Three-Part Test"[51] distributed by the U.S. Department of Education, Office of Civil Rights.

BROWN UNIVERSITY I AND II

The district court, in Brown University I, while assessing this university's compliance with Title IX, specifically addressed whether it accommodated effectively "the interest and abilities of students to the extent necessary to provide equal opportunity in the selection of sports and levels of competition available to members of both sexes."[52] The appellate court commenced by stating that it may not find a violation solely because there is a disparity between the gender composition of the educational institution and student constituency, on one hand, and its athletic programs, on the other.[53] The appellate court, however, stated that subsection (b) of Title IX also provides that it

> shall not be construed to prevent the consideration in any proceedings ... of statistical evidence tending to show that such

---

[49] Prior to trial on the merits of the Brown University cases, the district court granted the plaintiffs a preliminary injunction, ordering the women's volleyball and gymnastics teams be restored from club to university-funded status. See *Brown University I*, 809 F. Supp. at 1001. The first circuit upheld the district court's decision after reviewing the district court's analysis of Title IX and the implementing regulations. See *Brown University II*, 991 F.2d at 906. On remand, the district court found that Brown's intercollegiate program violated Title IX and the supporting regulations. See *Cohen v. Brown University*, 879 F. Supp. 185 (D.R.I. 1995) (*Brown University III*). Brown University appealed and on November 21, 1996, the First Circuit affirmed. See *Cohen v. Brown University*, 101 F.3d 155 (1st Cir. 1996) (*Brown University IV*), cert. denied, 520 U.S. 1186 (1997).

[50] 912 F. Supp. 892 (M.D. La. 1996).

[51] Letter from Norma Cantu, Assistant Secretary for Civil Rights, U.S. Dep't of Education, to Colleges and Universities (Sept. 20, 1995) (on file with author).

[52] *Brown University I*, 809 F. Supp. at 985.

[53] *Brown University II*, 991 F.2d at 895.

> an imbalance exists with the respect to the participation in, or the receipt of benefits of, any such program or activity by the members of one sex.[54]

The appellate court judges concluded that an institution satisfies prong one (proportionality) if the gender balance of its intercollegiate athletic program substantially mirrors the gender balance of its student enrollment.[55] Taking the view that the phrase "substantially proportionate" must be a standard stringent enough to effectuate the purposes of the statute,[56] the court said that Title IX established a presumption that discrimination exists if the university does not provide participation opportunities to men and women in substantial proportionality to their respective student enrollments.[57] It found that the numerical disparity between male and female athletes in Brown University's program, approximately 13 percent, was not "substantially proportionate" and was certainly not a mirror image of the gender of the respective male and female enrollments.[58] The court concluded that Brown University did not meet the requirements of prong one of the three-part test.[59]

With regard to prong two, the issue was whether the institution can show a history and continuing practice of program expansion which is demonstrably responsive to the developing interest and abilities of the members of the underrepresented sex.[60] Prong two illustrates that Title IX does not require the university to leap to complete gender parity in a single bound. It does, however, require an institution to show that it has a history and continued practice of program expansion

---

[54] *Id.*

[55] *Cohen v. Brown University* (*Brown University II*), 991 F.2d 888, 897 (1st Cir. 1993).

[56] *Id.*

[57] *Id.* at 898.

[58] *Id.*

[59] *Id.*

[60] *Id.*

to increase the number of underrepresented athletes participating in intercollegiate athletics.[61] The court stated that schools may not twist the ordinary meaning of "expansion" to find compliance under prong two when schools have increased their relative percentage of women participating in athletics by making cuts in both men's and women's sports.[62] Because Brown University had attempted to comply with prong two by reducing both men and women's sports to equalize proportionality, the court found it had failed the prong two test.[63]

The court said that prong three—interests and abilities—requires a relatively simple assessment of whether there is unmet need in the underrepresented gender that rises to a level sufficient to form a new team or require the upgrading of an existing one.[64] Thus, if athletes of the underrepresented gender have both the ability and interest to compete at the intercollegiate level, they must be fully and effectively accommodated.[65] Institutions need not upgrade or create a team where the interest and ability of the students are not sufficiently developed to field a varsity team.[66]

Brown University argued that "to the extent students interests in athletics are disproportionate by gender, colleges should be allowed to meet those interests incompletely as long as the school's response is in direct proportion to the comparative levels of interest."[67] In other words, Brown University claimed that it may accommodate *fewer* than all of the interested and able women if, on a proportionate basis, it accommodates *fewer* than all the interested and able men.

The court took considerable pains to address why this reading of Title IX was flawed. Brown University argued that they could

---

[61] *Id.*

[62] *Id.*

[63] *Id.* at 906.

[64] *Id.* at 898.

[65] *Cohen v. Brown University* (*Brown University II*), 991 F.2d 888, 898 (1st Cir. 1993).

[66] *Id.*

[67] *Id.* at 899.

read the third prong, providing for accommodation of interests and abilities, separately from prong one, requiring substantial proportionality. This view was rejected because the policy interpretation, which requires full accommodation of the underrepresented gender, draws its essence from the statute and requires an evaluation of the athletic program as a whole.[68]

Second, the court stated that any argument is wrong where prong three somehow countervails the meaning of prong one. Such a position overlooks the accommodation test's general purpose: to decide whether a student has been "excluded from participation in, or denied the benefits of" an athletic program on the basis of sex.[69] The test is whether the athletic program as a "whole" is reasonably constructed to carry out the statute.[70] Brown University's proposal would be contrary to the purpose of the statute. It would determine athletic interest and abilities of students in such a way as to take into account the nationally increasing levels of women's interest and abilities as related to their population in the student body. The court clearly did not agree that full and effective accommodation can satisfy the statute when prong-one proportionality is not found.

Brown University's reliance on student surveys of interest and abilities was also found at fault. *The Athletic Investigator's Manual* (The Manual) stated that the intent of its provisions was to use surveys of interest and abilities to follow a determination that an institution does not satisfy prong three:[71] they could not use it to make that determination in the first instance.[72] The court was also concerned that a survey of interests and abilities of the students at Brown University would not be a true measure of their interest and abilities because the school's recruiting methods could predetermine

---

[68] *Id.*

[69] *Id.* at 899–900.

[70] *Id.* at 900.

[71] *The Manual* at 9.

[72] *Brown University II*, 991 F.2d at 901.

such interests and abilities in the first place.[73] The judges noted that the test was full and effective accommodation in the whole program, not solely an accommodation of interests and abilities at the expense of disregarding proportionality.[74] Prong three would excuse Brown University's failure to provide substantial proportionate participation and opportunities only if the university fully and effectively accommodate the underrepresented sex. However, Brown University did not comply with prong three because it failed to increase the number of intercollegiate participation opportunities available to the underrepresented sex and also failed to maintain and support women's donor-funded teams at Brown University's highest level, thus preventing athletes on those teams from fully developing their competitive abilities and skills.[75]

Finally, the court found that far more male athletes were being supported at the university-funded varsity level than female athletes, and thus, women receive less benefit from their intercollegiate varsity programs as a whole than do men.[76]

BROWN UNIVERSITY IV—THE APPEAL

Brown University appealed the district court's order to effect changes (*Brown University III*)[77] and challenged the analysis of the three-part test employed by the district court in *Brown University I*, which was approved by the first circuit in *Brown University II*. The appeals court stunned Brown University by announcing it had squarely rejected Brown University's reading of the three-part test and that, under the "law of the case" doctrine, the court was precluded

---

[73] *Id.*

[72] *Id.* at 902–03.

[73] *Cohen v. Brown University*, 991 F.2d 888, 903 (1st Cir. 1993) (*Brown University II*).

[76] *Id.* at 904.

[77] *Cohen v. Brown University*, 879 F. Supp. 185, 186 (D.R.I. 1995) (*Brown University III*).

from relitigating the issues previously decided.[78] It affirmed the district court's finding concerning Brown University's obligation to fully and effectively accommodate the interests and abilities of women athletes.[79] The appellate court did, however, again take strong issue with Brown University's argument that it could meet prong three of the three-part test by failing to meet the interests and abilities of women to the same extent that it failed to meet the interests and abilities of men. If there is sufficient unmet interest and ability among the underrepresented sex, the institution necessarily failed the test, said the court.[80] "Brown University reads the 'full' out of the duty to accommodate 'fully and effectively.' Prong three 'demands not merely some accommodation, but full and effective accommodation.'"[81] Brown University's interpretation of full and effective accommodation is not in accordance with the law because it cannot withstand scrutiny on legal or policy grounds.

The appellate court again stressed the importance of the proportionality "mirror" image test by observing that a school creates a presumption if it is in compliance when it has achieved a statistical balance.[82] Further, when a statistical balance is not present, the school must fully and effectively accommodate women's interests and abilities even when that requires a larger slice of the athletic department pie go to women's programs.[83]

Finally, the court viewed with distaste Brown University's argument that there is a gender-based difference in the level of sports participation interest that should be considered to allow fewer participation opportunities for women. It viewed such a position as an attempt to ignore the purpose of Title IX and to

---

[78] *Cohen v. Brown University*, 101 F.3d 155, 167 (1st Cir. 1996) (*Brown University IV*), *cert. denied*, 520 U.S. 1186 (1997).

[79] *Id.* at 162.

[80] *Id.* at 174.

[81] *Id.*

[82] *Id.* at 175.

[83] *Id.* at 176.

rely on an outdated stereotyping of women's interests.[84] In the court's view, the perceived lack of interest evolves directly from the historical lack of opportunity for women to participate in sports; precisely what Title IX is designed to remedy. Several times the court pointed out that Title IX implementation deserves some credit for the showing of American women athletes in the Olympic summer games.[85]

THE DISSENT

Schools with football programs may find some comfort in the dissenting opinion in *Brown University* because, for the first time, a judge advocated that contact sports, like football, "should be eliminated from the calculus in determining membership numbers for varsity sports."[86] The judge cited 34 C.F.R. section 106.41(b), which states that a school may have separate teams for members of each sex "when selection is based on ... activity involving a contact sport."[87] In counting participation opportunities for comparison of proportionality, it does not make sense to compare athletes who participate in contact sports that include only men's teams, said the judge. He believed that not all sports are the same and the school should be able to choose those most beneficial.[88]

LOUISIANA STATE

In *Pederson v. Louisiana State University*,[89] the district court examined each prong of the three-part test in the context of whether the university had fully and effectively accommodated the interests and abilities of its female students. The plaintiffs argued that LSU

---

[84] *Id.* at 179.

[85] *Id.* at 180.

[86] *Id.* at 188 (Torruella, J., dissenting).

[87] 34 C.F.R. § 106.41(b) (1992).

[88] *Cohen v. Brown University*, 101 F.3d 155, 188 (1st Cir. 1996) (*Brown University IV*) (Torruella, J., dissenting).

[89] 912 F .Supp. 892 (M.D. La. 1996).

failed to accommodate its female athletes by providing greater athletic opportunities to its male students at a time when sufficient interest and ability existed in its female student population to justify increasing women's sports opportunities.[90] The specific complaint concerned a perceived failure to provide a women's fast-pitch softball team.

Relying on *Colorado State* and the foregoing *Brown University* cases, both plaintiffs and defendants asked the court to find that so long as males and females are proportionally represented in athletics as found in the general student undergraduate population and are given numerically proportionate opportunities to participate in advanced competition, the university should be deemed in compliance with Title IX. Further, if numerical proportionality is not found, the university should be deemed in violation of Title IX.[91]

The court rejected this proposition and specifically stated that it disagreed with the rationale of the *Brown University* and *Colorado State* opinions. "Title IX does not mandate equal numbers of participants. Rather, it prohibits exclusion based on sex and requires equal opportunity to participate for both sexes."[92] Therefore, ending the inquiry at the point of numerical proportionality does not comport with the mandate of the statute. Title IX specifically does not require preferential, disparate treatment based on proportionality.[93] Rather, those percentages should be considered as evidence "tending to show that such an imbalance exists with respect to the participation in, or receipt of benefits of, any such program or activity by members of one sex."[94] Consequently, the clear language of the statute prohibits the requirement of numerical proportionality and regarded the Brown University cases as a "safe harbor" for a university.[95]

---

[90] *Id.* at 904–5.

[91] *Id.* at 913.

[92] *Id.* at 914.

[93] *Id.* at 913.

[94] *Id.* (citing Title IX, 20 U.S.C. § 1681(a) (1972)).

[95] *Id.*

Clearly, the pivotal element of the LSU analysis is the question of effective accommodation of interests and abilities.[96] Given the foregoing, it was imperative that LSU be acquainted with the interests and abilities of its female students.

Because LSU had not conducted a survey of its female students, the court found that there was no credible evidence to establish their actual interests and abilities. LSU simply had no method, discriminatory or otherwise, by which a determination could be made. This school was, and had been, ignorant of the interests and abilities of its student population for some time.[97]

The trial evidence found that LSU's student population during the relevant period was approximately 51 percent male and 49 percent female and its athletic participation for the same period was about 71 percent male and 29 percent female.[98] Throughout the relevant period, LSU fielded a men's baseball team. The court accepted evidence that women's fast-pitch softball was the closest approximation to this sport.[99]

The plaintiffs established that since 1979, there was sufficient interest and ability at LSU to fill a successful Division I varsity fast-pitch softball team, and that in 1983, for some unknown reason, LSU disbanded that program. The plaintiffs also were able to establish that the interest in fast-pitch softball had increased since 1979.[100] Finally, and most critically, the plaintiffs established that intercollegiate play is provided for male students with similar interests and abilities by way of the varsity baseball team.[101] At the same time, LSU provided

---

[96] *Id.* at 913–15.

[97] *Id.*

[98] *Id.* at 915.

[99] *Pederson v. Louisiana State University*, 912 F. Supp. 892, 915–16 (M.D. La. 1996).

[100] *Id.* at 915.

[101] *Id.* at 916.

absolutely no opportunity for women to compete in fast-pitch softball at any level.

By not fielding a women's fast-pitch softball team, LSU failed to accommodate the female plaintiffs' interests and abilities individually because the interest and abilities to support a softball team existed in the student undergraduate population. The court's findings suggested that sex discrimination accounted for the discrepancy.[102]

The court then examined the history of expanding opportunities for women athletes at LSU and concluded that the university has demonstrated a practice not to expand its women's athletics before it became absolutely necessary to do so.[103] The court could find no evidence of a workable plan of action by the university to address the failure to accommodate interests and abilities of women students and concluded that LSU was in violation of Title IX, noting that LSU was a national leader in resisting gender equity.[104]

In a harsh assessment of the athletic department, the court wrote that its director's one-dimensional assessment of programs created an atmosphere of arrogance by management that had continued to be undaunted by the facts, up to the date of the trial.[105] LSU's action was seen as a direct result of the director's belief that his "women's athletics" program was "wonderful."[106] He equated winning teams, rather than participation, as accommodating interest and abilities. The judge interpreted the violations a result of an arrogant ignorance, and confusion regarding the practical requirements of the law, and a remarkably outdated view of women athletes which created the resistance to change.[107]

---

[102] *Id.* at 916–18.

[103] *Id.*

[104] *Id.*

[105] *Id.*

[106] *Id.* at 919.

[107] *Id.* at 916–18.

A comparison of *LSU* with *Brown University* clearly shows a potential split in the circuits concerning the proportionality requirement. According to the *LSU* court, the theory that numerical proportionality is a "safe harbor" contradicts the prescriptions of Title IX because it treats women as a class rather than as individuals.[108] This decision appears to support the use of surveys to determine the unmet interests and abilities of the student body. In contrast, *Brown University* shows surveys are inherently unreliable because they only reflect the predetermined interest of the student body.

POLICY GUIDANCE

On January 16, 1996, the OCR released its long overdue "Clarification of Intercollegiate Athletics Policy Guidance: Three-Part Test" as an enclosure to a letter from the assistant secretary for the OCR.[109] It begins by focusing on the athletics programs as a whole. This focus is interesting because the same language is adopted in *Brown University* and *LSU* as well as in the Clarification.[110] The Clarification states that an institution's failure to provide nondiscriminatory participation opportunities for the whole student body usually amounts to a denial of equal athletic opportunity.[111]

The Clarification appears to follow past policy interpretation concerning prong one of the three-part test. It states that

> where an institution provides intercollegiate level athletic participation opportunities for male and female students in numbers substantially proportionate to the respective full-time undergraduate enrollments, OCR will find that the institution

---

[108] *Id.* at 913–14.

[109] Office for Civil Rights, *Clarification of Intercollegiate Athletics Policy Guidance: The Three-Part Test* (Washington, D.C.: U.S. Department of Education, 1996), hereinafter *"The Clarification."*

[110] *Id.* at 1–2.

[111] *Id.* at 2.

is providing nondiscriminatory participation opportunities for individuals of both sexes.[112]

The so-called "safe harbor" test is still safe as far as the OCR is concerned, despite the reluctance of the *LSU* court.[113]

The test for part two remains essentially the same. Under part three, OCR says that the institution must provide equal athletic opportunity to its admitted and enrolled students. Accordingly, the policy interpretation does not require an institution to accommodate the interests and abilities of merely potential students. This would appear to mean an institution need not accommodate the interests and abilities of potential female athletes in its recruiting area. How does that advance the interest of the underrepresented sex? This question is left unanswered by the policy.

Among the factors OCR uses to determine whether female interests and abilities are being accommodated are requests by students and admitted students that a particular sport be added; requests that an existing club sport be elevated to intercollegiate team status; participation rates in particular or intramural club sports; interviews with students, admitted students, coaches, administrators, and others regarding interest in particular sports; results of questionnaires of students and admitted students regarding interest in sports; and participation in particular interscholastic sports by admitted students.[114]

Finally, the Clarification suggests that schools have flexibility in choosing a nondiscriminatory method of determining athletic interests and abilities provided they meet the appropriate requirements.[115]

DISCUSSION

Given the law, the Brown University case was properly decided because the university failed all three parts of the test, not just

---

[112] *Id.* at 5.

[113] See note 108 and accompanying text.

[114] *The Clarification* at 6.

[115] *Id.*

mandating proportionality. But there are several problems with both the courts' and the OCR's strong emphasis on a "substantially proportionate to female enrollment test."[116] First, failure to achieve strict proportionality need not be evidence of discrimination and therefore cannot be used as a short cut to determine whether an institution is unlawfully discriminating based on sex.[117] Congress explicitly held that proportionality alone was not relevant when it stated that the statute should not "be interpreted to require ... preferential or disparate treatment to the members of one sex on account of an imbalance which may exist with respect to the total number or percentages of persons of that sex participating in ... institutional programs."[118]

Second, the courts have no authority to impose liability under a federal antidiscrimination law like Title VI and VII unless a defendant has unlawfully discriminated.[119] Title IX simply provided that no individual may be excluded from a federally funded program on "the basis of sex."[120] A holding, as in *Colorado State*, that the lack of proportionality creates a disparate impact without considering the impact on accommodating interest and ability, runs contrary to cases that indicate that "a violation of Title VI requires an intentional discriminatory act and that disparate impact alone is not sufficient

---

[116] *Id.* at 192.

[117] The Supreme Court has strongly cautioned lower courts against comparisons to the general population when special interests or qualifications are required. See *Hazelwood School District v United States*, 433 U.S. 299, 308 n.13 (1977). In a recent voting rights case, the Supreme Court held that proportionality cannot serve as a shortcut to determine whether a set of districts unlawfully dilutes minority voting strength. See *Johnson v. Florida*, 512 U.S. 997 (1994).

[118] 20 U.S.C. § 1681(b) (1972).

[119] *St. Mary's Honor Center v. Hicks*, 509 U.S. 502, 514 (1993) (interpreting a Title VII employment discrimination claim). See also *Cannon v. University of Chicago*, 648 F.2d 1104, 1109 (7th Cir. 1981), *cert. denied*, 454 U.S. 1128 (1981) (stating that "a violation of Title VI requires an intentional discriminatory act and that disparate impact alone is not sufficient to establish a violation. We shall therefore adopt that standard under Title IX.").

[120] 20 U.S.C. § 168 1(b).

to establish a violation."[121] There must be a failure to accommodate interests and abilities for a violation to occur. Because Title IX provisions are virtually identical to those of Title VI of the Civil Rights Act of 1964, the court should look to Title VI cases which hold that the act only "reaches instances of intentional discrimination."[122]

Colorado State and, to some extent, *Brown University I, II,* and *IV* disregard the statute's plain meaning concerning proportionality. These decisions are not in the institutions' best interest subject to the law nor to the intended beneficiaries, female students. *Colorado State* holds conduct discriminatory that the statute does not prohibit and appears to specifically permit without regard to the actual interest of female students.[123] Educational and other institutions should be able to rely on reasonable implementation regulations promulgated by the responsible government agency. That agency has published regulations that contain the three-part test including accommodation of interest and abilities of members of both sexes. The OCR regulations explicitly provide that a sports team must be established when there is interest; ability to play the sport; likelihood that the team can be sustained for a number of years; and a reasonable expectation of

---

[121] *Cannon,* 648 F.2d at 1109.

[122] *Alexander v. Choate,* 469 U.S. 287, 293 (1985). Additionally, Title IX is patterned after Title VI. See *Grove City v. Bell,* 465 U.S. 555, 566 (1984). By setting up the same administrative structure and using virtually the same language, Congress intended that the interpretation of Title IX was to be the same as Title VI. See *Hearing Before the Subcomm. on Post Secondary Education of the House Comm. on Education and Labor,* 94th Cong. 16, 150 (1971).

[123] The Roberts Court was apparently relying on *Guardians Association v. Civil Service Commission of New York* to justify a holding that a federal agency, or in this case a court, may proscribe, as discriminatory, conduct which the statute itself does not prohibit. See *Roberts v. Colorado State Board of Agriculture,* 998 F.2d 824, 832 (10th Cir. 1993); *Guardians Association v. Civil Service Commission of New York,* 463 U.S. 582, 584 (1982). The court's reliance is misplaced because the *Guardians* court found that the authority was delegated to the agency by statute. Unlike *Guardians,* Congress in Title IX specifically withheld authority to take action on account of a statistical imbalance between the sexes. See 20 U.S.C. § 1981(b) (1972).

competition within the institution's normal competitive region.[124] Admittedly, it may be difficult in some instances to fashion an instrument to achieve a good measure of the interest and abilities in the particular area. However, a properly designed and conducted study of the institution's drawing and recruiting area can be used to accurately determine whether the interest and abilities of female athletes are being fully accommodated. Such a survey is a better, and more intellectually honest, measure of compliance with the intent of Title IX than an unreasoning reliance on numbers.

The analysis should focus on the athlete's interest and ability to participate in college sports. One cannot seriously argue that all students have the same ability to participate at the university level. Data collected must focus on the disparity between male and female athletes who have the interest in and ability to compete, rather than on the number of males and females in the entire educational community. A simplistic percentage comparison without considering competitive qualifications for varsity athletics lacks real meaning.[125] The rationale of *Colorado State* and *Brown University IV*, insofar as they are based solely on statistical disparity, does not allow the university reasonably to present possible interest and ability justifications.

Finally, a reasonable fact-finder should be able to listen to evidence and decide if a college is making a good faith effort to meet the "interests and abilities" test. In an article appearing in the *Arkansas Democrat-Gazette* regarding the lack of junior women golfers in the state of Arkansas, Arkansas State University's women's golf coach, Neil Able stated, "I would love to recruit girls from Arkansas, but they are not here. There is not a lot of emphasis on girls' golf, nobody seems to be pushing it. It is really a shame because if a girl can shoot between 78 and 82, she can get her education mostly paid for."[126]

---

[124] 34 C.F.R. § 106.41 (c)(1) (1992).

[125] *City of Richmond v. J.A. Croson Co.*, 488 U.S. 469,501 (1989); *Mayor of Philadelphia v. Educational Equity League*, 415 U.S. 605, 620 (1974).

[126] Todd Traub, *While Footing the Bill: Football Also Creates Title IX Imbalance*, Arkansas Democrat-Gazette (Little Rock, Ark.), November 14, 1996, p. C1.

Clearly, this kind of information would be relevant evidence of whether there is sufficient female interest and ability to justify a golf team in Arkansas. The bottom line is that when a college or university is honestly accommodating the interests and abilities of its female undergraduates and potential participants in its recruiting area, the intent of Title IX and OCR guidelines have been met.

ANALYSIS: WHAT DOES IT ALL MEAN?

Some athletic administrators, particularly at football-playing institutions with a majority female enrollment, have placed considerable faith, or maybe hope, in their ability to comply with Title IX by accommodating the interests and abilities of female athletes who have the ability to participate at the collegiate level. This faith, or hope, has been shattered by several courts' perceived reliance solely on proportionality, the first of the three factors used by OCR to assess the equality of opportunity for individuals of both sexes to participate in intercollegiate programs. In *Indiana University*,[127] *Brown University II & III*,[128] and *Colorado State*,[129] the courts found that the participation rates for male and female students were not proportionate to their respective enrollments. In analyzing these decisions, most commentators have focused solely on the first prong and concluded that effective accommodation always requires substantial proportionality of numbers. There has been an unquestioned acceptance that only the first part of the test is relevant.[130]

This analysis, however, is factually incorrect and even disingenuous. These decisions were compatible with the law: the three universities all failed to meet the participation opportunity, a history

---

[127] *Favia v. Indiana University of Pennsylvania*, 812 F. Supp. 578 (W.D. Pa. 1993), aff'd, 7 F.3d 322 (3d Cir. 1993).

[128] *Cohen v. Brown University*, 991 F.2d 888 (1st Cir. 1993) (*Brown University II*); Cohen v. Brown University, 879 F. Supp. 185 (D.R.I. 1995) (*Brown University III*).

[129] *Roberts v. Colorado State Board of Agriculture*, 998 F.2d 824 (10th Cir. 1993).

[130] See generally Denise K. Magner, "Judge Blocks Cal-State Bakersfield's Plan to Cap Size of Wrestling Team," *Chronicle of Higher Education*, March 12, 1999, p. A44.

and practice of program expansion, or fully and effectively accommodate the interests and abilities test. Because the three universities failed all three parts of the test, their cases offer no precedent relevant to a school which meets the interest and abilities test.

A compelling argument can be made that a college which meets the third part of the test—that is, accommodates the interests and abilities of its male and female students—is in compliance with Title IX. The statute's purpose is to provide equality of opportunity, as supported by *Louisiana State*.[131] Use of the proportionality test, without considering the interests and abilities of female students, would have little value in providing equal opportunity to the actual students who have the ability to play at the college level. What is the logical extension of the proportionality argument which does not include interests and abilities? Proportionality would demand female teams even if there were no interest on the part of the women students. Should a university force female students to participate in varsity sports in which they have no interest or ability? Substantial proportionality erroneously presumes that men and women in the general student body will have the same interest and ability to participate at the same rates in intercollegiate athletics. There is no valid statistical or any other kind of evidence to support that presumption. Additionally, a strict proportionality approach violates the Supreme Court's holding concerning the use of statistical analyses to support discrimination claims.[132] Finally, the purpose of the statute and its implementing regulations is to accommodate the interests and abilities of both male and female students who have the ability to participate in intercollegiate sports, not to establish some mechanical, numerical quota based on a student population ratio. The slavish and unreasoned reliance on numbers has already created an unfavorable backlash harmful to gender "equity."[133]

---

[131] See generally *Pederson v. Louisiana State University*, 912 F. Supp. 892 (M.D. La. 1996).

[132] See, e.g., *Hazelwood School District v. United States*, 433 U.S. 299 (1977); *Castaneda v. Partida*, 430 U.S. 482 (1977).

[133] For example, the backlash in football has been very strong. See generally Bob Holt, "Court Ruling Raises Alarm on Title IX: ASU'S Dowd Calls

There is another factor that should reduce administrators' comfortable reliance on the Athletic Investigator's Manual and the three-part test. This is the stated goal of the NCAA Gender Equity Task Force report that the numbers of male and female athletes should be substantially proportionate to their numbers in the institution's undergraduate population.[134] This report language may soon start appearing in future decisions, given the perceived rationale of *Indiana University*, *Brown University*, and *Colorado State*.

SUMMARY OF ISSUES FACING ADMINISTRATORS

Obviously, athletic administrators and boards of trustees are presently in an untenable position because of the dramatic conflict between the provisions of Title IX, its implementing regulations promulgated by the Office of Civil Rights, and the outcome of federal court cases, particularly *Colorado State* and *Brown University*. Certainly, the safe harbor approach is to insure a strict proportionality of percentages of female athletes compared with the number of females in the total university enrollment. The recent OCR clarification clearly underscores this. The strict proportionality approach, while attractive on its face, is, in fact, counterproductive to athletes who have the ability to participate at the collegiate level, and is contrary to the meaning of the statute and its implementing regulations. Many contend that female athletes have been subjected to discrimination in the past and in many

---

Decision 'Idiotic,'" *Arkansas Democrat-Gazette* (Little Rock, Ark.), Apr. 22, 1997, p. C1. Unfortunately, some schools have helped justify their decisions to cut men's sports by blaming Title IX, according to NCAA president Cedric Dempsey, and a recent GAO study shows a drop in men's participation in NCAA sports. See generally, "GAO Study Shows Drop in Men's Participation, but Reason Is Unclear," *NCAA News*, July 5, 1999, p. A1; Erik Lords, "More Women and Fewer Men Participate in Intercollegiate Athletics, Study Finds," *Chronicle of Higher Education*, July 9, 1999, p. A40.

[134] *The NCAA Gender-Equity Task Force Report* states that it should be the ultimate goal of each institution that the numbers of male and female athletes are substantially proportionate to their undergraduate population. See *The Report*, note 4, p. 3. *The Report* also stresses that maintaining current revenue-enhancing programs like football is essential to enhancing opportunities for women athletes (see *id*).

cases are still being victimized by institutions of higher learning. Even so, an unthinking reliance on proportionality at the expense of accommodating the interest of women who have the ability to participate at the collegiate level is not only contrary to the law, it is not even in the best interests of such female athletes.

When the federal courts are persuaded to carefully read the statute and its implementing regulations, and properly evaluate the intent of the statute and its impact on female athletes, as the court did in *Louisiana State*, they will conclude that a university may comply with the statute by effectively and fully accommodating the interest and abilities of female athletes.

A SOCIOBIOLOGICAL AND ECONOMIC CRITIQUE OF GENDER "EQUITY"

The goal of this section is to take issue with the OCR and to criticize the regulations against discrimination it has promulgated. In our view, the basic premise from which government "equity" laws proceed is that absent discrimination, all groups, whether based on race, ethnicity, or, in the present case, gender, would be exactly alike in all major regards;[135] that if virtually exact proportional representation of all categories of people in all activities and accomplishments has not been achieved, this is "inequitable;" and that this inequity represents an exploitation of the "victims" by the "privileged."

This politically correct perspective is so well entrenched in legal thinking that to even question it is to call forth the charge of irrational and "outdated stereotyping."[136] It is so inviolable that to question it is to open the critic to charges of "racism" or "sexism," which are fighting words in any person's lexicon. The view that all groups are equally endowed with all sorts of interests and abilities is so impregnable

---

[135] The conventional wisdom does make one set of exceptions in the case of sex: it "concedes" that men and women have different biological characteristics, and that only females can become pregnant and give birth. We applaud this concession to reality.

[136] See generally *Cohen v. Brown University*, 809 F. Supp. 978 (D.R.I. 1992) (*Brown University I*).

that to even mention evidence for the opposite contention is widely seen as rude, unseemly, or in some other way improper. Such claims are refuted not by providing evidence, but through *ad hominem* attacks. The findings of Thomas Sowell and Walter Williams,[137] which challenge this conventional wisdom, are dismissed not based on errors that have been found in the logic or empirical evidence they offer, but through personal attacks on these researchers.

Sowell points to the following facts about which "it is virtually impossible to claim that the statistical differences in question are due to discrimination:"[138]

- American men are struck by lightning six times as often as American women;

- Cognac consumption in Estonia was more than seven times, *per capita*, that of Uzbekistan;

---

[137] See generally Thomas Sowell, *Civil Rights: Rhetoric or Reality* (New York: William Morrow, 1984); Thomas Sowell, *A Conflict of Visions: Ideological Origins of Political Struggles* (New York: William Morrow, 1987); Thomas Sowell, *The Economics and Politics of Race: An International Perspective* (New York: William Morrow, 1983); Thomas Sowell, *Ethnic America* (New York: Basic Books, 1981); Thomas Sowell, *Pink and Brown People* (Stanford, Calif.: Hoover Institution Press, 1981); Thomas Sowell, *Race and Culture: A World View* (New York: Basic Books, 1994);Thomas Sowell, *Race and Economics* (New York: Longman, 1975); Thomas Sowell, *The Vision of the Anointed* (New York: Basic Books, 1995); Walter E. Williams, *South Africa's War Against Capitalism* (New York: Praeger, 1989); Walter E. Williams, *The State Against Blacks* (New York: McGraw-Hill, 1982); Thomas Sowell, "Preferential Policies," in *Thinking about America: The United States in the 1990s*, Annelise Anderson and Dennis L. Bark, eds. (Stanford, Calif.: Hoover Institution Press, 1988); Thomas Sowell, "Weber and Bakke and the Presuppositions of 'Affirmative Action'," in *Discrimination, Affirmative Action, and Equal Opportunity*, Walter Block and Michael Walker, eds. (Vancouver, British Columbia: Fraser Institute, 1982); Walter E. Williams, "On Discrimination, Prejudice, Racial Income Differentials, and Affirmative Action," in *Discrimination, Affirmative Action, and Equal Opportunity*.

[138] Sowell, *The Vision of the Anointed*, p. 33.

- In the 1960s, members of the Chinese minority in Malaysia received over 400 degrees in engineering, compared to only 4 for the majority Malays;

- Afrikaners in 1946 South Africa earned less than half the income of the less politically powerful British;

- Orientals in the United States in 1985 scored over 700 on the mathematics SAT at twice the rate of whites;

- Germans were only 1 percent of the population of czarist Russia but accounted for some 40 percent of that army's high command;

- Japanese immigrants accounted for more than 66 percent of potato and 90 percent of tomato production in the Brazilian state of Sao Paulo;

- In the 1850s, over 50 percent of Melbourne's clothing stores were owned by Jews, who were less than 1 percent of the Australian population.[139]

All of these facts are simply incompatible with the "vision of the anointed" that absent anything untoward, there would be homogeneity of all groups of people over all activities. Sometimes, this basic premise has annoying, and perhaps even infuriating, results, but mostly on an intellectual plane. An example might be its influence generally in the United States at the close of the twentieth century, and particularly the debate over female participation in college athletics. At other times, however, this flawed philosophy has had far more serious repercussions. For example, the Nazi attempt to exterminate the Jews was, at bottom, due to Hitler's resentment that this minority was more than proportionately represented among German bankers, professors, university students, playwrights, businessmen, doctors and lawyers, and was far more wealthy than the average citizen.[140]

---

[139] *Id.*, pp. 35–57.

[140] See generally Steven Farron, "Prejudice is Free but Discrimination has Costs," *Journal Libertarian Studies* 14, no. 2 (Summer 2000): 179–245.

It is crucial to realize that there is a notion of proportionality of representation as the norm at work in both examples.[141]

It is a matter of great interest that failure to register statistical homogeneity should be interpreted as discrimination in some cases, but not others. Returning to our focus on athletics, consider this statement by Sowell: "No one regards the gross disparity in 'representation' between blacks and whites in professional basketball as proving discrimination against whites in that sport."[142] Were it not for the miasma of political correctness, this statistical disparity would occasion as much criticism as any other. That this situation is not widely resented is thus more than passing curiosity.

What are the facts of the case? Let us consider both professional basketball and football:

RACIAL AND ETHNIC COMPOSITION OF PROFESSIONAL ATHLETIC EMPLOYMENT (IN PERCENT)[143]

		White	Black	Hispanic	Other
Total Population		73	12	11	4
NBA	Players	20	79	0	0
	General Managers	72	28	0	0
	Coaches	67	33	0	0
	Staff	77	17	2	3
NFL	Players	31	66	1	0
	General Managers	83	17	0	0
	Coaches	75	24	1	0
	Staff	80	15	3	2

---

[141] One might expect Jews to be among the most vociferous opponents of affirmative action, given their historical experiences with this phenomenon. Why this is not the case is explored by Walter Block, "The Mishnah and Jewish Dirigisme," in *International Journal of Social Economics* 23, no. 2 (1996): 35–44; Milton Friedman, "Capitalism and the Jews," in *Morality of the Market: Religious and Economic Perspectives*, Walter Block, Geoffrey Brennan, and Kenneth Elzinga, eds. (Vancouver, British Columbia: The Fraser Institute, 1985), pp. 429–42.

[142] Sowell, *The Vision of the Anointed*, p. 35.

[143] Michael Lynch and Rick Henderson, "Team Colors," *Reason*, July 1998, p. 21.

As indicated in the table, the roster of professional athletes includes far fewer whites than would occur were they distributed to this employment slot from a random sampling of the population; and, obversely, we must also reject the null hypothesis that blacks are randomly distributed as well. Yet there is not one person in a million who thinks that the owners of these sports leagues (100 percent white) engage in anti-white, pro-black prejudice; that they turn away better scoring, higher jumping, stronger whites to make room on their rosters for weaker, smaller, less athletic blacks. The thought never occurs that black success in this field is due to anything but the fact that blacks bring to the table a great amount of athleticism, power, strength and grace.[144]

Having introduced our topic with a discussion of the fallacious homogeneity hypothesis, and applied it to male sports, let us now consider how it applies to females *vis-à-vis* males.

First, if we are to take seriously the non-discrimination ethic, there should be no division between female and male sports programs. Given the feminist contention[145] that the genders are alike (apart from unimportant biological matters), it is an egregious matter of segregation to separate the sexes into two different categories.

---

[144] Ibid., p. 20. It is often charged that while blacks are hired as players in professional sports leagues, there is in effect a "glass ceiling" which prevents them from rising to management, coaching, and other staff positions after they retire as athletes. This contention cannot be supported by the reported facts. Blacks comprise only 14 percent of the U.S. population. See U.S. Census Bureau, *Statistical Abstract of the United States: 1998*, p. 14, table 13 (1998). Thus, they are statistically overrepresented in the NBA and NFL not only as players, but also as managers, coaches and staff. Therefore, were employment equity strictly applied to the professional athletics industry, at least insofar as these two leagues are concerned, there would be a massive firing of blacks as players, as well as roughly half of the black general managers and coaches in the NBA, and coaches in the NFL would have to be dismissed.

[145] For antidotes, see generally Richard A. Epstein, *Forbidden Grounds: The Case against Employment Discrimination Laws* (Cambridge, Mass.: Harvard University Press, 1992); Michael E. Levin, *Feminism and Freedom* (New York: Transaction Books, 1987).

Gender integration is now commonly practiced for children's soccer leagues, and based on the premises of the anointed, there is no reason not to follow this practice at the university level.

The problem here is that while seven-year-old girls are reasonably competitive with boys of that age, the same does not at all apply to adult men and women. A perusal of any of the male and female world's records in activities such as swimming, running, throwing, jumping, rowing, skiing, skating, and bicycling suggests that were there no segregation by sex, there would be virtually no females with the requisite strength, speed or other physical attributes to even earn a berth on a university team.[146] In order to be competitive, males and females of very different vintages must confront one another (e.g., the famous tennis match between Billie Jean King, then at the apex of her tennis game, versus Bobby Riggs, who was long past his prime and never had attained stature among men comparable to King's stature among women, even at the apex of his abilities). Surely it is inequitable, in at least some reasonable senses of the word, to have special categories for female athletes at all. Were there not any such categories, and universities wished to field as many athletes as they now do, there would be a large number of relatively mediocre male athletes who could instead enjoy this experience. On this basis, then, women "athletes" are favored when universities spend any money on these pursuits, for in a purely "fair" world, where slots on teams were awarded strictly in accordance with ability, few women would be able to break through the "sports ceiling."

Clearly, we believe this state of affairs is not due to the early conditioning of "culture," or of females by male misogynist fathers.

---

[146] Golf may well be an exception. If so, and to that extent, its pedigree as a legitimate athletic event comes into question. In other words, we may perhaps distinguish between "real" sporting activities and mere "play" on the basis of whether adult males and females are competitive with each other. True, female Olympic athletes of 1998 can swim rings around males of an earlier era (e.g., Buster Crabbe, Johnny Weismuller), but records have been significantly improving over the intervening decades. These two swimmers, Crabbe and Weismuller, who later played the role of Tarzan in the movies, could best their female contemporaries of the day by similar margins as men now outdistance women in the pool.

Mothers do most of the early childhood rearing, of both boys and girls.[147] Nor is it due to "self-hating" mothers, who conspiratorially undermine athletic abilities on the distaff side. Instead, there are good and sufficient sociobiological reasons why females should be weaker and slower, on average, than males, and therefore make poorer athletes.

According to scholars of sociobiology and evolutionary psychology, we are the way we are now in large part because of what it took to survive and leave progeny hundreds of thousands of years ago. In those days, and at present as well, for that matter, women were the genetic bottleneck. Or, to put this the other way around, most males were genetically superfluous. That is, one man could fertilize hundreds of women; the others were, biologically speaking, in effect, drones. In contrast, each female was precious in terms of preserving the human race, in that she could leave progeny with the genetic contribution of a single male. Suppose, a long time ago, there were two tribes of (pre-) humans: one of which sent the women out hunting (which sharply penalized non-athleticism) and accorded the men the role of staying in the relatively safer caves with the children while the other group inverted this process. Which of them would survive and leave descendants? To ask this question is to answer it. In fact, we have a name for the first (presumably imaginary) tribe: "extinct."[148]

---

[147] Lillian B. Rubin, *Families on the Fault Line: America's Working Class Speak About the Economy, Race, and Ethnicity*, 1st ed. (New York: Harper Collins, 1994); Rodney Stark, "Socialization and Social Roles," in *Sociology*, 7th ed. (1998), pp. 160–62.

[148] See generally Robert M. Axelrod, *The Evolution of Cooperation* (New York: Basic Books, 1984); David M. Buss, *The Evolution of Desire: Strategies of Human Mating* (New York: Basic Books, 1994); Richard Dawkins, *River out of Eden: A Darwinian View of Life* (New York: Basic Books, 1995); Richard Dawkins, *The Selfish Gene* (Oxford University Press, 1989); R.H. Frank, *Passion within Reason: The Strategic Role of the Emotions* (London: Norton, 1988); Donald Symons, *The Evolution of Human Sexuality* (Oxford University Press, 1979); Robert Trivers, *Social Evolution* (Menlo Park, Calif.: The Benjamin Cummings Publishing Company, 1985); E.O. Wilson, *Sociobiology: A New Synthesis* (Cambridge, Mass.: Harvard University Press,

Thus, the reason men are now far better athletes than women is that males without such attributes were weeded out of the genetic stock to a far greater extent than females. Stated differently, male, but not female, athleticism contributed to evolutionary success.

With success, of course, comes interest. That is, there tends to be a positive correlation between what we do well at and what we are interested in. Nerds and geeks tend to be interested in computers and mathematics because they succeed in mastering their intricacies. And, of course, there is a positive feedback loop between them where interest breeds success which, in turn, leads to yet greater involvement. Likewise, those who achieve in athletic arenas tend to focus on them and are positively reinforced for doing so. This being the case, it should not occasion any surprise that boys are not only better at sports, but also more occupied with them as well.

But sociobiology is merely an explanation of the human (and other species') condition. We can transcend our "selfish genes"[149] if we wish. That is, this academic discipline can only account for the fact that girl students would have less interest and ability to pursue intercollegiate competition than boys. However, it is not at all prescriptive. Just because female athletes are vastly inferior to their male counterparts does not mean that their desires to indulge in such activities, lesser though they be, should not be accommodated in modern society. On the other hand, given these sociobiological insights, it is difficult to credit the findings of various courts that lesser support for female athletic programs is evidence of sexist discrimination on the part of university administrations.

1975); Robert Wright, *Moral Animal: The New Science of Evolutionary Psychology* (New York: Vintage, 1994); R. Axelrod and W.D. Hamilton, "The Evolution of Cooperation," *Science* 211 (1981): 1390–96; John Tooby and Leda Cosmides, "Evolutionary Psychology and the Generation of Culture," *Ethnology and Sociobiology* 10 (1989): 375–424; John Tooby and Leda Cosmides, "On the Universality of Human Nature," *Journal of Personality* 58 (1990): 17–67; R. Wright, "Feminists, Meet Mr. Darwin," *New Republic*, Nov. 28, 1994, p. 43.

[149] Dawkins, *The Selfish Gene*, p. 1.

How, then, would the more limited interests of females in athletic pursuits be accommodated, absent the Office of Civil Rights, Title IX of the Education Amendments of 1972, the Civil Rights Law of 1964, Gender "Equity" Task Forces, and all the rest of the panoply of government intervention into private arrangements? Access to athletics would be allocated through the free-enterprise system, just as access to health clubs and golf courses is now allocated in the world beyond colleges.

Even though men have very little interest in wearing women's clothes, this has not prevented a gigantic industry from arising, dedicated to satisfying women's desires in fashion. Industries which provide makeup, hair styling, nail polish, hair removal, and weight loss services are similarly "biased" in the direction of females: they disproportionately serve women. These phenomena would be very difficult to understand on the feminist model that female wants are ignored or deprecated in the male's favor.

Why is it that the market is led by "an invisible hand"[150] to provide goods and services for women, who are not "dominant," or "aggressive" and are thought to be "victims" of discrimination? It is based on profit and loss. The market provides goods and services in proportion to the dollars which are "voted" in their behalf.[151]

---

[150] See generally Adam Smith, *An Inquiry in the Nature and Causes of the Wealth of Nations* (New York: Modern Library, 1965). The invisible hand was thought by Smith to be God's ordering of the human condition such that we are automatically led, by selfish interest and even greed, to do that which is in the best interests of our fellow human beings.

[151] For an economic account of male/female earnings differentials in terms of unequal sharing of family, household, and child rearing tasks, see generally Walter Block and Michael A. Walker, *Focus on Employment Equity: A Critique of the Abella Royal Commission on Equality in Employment* (Vancouver, British Columbia: The Fraser Institute, 1985); Walter Block and Walter Williams, "Male-Female Earnings Differentials: A Critical Reappraisal," *Journal of Labor Research* 2, no 2 (Fall 1981): 385–88. But doesn't this just put back the real question? The claim might be made that women have fewer dollar votes in the first place because of male discrimination in the labor market. Even if, then, goods and services are provided according to spending power, females still get the short end of the stick due to this prior injustice.

If, for example, females have 55 percent of the spending power, then this proportion of the GDP will tend to be allotted to their demands, and 45 percent to that of males. This can be proven by the following considerations. Suppose that, given this division of income, the market has somehow produced 70 percent of its wares according to males' tastes, and only 30 percent in the direction of female wants. This would imply relative satiety for things such as golf clubs, baseball bats, power boats, and beer, but an under-supply relative to demand for makeup, high-heeled shoes, and jewelry. Profits would rise in the latter industries and fall in the former ones. Entrepreneurs would be led by Adam Smith's invisible hand into producing more products that appeal to females and fewer that appeal to males. If they failed to do so, there would continue to be more bankruptcies among firms serving preponderantly male needs.

A similar analysis applies to male and female sports programs at the university level. Assume that such spending for each gender was on a 50:50 basis. Suppose, for argument's sake, that the optimal proportion of expenditure for women's and men's teams is 25:75 in terms of actual demand. Then, on the assumption of private schools which are subjected to the market forces of profit and loss, educational "firms" (e.g., universities) would be led to conform their practices to this proportion. The same principle applies no matter what the statistical assumption. If tastes somehow change, and women athletes now are willing to spend, say, 70 percent of the sports dollar, and men only

---

This may well be the popular view, but it is erroneous. Wages tend to be proportional to productivity, and male and female productivity is roughly equal. Why, then, do women earn less in the market? This is not because of favoritism toward males. Rather, it is due to the fact that females have less attachment to the labor force, and have invested in less work-specified human capital. And the explanation for this state of affairs, in turn, is the unequal sharing of child rearing and household tasks in marriages. Again there are good and sufficient sociobiological reasons why this should be the case, but whether or not this explanation for unequal household duties is true, it is a bit of a stretch to blame this state of affairs on the market, or capitalism, or employers, or discrimination, or any other of the feminists' whipping boys.

30 percent, then a similar shift would again occur, this time in the direction of more money for female teams.

The assumption of private universities is crucial for the case that government intervention is not needed to fully accommodate the demand for intercollegiate sports teams. To the extent that there are public institutions of higher learning, we can no longer rely on market forces to bring about any such result. Thus, any feminists who pay attention to economics should advocate the privatization of higher education.[152] In public universities, there is no economic profit and loss oversight to counteract any tendencies toward anti-female discrimination.

So far, we have been discussing sexual discrimination from a biological and economic perspective. Let us now conclude with a normative analysis. Setting aside the causes and effects of gender discrimination, and the issue of whether it exists on college campuses (or is due to lesser female interest in sports teams), let us ask the question of whether schools should have a right to discriminate in this regard. Nondiscrimination rules apply to "public" accommodations,[153] such as stores, hotels, and movie theaters, but not to certain private choices. That is, it is illegal for a commercial firm's owner to discriminate on the basis of sex,[154] race, ethnicity, etc., but this may be done, and

---

[152] This is on the assumption that the feminist agenda is actually one of promoting the welfare and best interests of women. An alternative hypothesis emanates from the Public Choice School of Economics, according to which there may be, in addition or possibly instead, a hidden agenda. The disparate treatment accorded President Bill Clinton and Supreme Court Justice Clarence Thomas suggests that it is to promote Democrats, or socialists, at the expense of Republicans, or conservatives, and not at all to help females. See generally James M. Buchanan and Gordon Tullock, *The Calculus of Consent: Logical Foundations of Constitutional Democracy* (Ann Arbor: University of Michigan Press, 1971); Christina Hoff Sommers, *Who Stole Feminism? How Women have Betrayed Women* (New York: Simon and Schuster, 1994).

[153] This is a bit of a misnomer, since enterprises of this sort are *privately* owned. Nor are they necessarily "open to the public." On the contrary, this is precisely the point at issue.

[154] Both heterosexuals and homosexuals discriminate in their choice of bed partner on the basis of gender. Of all groups, only bisexuals are completely

commonly is done, in dating, friendship patterns, and marriage. If discrimination is such an utter evil, why should it be countenanced in any realm of human endeavor?

Second, even within the area of commerce, there is a curious lack of symmetry. Customers are allowed to discriminate between, say, restaurants selling Chinese, Italian, Indian and Mexican food, while none of these establishments would be allowed by law to reciprocate in a similar manner. That is, none of them could legally restrict their clientele to any one ethnic group, or, indeed, exclude any of them.[155]

CONCLUSION

So the philosophical premise upon which gender equity is built, far from being impregnable, is, in our view, intellectually incoherent. Perhaps, then, an alternative may one day come to take its place: the right of free association. According to this doctrine, people should be free to associate with whomever they wish, on whatever basis they choose; there should be no law compelling them to deal with those they wish to avoid. Strong historical and moral precedent exists for this approach. It is the philosophy upon which the anti-slavery movement is built.[156] The kidnapping of innocent people is the paradigmatic case of the violation of the law of voluntary association. Forcing individuals to interact with one another when it is not on a mutually agreeable basis is a form of slavery. This basic principle still resonates widely, even in this benighted age of gender "equity."

---

without sexual bias. The law, if logically consistent, would thus impose this practice upon us all. But even bisexuals discriminate on the basis of other characteristics: beauty (they are guilty of "lookism"), talent, sense of humor, intelligence, etc. It would appear that there are no people innocent of prejudice in this regard. Perhaps all of humanity ought to be incarcerated on this ground.

[155] Civil Rights Act of 1964, 42 U.S.C. § 2000c to 2000c-17.

[156] *The Antislavery Argument*, W. and J. Pease, eds. (New York: Bobbs-Merrill, 1965), citing William Lloyd Garrison, *Declaration of Sentiment of the American Anti-Slavery Convention* (Boston: R. F. Wallcut, 1833).

32. The Feminist Competition/Cooperation Dichotomy: A Critique

"The function of battle is destruction; of competition, construction."
– Ludwig von Mises

FEMINIST LITERATURE OFTEN POSITS THAT COMPETITION AND cooperation are opposites. Exchange is seen as competitive, not cooperative (Strober 1994; Hartsock 1983; Gross and Averill 1983).[1] The dichotomy is important in that it is often invoked in order to explain why mainstream economics has focused on market activity to the exclusion of non-market activity, and why this fascination is sexist. Since resource allocation through markets is determined by competition for monetary profits, if this process can be interpreted as sexist, then reliance on markets is sexist as well.

This paper addresses the conclusions of both the "feminist empiricist" position and the "feminist difference" position, as

---

Deborah Walker, Jerry W. Dauterive, Elyssa Schultz, and Walter Block, *Journal of Business Ethics* 55, no. 3 (December 2004): 241–52. In-text references can be found in the bibliography section of this book.

[1] Sometimes the idea of cooperation is expressed as being "natural" or from nature (Gross and Averill) and is therefore defined as a "relationship," while competition is defined as a "struggle." This follows from another popular theme in feminist literature which criticizes mainstream economics on the grounds that its theories ignore nature in favor of artificial constructs; or that instead of living in peace with nature, nature is to be conquered.

explained by Marianne A. Ferber and Julie A. Nelson.[2] Both of these feminist views have described cooperation and competition as opposing ways of organizing society or of solving social problems. With respect to the feminist empiricist position, it is not male economists' theories *per se* that are patriarchic, "but the questions male economists have asked and the conclusions they have drawn" (Ferber and Nelson 1993, p. 8). To the extent that male economists *choose* to focus on and study competitive means to achieve social goals to the exclusion of cooperative means, they may be viewed as sexist. Competitive behavior is defined in the present paper as rivalrous (Kirzner 1973); e.g., individuals try to out-do others in order to achieve their goals. In contrast, individuals agreeing with and working with others to achieve their goals, is seen as cooperative. The exclusion of cooperation in the analysis of these male economists might be due to activities often performed by women. But if by focusing on competition the economist is also, of necessity, studying cooperation, then the argument that a focus on competition is biased (at least against cooperative "feminine" behavior) is dissolved.

On the other hand, the feminist difference position posits that male economists study and define competition in a given way because of the methods they have developed over time; methods which do not incorporate "women's 'ways of knowing'" (Ferber and Nelson 1993, p. 8). If the methodology used leads male economists to study competition to the exclusion of cooperation, such methods may be fostering sexist analysis. Even if the strict methodology of mainstream economists does not allow for an analysis of competition which includes both rivalrous and cooperative behavior,[3] we argue that once we depart

---

[2] Ferber and Nelson explain the feminist empiricist position: "it is not the tools of the discipline [of economics] that need improvement, only the way they are applied" (Ferber and Nelson 1993, p. 8); the feminist difference position emphasizes "distinctions between men and women," such that, "the failures and biases of men's past inquiry are the result of their 'masculinist methods'" (ibid.).

[3] We are referring here to the model of perfect competition, which we explain further later in the paper. This model concludes that cooperative behavior

from this methodology, the analysis of competition is *not* separate from that of cooperation. Therefore, insofar as feminists[4] treat the two as separate (after they have stepped outside of mainstream methodology) they are incorrect in doing so.

Once it is demonstrated that the competition/cooperation dichotomy is false, it will be shown, *pari passu*, that competition and cooperation, at least in the context of free markets, are not mutually exclusive but are, instead dependent upon one another. That being the case, if economists focus on market activities to the exclusion of non-market activities, it is not because of a predisposition to focus on competitive activities over cooperative ones; nor does it stem from any sexism, whether explicit or implicit.

THE COMPETITION/COOPERATION DICHOTOMY

The theoretical idea that competition and cooperation are mutually exclusive and, in fact, are polar opposites of one another, is not a new one. Modern feminist literature builds upon a tradition dating back to the early socialist feminists, including Robert Owen, William Thompson, Anna Wheeler, and August Bebel.[5] In their critiques of individualism in general, the idea of competition as a principle of societal organization was discouraged because of the kind of character it would presumably promote among the people. Instead, cooperative efforts of all kinds would foster good character and habits and lead to "prosperity and happiness."[6] With respect to

---

between firms is, by definition, anti-competitive. We do not agree, however, that this model is sexist in nature.

[4] In this paper, we use the term "feminist" to refer to the views of those with whom we disagree. A better appellation for economists with this perspective might be "left-wing feminists," or "anti-market feminists" to distinguish them from feminists who support markets and capitalism. See on this: http://www.zetetics.com/mac.

[5] Nancy Folbre (1993) for a synopsis of the ideas of these writers with respect to the self-interest assumption of economics and its relation to competition.

[6] Owen was articulate on the idea "that the character of man is, without a single exception, always formed for him. ... Man, never did, nor is it possible he ever can, form his own character" (1950, pp. 91–92).

women in particular, competition was seen as detrimental and unfair. This was because men could compete without being interrupted "by gestation" (Thompson 1963, p. 1824).

It is interesting to note that Bebel, who termed competition "rivalry," did not condemn the activity *per se*, but saw it as beneficial depending upon the motives and circumstances of those engaged in it (Bebel 1910).[7] Therefore, it was possible that "common interest will cause all to seek to improve, simplify and hasten the process of work" (ibid., p. 375). Bebel did see, therefore, something positive in rivalry, but only outside the profit-seeking mode of organization. With profit-seeking, the rivalry produces negative outcomes: "Ambition is harmful only when it is satisfied at the expense of others or to the detriment of society" (ibid., p. 375 fn.). While rivalry has the potential to produce societal benefits, competition in the marketplace produces only individual gain.

The socialist roots of the competition/cooperation dichotomy have been emphasized in modern feminist literature, especially with regard to competition's effects on women:

> Women's interests are disadvantaged by the centrality in economic theory of the concepts of scarcity, selfishness, and competition. The feminist rethinking of these concepts benefits not only women, but also economic theory and policy. (Strober 1994, p. 145)

In many social-economic situations, for instance in the workplace, it is thought by those of this methodological persuasion that the existence of scarcity (of people, money, markets, goods, services, etc.) is an artificial construct men seem to impose in order to establish a competitive and hierarchical situation (competitive against one another and against the milieu which they define as "external") (Gross and Averill 1983, p. 88 fn.). Part of the milieu defined as

---

[7] Bebel goes on to say, "The persons vying with each other [in a non-capitalistic mode of production] are indeed impelled by the ambition of serving the common cause and of winning recognition. But this sort of ambition is a virtue since it serves the common good and at the same time gives satisfaction to the individual" (1910, p. 375).

external by men is cooperative behavior. Competition is therefore viewed as "an increasing capacity to manipulate nature, a constant struggle for occupation and control of territory" (ibid.), an attempt to destroy, or rivalry with a purely selfish intent. Furthermore, it is "masculine" in nature. Competition conjures up an image of fighting, of conflict; of, in Hobbesian (1943) terminology, life being "solitary, poor, nasty, brutish and short."

Cooperation, on the other hand, is defined as a "relationship" which is other-directed and socially driven. It is also "feminine." "For example," as Julie Nelson explains, "it might be considered more 'feminine' to model a particular phenomenon in terms of its aspects of cooperation rather than in terms of its aspects of *competition or conflict*" (Nelson 1992, p. 121, emphasis added). In this way, cooperation is not a competitive strategy but is a means to more desirable social arrangements in and of itself. Or at least, "cooperation that cannot be reduced to a competitive strategy is of special interest" to feminists (Held 1985, p. 301). By emphasizing cooperation rather than competition, one outcome is that "a number of alternative conceptions of economic relations focus on giving and the satisfaction of human needs, concepts obscured by the standard economic metaphors tied to separative conceptions of selfhood" (Strassmann 1993, p. 62).

Since competition, especially market competition, is seen as separative, other market phenomena are also viewed as non-cooperative. The exchange relationship is seen as a direct result of competition and is thus a purely individualistic, self-centered action. Since men, not women, have traditionally engaged in the activity of market exchange, the concept can be seen as masculine.[8] In fact, Nancy Hartsock views the masculine market environment as analogous to a battleground:

> If the community of exchangers (capitalists) rests on the more
> overtly and directly hostile death struggle of self and other, one

---

[8] It is highly debatable as to whether or not women have engaged in market relations less often than men have. In any case, feminists often claim that when women do engage in exchange, it is usually as exploited laborers or passive consumers.

might be able to argue that what underlies the exchange abstraction is abstract masculinity. (1983, p. 305)

This exchange abstraction, according to Hartsock, becomes even more revealing when viewed as a battle. She therefore concludes,

the male experience when replicated as epistemology leads to a world conceived as, and (in fact) inhabited by, a number of fundamentally hostile others whom one comes to know by means of opposition (even death struggle) and yet with whom one must construct a social relation in order to survive. (1983, p. 298)

Exchange is a social relationship, but it is one that arises out of necessity rather than cooperation *per se.*

Susan Feiner further maintains that the actors in standard economic theory are always engaging in exchange, that is, "Every behavior is a giving up in order to receive" (1995, p. 151). A "psychoanalytic reading" of this exchange relationship, according to Feiner, "sets the stage for a new, feminist understanding of economics which has the potential to recast the human activities of production, distribution, and consumption as relations of *sharing* rather than as relations of exchange" (ibid., emphasis added).[9]

Also important are the consequences of competition and exchange as compared to those consequences of cooperation. Competition with selfish intent can be viewed as harmful because it produces unequal outcomes, in this view. Those who are best equipped to compete (destroy) will gain, at the expense of those who are not. Competition, from a societal point of view, is seen as a negative-sum game. As more and more competitors are destroyed, the proportion who cannot successfully compete increases, thus widening the gap between the "haves" and the "have nots." The outcome of such competition is an inequitable distribution of wealth. Therefore, "When Owen, Thompson,

---

[9] Feiner explains that since markets fulfill our wants, just as our mothers did when we were infants, the neoclassical model, which emphasizes individu-alized market exchange, therefore "functions to relieve separation anxieties" (from having been separated from our mothers) (1995, p. 161).

Wheeler, and Bebel railed against competitive individualism, and called for greater social cooperation, they invoked moral categories of right and wrong, fair and unfair" (Folbre 1993, p. 106).

And again, this inequitable distribution of wealth especially impacts women, as Strober emphasizes:

> Since women are disproportionately represented among the "have nots," women stand to benefit from a world view that is less centrally focused on scarcity, selfishness, and competition. As economics begins to include abundance, altruism, and cooperation in its analyses, there will be more emphasis on redistribution of goods and services and more emphasis on an improvement in women's economic situation. (1994, p. 145)

Competition is inherently sexist. This is so not because men are more competitive and women more cooperative (if indeed this is even true whether by socialization or "nature"), but because (probably for power reasons) men have usually occupied the competitive realms of society while women have occupied the cooperative ones. Markets, being competitive, will naturally attract men. If economists focus on competition (rather than cooperation), they will address markets, and will thus study what is masculine, not feminine. The strict neoclassical model, with its emphasis on competition and exchange,

> displaces classical concerns for concrete, embodied activities like labor and production. These inescapably physical activities—some would even say womanly—vanish, replaced by autonomous, rational, choosing minds. (Feiner 1995, p. 161)

Market competition is also sexist because it supposedly perpetuates a redistribution of wealth from women to men. If individuals were to focus instead on cooperative means of resource allocation, a more equitable pattern of wealth would arise in society (Strober 1994). The sexist and inequitable distribution of wealth in market economies arises because economists as well as the general public look to competition for progress and success. And, because markets are inherently competitive, not cooperative, it is through them that individuals gain power and wealth. Since markets have traditionally been under the dominion of men, they have been in a position to become powerful and wealthy at the expense of women, who have traditionally occupied other arenas.

As men gained power, they deliberately perpetuated the concept of competition as the means not only to attain individual success, but social progress as well, in order to remain in control. Many social institutions are therefore seen as being deliberately constructed in order to maintain masculine power. The stereotypical "domain" of women—household activities and family responsibilities—is relegated to the unimportant areas of social life. Here, we do not find competition, but rather nurturance, tolerance, benignancy, sharing, and cooperation. These characteristics or kinds of behavior are deemed unimportant to the progress of society, as well as to those studying it. Hence, both the very process of competition, itself, and those who examine it without seeing its drawbacks, notably mainstream economists, are "sexist."

Some feminists trace this line of thought back to liberalism in political philosophy. Under this tradition:

> women's work was taken for granted, seldom discussed, and excluded from political theory, because these authors viewed women and their work as "part of nature" within a metaphysic that denigrated nature. Moreover, women's activities did not count as "moral," since only exercising "autonomy" in the public sphere counted as "moral." Thus the separative self was valued while nurturant connection either was ignored or deprecated. (England 1993, p. 40)

THE CRITIQUE

The feminist claim—that neoclassical economics (with its focus on the self-interested individual in competitive markets) ignores much of what is interesting and important—*does* have validity.[10] The

---

[10] For a response to feminist economists from a neoclassical point of view, see Reder (1999, pp. 139–40).

model of perfect competition, for example, tells us nothing about reality—especially about the existence of competition. As F.A. Hayek explains, "'perfect' competition means indeed the absence of all competitive activities" (1948, p. 96). The model of perfect competition assumes homogeneous products produced by a large number of small firms that can enter and exit the industry without cost. The model also assumes perfect information on the part of economic agents. It is only when competition is viewed as rivalry, however, that Hayek's point makes sense. To compete means to differentiate one's product and, in the process of competing, we learn what is and is not a competitive (profitable) activity. But, it is through this competitive process, and only in this way that we can gain such knowledge.[11]

Paradoxically, in the realm of perfect competition, no real competition ever takes place. Firms do not so much as see themselves as rivals with one another. There is no sense of winning and losing, or triumphing over a competitor. Rather, abstracting from entry and exit, each firm believes that it can produce all it wishes; its offerings comprise so small a part of total industry output that every one of them supposedly acts as if it faces a flat demand curve. The point is that while the feminists do have something of a legitimate criticism to level against the neo-classical model of perfect competition, this does not at all apply to the Austrian perspective[12] of rivalrous competition.

There are also important policy implications that follow from perfect competition.[13] Cooperative ventures between firms in the same industry, for example, are interpreted by it as (at least) potentially monopolistic, if not *per se* evidence in this regard. In fact, this

---

[11] For the view that appraisement, not information, lies at the core of the Austrian contribution to the socialist calculation debate, see Gordon (1990), Hoppe (1989, 1996), Mises (1981), Rothbard (1991), and Salerno (1990a, 1990b).

[12] For critiques of feminist economic theory from a praxeological point of view, see Horwitz (1995), Vaughn (1994), and Walker (1994).

[13] It is usually through what is known as the "structure-conduct-performance" paradigm that antitrust policies are considered to be necessary means to increasing competition in markets.

model, by its very nature, defines cooperative behavior among firms as anti-competitive. The further an industry deviates from the "ideal structure" (an indefinitely large, not to say "infinite" number of small firms with no control over price on the part of any of them), the more likely it is to have "monopoly power." Furthermore, by focusing on scarcity and choice in a world of given preferences, the concept of society is, to a degree, nonexistent. Coordination in a social setting, where individuals make choices under uncertainty, is pushed aside in order to formalize individual decision-making.

It is certainly reasonable to share with feminists some substantive criticisms of neoclassical theory (Horwitz 1995). Basing economic analysis on purposeful action, the individual does not have prede-termined preference functions and perfect knowledge. Quite the contrary, humans are social beings, with imperfect knowledge, subjective tastes, and an (albeit limited) ability to learn.

As Hayek explains, "The economic problem of society is thus not merely a problem of how to allocate 'given' resources ... it is a problem of the utilization of knowledge which is not given to anyone in its totality" (1948, pp. 77–78). The knowledge that exists in an economy is dispersed among individuals, is subject to time and circumstances, and is constantly changing. Therefore, the problem is widened from the utilization of existing knowledge to the discovery of new and better knowledge. Given this dispersed and limited knowledge, *coordination* of individual plans is imperative.

Feminists should welcome such an emphasis on coordination rather than scarcity and choice *per se*. Myra H. Strober notes that "many problems are not a result of scarcity but of maldistribution" (Strober 1994, p. 145), and Julie Nelson writes that "economic provision" should be "the center of study" in economics (Nelson 1992, p. 119). However, Strober and Nelson appear to have a particular distribution or provision of goods in mind as a goal to their analyses, whereas Hayek would argue that it is impossible to achieve a predetermined outcome when dealing with something so complex and spontaneous as a social economic order. But a focus on coordination in society can help us understand why a particular pattern of distribution arises.

With such a focus on knowledge and coordination, institutions play a crucial role in the analysis. Which ones better enable people to utilize information? How do these institutions come about? Changes in the institutional framework of society (the "rules of the game") can have far-reaching effects on economic coordination—another point supported by feminist dismal scientists (but often ignored by neoclassical economists). However, regarding the competition/cooperation dichotomy, a critical departure from the feminist approach occurs with respect to these rules of the game.

First, at the most basic level, competitors within markets certainly try to out-perform one another—there is rivalry.[14] But individuals in markets compete under a given set of rules; before the rivalry can take place, they must be made clear. Insofar as there is agreement to abide by the rules of the game, there is also cooperation. If this agreement does not exist, then cooperation is impossible, nor will its usual outcomes result.

For example, assume a society of three individuals. Two of them may agree to a given rule and one may not. If each has already consented at a "constitutional" level (Buchanan and Tullock 1971) that in any given case where there is disagreement, the majority can "force" the minority (with an actual threat of violence, if need be) to abide by the rules, then in essence, there is still agreement or cooperation (on, at least, the making of the rules). If, on the other hand, all three do not agree on the process of the making of the rules or on what rules to abide by, then there is no cooperation. Instead, coercion is the only option.

The key lesson from this argument is that in the absence of coercion, rivals must cooperate before they can compete. Just as the constitution level of law making underlies debate over specific laws, so, too, does cooperation serve as the very foundation of the

---

[14] This is the definition used by Austrian economists for competition, not the model of perfect competition of the neo-classical school. See on this Armentano (1991), Block (1994), DiLorenzo (1997), Boudreaux and DiLorenzo (1992), High (1984–1985), Kirzner (1973), McChesney (1991), Rothbard (1970), Shugart (1987), and Smith (1983).

rivalry that occurs in markets. Indeed, in any interaction or "game" involving commercial competition, cooperation is necessary. While players in most games compete against each other either individually or in teams, they do so in a cooperative framework established by common rules which ensure that success is achieved either by skill or luck or some combination of the two. Cooperation on this (often unspoken and even unconscious) level is a precondition of the pleasure and profit that we derive from any such activity.

There is no need for each participant in the market to have the same goals or objectives for cooperation (and the benefits derived thereof) to take place. The market is an institution "that maximizes the opportunities for interaction without at every turn calling into question the values of others or the legitimacy of the ends they seek" (Coleman 1987, p. 86). As Frank Knight explains:

> The supreme and inestimable merit of the exchange mechanism is that it enables a vast number of people to cooperate in the use of means to achieve ends as far as their interests are mutual, without arguing or in any way agreeing about either the ends or the methods of achieving them. It is the "obvious and simple system of natural liberty." The principle of freedom, where it is applicable, takes other values out of the field of social action. In contrast, agreement on terms of cooperation through discussion is hard and always threatens to become impossible, even to degenerate into a fight, not merely the failure of co-operation and loss of its advantages. The only agreement called for in market relations is acceptance of the one essentially negative ethical principle, that the units are not to prey upon one another through coercion or fraud (1956, p. 267).

Thus, the game played in markets does not require that participants agree upon a long list of rules, but instead, on only one basic rule. This makes agreement (and therefore cooperation) more likely because the generality of the (no coercion/no fraud) rule leaves the door open for all to pursue very different ends under the same rule. As Jules Coleman notes, with the principle of freedom as its basis, Knight argued that individuals would choose to use markets for social interaction because of "social stability" (1987, p. 85). If consensus and widespread cooperation on the rules of the game are necessary for stable social arrangements, then markets will be selected over any other alternative whereby agreement on ends or values must be dealt with constantly if people are "free to choose" (Friedmans 1980). The rules necessary for competitive markets are broad or general ones and are, therefore, more likely to be stable over time.

Once cooperation regarding the rules of the game exists, the game of competition will foster social well-being (and economic productivity). This is another way in which market competition is fundamentally cooperative. Certainly, individuals exchange to make themselves better off, but that does *not* imply that anyone engaging in the exchange is made worse off. In fact, it is quite the opposite. Both parties enter a voluntary exchange in order to improve their positions. An individual cannot make an exchange unless someone else agrees to take part in it. In this way, market exchange is a social activity that is at one and the same time both cooperative (both parties must agree to make an exchange) and competitive (both parties will try to get the "best deal").

Far from being "exploited" by commercial interaction, each party gains. In the *ex ante* sense of anticipations, both buyer and seller *necessarily* improve their welfare; they would scarcely agree to take part if they didn't expect to profit thereby. It cannot be denied that, in the *ex post* sense, one cannot apodictically conclude that *emptor* and *vendidor* will always benefit. But even here, the presumption, particularly for repeat business, is that this is still the case.

Market competition is thus dependent upon social cooperation. The one cannot take place without the other. Market competition is not anti-social or anti-cooperative—quite the opposite. It is not a "fight to the death" as sometimes described in the feminist literature. As Mises explains:

> Fighting in the actual original sense of the word *is* anti-social. It renders co-operation, which is the basic element of the social relation, impossible among the fighters, and where the co-operation already exists, destroys it. Competition is an element of social

collaboration, the ruling principle within the social body. Viewed sociologically, fighting and competition are extreme contrasts. (1981, p. 286)

Mises's idea that "competition is an element of social collaboration" can be taken to an even more fundamental level. He begins with the division of labor: "The fundamental social phenomenon is the division of labor and its counterpart human cooperation" (1966, p. 157). Isolated yet rational humans learned through experience that "cooperative action is more efficient and productive than isolated action" (Mises 1966, p. 157). Humans learned that specialization increased productivity and made social progress possible, but it also made individuals dependent upon others. Exchange became the means to dealing with the dependency. At the same time, trade increased socialization. Apart from hand-to-mouth hermits, individuals *must* cooperate with one another if they are to survive, let alone prosper.

Both the division of labor and exchange (cooperative efforts) are enhanced by competition. This process provides the knowledge from which people determine how labor should be divided, what labor should produce, and which production techniques should be utilized. Without this process of competition, society would remain stagnant. As Hayek explains:

> But which goods are scarce goods or which things are goods, and how scarce or valuable they are—these are precisely the things which competition has to discover... . Utilization of knowledge widely dispersed in a society with extensive division of labor cannot rest on individuals knowing all the particular uses to which well-known things in their individual environment might be put. (1978, pp. 181–82)

In other words, "competition is a discovery procedure" (Hayek 1978, p. 179). It is through the very act of competing that we discover better ways of doing things: of producing, of pleasing consumers, and, in fact, better ways of cooperating. Exchange is beneficial to the parties involved because the competitive process has provided producers with more knowledge regarding what consumers want and where scarce resources should be utilized. Therefore, cooperation (division of labor and exchange) is *dependent upon* competition.

Without the competitive process and the prices that flow from it, economic coordination becomes virtually impossible, as the failure of planned economics has everywhere empirically demonstrated (Boettke 1991; Conway 1987; Ebeling 1993; Foss 1995; Gordon 1990; Hoppe 1989, 1996; Horwitz 1996; Klein 1996; Lewin 1998; Mises 1981; Reisman 1996; Reynolds 1998; Rothbard 1991; Salerno 1990a, 1990b; Steele 1981, 1992). Economic competitors cooperate with one another through a constant flow of information provided by prices. Commercial rivals are constantly fed indicators of their relative successes or failures by the prices that they are able to charge compared to others. The supply of such information allows each participant to cooperate and seek new opportunities and efficiencies—even though on another level they are each trying to outdo each other in terms of rivalrous business success. Economic coordination and the exchanges it makes possible are dependent upon a competitive order. If, at the fundamental level, competition is dependent upon cooperation—while at the same time cooperation is dependent upon competition—how can they be a dichotomy? Instead, *competition and cooperation are two necessary components of economic social organization.*

It is reasonable to assume that for many, if not for all, cooperation is a personal goal. If we truly are social beings, in need of nurturing and personal interrelations as much as the increased material wealth brought about by the division of labor, then it makes more sense to think of cooperation as our ultimate goal, not competition. There is then no reason to think that humans are not, by nature, social and cooperative and that sometimes, therefore, the "end" sought could easily be some form of cooperation (instead of, for example, increased efficiency or material progress). It is on this cooperative nature of human beings, and not the self-interested competitive nature, that feminists want to focus.

Economists should have no problem with the idea that social cooperation is a human goal, or with addressing the issue of how we enhance social cooperation. But, if we do focus on this (and not productivity *per se*), we still face the "knowledge problem." Whether we are trying to coordinate resources and enhance cooperation through exchange or to coordinate human beings and enhance cooperation *per se* (for example, in relationships, in marriages, or in families, where women have usually been the main actors), we still must find ways of dealing with our limited knowledge. This is especially true with respect to what others expect or want from cooperative efforts and regarding new forms of cooperation. The same process of competition that enhances knowledge utilization and discovery in the marketplace applies to social institutions in general. More cooperative institutions (enhancing human life) can only be found through a process of trial and error, of social experimentation, of persuasion—which are often forms of competition.

Certainly, for example, in choosing a partner for marriage, selecting among alternatives increases the likelihood that any given choice will form a more cooperative union than if there are no alternatives, i.e., no rivalry. Competition provides alternatives by which individuals can experiment and learn more about what they need from a marital relationship—or indeed, whether they need one at all. If a person's goal is cooperation, a competitive process will certainly aid in achieving it.

If one goal of feminists is to persuade economists to focus more on non-market activities, using the competition/cooperation dichotomy is not a compelling argument. Since this distinction is only a superficial one, a focus on competition does not lead one to favor market activities *vis-à-vis* non-market ones. Capitalist behavior is every bit as cooperative as it is competitive. Therefore, in the feminist sense, it is just as "feminine" as "masculine." If market activities are emphasized, it is for some other reason. And if focusing on markets is sexist simply because we find more men than women taking part in markets, the male domination of markets (the extent of which is a debatable, and ultimately empirical, issue) is *not* because market relationships are competitive rather than cooperative in nature.

Certainly the importance of social relationships to the human condition cannot be overstated.[15] For this reason, feminists would be well advised to embrace the tools of economic analysis that focus on purposeful human action as it relates to knowledge and coordination in society.[16]

There is, of course, a difference between explicit and implicit cooperation. The latter, we have argued, is the province of the free marketplace. But even the former, comprised of voluntary charity, voluntary socialism, and other such institutions, are *also* part of the free-enterprise system, albeit they cannot be characterized as markets. Take voluntary charity first; to which sector is it properly to be most likened? That is, common parlance has it that there are three categories of an economy: the private market place, government, and the third or voluntary sector. Suppose that, for some reason, we were allowed only a bipartite distinction, instead of this tripartite one; into which category would private charity fall? That is, is charitable giving more like market or government behavior?

The answer is clear: the former is correct. For what markets and voluntary charity share is the non-coercive elements that are common to both; the same cannot be said for government. When the state comes to collect money for what it needs, it does so on the basis of compulsion: if you do not pay your taxes, force and violence are visited upon you.[17] In very sharp contrast indeed, both business

---

[15] And perhaps many feminists are correct in their assessment that as more women enter the economics profession, those institutions usually dominated by women will become more important in the study of economics.

[16] Austrian economists, following Mises, define economics as the study of purposeful human action. At least theoretically, action within households, child-rearing activities and the like, are as much up for discussion as are actions in markets. What women mostly do, and what men mostly do, insofar as they differ, are of equal importance.

[17] This is contrary to the Public Choice (Buchanan and Tullock 1971) argument that we have all agreed to be taxed at the constitutional level, and that therefore, if you look beneath the superficialities, these payments are really

firms and charitable organizations have to *seduce* their clients, they cannot force them to do their bidding.

States Williams (1998, p. 640) in this regard:

> The test for moral relations among people is to ask whether the act was peaceable and voluntary or violent and involuntary. Put another way, was there seduction, or was there rape? Seduction (voluntary exchange) occurs when we offer our fellow man the following proposition: I will make you feel good if you make me feel good. An example of this occurs when I visit my grocer. In effect I offer, "If you make me feel good by giving me that loaf of bread, I will make you feel good by giving you a dollar." Whenever there is seduction, we have a positive-sum game; i.e., both parties are better off in their own estimation.

> Rape (involuntary exchange), on the other hand, happens when we offer our fellow man the following proposition: "If you do not make me feel good, I am going to make you feel bad." An example of this would be where I walked into my grocer's store with a gun and offered, "If you do not make me feel good by giving me that loaf of bread, I am going to make you feel bad by shooting you." Whenever there is rape, we have a zero-sum game, i.e., in order for one person to be better off, it necessarily requires that another be made worse off.

> For those of us who think that the democratic principle of majority rule establishes the morality of government actions, I would caution that gang rape is no more morally acceptable than individual rape. In other words, a majority vote to rape someone does not make rape moral.

> Widespread private control and ownership of property is consistent with seduction and the minimization of rape. Widespread government ownership and/or control over property is consistent with rape-maximization. Government is the major source of rape-like exchanges. In addition, private ownership and control of property leads to the dispersion of power. Government control

---

voluntary. For a critique of this view, see Block and DiLorenzo (2000, 2001), DiLorenzo and Block (2001), DiLorenzo (1988), and Rothbard (1997).

and ownership leads to consolidation of power and increased potential for abuse.

Next, consider socialism. It, too, or at least one of its variants, can properly be considered as legitimate a part of free enterprise as any explicit market. In order to see this, consult the diagram below. There, it will be seen that there are not one but rather two versions of socialism, and the same applies to capitalism. That is, each system can be organized along either voluntary or coercive principles.

	Voluntary	Coercive
Socialism	A	B
Capitalism	C	D

If the former, then that system is compatible with *laissez-faire* capitalism, if the latter, then not. For example, under category A, we find such institutions as the kibbutz,[18] the monastery, the nunnery, the food or baby-sitting co-op, etc. In B, there are unions and communist countries such as the old U.S.S.R., and present-day Cuba and North Korea. These are miles apart in terms of political philosophy, and there is the question as to why they should even share an appellation. C is of course the domain of *laissez-faire* capitalism, where all acts take place between consenting adults, and D is economic fascism, in which there is a veneer of free enterprise and private property rights, but the basic reality is one of compulsion and intimidation. There are, unfortunately, no real-world examples of the former, but fascist Italy and Nazi Germany readily depict the latter.

The point is that the economic debate is not really between socialism (A + B) and capitalism (C + D) as the feminists we are criticizing implicitly believe. Rather, the contending forces are the institutions devoted to peaceful interaction (A + C) versus those predicated upon the opposite philosophy (B + D).

---

[18] This assumes, contrary to the actual practice of most such organizations in Israel, that it is funded solely by its own members, and not on a coercive basis by unwilling participants.

CONCLUSION

This essay began with a quotation by Mises: "The function of battle is destruction; of competition, construction" (1981, p. 285). As Hayek's work demonstrates, without competition we could not discover or utilize knowledge in society. The outcome of competition (more and better knowledge) enhances, and in some cases, makes cooperation possible in the first place. Contrast this to the feminist view that the outcome of competition is an unequal distribution of wealth in favor of men and that a world that was cooperative rather than competitive would produce a more equal outcome. By focusing on processes and not on particular outcomes *per se*, one does not try to manipulate institutions such that a particular distribution of wealth will ensue in society. Even if desirable, this is impossible due to the complexity of the economic order.

Certainly, if market competition is dependent upon cooperation through agreement on rules, women should not only be subject to them but also have the ability to agree (or disagree) with them. This is fundamental to a just society. If women are part of the process by which the fundamental rules of society are decided upon, then it need not be sexist. However, to the degree that women have not been allowed to fully participate in that process,[19] sexism has reigned. Perhaps it has been the asymmetric application of rules in society that has gone a long way toward producing the distribution in wealth that feminists find so disturbing. Because it is impossible to determine what the societal outcome (such as with respect to wealth distribution) would have been had men and women always been subject to the same rules, our policy prescriptions would only entail according the same legal treatment to both men and women. As Hayek explains, "The only common aim which we can pursue by the choice of this technique of ordering social affairs is the general kind of pattern, or the abstract character, of the order that will form itself" (1978, p. 184). In other words, we cannot hope to bring about *specific* results, nor would it be just to do so by force. Empirically,

---

[19] For example, not being allowed to own property, to sign contracts, as was the case in the U.S. in a bygone era, and still obtains in many places.

it is a question as to how this change alone already has and will continue to impact social institutions in general (as well as wealth distribution). Undeniably, however, this change implies a process of *both* competition and cooperation.

33. REVIEW OF MICHAEL LEVIN'S *FEMINISM AND FREEDOM*

WHEN I WAS BROUGHT UP AS A YOUNG LAD, ONE OF THE MORAL imperatives instilled in me was, "Don't hit girls."

Although I have rebelled against many of the early teachings to which I was exposed, that one always seemed reasonable. I have followed this bit of folk wisdom in my own life and have attempted to pass it along to my son, now aged ten.

The only problem is, things are now a bit more complicated on the not-hitting-girls front than they were in my own youth. We are all now faced with the results of the so-called women's liberation movement which has permeated our society. It has been argued vehemently, and with no small measure of success, that men and women are, for all intents and purposes, the same. If this is true, then boys and girls must also be equal. But, if it is legitimate for my son to hit back at boys, then why not at girls too?

In this case, there is a further complication. He is enrolled in a karate class along with equally young people of the female persuasion. Undoubtedly, as part and parcel of feminist inroads into our culture, he is urged by his teacher to engage in combat with them; if he demurs at my suggestion, he loses face.

It is against this background that we consider Michael Levin's response to the feminist invasion of the world of ideas. We are all in

Nomos 7, no. 1 (Spring 1989): 25–26.

great debt to him, especially those among us who are libertarians. This book is monumental in its coverage, refuting the claims of the feminists in just about every area in which they have staked a claim: innateness, sex differences, affirmative action, comparable worth, education, "women's studies," sports, law and order, language, the family. It is masterful in its insights, using an interdisciplinary approach which brings to bear the findings of economics, politics, philosophy, anthropology, sociology, logic, history, and biology. It is ambitious in that it is the only study to my knowledge dedicated to a refutation of feminism in its totality. It is extremely well written. I waged a continual struggle with myself to read more slowly; as with a riveting novel, I didn't want the book to end.

Given the long march toward statism, we libertarians are especially indebted to Professor Levin for this book, which constitutes a spirited defense of freedom from the many attacks made upon it by the feminists.

Above all, *Feminism and Freedom* is the work of a supremely courageous individual. This is so for several reasons. Women's liberation has so permeated the universities that this volume must create personal difficulties for its author, a Professor of Philosophy at the City University of New York, a hotbed of feminism if ever there was one. Then, too, there is the courage that one must amass when he takes on not just a single author, nor even a few dozen, but a movement which comprises literally hundreds of thousands of intellectuals, artists, writers, and people from all walks of life. Beyond this, however, is the even more superlative courage it takes to "hit back at girls," not physically, of course, but intellectually and morally. I contend that it is deeply embedded in our very beings that we refrain from engaging in such activities.

I suspect that a large part of the reason for the success of the feminist movement is that it is mainly comprised of women. Our chivalrous instincts cry out in protest against any spirited attack on people of the weaker sex. I speculate that were the identical arguments brought to bear by any sub-group other than women, they would long ago have been given the short shrift they so richly deserve.

What, then, are Levin's arguments against the feminists? At the core of his contribution is the denial of their thesis that men and women are exactly alike, except for reproductive elements. On the face of it, this might not sound like much. Indeed, it can only be considered the merest of common sense. However, an entire public policy has been erected based upon either the denial or neglect of this elementary insight.

Consider the analysis of *Berkman v. NYFD* with which the book begins. In 1977, all 88 women who took the New York City Fire Department's entrance examination failed its strength component, while only 54 percent of the men did not pass. In the ensuing class action, sex discrimination lawsuit, the court, utilizing the guidelines set down by the Equal Employment Opportunity Commission, asked "how likely it would be, in the absence of discrimination, that none of the 88 women passed, while 46 percent of the men did.

"As the court correctly noted," states Levin,

> the pass rates were separated by more than eight standard deviations," and the probability that this could happen is so small—less than one in 10 trillion—as to amount to virtual impossibility. The court's conclusion that discrimination must have occurred is entirely cogent, if strength is assumed to be uncorrelated with sex. A difference in failure rates on a strength test is consistent with the absence of bias if it is allowed that men are on average stronger than women. The court found the outcome. ... unacceptably improbable because it adopted the hypothesis that gender and strength are independent variables. ... Since women are the same as men, the EEOC and the court reasoned, special steps must be taken to compensate for their manifest differences.

I could trace Levin's reasoning throughout the book, where he eviscerates fallacy after fallacy in similar manner. And, indeed, I am tempted to do this, if only to afford the reader the enjoyment of his analytical mind. I have a better suggestion, though. Let the reader buy this book for himself, and derive the full benefits thereof.

There is, however, one further implication of the Levin thesis that I absolutely cannot resist describing: that regarding language, specifically the substitution of "he or she" or "(s)he" for "he," and the use of the appellation "Ms." as a substitute for "Mrs." and "Miss." It is important to me that I relate his contribution on the language front because, I confess, I had been taken in by the feminists on this one, and have now resolved to struggle mightily to overcome my previous error.

Before reading *Feminism and Freedom*, I had tried not to use the words "he," or "man" when referring to all people. I told myself that it was an unfair denigration of the female gender. How would I like it, after all, if everyone used "she" or "woman" to refer to all persons? In like manner, I tried to accustom myself to "Ms." and to eschew the "sexist" "Mrs." and "Miss."

But I now see this issue very differently, thanks to Professor Levin's book. In this area, too, the feminists are, in effect, arguing that there are no important differences between men and women. What is sauce for the goose is sauce for the gander. If people cannot tell from a man's title (Mr.) whether or not he is married, they should not be able to garner this information with regard to a women. "Ms." puts the woman on equal non-informational footing with "Mr."

However, men are very different from women. For one thing, due to the number of sperm available, the most efficient male strategy for propagating his gene pattern is one of promiscuity: the more children he fathers, the better. But the female has far fewer opportunities to leave heirs. The maximum biological limit is only a few dozen; in actuality, most females bear far fewer children than this. Her ideal strategy, then, is not one of promiscuity; instead, she must be far more careful and choosy, picking as a mate someone upon whom she can rely, who will help her raise her offspring.

From these undoubted biological facts stem sociological patterns which are deeply embedded in us. This includes the physical protection of the female alluded to at the outset of this review, the importance of the family, and the discouragement of males from wasting time making indiscriminate passes at married women when they could (and should, from the point of view of propagation of the human species) be courting single women. Anything, then, that encourages inter-familial sexuality is to be counted as a positive. But this includes such things as the wearing of wedding rings, and, to return to our point, the clarity as to female marital status by use of the distinction between Mrs. and Miss.

Says Levin,

> The wish to collapse "Miss" and "Mrs." into Ms's is the wish that women be thought of as selecting sexual partners in the way and with the purposes characteristic of men. It is a wish for the terms of address and marital status that would have evolved had there been no differences in the sexual nature of men and women.

As well, Levin points to the Orwellian historical examples of which the Ms. caper is only the latest. During the French Reign of Terror, all persons were addressed as "citizen"; during and after the Bolshevik Revolution, all Russians became "comrades." Nor can it be objected that in these historical cases, but not in the present, people were coerced into using the new appellations through force of law. Although the full force of the law has not as yet landed upon those intemperate enough to insist on their right to use "sexist" language, the courts are moving in the direction of a finding that the use of this language is sexually discriminatory, and even comprises sexual harassment, both of which practices are illegal.

I recommend this book without any reservation. Its positive contributions are great, and its flaws do not at all detract from its central thesis. On the contrary, they are peripheral, although interesting, issues. (Levin is a conservative, not a libertarian; hence he takes positions on several issues—government roads and education, land reform, the draft, abortion—that are not strictly compatible with freedom.)

I conclude that if you have any love at all for freedom and want to help protect it against the feminist onslaught, go out and get this book! Now! It is the only exhaustive, in-depth, utter refutation of the feminist argument presently in existence.

34. LEVIN ON *FEMINISM AND FREEDOM*

MICHAEL LEVIN'S *FEMINISM AND FREEDOM*[1] IS THE WORK OF a supremely courageous individual. Women's liberation has so permeated the universities that any attack on this philosophy is bound to create personal difficulties for a male author.

Professor Levin denies the feminist thesis that men and women are exactly alike except for reproduction. On the face of it, this might not sound like much; indeed, it can only be considered the merest of common sense. However, an entire public policy agenda has been erected on either the denial, or neglect, of this elementary insight. Levin shows that the feminist program is entirely incompatible with freedom. Equal pay, affirmative action, nondiscrimination statutes, women's studies departments, set-asides, quotas, equal opportunity laws, anti-harassment enactments—indeed, a whole panoply of modern public policy—are *all* intolerable attacks on human liberty.

Consider just the charge of sexism, the veritable tip of the iceberg: Levin gives the example of a male faculty member who asks a female graduate student for a date, or a foreman who invites one of his employees for coffee, and is refused. The professor or foreman takes the rejection with good grace, and does not in any way retaliate. Nevertheless, his mere invitation can subject him to charges of

---

Journal of Libertarian Studies 10, no. 1 (Fall 1991).

[1] Michael Levin, *Feminism and Freedom* (New Brunswick, N.J.: Transaction Books, 1987).

harassment. This has a chilling effect, to say the least, on our rights of free speech—to say nothing of normal social interaction.

I like this book, and very much so. I recommend it highly to all those who are concerned with human liberty and with the feminist attack on these principles.[2] As in the nature of such things, however, I have found numerous details to which I can object. None of them invalidates his main thesis, but these small points will certainly be of interest to libertarians. Most of my disagreement stems from the fact that Levin is a conservative, not a libertarian, and while he is innovative and brilliant in coming to grips with the feminist attack on freedom, his refutations open him up to violations of liberty on numerous other grounds. So without any further ado, I consider those parts of the Levin volume with which I disagree.

1. The author states that "[p]rivate discrimination against women has been illegal since 1964," in a context which implies he favors such legislation.[3] Certainly, he does not criticize this state of affairs, while castigating almost everything else favored by feminists. From this, we can deduce that he is not opposed. If so, however, this is clearly counter to the dictates of morality, to say nothing of common sense. For surely the basic right of free association allows us the privilege of not only interacting with those we choose to, but also refusing to associate with those we wish to avoid. Yet, if private discrimination against women were legally prohibited, then organizations such as the Boy Scouts, Rotary, Lions, Moose, and Elks Clubs, and the Chamber of Commerce, to say nothing of the dozens of other men's only luncheon, supper, and athletic clubs, would be outlawed. And what of male homosexuals? Their discrimination against women would

---

[2] For a review of Levin's book that focuses entirely on its positive elements, see my review in *Nomos* 7, no. 1 (Spring 1989): 25–26.

[3] Levin, *Feminism and Freedom*, p. 4. See also ibid., p. 282, for another failure to object to the legal prohibition of private discrimination.

have to be brought to an abrupt halt, to the utter denigration of their liberties. Strictly speaking, disallowing
private discrimination against women would also rule out
the possibility of separate men's washrooms.

In addition, if private discrimination against men were by
the same token also disallowed, then this would mean the
end of women-only groups, such as the Y.W.C.A., feminist
consciousness-raising groups, lesbian organizations, and
large parts of the women's liberation movement itself.
(I'm tempted to say: Hey, maybe this isn't such a bad
idea after all; except for the fact that women, and men
too, have a right to assemble together with those of their
choice, and to exclude all others.)

Similarly, our author lists segregation, along with slavery
and the lynch mob, as examples of wrongs perpetrated
upon blacks.[4] According to libertarian principles, however,
people have a right to live in segregated housing (i.e.,
to refuse to sell to members of certain racial or ethnic
groups), but certainly not to invade others as in the case
of enslavement or lynching. Suppose we were to list the
three "crimes" of enslavement, segregation, and lynching,
and then to ask the man in the street "Which one does
not belong with the others?" Is there any doubt he would
pick segregation?

2. Levin accepts without demur the claim that "getting
everyone to drive on the same side of the road [is] a
paradigm coordination problem solved by state action."[5]
But surely private road owners were able to get everyone to
drive on the same side of the road when property rights in
highways were allowed, and would be able to do so again
should we ever move toward road privatization again. And
not only could private enterprise get everyone to drive on

---

[4] Ibid., p. 113.

[5] Ibid., p. 82.

the same side of the road, the government cannot—at least to judge by our stupendous traffic fatality rate.[6]

3. While Levin is sound on the question of forced equality for women, he leaves something to be desired in regard to what I would consider the identical issue of forced equality for racial minorities. He states that "unlike the case for racial quotas, which is merely unsound, the case for gender quotas is an intellectual scandal." In his view, there are relevant differences between the two. At one juncture, he points to the innate differences between the sexes. But are there no innate differences between the races? And even if it could be shown that there are innate differences between the sexes, but not the races, it would still not follow that this is a relevant *moral* distinction. The libertarian non-aggression principle, for example, would still apply in both cases.[7]

Elsewhere he claims it as a relevant difference that blacks have been more heavily victimized by violence (slavery, segregation, lynching) than have women.[8] We have already dealt with the segregation issue; but what of the feminist rejoinder that women have been victimized by rape? To this, Levin cavalierly notes that "there is no evidence that rape adversely affects female acquisition of job skills." One might think the reason there is no evidence is that the causal chain is so obvious it never occurred to anyone to go out and find evidence on this matter. Rape is so savage and bestial an attack that it

---

[6] For a demonstration that the market would be able to reduce the accident, fatality, and injury rates on the highways, see Walter Block, "Free Market Transportation: Denationalizing the Roads," *Journal of Libertarian Studies* 3, no. 2 (Summer 1979): 208–32; idem, "Theories of Highway Safety," *Transportation Research Record* 912 (1983); Murray N. Rothbard, *For a New Liberty* (New York: Macmillan, 1983), pp. 202–18.

[7] Levin, *Feminism and Freedom*, pp. 104, 41–42.

[8] Ibid., p. 113.

cannot help but have a negative impact on all aspects of life. For that matter, is there any evidence of the fact that lynching or slavery "adversely affects black acquisition of job skills?" Furthermore, there are no blacks being lynched or enslaved today, while women, unfortunately, are still being raped.[9]

In any case, what is the *relevance* of past victimization to present rights? Surely, we all have an equal right not to be aggressed against at present, and no other rights than that, regardless of the amount of victimization suffered by our forebears in the past.

4. Although Levin does not go so far as to advocate preventive incarceration for all eighteen-year-old males in order to reduce the crime rate (indeed, he repudiates this), he does claim the legitimacy of preventative coercion on the part of the state "only in emergencies."[10] The forces of law and order, he claims, need not wait until an actual crime is committed; the threat thereof, or the opening stages (like the pointing of a gun), will suffice.[11] But the libertarian moral code legitimizes force only as a reaction to prior force—one may not assault another who has engaged in no coercive activities simply on the assumption that he may do so later. Preventive coercion is thus never justified, emergency or not.

5. Levin objects to governmentally enforced quotas on the ground that "rights originally promised on the basis

---

[9] This, of course, is largely a matter of there being altogether too much public property and not enough private property (it is no accident that more women are raped in Central Park than in Disney World). It is also traceable to the fact that the institutions ostensibly set up to eradicate rape (the police, the courts) are unfortunately in the intrinsically inefficient public sector.

[10] Levin, *Feminism and Freedom*, p. 106.

[11] Murray N. Rothbard, *Ethics of Liberty* (Atlantic Highlands, N.J.: Humanities Press, 1982).

of seniority are subordinated to the need to 'preserve the gains' of affirmative action."[12] But these seniority "rights" were gained through an illegitimate process of their own; that is, through coercive unionism.[13] It is an interesting speculative venture to choose between two such illegitimate rights, but it is ultimately meaningless. Suppose you had to judge which of two persons was the rightful owner of a wallet. One gave as his reason that he is 5'8" tall and wears a red coat, while the other justified his claim on the ground that he weighs 160 lbs. and wears a blue coat. All you could do is throw up your hands in dismay.

6. States Levin: "The common law will not dispossess the current holders of land that has been transferred in good faith for a number of generations, despite proof from a claimant that the land was stolen from his ancestors; too much honest labor is now part of the land."[14] This is a particularly infuriating argument, because the author does not even openly agree with the assessment; instead, he hides behind a declarative sentence concerning the common law. We are forced to deduce from the fact that he does not object to it—that he indeed cites it to buttress his own argument—that he actually favors it.

But there is no statute of limitations on justice.[15] If my grandfather stole your grandfather's watch, it is unjust if

---

[12] Levin, *Feminism and Freedom*, p. 112.

[13] W.H. Hutt, *The Strike-Threat System* (New York: Arlington House, 1973); Emerson P. Schmidt, *Union Power and the Public Interest* (Los Angeles: Nash, 1973).

[14] Levin, *Feminism and Freedom*, p. 115.

[15] Rothbard, *Ethics of Liberty*, pp. 63–68. For a debate on this issue between the present author on the one hand, and Milton Friedman, David Friedman, and Paul Heyne on the other, see Walter Block, Geoffrey Brennan, and Kenneth Elzinga, eds, *Morality of the Market: Religious and Economic Perspectives* (Vancouver, British Columbia: The Fraser Institute, 1985), pp. 490–510.

I am allowed to keep it, no matter how many times my
father may have polished it and otherwise cared for it. It
is stolen property which never should have passed from
my grandfather to my father, or from him to me. And the
same analysis applies to land, or any other good.

7. Not content with attacking the feminists, Levin also
launches into a critique of right-wing opponents of
women's liberation—for being insufficiently radical. This
is all well and good; anyone who publishes anything, on
whatever side, must bear the scrutiny of all subsequent
writers. Furthermore, most of his shots hit their mark.
But there are several places where he is off target. First,
Levin upbraids Thomas Sowell (without directly quoting
him), for what he calls Sowell's implicit acceptance of
the view "that quotas 'work' if they increase the number
of blacks and women in high-level positions." But all
Sowell says, according to Levin, is that "affirmative
action does not work because it rewards well-credentialed
blacks and women whom firms are eager to hire without
helping poorly-credentialed blacks."[16] By this quote,
though, Sowell does not necessarily indicate that he has
accepted the feminist premise. All he is doing is claiming
that even given the viability of this feminist premise,
affirmative action is still not an effective means toward
that end.[17] In other words, Sowell finds that the women's
liberation movement is acting inconsistently with its own
goal in championing affirmative action. I find nothing
wrong with that.

Second, Levin reprimands Carl Hoffman (again, without
directly quoting him) for accepting "wholly environmental

---

[16] Levin, Feminism and Freedom, p. 118.

[17] Thomas Sowell, "Weber, Bakke, and the Presuppositions of Affirmative
Action," in Walter Block and Michael Walker, eds., *Discrimination, Affir-
mative Action, and Equal Opportunity* (Vancouver, British Columbia: Fraser
Institute, 1982), pp. 37–63.

explanations of sex differences in economic behavior." Specifically, Levin complains that Hoffman "objects to comparable worth because it penalizes employers who 'had nothing to do with producing ... female inhibition.'"[18] But why is this equivalent to accepting a wholly environmental explanation of sex differences? All Hoffman[19] is saying is that employers are punished, even though they are entirely innocent of whatever it is that is causing female inhibition. As I read this, it is entirely consistent with the denial of a wholly environmental explanation.

Third, Levin admonishes Ma Block's favorite and only son. Once again, his usual scholarly scrupulousness deserts him, and he fails to quote me directly. What is his complaint? "Walter Block explains sex differences in economic characteristics in terms of a 'fear of success' which besets girls in high school."[20] In fact, however, I was not offering this as an explanation of my own, but rather citing a whole host of feminist writers to this effect.[21] In any case, why is this necessarily equivalent to a wholly

---

[18] Levin, *Feminism and Freedom*, p. 143.

[19] Actually, reference is presumably being made to Carl Hoffman and John Reed, "When is Imbalance Not Discrimination," in Block and Walker, *Discrimination, Affirmative Action, and Equal Opportunity*, pp. 187–216.

[20] Levin, *Feminism and Freedom*, p. 144.

[21] Since Levin does not quote me, I cannot be sure of the exact context, but I assume his reference is to footnote 21 of "Economic Intervention, Discrimination, and Unforeseen Consequences," chapter 18 in this book.. This footnote stretches on for three pages, wherein I cite numerous feminist writers who give dramatic testimonial to the fear of success of many, many accomplished women. My motivation for reviewing this Literature was similar to that of Sowell: I wanted to catch the women's liberationists in a contradiction. On the one hand, they explain the female-male wage gap in terms of employer sexism; on the other hand, they testify to the fear of success of many women. They utterly fail even to consider that the latter could be at least part of the cause of the wage gap.

environmental explanation? Couldn't it be that this fear of success stems from biological antecedents?

8. The author of *Feminism and Freedom* accepts without criticism the myth that government can be productive, in the ordinary economic sense.[22] This is unremarkable in a conservative; no better can be expected. However, he does take the view that "people should not be forced to finance what they abhor";[23] from this, one might expect him to reason that if people are forced to do so, the result cannot be productive from their point of view (otherwise they would have financed the projects voluntarily), and that since government revenues are derived through force, the state cannot be productive. Alas, the very opposite of this conclusion was drawn by him.

9. Levin opines that as long as all large firms are forced to engage in affirmative action, none need fear loss of profits. General Motors need not worry about transmitting costs to the consumer in the form of higher prices as long as Ford and Chrysler must do the same. But what about small firms, not covered by this pernicious legislation? Can they not take market share away from all the large but encumbered firms?

10. Libertarians hold that discrimination should be allowed, on any basis, in the private sector, but not at all, on any basis, in the public sector. The reasoning is that if people are forced to pay taxes without discrimination, then they should be allowed to seize whatever benefits they see in government operation, also without discrimination. But the types of discrimination envisaged in this principle include far more than what is usually supposed. In addition to the usual race, sex, ethnicity, etc., it also includes everything else conceivable: strength, agility, intelligence, endurance, speed, and so on. The point is

---

[22] Levin, *Feminism and Freedom*, p. 120.

[23] Ibid., p. 111.

that if both the weak and the strong are forced to support the state, on a non-discriminatory basis, then the state must deal with each in the same manner.

Consider the case of the fireman with which Levin begins his book. By establishing physical requirements for fire fighters, the government is discriminating on behalf of the strong and agile—those, in other words, who are best suited to fighting fires and rescuing fire victims. This is entirely illegitimate, however, in that the state is discriminating against the elderly, those in wheelchairs, the weak, the blind, etc.; in a word, against all those unable to function adequately as firemen. Naturally, of course, without such discrimination, public-sector fire protection would he fatally compromised. But that is of no concern at all to the libertarian. Indeed, this state of affairs would be positively welcomed! For it would undermine the present nationalization of this vital service, and tend to place it back in private hands, where it belongs.

11. The same goes for education, despite Levin's chapters 7 through 9, where he deals with such matters. How is it warranted for the state to hold entrance exams for public universities, when these discriminate in favor of the most intellectually able? Ignorant and stupid people also pay the taxes used for these institutions of learning. They deserve representation at the finest public universities, and on a proportional basis; or at least on one that does not discriminate on any basis whatsoever. Of course, all entrance exams have to discriminate on some basis, so the argument in effect calls for the cessation of all entrance exams for public universities. Remember, we are searching for a moral way for goods and services that have been taken from people against their will to be ethically returned to them. And surely it cannot be on any basis irrelevant to the manner in which such things were taken.

Levin, in sharp contrast, avers that government is justified in supplying public education, provided that it teaches children good citizenship and steers clear of controversy. He does so despite his recognition that "public education forces parents to send their children to ... school," that people obviously abhor being forced to do things against their will, and that "people should not be forced to finance what they abhor."[24] Even his restriction upon the state not to engage in controversy is logically flawed. He holds that "the state can legitimately press literacy, numeracy, and basic factual information on children" and that "the public schools could teach industriousness and honesty, but they could not take sides in controversies.[25] But not all taxpayers favor honesty; some are thieves. Not all favor industriousness; some are lazy. Not all favor literacy; some are illiterate.[26]

12. Our author favors wage-control legislation. He says that "the question ... [of] whether women ... receive the same pay as men for the same work ... was settled in 1963 when the Equal Pay Act made it illegal to pay a woman less than a man for the same job."[27] Well, this may well be settled in the minds of some advocates of government intervention, but there are still those of

---

[24] Ibid., pp. 194–95, 111.

[25] Ibid., pp. 194–95.

[26] Levin also champions academic freedom, and does not even restrict this "right" to private institutions. For a critique of his views concerning academic freedom, see Walter Block, *Defending the Undefendable* (New York: Fleet Press, 1976), pp. 54–57. He also favors the legal prohibition of blackmail (Levin, p. 261). For an alternative view, see Block, *Defending the Undefendable*, pp. 44–49; Block, "Trading Money for Silence," *University of Hawaii Law Review* 8, no. 1 (Spring 1986): 57–73; and Block and David Gordon, "Extortion and the Exercise of Free Speech Rights: A Reply to Professors Posner, Epstein, Nozick, and Lindgren," *Loyola of Los Angeles Law Review* 19, no. 1 (November 1985): 37–54.

[27] Levin, *Feminism and Freedom*, p. 131.

us who yearn for a world of economic freedom, one of contract, not status. If an employer wishes to pay a man twice as much for doing the same exact work as a woman, that is his natural right. We could interpret the extra pay as a gift; or we could determine that the jobs are not really exactly equal, if only because the employer is more comfortable with the man in his employ than with the woman. But these scenarios are beside the point. The bottom line is that, in a free society, there should be no restrictions whatsoever on the free contractual rights of consenting adults. If an employer can find a woman willing to accept half the salary of a man for the same job, it is their right to agree to a wage contract which stipulates this.[28]

13. Perhaps Levin's most serious breach of the libertarian legal code involves his defense of conscription. In his view, "if the all-volunteer force is unable to attract enough men, an obvious solution is [a] return to all-male conscription."[29] But an obvious moral alternative is to raise pay scales until enough men are willing to supply their labor for this enterprise, assuming in the first place it is a legitimate one.

14. He also opposes a woman's right to abortion on the "fundamental Kantian rule against initiating aggression."[30] He rejects the familiar Judith Jarvin Thomson analogy of someone who wakes up to find another person attached to himself, dependent upon the use of his kidneys. Levin rejects this on the grounds that "the person who

---

[28] An employer who engages in this practice on a large scale is of course risking bankruptcy, but that is an entirely different matter.

[29] Levin, *Feminism and Freedom*, p. 229.

[30] Too bad he does not take this fundamental Kantian or libertarian axiom more seriously, especially in the cases of taxation, public enterprise, and conscription.

withdraws his assistance is not completely responsible for the dependency on him of the person who is about to die, while the mother is completely responsible for the dependency of her fetus on her."[31] But this will not do. Surely the victim of rape is in no way responsible for her fetus's dependency on her. And just as surely all fetuses, whether the result of rape or not, have equal rights with one another.[32]

To sum up: I have praised the book to the skies, and then, that being my nature, have registered quite a few disagreements with it. But it should be obvious that I recommend reading this book: It is the only exhaustive, in-depth, utter refutation of the feminist argument presently in existence. Its positive contributions are great, and its flaws do not detract from its central thesis. On the contrary, they are peripheral, although interesting, issues.

---

[31] Levin, *Feminism and Freedom*, p. 288.

[32] For a defense of fetus eviction, not abortion, see Walter Block, "Abortion, Woman and Fetus: Rights in Conflict?" *Reason*, April 1978, pp. 18–25.

DISCRIMINATION AND THE LAW

WHEN IT COMES TO DISCRIMINATION, GOVERNMENT IS OFTEN quick to act—for better or for worse. In some instances, government acts to end what it perceives as discrimination against women, minorities, people with alternate lifestyles, and others.

However, in other instances, government itself engages in discrimination, such as when state universities discriminate against students with low test scores, when government programs offer job training for people in some industries but not others, or when the law mandates that members of certain groups be hired before members of other groups.

This section of the book is comprised of four journal articles, three of which are co-authored. As will be seen, in all cases, the free market will provide justice.

35. COMPROMISING THE UNCOMPROMISABLE: DISCRIMINATION

SHOULD PEOPLE BE FREE TO DISCRIMINATE AGAINST OTHERS?[1]
At first glance, the only proper answer to this question would appear to be a resounding (and horrified), "No!" However, on further reflection, things are not quite so simple.

A few preliminary remarks. The liberals, who are most associated with this lofty reply in the public mind, by no means give total assent to it. Their protestations notwithstanding, they actually favor discrimination on racial[2] grounds—as long as it favors the underdog *vis-à-vis* the "overdog." They might not choose to accept this description, but their advocacy of affirmative action, quotas, "goals," set-asides, preferences, norming, and all such other programs

---

American Journal of Economics and Sociology 57, no. 2 (April, 1998): 223–37.

[1] Discrimination occurs on the basis of race, gender, sexual preference, national origin, handicap status, baldness, citizenship, beauty, intelligence, height, weight, sense of humor, left or right handedness, and dozens of other criteria. The law singles out the first five of these for special protection, leaving the "victims" or "undesirables" in the latter categories to fend for themselves. Presumably, public choice considerations (Buchanan and Tullock 1971, 1980; Gwartney and Wagner 1988), not any intrinsic characteristics of these groups, can account for this selection bias.

[2] Although we mention race alone in the text, this could stand in for any characteristic on the basis of which certain people are distinguished from others and are reacted to in different ways.

amounts to discrimination—no more, no less. They of course do this for the "best" of reasons, or at least for reasons that seem good and sufficient to them, but the same might be said of anyone at all who acts (Mises 1966). In summary, "progressives" favor discrimination on behalf of downtrodden groups as a matter of principle, and, presumably, act in this manner in their own lives.[3]

What of the conservatives? Nowadays, they speak out in favor of something called "color blindness" (Bolick 1996; Eastland 1996). This amounts to a restoration of the Civil Rights Act of 1964, and Martin Luther King's dream of a society in which decisions are made on the basis of people's characters, not the color of their skins.[4] This, too, sounds nice. What could be more fair or just? Treat all people based on their merits.

But this position is also philosophically flawed. First of all, merit is merely another characteristic on the basis of which people can discriminate against each other. Because merits of different types and varieties are statistically correlated with different groupings, including racial, preferences for people on this basis are not at all distinguishable, at least in effect, from choices made with respect to race or color. If true colorblindness is the goal, allowing discrimination on the basis of merit will hardly achieve it (Gottfredson 1987, 1988; Herrnstein and Murray 1994; Levin 1997; Rushton 1988; Seligman 1992; Sowell 1975).[5]

---

[3] Or not. Many liberals champion racial integration yet live in white-only neighborhoods themselves; others favor public schools but (e.g., the Clintons) send their children to exclusive private schools.

[4] Conservatives, of course, did not always pursue this policy. Once upon a time, they were in favor of discrimination—racial preferences—for the overdog, on a compulsory basis, for example, Jim Crow legislation. (At this time the liberals favored colorblindness.) Then the conservatives went through a period of advocating separate but equal separation. Only lately have the conservatives adopted the liberal democratic policies of the 1960s.

[5] To be fair to the conservatives, they would be philosophically satisfied if, by adhering strictly to merit, racial disparities were to arise on a statistical basis. The explication is that conservatives see colorblindness as an end in itself, not merely as a means (e.g., to a statistically representative society), as do the liberals.

Secondly, neither liberals nor conservatives are really serious about this goal, at least for the personal if not the business arena. If color-blindness is truly virtuous, and for some reason should be required by law, then why confine this compulsion to one or another aspect of our lives? Why not compel it throughout? If a person must hire employees on the basis of character or merit or on the basis of anything but skin color and must apply this criterion to firing, investing, selling, buying, and so on, then why should this basic element of morality not be applied to private life as well? Why not prohibit racial discrimination in the choice of friends, dating partners, or marriage partners? The conservatives (at least nowadays) talk a good colorblindness line, but their adherence to it is only skin deep. Even the conservatives jettison the whole perspective as applied to their whole lives.[6, 7]

---

[6] Were colorblindness applied to personal life, then the state, before granting a marriage license, would have to query citizens as to whether they had dated people from other races. If not, why not? If blacks are 15 percent of the popu-lation, and Jews are 3 percent, then each should intermarry with all others at about that percentage. If not, racism (e.g., non-colorblindness) is presumed to be the cause. (This is true at least if we follow the same pattern in personal life as we do for business practices). Surely, no rational commentator reflecting on this issue for one moment can deny that non-colorblindness is rife in personal relationships. If the civil rights law of 1964 is morally required, and no relevant difference between commerce and personal relations can be adduced, then it should be used to stamp out these racist patterns. If this is not a powerful *reductio* of the whole idea, then there is no such thing as a *reductio*.

[7] Another "feel-good" notion is that of equality of opportunity rather than outcome. But what, precisely, does this mean? If all it means it that the government must not interfere with the free choices of individuals, it is entirely vacuous. More exactly, it means, then, no more than free enterprise, and we already have a perfectly good phrase to express that idea. On the other hand, if it means more than this, if it is applied to race or sex discrimination, it is a positive evil. This can be shown by subjecting it to the personal life test. To wit, equality of opportunity must mean that, for example, heterosexuals must date others of their own gender (we've got to give these people an equal opportunity to marry us, after all). Similarly, homosexuals must be forced—this is the law, after all—to date members of the opposite sex. As well, whites and blacks must be forced to date one another. None of these three groups need marry each other (that requirement can be deduced from a law prohibiting discrimination in marriage, not from "equality of opportunity, not of outcome"), which would be to compel equality of outcome, not merely

LIBERTARIAN COMPROMISE

What, then is the Libertarian Compromise? For this position, we must make a sharp and deep distinction between the public and the private sectors not only of the economy but of the society as well. The libertarian sees an unbridgeable philosophical chasm between the government, which is necessarily based on force and compulsion, and the private sphere, which consists of voluntary interaction.[8]

This being the case, the compromise must come in two sections, one devoted to each of these spheres. In the private sector, the rule is not race preference to the underdog of the progressives, nor is it the color-blindness of the conservatives. Instead, it is one of completely voluntary association, where each person is "free to choose."[9] All people are or should be free to make up their own minds about how they will choose their spouses, friends and neighbors, customers, employees, employers, and other business associates. The clear implication is that the Civil Rights Act of 1964 must be repealed, as it is inconsistent with the total freedom to choose one's associates in *all* spheres of life.

Some people might recoil in horror from turning the clock on race relations back to the pre-1964 period. They would object that if a majority were free to discriminate against a minority, the latter would be greatly disadvantaged. That is, if, for example, whites, were to refuse to buy from, sell to, hire, work for, invest with, for example, blacks, the latter would be unemployed, homeless, and starving.

---

opportunity. Nevertheless, it is entirely noxious, at least for the libertarian, to force people to do *anything* against their wills (apart from requiring them to keep their hands to themselves, of course).

[8] From this fact, the anarcho-libertarians (Benson 1989, 1990; Friedman 1989; Hoppe 1989, 1992; Rothbard 1973, 1982) draw the conclusion that government must be banned totally, root and branch. In contrast, the minarchist libertarians (Epstein 1985; Nozick 1974) deduce that "government is best which governs least." Arguing from the premise that a certain minimal amount of coercion is necessary for the functioning of society, this latter group maintains that if force cannot be eliminated, at least the state should be limited to the basic tasks of protection of person and property, for which government, courts, armies, and police are needed, and nothing much else.

[9] The title of Friedman's 1981 work.

But this position is economically erroneous. All such scenarios fail to take into account the market's fail-safe mechanism that helps those subjected to discrimination. Consider employment. If white racists rebuffed black workers, the first effect would indeed be unemployment or lower wages for the latter group. But this situation is only temporary, a mere first stage in the mental experiment we are now considering.[10] For with lower wages or greater unemployment, some whites[11] would be sorely tempted to employ these blacks, because they can earn additional profits exploiting workers who are underpaid or idled.

TABLE 1

	Marginal Productivity	Wage
Black	$10	$10
White	$10	$10

Consider a two-stage numerical example. Initially, there is no racism, and white and black workers are all employed at $10 per hour (Table 1). We assume that marginal revenue product, marginal productivity, or just plain old productivity was also equal to $10 for both groups; thus we start out at a competitive equilibrium. All employers are of course seeking profits, but, because they rival for workers, wages are bid up to productivity levels and no profits are actually made.

Now, in the second stage, we introduce racism into the analysis. This means, if it means anything, that while the demand curve for white workers remains intact, that for blacks shifts to the left (Figure 1). This, in turn, implies that while white wages and employment levels remain as they were before, the number of blacks hired, and their compensation levels, falls.

---

[10] For an economic analysis of discrimination, see the works of Becker (1957); Block (1982a, 1982b, 1992); Block and Williams (1981); Demsetz (1965); Higgs (1977); and Sowell (1975, 1981a, 1981b, 1994).

[11] Also, blacks with savings who were on the margin of being an employer or an employee, plus those blacks who were already employers.

FIGURE 1

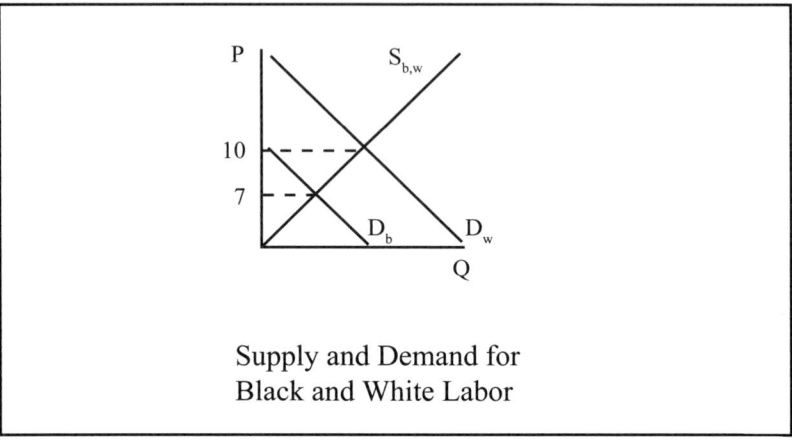

Supply and Demand for
Black and White Labor

Let us suppose that it decreases to $7 per hour (Table 2). But this, clearly, is untenable and cannot endure for long. If an employer hires a white, he earns zero profit;[12] in contrast, if he hires a black, he will net $3 additional per hour. Some employers, blinded by their race prejudice, will still insist on hiring only whites.[13] However, in the competitive struggle, those who either have no race prejudice, or choose not to indulge in it, will hire the equally productive blacks[14] at $3 per hour less. On this basis, they will be able to manufacture the product at lower cost. Then, they will either keep prices the same and

---

[12] We assume the employer can just stay in business, even with zero profit, because, by assumption, the employer still can do just as well as the next best alternative, say, working for someone else, and investing his or her capital in another business.

[23] We assume away as a complication that does not affect the main line of analysis the possibility that customers or other employees object to being served by, or working next to, blacks. On this see Becker's (1957) work.

[14] If blacks are not equally productive, then that will account for their lower wages, not discriminatory behavior on the part of their employers, as we have been assuming.

pocket additional profits, or lower their prices. In either scenario, there can be only one result: The racists will be driven out of business.[15]

TABLE 2

	Marginal Productivity	Wage
Black	$10	$7
White	$10	$10

A similar analysis could be applied to every other arena of commercial endeavor. If blacks are not sold houses (or food, or clothing), the price they must pay will rise, making them better buyers from the point of view of lenders,[16] others will jump into the breach. If blacks are not given loans, the interest they will be forced to pay will increase, rendering them better borrowers; others, blacks as well as whites, will be more than happy to "exploit" these blacks, by lending to them.[17]

But is this not unfair to blacks? Why should they have to endure the indignity of lower wages and unemployment (or higher prices for food, clothing shelter, loans, etc.), even if it is only temporary? One

---

[15] This is according to the old saw that there is a sucker born every minute. This may well apply to racists too, that there is a racist born every minute. If so, racism will always exist, even though the market continually weeds them out. This is one answer to the question of why racism still exists if these beneficial effects of the market are really operational. The other reply is that full free enterprise—*laissez-faire* capitalism—does not now apply. Instead, the government interferes in all sorts of ways, the effect of which is harming blacks, for example, the minimum wage law, unionism, laws compelling union rates of pay, and so on. On this see the work of Williams (1982).

[16] We here implicitly assume that the costs of servicing these two groups (pilferage rates, etc.) are equal. If they are not, then this factor, not racism, would account for the longevity of differential prices.

[17] We here implicitly assume that the likelihood of paying back the debt is invariant between white and black. If it is not, then this factor, not racism, would account for the longevity of differential rates of interest.

answer to this very reasonable challenge is to realize that the enemy is not the market, which is riding to the rescue of the downtrodden group (by first allowing it to suffer, and then, in effect, making this suffering the key to their economic salvation). Another perhaps better answer is that this scenario is a hypothetical construct, articulated in terms of two stages, separate in time, and mainly for heuristic purposes. That is, to clarify the process, we purposefully assume that there would be two stages; in the first, the position of blacks is worsened, to show that in the second they would be rescued. In actual point of fact, there are no such two stages. Any time the wages of blacks (or anyone else) dips below their productivity levels, even by a tiny amount, there are immediate profit incentives to hire them, which starts their wages up on an upward spiral back toward equality.[18]

Let us now summarize this part of our discussion. For the libertarian, there is a compromise between the conservative's call for colorblindness and the liberals advocacy of equal representation of all groups in all possible niches of the economy. This compromise is, simply, that no one is forced to discriminate, but no one is prevented from so doing either. People are totally free to choose. There is complete freedom of association, and this applies to both the spheres of business and personal life. This is as a matter of right. As a matter of utility, the claim which emanates from this sector of the political-economic spectrum is that discrimination is impotent to do any real damage to its supposed victims. This is because any time any group is subjected to discrimination, its economic status makes its people more acceptable to others, and these others can bankrupt the discriminators.

---

[18] Why, then, do wages of blacks lag behind those of whites, and females behind males? It is because, contrary to our assumption in the text, productivities are not at all equal. In the case of racial differences, several theories account for the gap—the history of slavery, the Jim Crow law and other incidences of statist repression, and lower IQ (Herrnstein and Murray 1994, where they control for this variable and find that the pay gap has all but disappeared). In the case of differences between the sexes, empirical research suggests the differences are due to differences in marital status: Marriage lowers female productivity in the market and raises that of males. See the work of Block (1982a), Block and Williams (1981), Levin (1984, 1987), and Sowell (1975), which show that when marriage is factored out of the equation and the wages of never-married males and females are compared, there is virtually no wage gap.

PUBLIC SECTOR

Now let us move to the second stage of our analysis, and consider the libertarian compromise in the case of the public sector. For the libertarian anarchist, this compromise is a very simple one. Because there is no public sector at all, the question of whether it should or should not discriminate on any basis simply does not arise.

The response from the limited government libertarian is greatly simplified as well. For this position, the application of the question is very much reduced (although not completely eliminated); it no longer applies to virtually the entire economy, as at present, but instead is limited to police, armies, and courts. In this system, all people are forced to pay taxes for the upkeep and maintenance of the government; therefore, all of them should have an equal legal right to work for it in these three realms. Here, the libertarians borrow a leaf from conservatives: colorblindness and merit.[19] This does not mean, however, that all racial, sexual, or other designated groups should be assigned jobs in proportion to their percentage of the population, as the liberals would have it.[20] Rather, as the purpose of government in this philosophy is to maintain civil order and protect person and property, then the people who can best achieve these goals, whatever their background, should be hired for them.

---

[19] The only exception is if skin color or gender are relevant to doing the job. For example, if the police want to infiltrate, for example, a black gang or the Mafia, then they must use, say, blacks or Italians. Obviously, to prevent female prostitution, female decoys would have to be used. (However, because prostitution would be legal in the libertarian society, this is a moot point.)

[20] The liberals claim that a logical implication of total non-discrimination would be a proportional share of all jobs, housing locations, income, wealth, etc., to all racial, ethnic, sexual, etc., groups. That is, if blacks are 15 percent of the population and women are 51 percent of the population, then blacks should comprise 15 percent and women should comprise 51 percent of all professors, doctors, merchants, actors, and so on. For a critique of this view, see the works of Sowell (1975, 1981a, 1994). Interestingly enough, the liberals never apply this theory to high-status and high-paying occupations in which blacks are statistically overrepresented (e.g., the National Basketball Association, the National Football League, etc.).

AN OBJECTION[21]

The implication of this paper is that the Civil Rights Act of 1964 was unjust,[22] was enacted to correct a problem that was not really a problem, and was, therefore, unnecessary.

But an immediate objection arises: Can we not think of this legislation as a form of reparations? After all, suppose you are a member of a minority race and a majority comes along and captures you, forcing you to work as a slave. This system lasts for hundreds of years. Then, happily, you and your people are freed. After that, you are allowed to trade and exchange freely, but virtually all of the means of production have been taken up by others; more specifically, the land ownership rights are almost totally owned by the majority. Why should you consider this allocation of property rights a legitimate starting out point for trade and exchange? Would justice not consist of the majority's giving up some of its wealth, property, and privileges, by force if need be, so that the minority could reclaim at least some of the fair market value of what had been confiscated from them?

The starting out point, then, is crucial for the analysis of markets. If the minority were brought back to the *status quo ante*,[23] then, perhaps, the argument might go, there would be no need for the Civil

---

[21] I wish to thank Laurence Moss for forcibly bringing to my attention the importance of addressing this issue, and, as well, for the form of this objection, which is based, almost verbatim, on his words.

[22] Support for this contention is given by Levin (1982, p. 85), who analyzes the situation of "giving someone a job he was denied because he was discriminated against" as follows:

> This is current policy, as reflected in the Civil Rights Act's ban on racial discrimination in employment. ... It is, however, arguable that employers do not owe anyone jobs. An employer, on this argument, is *choosing* whom to give his job to, and is entitled to choose on criteria that most people would find objectionable. His right to liberty overrides his obligation not to indulge prejudice. If so, the Civil Rights Act curtails freedom impermissibly.

[23] This is impossible, strictly speaking. But if they were at least compensated by a good faith effort.

Rights Act of 1964. But, as this has not occurred, that legislation is justified, at least as a second-best policy.

The liberal-egalitarians would deny there is any need for reparations. They think that income should be equalized among all people in any case. So, there is no warrant for transferring funds to them based on considerations of the past. Suppose there were two groups of poor people, one victimized unfairly in the past, the other not. The consistent egalitarian would not wish to elevate the former over the latter; rather, he would want to bring up the income of both groups, so that it attained the level achieved by everyone else. The conservatives too would deny there is any need for reparations. Some would argue that none of the people alive in 1964, and even more certainly not at the time of this writing, were actually slaves. They are only the descendants of such people. Therefore, restitution should only be given to those who were direct victims of injustice; as there are no such people alive any longer, compensation for slavery is not justified. Others correctly see the demand for restitution as a demand for justice. However, remarkably, they either deny that there is any such thing as justice, or maintain that "the search for justice will destroy the world."[24]

In contrast, the libertarian position is that amends of the income transfer variety are most certainly justified. For example, I advocated just this in a case analogous to slavery, stating (Block 1985, p. 496):

> According to the [John Lockean] theory of property rights, the peasants who tilled the soil are the rightful owners of the land. The conquistadores who conquered them stole this land. Their

---

[24] This was Milton Friedman's recitation of a favorite saying of his "old teacher" Frank Knight. Friedman (1985, p. 498) interpreted Knight as saying: "Justice is in the eye of the beholder," and went on to assert on his own account in 1982 that

> there are no really objective standards of justice. And there's no way other than force, ultimately, of mediating different claims of justice. It's a search for justice that animates Khomeini's Iran today. ... So, I believe that it is very dangerous to base any judgment of social policy upon the objective of searching for justice.

descendants, many of the large land owners in South and Central America, thus hold unjust title to their land.[25]

Note that not every type of reparation is justified under libertarianism. For restitution to be proper, it must meet certain criteria. Foremost, the land or other valuable consideration must be taken away from the actual thieves or from their descendants,[26] not from innocent people,

---

[25] My response (Block 1985, p. 498) to Friedman was to

> take the latifundi in the Third World where, as far as I am concerned, the historical facts show that it was the conquistadores who, at one time, took over the land, kicked the peasants off, or allowed the peasants to stay there, but claimed ownership of it. And, on the other hand, you have a bunch of peasants who had, according to the Lockean theory, been the true owners of it. Now, if you say that there is no such thing as justice, and we must couch everything in terms of what is, then clearly the people who are working as peons there have no right to take over the land which I contend should really belong to them.

[26] David Friedman (1985, pp. 501–02, 505) makes the following response to me:

> The point where I would want to agree with my father [Milton Friedman] ... against Walter Block or at least make an argument on [the side of the latter], goes back to the latifundi. It seems to me entirely possible ... that as a matter of abstract justice, if I were a judge in a court, I would agree that the peasants were in the right. But second, that it would be better for the world, including the peasants, if they forget about the past. Fighting over their claims to justice will get people killed. There is no particular reason to think that the most just people will win the war. Fighting tends to create unjust situations. So, it seems to me quite plausible to argue both that here is an abstract principle of justice, which in principle could be applied; and that as a matter of practical, social reality we accept what is and work from there.

> If by "justice" we are concerned with initial ownership of things, I think in the long run that isn't enormously important. In the U.S. at the moment, if you gave the country back to the Indians, in some fair way where you didn't give them the buildings that are built on it, but just the land; and divided it fairly evenly among the Indians, it would not noticeably affect the distribution of income in the U.S. It wouldn't much affect how well off I am, and so forth.

> Starting with either a "just" or an "unjust" distribution of property, in a generation or two you end up in not very different circumstances, except in very extreme cases.

or all people including the innocent. Second, the burden of proof always rests on those who would overturn extant property titles. As the lawyers say, possession is nine-tenths of the law. If redress is due, the claimant must offer proof, not mere allegation.

Unhappily for the objection we are now considering, these criteria do not apply to the Civil Rights Act of 1964 nor to any welfare scheme that transfers funds, on net balance, from whites to blacks in the modern era,[27] because forcing present day whites to integrate with blacks, or to in any other way give up their right of free association, is to punish innocent people for the evil deeds of their grandparents. But in the libertarian legal code, a person can be punished only for his own rights violations. In any case, there are many whites now in the country whose grandparents were in Europe or in Asia and had absolutely nothing to do with slavery.

In sharp contrast, however, there is a strong case that can be made for the transfer of *some* property now owned by whites to *some* blacks. Had justice been attained in 1865, the slave owners would have been punished[28] for the crime of slave owning.[29] Certainly, their

---

[27] Here is my response to David Friedman (Block 1985, pp. 505–06):

> Milton and I were distinguishing ourselves on a "normative" question. David replied in a "positive" vein, with which I happen to be in full agreement. That is, I agree that the Indians or the natives would probably be better off if instead of worrying about their lost endowments of property, they were just concerned with creating a libertarian society from hence forward.

[28] My point is still worth making:

> Those people owned that property. ... Here we are supposed to be defenders of property rights; and yet, grant me the facts of the case, massive theft has taken place; and we're giving ... a positive statement with which I happen to agree: that this stolen property is economically unimportant. But I think it's very inadequate to (make) that positive statement. What we have to make is the normative statement, too. Both. We have to say, "Yes, in justice, that property belongs to you." Namely, the free market advocate is not just in favor of the *status quo*, where blatant theft has taken place.

[39] I conclude from all of this that the starting point might be crucial to the descendants of black slaves, or it might not. That is merely an empirical issue. The far more important point is that they have a right to start out as fairly as

property would have been seized from them and given over to their ex-slaves, as (partial) compensation for the years of misery inflicted on them. The slave owners, unfortunately, are beyond the reach of present day justice. However, their lands, plantations, other holdings, never should have been given to their children, and, through further inheritance, to those who hold these properties at the turn of the 21st century. In justice, they should be given back, provided that specific present day blacks can prove they are the descendants of slaves who worked on precisely located land. With historical records, including notations on family Bibles, this should not prove impossible. Of course, it would have been somewhat easier to offer such proofs in 1964, because records tend to become lost as time passes.[30]

Levin (1982, p. 85) addresses the dichotomy these two options present, saying, "The difference between the two policies is the difference between restoring a robbery victim's property to him, and hunting up the descendants of robbery victims and giving them goods at the expense of people who robbed no one." Levin "has no quarrel with the former, many quarrels with the latter."[31] But we can see that he must necessarily have a quarrel with the libertarian view of reparations. The descendants of the white slaveowners robbed no one. According to Levin, it is therefore unjust to find the descendants of slaves and give them the plantations and other property on which their great-grandparents worked. However, even though the present white holders of these plantations themselves

---

possible. Fighting, in any case, is not really an issue here. In answering this question, I am implicitly considering a historical state of affairs alternative to the one which brought us the Civil Rights Act of 1964. In it, reparations based on the libertarian code would have been made instead.

[30] If my great-grandfather stole something from yours, and then I inherited it, my claim to it is no more justified than his. Because his claim was improper, so is mine. If you sue me for the property, then libertarian justice would require that I turn it over to you. I cannot be imprisoned, because I did not do the initial stealing. I am, in this case, akin to the innocent holder of stolen goods; I cannot keep them, but I am not guilty of theft.

[31] Levin (1977) rejects compensation to blacks from whites on grounds very different from those of our discussion.

robbed no one, they never should have been given these lands in the first place, and, in justice, ought to be made to give them up in favor of the great-grandchildren who would have inherited them, had their slave ancestors been given them in 1865. These people might not have robbed anyone, but they are in effect (innocent) holders of stolen property, and must in justice be forced to disgorge them. But this holds true if and only if their rightful owners can be determined, and the burden of proof rests with the latter.[32]

---

[32] The implication of the libertarian theory of reparations, thus, is that the further back in history the initial injustice occurred, the more difficult it is to justify such acts, because in addition to the fact that the passage of time causes records to deteriorate, the further back one goes, the less likely it was that written records were kept. For both these reasons, restitution based on theft from Japanese-Americans during World War II would be far easier to make than restitution for crimes that occurred 2000 years ago in the Middle East. Similarly, it would be easier to give justice to American blacks than to Native Americans.

36. SHOULD THE GOVERNMENT BE ALLOWED TO ENGAGE IN RACIAL, SEXUAL, OR OTHER ACTS OF DISCRIMINATION?

EXTANT LAW AND ITS COMPATIBILITY WITH THE UNITED STATES CONSTITUTION

A. THE LAW OF ARKANSAS

THE STATE OF ARKANSAS PROVIDES TO GRADUATES OF ARKANSAS secondary schools who demonstrate "extraordinary academic ability" a full academic scholarship for enrollment in a state-approved public or private Arkansas institution of higher education.[1] The sole measure of the graduate's "extraordinary ability" is demonstrated by scoring 32 or above on the American College Test (ACT), or at least 1410 on the Scholastic Aptitude Test (SAT), and selection as a finalist in the National Merit Scholarship competition or achievement of a high school grade point average of at least 3.5 on a scale of 4.0.[2] The purpose of the Governor's Scholarship Program, according to the enabling legislation, is "that outstanding students are an essential ingredient for the economic and social benefit of the State

Walter Block and Roy Whitehead, *Northern Illinois University Law Review* 22, no. 1 (Fall 2001): 53–84.

[1] Ark. Code Ann. § 6-82-305 (Michie 1996 and Supp. 1999), *amended* by 2001 Ark. Acts 1761.

[2] Ark. Code Ann. § 6-82-302(a) (Michie 1996), *amended* by 2001 Ark. Acts 1761.

of Arkansas. Benefits accrue to the state when a majority of National Merit Scholars, National Achievement Scholars, and superior students attend Arkansas institutions of higher learning and remain in the state."[3] The scholarship award dollar amount equals the tuition, room and board, and mandatory fees charged for a regular full-time student by the approved institution of higher education in which the student is enrolled.[4] For students who are first-time entering freshman after July 1, 2002, a new $10,000.00 maximum will be in effect.[5] There are eight public and seven private, church-related, approved institutions participating in the program.[6]

The dollar value of the scholarship award varies considerably between public and private institutions. It is estimated, for example, that a scholarship recipient enrolled in Hendrix, a private church-related institution, costs the state about $15,474 per year. In contrast, a distinguished scholar enrolled at Southern Arkansas University, a public institution, will cost the state only about $5,088 per year.[7] It is critical to understand that the scholarship funds are disbursed from the state directly to the approved public and private, church-related institutions.[8] No funds are sent to the parents or recipients.[9] The responsibility for selecting the scholarship recipients rests with the Arkansas Department of Higher Education (DHE).[10]

---

[3] Ark. Code Ann. § 6-82-301 (Michie 1996 and Supp. 1999), *amended* by 2001 Ark. Acts 1761.

[4] Ark. Code Ann. § 6-82-312(b) (Michie 1996 and Supp. 1999), *amended* by 2001 Ark. Acts 1761.

[5] Ark. Code Ann. § 6-82-312(c) (Michie 1996 and Supp. 1999), *amended* by 2001 Ark. Acts 1761.

[6] Arkansas Department of Higher Education, Student Enrollments, Table III, State Appropriations Per Student for Arkansas Governor's Distinguished Scholars for 1999–00 Fiscal Year, May 2000.

[7] *Id.*

[8] Arkansas Department of Higher Education, Program Rules and Procedures, Rule 5.

[9] *Id.*

[10] Ark. Code Ann. § 6-82-304 (3) (Michie 1996), *amended* by 2001 Ark. Acts 1761.

As a condition of participation in the program, each institution of higher education, public or church-related, has to agree to provide to the state the same level of administrative services in administering the program. Among these services are the following: appointing an institution representative to act as administrator of the program for that campus; receiving all disbursements; completing all forms and rosters; verifying all data; and ensuring compliance with all DHE program rules and regulations.[11] In addition, the institution, public or private, must do the following: maintain disbursement records; prepare an annual Institutional Financial Information Sheet for all programs administered by DHE; prepare a list of program drop-outs; certify full-time enrollment; provide DHE with an institutional verification of compliance at least twice yearly; and, finally, submit from time to time to a DHE review of the institution's records to demonstrate its due diligence as a *steward of state funds*.

The program has been much used. The state awarded a total of 808 Distinguished Governor's Scholarships for the 1997–98, 1998–99, and 1999–2000 academic years.[12] Of those, 425 (52.6 percent) chose to attend a public institution, and 383 (47.4 percent) chose to attend a private, church-related institution. The approximate expenditure of state funds for the scholarship program has resulted in disbursements of $6,149,087.00 to the private, church-related institutions and $3,666,371 .00 to their public counterparts.[13] As a result, 62.6 percent of the total state distinguished scholarship funds were forwarded directly to the former, and 37.4 percent to the latter.[14] Of the scholarship recipients, 4 (0.4 percent) were African American, 19 (2.0 percent) Asian, 5 (0.5 percent) Native American, 885 (94.6 percent) Caucasian, 3 (0.3 percent) Hispanic, and 20 (2.1

---

[11] Arkansas Department of Higher Education, Rules and Procedures, Rule 5.

[12] Arkansas Department of Higher Education, Student Enrollments, Table 1, Comparison of The Number of Arkansas Governor's Distinguished Scholarship Awards by Institution for the 1997–98 Through 1999–00 Academic Years.

[13] Arkansas Department of Higher Education, Table II, Amount of Arkansas Governor's Distinguished Scholarship Awards by Institution.

[14] *Id.*

percent) were other or unknown. Finally, 532 (56.8 percent) of the scholars were male, and 404 (43.2 percent) female.[15]

B. FEDERAL GOVERNMENT JURISDICTION OVER STATE DISCRIMINATION

Does the federal government have jurisdiction over states when and if they engage in racial discrimination against their citizens? Some argue that state courts lack jurisdiction over a plaintiff's federal damage claims under §1983 because states are not persons amenable to suit under §1983.[16] See 42 U.S.C. § 1983 (1994). However, it is well-settled in the judicial circuit including Arkansas that, to survive a motion to dismiss, all a plaintiff must do is plead that a facially neutral practice's adverse effects fall disproportionately on a group protected by Title VI.

As the Court of Appeals for the Eighth Circuit explained in the Fair Housing Act discrimination case of *Ring v. First Interstate Mortgage*,[17] "the prima facie case under [disparate impact] analysis is an evidentiary standard—it defines the quantum of proof plaintiff must present to create a rebuttable presumption of discrimination."[18] According to the Federal Rules of Civil Procedure, "an evidentiary standard is not a proper measure to determine whether a complaint fails to state a claim."[19]

Additionally, the Supreme Court has stated, "[W]hen a federal court reviews the sufficiency of a complaint ... the issue is not whether the plaintiff will ultimately prevail but whether the claimant is entitled to offer evidence to support such claims."[20] The State of Arkansas has promulgated a program that clearly has a disparate impact on

---

[15] *Id.*

[16] See 42 U.S.C. § 1983 (1994).

[17] 984 F.2d 924 (8th Cir. 1993).

[18] *Id.*

[19] *Id.* at 926.

[20] *Scheuer v. Rhodes*, 416 U.S. 232, 236 (1974).

black students.[21] They are underrepresented among the scholarship winners.[22] Given this, a clear implication exists that they are entitled under *Ring* to offer evidence to support their claims.

C. GETTING PAST THE NOTION OF STATE IMMUNITY

Under certain circumstances, the United States Congress can pass laws that give individual citizens a right of action in federal court against an non-consenting state. The circumstances require, first, that "Congress has 'unequivocally expressed its intent to abrogate the immunity,'"[23] which "must be obvious from a 'clear legislative statement.'"[24] Second, Congress must have acted "pursuant to a valid exercise of power."[25] The Supreme Court has held that Congress can abrogate state immunity when it acts pursuant to Part 5, the enforcement provision of the Fourteenth Amendment, which provides that "the Congress shall have the power to enforce, by appropriate legislation, the provisions of this article."[26]

Congress, through the legislation that established Title VI, abrogated state immunity in order to give effect to the provisions of the Fourteenth Amendment of the United States Constitution.[27] A private right of action under a federal statute requires analysis of the factors set forth in *Cort v. Ash*.[28] The *Cort* factors ask:

> First, is the plaintiff "one of the class for whose *especial* benefit the statute was enacted"—that is, does the statute create a federal right in favor of the plaintiff? Second, is there any indication

---

[21] See text accompanying notes 13–19.

[22] See note 13.

[23] *Seminole Tribe of Florida v. Florida*, 517 U.S. 44, 55 (1996) (quoting *Green v. Mansour*, 474 U.S. 64, 68 (1985)).

[24] *Id.* at 55.

[25] Seminole Tribe, 517 U.S. at 55.

[26] U.S. Const. amend. XIV, § 5.

[27] See *Atascadero State Hospital v. Scanlon*, 473 U.S. 234, 246–47 (1985).

[28] 422 U.S. 66 (1975).

of legislative intent, explicit or implicit, either to create such a remedy or to deny one? Third, is it consistent with the underlying purposes of the legislative scheme to imply such a remedy for the plaintiff? And finally, is the cause of action one traditionally relegated to state law, in an area basically the concern of the States, so that it would be inappropriate to infer a cause of action based solely on federal law?[29]

Plaintiffs fit squarely under the *Cort* rationale.

D. A PRIVATE CAUSE OF ACTION FOR ARKANSAS PLAINTIFFS

An individual affected by the disparate impact of the Arkansas scholarship distributions fits squarely within the circumstances where private citizens have a right of action in federal court. Section 601 of Title VI of the Civil Rights Act of 1964 provides that "No person in the United States shall, on the grounds of race, color, or national origin, be excluded from participation in, be denied the benefits of, or be subjected to discrimination under any program or activity receiving Federal financial assistance."[30] Moreover, section 602 of Title VI authorizes and directs federal departments and agencies that extend federal financial assistance to particular program or activities to effectuate the provision of 2000d by issuing rules, regulations, or orders of general applicability.[31]

The Department of Education, in exercising statutory authority under section 602, promulgated such a regulation, which prohibits a funding recipient from "utiliz[ing] criteria or methods of administration which have the effect of subjecting individuals to discrimination because of their race, color, or national origin, or have the effect of defeating or substantially impairing accomplishment of the objectives of the program as respect individuals of a particular race, color, or national origin."[32] So any action alleging disparate

---

[29] *Id.* at 78 (citations omitted).

[30] Civil Rights Act of 1964, 42 U.S.C. § 2000d (1994).

[31] *Id.*

[32] 34 C.F.R. § 100.3(b)(2) (2000).

impact resulting from administration of the Arkansas Distinguished Scholarship Program [hereinafter Program] would be fairly based on the foregoing statutes and regulations prohibiting discriminatory effects in educational programs.

While it is well established that a private cause of action exists under § 601 of Title VI of the Civil Rights Act of 1964 to redress intentional discrimination,[33] the Supreme Court has never specifically ruled that a private right of action exists where regulations promulgated under § 602 have resulted in disparate impact as opposed to intentional discrimination.[34] In fact, in *Alexander v. Sandoval* the Supreme Court recently found there is no such private right of action under § 602, a decision referred to in the dissent as "unfounded in our precedent and hostile to decades of settled expectations."[35]

While this recent Supreme Court decision precludes a private cause of action for Arkansas plaintiffs under § 602, a viable claim under 42 U.S.C. § 1983 nevertheless still exists. In *South Camden Citizens in Action v. New Jersey Department of Environmental Protection*,[36] the United States District Court of New Jersey acknowledged the *Sandoval* ruling that no private right of action exists under § 602.[37] The *Camden* court went on to find that, "[I]t is equally clear that *Sandoval* did not address, nor does it affect, Plaintiffs' right to bring a claim for disparate impact discrimination in violation of the § 602 regulations under § 1983."[38]

With respect to whether the plaintiffs would have a claim under 42 U.S.C. § 1983, we begin with the statute:

---

[33] *Alexander v. Sandoval*, 121 S.Ct. 1511, 1516 (2001) (5–4 decision) (Stevens, J., dissenting).

[34] *Id.* at 124 (Stevens, J., dissenting).

[35] *Id.* at 124 (Stevens, J., dissenting).

[36] *Camden Citizens in Action v. N.J. Department of Environmental Protection*, 145 F. Supp. 2d 505, 518 (D.N.J. 2001).

[37] *Id.*

[38] *Id.*

Every person who, under color of any statute, ordinance, regulation, custom, or usage, of any State or Territory or the District
of Columbia, subjects, or causes to be subjected, any citizen of the
United States or other person within the jurisdiction thereof to the
deprivation of any rights, privileges, or immunities secured by the
Constitution and laws, shall be liable to the party injured in an action
at law, suit in equity, or other proper proceeding for redress.[39]

A § 1983 action has two essential elements: (1) that the conduct
complained of was committed by a person acting under color of state
law; and (2) that this conduct deprived a citizen or other person of
rights, privileges, or immunities secured by the Constitution or laws
of the United States.[40]

When a § 1983 plaintiff seeks damages against state officials in
their official or personal capacities, the action may be maintained
even if a named individual acted in his official capacities in the matter
at issue.[41] A "government official in the role of personal capacity ...
fits comfortably within the statutory term 'person.'"[42] The Supreme
Court has held that a state official sued for injunctive relief is a
person under § 1983 because the action of prospective relief is not
treated as a suit against the state.[43] "[A] state official in his official
capacity when sued for injunctive relief, would be a person under §
1983 because 'official-capacity actions for prospective relief are not
treated as actions against the State.'"[44]

Once a plaintiff has identified a federal right that has allegedly
been violated, there arises a "rebuttable presumption that the right is
enforceable under § 1983.[45] The presumption is rebutted "if Congress

---

[39] 42 U.S.C. § 1983 (1994 and Supp. 1999).

[40] See *Powell v. Ridge*, 189 F.3d 387, 400 (3d Cir. 1999).

[41] *Hafer v. Melo*, 502 U.S. 21, 27 (1991).

[42] *Id.* (quoting *Will v. Michigan Department of State Police*, 491 U.S. 58, 71
n.10 (1989)).

[43] *Will v. Michigan Department of State Police*, 491 U.S. 58, 71 n.10 (1989).

[44] *Id.* (quoting *Kentucky v. Graham*, 473 U.S. 159, 167 n.14 (1985)).

[45] *Blessing v. Freestone*, 520 U.S. 329, 341 (1997).

'specifically foreclosed a remedy under § 1983 ... [either] expressly, forbidding recourse to § 1983 in the statute itself, or impliedly, by creating a comprehensive enforcement scheme that is incompatible with individual enforcement under § 1983."[46]

Neither Title VI, nor the regulation promulgated there, restricts the availability of relief under § 1983. Thus, defendants must make the difficult showing that allowing a § 1983 action to go forward in these circumstances would be inconsistent with Congress's carefully tailored scheme.[47] Neither Title VI, nor the Department of Education regulations, establishes an elaborate procedural mechanism to protect the rights of plaintiffs.[48] Plaintiffs in such a case would have identified and pled disparate impact discrimination, the Fourteenth Amendment "evil" or wrong that Congress intended to remedy by Title VI.[49] It is thus clear that the propriety of the Section 5, Fourteenth Amendment legislation must be judged with reference to the historical reference of racial discrimination it reflects.[50] Consequently, given the historical record of racial discrimination in violation of the Fourteenth Amendment's Equal Protection Clause, arising from the State of Arkansas' Program, plaintiffs would be entitled to maintain their § 1983 action against the individual defendants pursuant to the enforcement provisions of the Fourteenth Amendment.

E. RIPENESS

The doctrine of ripeness poses the query of "whether the harm asserted has matured sufficiently to warrant judicial intervention."[51] The Supreme Court has held that the ripeness doctrine's purpose

---

[46] *Id.* (quoting *Smith v. Robinson*, 468 U.S. 992, 1005 n.9 (1984).

[47] *Blessing*, 520 U.S. at 341 (1997).

[48] *Id.*

[49] See *College Savings Bank v. Florida Prepaid Postsecondary Education Expense Board* 527 U.S. 627, 639–40 (1999).

[50] *Id.*

[51] *Sierra Club v. Marita*, 46 F.3d 606, 611 (7th Cir. 1995) (quoting *Warth v. Seldin*, 422 U.S. 480, 499 n.10 (1975)).

is "to prevent the courts, through avoidance of premature adjudication, from entangling themselves in abstract disagreements over administrative policies, and also to protect the agencies from judicial interference until an administrative decision has been formalized and its effects felt in a concrete way by the challenging parties."[52]

In *Columbia Broadcasting System v. United States*,[53] the Court held ripe for review a Federal Communications Commission regulation that pronounced that the agency would not license local stations that maintained certain contracts with chain broadcasting networks.[54] The Court stated, although the rule was only a statement of intentions and that no license had yet been denied or revoked, this type of regulation had the effect of law both before and after its sanctions were enforced.[55] The regulation could be challenged because expected conformity to the rule caused an injury that a court could recognize.

In *Frozen Food Express v. United States*,[56] an order of the Interstate Commerce Commission exempting vehicles that carried certain commodities from licensing regulations was held reviewable. The Court held that the order was a final agency action under the A.P.A. *Frozen Food* holds that "where there has been formal action, as the adoption of a regulation ... presumptively the action is reviewable."[57]

In *Abbot Laboratories*, the Supreme Court observed that "the cases dealing with judicial review of administrative action have interpreted the 'finality' element in a pragmatic way"[58] and concluded that there was no reason to deviate from those precedents. In that case,

---

[52] *Abbott Labs. v. Gardner*, 387 U.S. 136, 148–149 (1967).

[53] *Columbia Broad. Systems v. United States*, 316 U.S. 407 (1942).

[54] *Id.*

[55] *Id.*

[56] 351 U.S. 40, 44–45 (1956).

[57] Louis L. Jaffe, *Judicial Control of Administrative Action* 407 (1965).

[58] *Abbott Labs.*, 387 U.S. at 149.

regulations published by the Commissioner of Food and Drug were found to be a final agency action and, thus, subject to judicial review under the A.P.A. and the Declaratory Judgment Act.

F. FITNESS OF ISSUES FOR JUDICIAL REVIEW

The issues raised by the type of lawsuit contemplated by this paper are fit for judicial decision because Arkansas has enacted the Governor's Distinguished Scholarship program into law. This law, and the connected implementing regulations, has been in effect for a period of over three years. The critical and concrete factor dispositive of the issue of justiciabililty is that there has been formal action on the part of the Arkansas General Assembly, the Governor of Arkansas, and the Arkansas Department of Higher Education.[59] The law and DHE regulations have a concrete and lasting effect on the citizens of Arkansas. It is entirely appropriate that the state's formal action be reviewed by a court, particularly in light of the seriousness of the continuing disparate impact on minority citizens of the state.

G. HARDSHIPS TO THE PARTIES CAUSING ACTIONABLE HARM

A hardship has been suffered by plaintiffs because, as stated in *Columbia Broadcasting System v. United States*,[60] the "expected conformity" to the rule causes an injury that a court can recognize.[61] The authors of *Griggs v. Duke Power Co.*[62] and of *Connecticut v. Teal*[63] would be astonished if the continuing disparate impact on African Americans resulting from conformity to the present regulations of this program were not considered to cause them actionable harm.

An even stronger argument that harm has occurred to African American students in Arkansas because disparate impact is found

---

[59] See *Frozen Food*, 351 U.S. at 44–45.

[60] *Columbia Broad. Systems v. United States*, 316 U.S. 407 (1942).

[61] *Id.* at 418–19.

[62] 401 U.S. 424, 431 (1971).

[63] 457 U.S. 440, 448–49 (1982).

in a Pennsylvania school funding case. The Third Circuit, in *Powell v. Ridge*,[64] decided all the plaintiff must do is plead that the adverse effects of a facially neutral practice fall disproportionately on a group protected by Title VI and its implementing regulations.[65] That court cited *Guardians Association v. Civil Service Commission* for the proposition that administrative regulations incorporating disparate impact standards (like the regulations of the Department of Higher Education) are actionable.[66] The law and regulations are final, and the plaintiffs have suffered the egregious harm of disparate impact. Consequently, the matters raised in the complaint are ripe for judicial review. In a recent case, the Supreme Court held that a school official's deliberate indifference to discrimination amounted to an intentional violation of Title IX.[67]

H. VIOLATION OF THE ESTABLISHMENT CLAUSE

The First Amendment to the United States Constitution says "Congress shall make no law respecting an establishment of religion, or prohibiting the free exercise thereof."[68] It is settled that "the Fourteenth Amendment has rendered the legislatures of the states as incompetent as the Congress to enact such laws."[69] Consequently, the Arkansas General Assembly is constitutionally prohibited from enacting laws respecting an establishment of religion. But what sort of state action offends the Establishment Clause? Does the Distinguished Scholarship Program that provides for direct payment of state funds to private, church-related institutions of higher education offend the prohibitions of the First Amendment? The answer lies in the intent of the founders and the relevant cases.

---

[64] *Powell v. Ridge*, 189 F.3d 387 (3d Cir. 1999).

[65] *Id.* at 393.

[66] *Guardians Association v. Civil Service Commission*, 463 U.S. 582, 607 (1982).

[67] *Davis v. Monroe County Board of Education*, 526 U.S. 629, 653 (1999).

[68] U.S. Const. amend. I.

[69] *Cantwell v. Connecticut*, 310 U.S. 296, 303 (1940).

First, let us visit James Madison. Thomas Jefferson's famous letter about the separation of church and state to the Danbury Baptist Association is often cited as the primary authority regarding the intent of the Establishment Clause. However, two Madison veto messages and a letter to the Baptist Churches of Neal's Creek and Black Creek, North Carolina, are arguably more revealing of the intent of the writers of the Constitution and the First Amendment. Jefferson's letter reflected his concern over the establishment of a state religion. Madison's veto messages and letter dealt with situations like the Arkansas scholarship program and revealed his notion that religious societies should remain pure and apart from government influence.

In 1811, Congress passed a bill giving certain powers to an Episcopal Church in Virginia.[70] Among them was the authority to provide for the support of the poor, and the education of their children.[71] On February 11, 1811, President Madison returned the bill to Congress with a veto message. Madison argued that the government had no authority over the affairs of the church because of the Establishment Clause. He said the bill violated the Constitution because it "would be a precedent for giving religious societies, as such, a legal agency in carrying into effect a legal and public duty."[72] Again, in February, 1811, Madison vetoed another bill that, in part, reserved a parcel of government land in the Mississippi Territory for the Baptist Church at Salem Meeting House. He maintained that the bill violated the principle of the Establishment Clause prohibiting the use of government money to support religious societies.[73] Shortly thereafter, Madison received a letter from two Baptist churches in North Carolina indicating approval of his veto of the bill to provide support to the Mississippi Baptist church.[74] In his response, Madison wrote that "having regarded the practical distinction between

---

[70] 22 Annals of Cong. 982–85 (1853).

[71] *Id.*

[72] *Id.*

[73] *Id.*

[74] *Id.*

Religion and Civil Government as essential to the purity of both and as guaranteed by the Constitution of the United States, I could not have otherwise discharged my duty."[75]

It is clear that Madison believed that government possesses no authority to impose a duty or responsibility on a religious body. Nor is it authorized, as evidenced in the Baptist Church at Salem Meeting House matter, to use government funds to directly support a religious society. Madison believed that the Constitution granted the government absolutely no power over religion. Religion was to be entirely removed from governmental influence, and the best way to separate them is to forbid the government from imposing any responsibilities or duties on religious societies. To maintain this "purity," government was given no constitutional authority or cause to directly support religious societies. This attitude arose not from hostility to religion, but from a desire to protect it from the heavy hand of government regulation. Why? Because we know that government regulation follows government funds. What better witness than Madison himself?

How has the Supreme Court dealt with this issue? In *Lemon v. Kurtzman*, the Supreme Court announced a three-pronged test to determine whether the Establishment Clause had been violated.[76] According to *Lemon*, a statute does not violate the Establishment Clause when: (1) it has a secular legislative purpose; (2) its primary effect neither advances nor inhibits religion; and (3) it does not excessively entangle government with religion.[77] In *Lemon*, the Court considered a Pennsylvania statute that authorized the state to "[purchase] certain 'secular educational services' from nonpublic schools, directly reimbursing those schools solely for teacher salaries, textbooks, and instructional materials."[78] Most of the schools were

---

[75] *Id.*

[76] *Lemon v. Kurtzman*, 403 U.S. 602, 612–13 (1971).

[77] *Id.*

[78] *Id.* at 602 (citations omitted).

affiliated with the Roman Catholic Church.[79] These schools were subject to state audit and had to "identify the 'separate' cost of the 'secular educational service'" to receive reimbursement.[80]

Here, the Court decided that the State statute violated the Establishment Clause because "schools seeking reimbursement must maintain accounting procedures that require the State to establish the cost of the secular as distinguished from the religious instruction."[81] The court then warned of the dangers of providing state financial aid directly to a church-related school citing *Waltz v. Tax Commission*[82] for the proposition that "obviously, a direct money subsidy would be a relationship pregnant with involvement and, as with most government grant programs, could encompass sustained and detailed administrative relationships for enforcement of statutory or administrative standards."[83]

According to the Supreme Court, the history of government grants reveals that they typically result in various measures of government control and surveillance.[84] Here, the state's power to audit, inspect, and evaluate a church-related school's expenditures creates an intimate and continuing relationship between church and state.[85] The Pennsylvania arrangement violated the First Amendment because the intent of the Establishment Clause is to protect religion from government interference or supervision.[86] Direct payments and state supervision would certainly violate Mr. Madison's expressed "purity" view of the proper relationship between church-related schools and the state.

---

[79] *Id.*

[80] *Id.* at 609–10.

[81] *Id.* at 620.

[82] *Waltz v. Tax Commission*, 397 U.S. 664, 675 (1970).

[83] *Lemon*, 403 U.S. at 621.

[84] *Id.*

[85] *Id.* at 621–22.

[86] *Id.* at 623.

In *Committee for Public Education and Religious Liberty v. Nyquist*,[87] the Supreme Court dealt with a program that provided direct money grants to certain nonpublic schools for the following: repair and maintenance; reimbursements to low-income parents for a portion of the cost of private school tuition, including sectarian school tuition; and granting to other parents certain tax benefits.[88] The Justices decided that the maintenance and repair provisions of the New York statute violated the Establishment Clause because its effect was to subsidize and advance the religious mission of sectarian schools.[89] The Court also held that the tuition reimbursement plans, if given directly to sectarian schools, would similarly violate the Establishment Clause.[90] This was notwithstanding the fact that the grants were delivered to the parents rather than the schools, as the effect of the aid is unmistakably to provide financial support for nonpublic sectarian institutions.[91]

The *Nyquist* holding concerning payments to parents was substantially weakened with respect to vouchers by *Agostini v. Felton*.[92] Here, the Supreme Court stated, "we have departed from the rule … that all government aid that directly aids the educational function of religious schools is invalid."[93] The Court rejected the argument that government and religion are too closely linked merely because a school voucher program transfers money from the government to sectarian schools.[94] It stated, "we reject the argument, primarily because funds cannot reach a sectarian school unless the parents or

---

[87] *Commission for Public Education and Religious Liberty v. Nyquist* 413 U.S. 756 (1973).

[88] *Id.* at 756–57.

[89] *Id.* at 779–80.

[90] *Id.* at 780.

[91] *Id.*

[92] 521 U.S. 203 (1997).

[93] *Id.* at 225.

[94] *Id.* at 226.

student decide independently of the government, to send their child to a sectarian school."[95]

Consequently, *Agostini* supports the proposition that when parents or students choose to use funds provided to them by the state to attend a church-related school, the Establishment Clause is not offended. This is because the state funds are paid to the student or parent rather than directly to the church-related school. The state, then, has no call to compel a church-related school to perform administrative tasks for it, or submit to its audit. This benefit-to-the-parent approach (allowing a tax deduction for parents for certain educational expenses whether they were incurred in private, church-related or public schools) is also seen in *Mueller v. Allen*.[96] The Court stressed that all the decisions invalidating aid to parochial schools have involved direct transmission of assistance from the states to the schools themselves.[97] However, the decision left the *Nyquist* prohibition of aid "directly" paid to a church-related school unaffected.

In *School District of the City of Grand Rapids v. Ball*[98] the Supreme Court dealt with a district that adopted a shared time and community education program with nonpublic schools.[99] The program was conducted for nonpublic school children at state expense in classrooms located in, and leased from, the private schools. It offered state-funded classes during the regular school day that were intended to supplement, for the private school students, the "core curriculum" courses required by the state.[100] The shared-time teachers were full-time employees of public schools.[101] Of the forty-one private schools involved in the program, forty were church related.[102]

---

[95] *Id.* at 230.

[96] *Mueller v. Allen*, 463 U.S. 338 (1983).

[97] *Id.* at 399.

[98] *School District Of Grand Rapids v. Ball*, 473 U.S. 373 (1984).

[99] *Id.*

[100] *Id.* at 375.

[101] *Id.* at 376.

[102] *Id.* at 379.

The Supreme Court decided that this initiative had the "primary or principal" effect of advancement of religion, and, therefore, violated the Establishment Clause.[103] According to the Justices, even the praiseworthy secular purpose of providing for the education of school children "cannot validate government aid to parochial schools when the aid has the effect of promoting a single religion or religion generally or when the aid unduly entangles the government in matters religious."[104] They said:

> The symbolic union of church and state inherent in the provision of secular state-provided public instruction in the religious school buildings threatens to convey a message of state support for religion to students and to the general public ... the programs in effect subsidize the religious functions of the parochial schools by taking over a substantial portion of their responsibility.[105]

The Court also said that the Establishment Clause "rests on the belief that a union of government and religion tends to destroy government and degrade religion."[106] Clearly, the most instructive case for our purposes is *Witters v. Washington Department of Services for the Blind.*[107] In *Witters*, the Supreme Court ruled on the denial of funds to Mr. Witters under the state of Washington's vocational rehabilitation program for the visually handicapped.[108] The funds were sought to finance petitioner's training at a Christian college.[109] The record showed that, were assistance provided to Mr. Witters, the funds would have gone directly to the student, who would then have transmitted them to the educational institution of his choice.[110]

---

[103] *Id.* at 379.

[104] *Id.* at 382.

[105] *Ball*, 473 U.S. at 397.

[106] *Id.* at 398.

[107] 474 U.S. 481 (1986).

[108] *Id.*

[109] *Id.* at 482.

[110] *Id.* at 487.

The Washington statute authorized the state to "'provide for special education and/or training in the professions, business or trades' so as to 'assist visually handicapped persons to overcome vocational handicaps and to obtain the maximum degree of self-support and self-care.'"[111] Mr. Witters, who suffered from a progressive eye disease, was eligible for vocational rehabilitation assistance under the terms of the statute. He attended Inland Empire School of the Bible, a private Christian College in Spokane, Washington.[112] He was studying the "Bible, ethics, speech, and Church administration in order to equip himself for a career as a pastor, missionary, or youth director."[113]

The Washington court ruled that the "principal or primary effect" of the state financial assistance to Witters was to train him to become a pastor, missionary, or church youth director.[114] In the view of the court, the state aid clearly had the primary effect of advancing religion and violated the Establishment Clause.[115] On appeal, the Supreme Court reversed this decision. It said:

> It is well settled that the Establishment Clause is not violated every time money previously in the possession of a State is conveyed to a religious institution. For example, a State may issue a paycheck to one of its employees, who may then donate all or part of that paycheck to a religious institution, all without constitutional barrier; and the State may do so even knowing that the employee so intends to dispose of his salary.[116]

The Court continued, "[i]t is equally well settled, on the other hand, that the State may not grant aid to a religious school, whether

---

[111] *Witters*, 474 U.S. at 483 (quoting Wash. Rev. Code § 74.16.181(1981)).

[112] *Id.*

[113] *Id.*

[114] *Id.* at 485.

[115] *Id.* at 484–85.

[116] *Id.* at 486–87.

cash or in kind, where the effect of the aid is 'that of a direct subsidy to the religious school' from the State."[117] The issue "is whether, on the facts ... [the] extension of aid to petitioner and the use of that aid by petitioner to support religious education is a permissible transfer similar to the hypothetical salary donation described above, or is an impermissible *direct* subsidy."[118]

In the opinion of the United States Supreme Court, the facts central to the inquiry in the *Witters* case were the following: whether "[a]ny aid provided under Washington's program that ultimately flows to religious institutions does so only as a result of the genuinely independent and private choices of aid recipients";[119] that "it is not one of 'the ingenious plans for channeling state aid to sectarian schools that periodically reach this Court'";[120] that "[i]t creates no financial incentive for students to undertake sectarian education";[121] that "[it] does not tend to provide greater or broader benefits for recipients who apply their aid to religious education";[122] and that "[in] this case, the fact that aid goes to individuals means that the decision to support religious education is made by the individual, not the State."[123]

Importantly, "nothing in the record indicates that ... any significant portion of the aid expended under the Washington program as a whole will end up flowing to religious education."[124] The Court stated, "*amici* supporting respondent are correct in pointing out that aid to a religious institution unrestricted in its potential uses, if properly attributable to

---

[117] *Witters*, 474 U.S. at 487 (quoting *School District of Grand Rapids v. Ball*, 473 U.S. 373, 394 (1985)).

[118] *Id.*

[119] *Id.*

[120] *Id.* at 488 (quoting *Nyquist*, 413 U.S. 756, 782–83, n.38 (1973)).

[121] *Id.* (quoting *Nyquist*, 413 U.S. at 785–86).

[122] *Witters*, 474 U.S. at 488.

[123] *Id.*

[124] *Id.*

the State, is 'clearly prohibited under the Establishment Clause.'"[125] But the respondent's argument did not apply in that case because there was no *direct aid* to the religious school.[126] The Court decided, on the facts presented, the Washington program did not constitute sufficiently direct support of religion so as to violate the Establishment Clause.[127] Justice Powell, concurring, said that the Washington scheme was constitutionally permitted because the student or parent directly received the State payments. He cited *Mueller v. Allen* for the proposition that payments directly to parents are constitutional because any benefit to religion results from "numerous private choices of individual parents of school-age children."[128]

Before we turn to the Arkansas scholarship program, it will be helpful to review the common threads woven through these cases that bind them together. First, requiring church-related schools to maintain administrative and accounting procedures for review by the state offends the Establishment Clause.[129] Second, payment of financial aid directly to a church-related school offends the Establishment Clause.[130] Third, when there is a disparity in the amount of state funds spent on public and church-related students, the Establishment Clause is offended.[131] Fourth, the Establishment Clause is offended if the scholarship program creates a financial incentive for the student to attend a church-related school.[132] Finally, perhaps the most troubling issue is whether the Arkansas Program is

---

[125] *Id.* at 489 (quoting *School District of Grand Rapids*, 473 U.S. at 395).

[126] *Id.*

[127] *Id.*

[128] *Mueller* at 388, 399.

[129] *Lemon*, 403 U.S. 602, 620 (1971); *Agostini v. Felton*, 521 U.S. 203, 221–22 (1997).

[130] *Lemon*, 403 U.S. at 607; *Nyquist*, 413 U.S. 756, 779–80 (1973); *School District of Grand Rapids*, 473 U.S. at 397; *Mueller*, 463 U.S. at 400; *Witters*, 474 U.S. at 487; see also *Waltz*, 397 U.S. 664, 675 (1970).

[131] See *Witters*, 474 U.S. at 488.

[132] *Id.*

an ingenious scheme designed to channel state aid directly to church-related schools, a practice condemned by the decision in *Committee For Public Education and Religious Liberty v. Nyquist.*[133]

I. ARKANSAS LAW AND THE ESTABLISHMENT CLAUSE

The State of Arkansas attempts to cloak itself in the recent case of *Mitchell v. Helms.*[134] Unfortunately for the State of Arkansas, the cloak does not fit because the *Mitchell* case concerned Chapter II of the Education Consolidation and Improvement Act of 1981.[135] Chapter II channels federal funds to the local educational agencies, which are usually public school districts, through state educational agencies, to implement programs to assist children in elementary and secondary schools. Among other things, Chapter II provides aid for "the acquisition and use of instructional and educational materials, including library services and materials (including media materials), assessments, reference materials, computer software and hardware for instructional use, and other curricular materials."[136] In effect, the Chapter II program was a neutral, per capita aid program. In sharp contrast, however, the Arkansas scholarship program is clearly not a per capita aid program.

Further, as Justice O'Connor highlights in her concurring opinion, Justice Thomas, writing for the *Mitchell* plurality, did not even consider issues important and decisive to Arkansas plaintiffs.[137] The issues for litigation in Arkansas are: whether any aid provided under the Arkansas program that ultimately flows to a religious institution does so only as a result of the genuinely independent private choices of scholarship recipients; whether or not the program is one of the ingenious plans for channeling state aid to sectarian schools that periodically occur; whether or not it creates a financial incentive

---

[133] See *Nyquist*, 413 U.S. at 785; *Witters*, 474 U.S. at 488.

[134] 530 U.S. 793 (2000).

[135] 20 U.S.C. § 7301–7373 (1994).

[136] 20 U.S.C. § 7351(b)(2) (1994).

[137] *Mitchell v. Helms*, 530 U.S. 793 (2000) at 841 (O'Connor, J., concurring).

for students to undertake sectarian education; and whether or not it intends to provide greater or broader benefits for recipients who apply their aid to religious institutions.

As Justice O'Connor wrote in concurring with the plurality in *Mitchell*, "Specifically, we decided *Witters* and *Zobrest* on the understanding that the aid was provided directly to the individual student who, in turn, made the choice of where to put that aid to use. ... Accordingly, our approval of the aid in both cases relied to a significant extent on the fact that '[a]ny aid ... that ultimately flows to religious institutions does so only as a result of the genuinely independent and private choices of aid recipients.'"[138]

Justice O'Connor continued by saying she believed that the distinction between a per capita school aid program and a true private choice program is significant for the purposes of endorsement.[139] "In terms of public perception, a government program of direct aid to religious schools based on the number of students attending each school differs meaningfully from the government distributing aid directly to individual students who, in turn, decide to use the aid at the same religious schools."[140]

Finally, Justice O'Connor wrote that "the distinction between a per capita aid program and a true private-choice program is important when considering aid that consists of direct monetary subsidies."[141] The Supreme Court has recognized special Establishment Clause dangers when the government makes direct money payments to sectarian institutions.[142] Consequently, there are important distinctions between the issue dealt with in the *Mitchell* case and the line of cases finding direct payments of state monies to church-related institutions offensive to the Establishment Clause.

---

[138] *Id.* (quoting *Witters*, 474 U.S. at 487).

[139] *Id.* at 482.

[140] *Id.* at 842–43.

[141] *Id.* at 843.

[142] *Id.*

A reasonable conclusion is that the Arkansas Distinguished Scholarship Program violates the Establishment Clause for a wide variety of reasons. First, the program requires church-related institutions to agree to perform administrative tasks and ensure compliance with state regulations.[143] The institution must submit to a review of its records and demonstrate its due diligence as a *steward of state funds*.[144] One would reasonably believe that the administrators of church schools would strongly object to the grubby hands of state officials thumbing through their private school files. Does this mean they agree to have the Legislative Audit look at their books? Apparently, yes! In any case, the regulations clearly offend the Establishment Clause holdings that the state may not compel religious societies to perform state administrative tasks.[145]

Second, the state funds are paid directly to church-related institutions.[146] This direct aid offends the Establishment Clause.[147] If there is one thing certain under all these cases, it is that state money paid directly to a church-related school is unconstitutional. This is so because the scholarship funds are a direct subsidy condemned in all the cases cited. This issue was not even raised in *Mitchell*.[148]

Third, there is a considerable disparity between the amount of state funds per distinguished scholarship provided church-related institutions and public institutions under the program. Recall that, for example, Hendrix will typically receive $15,000 and Southern Arkansas $4,730 per scholarship student.[149] There is also a disparity

---

[143] Revised Rules and Regulations for the Arkansas Governor's Scholarship Program, D.H.E. Rule 56.1.H (2001).

[144] *Id.*

[145] *Lemon*, 403 U.S. 602, 620–22 (1971).

[146] Revised Rules and Regulations for the Arkansas Governor's Scholarship Program, D.H.E. Rule 5.1.A.

[147] *Lemon*, 403 U.S. at 621; *Waltz*, 397 U.S. 664, 675 (1970); *Nyquist*, 413 U.S. 756, 780 (1973); *Witters*, 474 U.S. 481, 487 (1986).

[148] *Mitchell.*

[149] See generally Ark. Code Ann. § 6-82-312(b) (Michie Supp. 1999) (establishing guidelines for calculating scholarship amounts).

in the total funds sent to private and public schools. Church-related schools received $2,182,000 and public institutions $1,334,000 in the years 1998–99.[150] This disparity in treatment of public and church-related institutions offends the Establishment Clause.[151]

Fourth, the program creates a financial incentive for the Distinguished Scholarship student to attend a church-related school because the program provides more funds to do so. The state formerly paid whatever the church-related institution considered a reasonable level of tuition and fees, and now only caps that amount at $10,000.[152] The state sponsored creation of a considerable financial incentive to attend a church-related school is offensive to the Establishment Clause.[153]

Finally, the distinguished scholarship program, if newspaper reports are accurate, may be a scheme to channel state aid directly to church-related schools, offending the Establishment Clause under *Witters*.[154] This is most disturbing. According to Doug Smith, the impetus for the distinguished scholars program did not emanate from the Department of Higher Education.[155] Rather, state senators proposed it.[156] The legislation that came back was not that proposed to the General Assembly by the DHE. The DHE had little choice because thirty-five senators sponsored the enabling legislation. One of its sponsors is quoted as stating that the bill was brought to him by the President of the Independent Colleges and Universities Association, and by the Association's lobbyist.[157] This certainly raises the

---

[150] *Id.*

[151] *Witters*, 474 U.S. at 487.

[152] Ark. Code Ann. § 6-82-312(b), (Michie 1996 and Supp. 1999), amended by 2001 Ark. Acts 1761.

[153] *Witters*, 474 U.S. at 487.

[154] *Id.*

[155] Doug Smith, "Pushing and Shoving For the State's Top Scholars," *Arkansas Times*, (August 27, 1999), p. 13.

[156] *Id.*

[157] *Id.*

issue of a scheme to support religious schools. It will be interesting to see why the Association would want the State rummaging around in their private, church-related educational programs to determine stewardship of state funds. The North Carolina Baptists who wrote to Mr. Madison would surely be offended.[158]

Mr. Madison would be saddened by the abuse of his Amendment on the part of the DHE of the State of Arkansas. His two veto messages, and letter to the Baptist Churches of Neal's Creek and Black Creek, North Carolina, in 1811, sent a powerful message that government has no (none at all) business regulating a religious society, giving a religious society legal agency to carry into effect a public duty, or giving direct aid to a religious society.[159] The Arkansas Distinguished Scholars Scholarship Program has the unique and dubious distinction of offending all of Madison's notions of separation of religion from influence and regulation by the government.

This was not so because of hostility toward religion but rather to protect religion from the government. He believed that the Constitution granted government no power over religion. It surely follows, as in the Arkansas example, that when a religious society accepts government funds in this manner, the heavy hand of government regulation is sure to follow.[160] It makes no Constitutional difference that church-related schools volunteer for regulation. It still offends the Constitution!

POLITICAL PHILOSOPHY

In this section, we will review the issue of discrimination from a libertarian point of view. We will utilize that perspective in order to focus on the issue of whether the government should be allowed to discriminate between its citizens, and if so, on what basis. In this section, we take a much broader perspective than that of the Constitution as it applies to racial discrimination by the government in the field of education in one state. We apply this theory, generally,

---

[158] See 22 Annals of Cong. 982–85 (1853).

[159] *Id.*

[160] *Id.*

to all discrimination, be it federal, state, or local government, in any field, on any basis.

A. LIBERTARIANISM

Since we shall be applying libertarianism to this thorny terrain, it behooves us to begin with a review of that philosophy. Libertarianism is the political philosophy which maintains that justice can only be attained by an adherence to the non-aggression axiom: all acts are legitimate, except those that transgress against a person or his legitimately owned property. That is, murder, kidnapping, rape, theft, trespass, fraud, assault and battery, and all such other invasive acts should be illegal, but no other deeds should be prohibited by law. Included in the latter category are victimless crimes such as pornography, prostitution, gambling, drug abuse, homosexuality, etc.[161]

What is the proper role of government in this system? For most libertarians, it consists solely of the duty to protect persons and property from invasion.[162]

---

[161] See Walter Block, *Defending the Undefendable* (1985); Walter Block, "Libertarianism vs. Libertinism," *Journal of Libertarian Studies* 11 (1994): 117.

[162] For some, there is no legitimate role for the government at all. On this, see Terry L. Anderson and P.J. Hill, "An American Experiment in Anarcho-Capitalism: The Not So Wild, Wild West," *Journal of Libertarian Studies* 3 (1979): 9; Randy E. Barnett, *The Structure of Liberty: Justice and the Rule of Law* (1988); Bruce L. Benson, "Enforcement of Private Property Rights in Primitive Societies: Law without Government," *Journal of Libertarian Studies* 9 (1989): 1, 1–26; Bruce L. Benson, "The Impetus for Recognizing Private Property and Adopting Ethical Behavior in a Market Economy: Natural Law, Government Law, or Evolving Self-Interest?" *Review of Austrian Economics* 6 (1993): 43; Bruce L. Benson, To Serve and Protect (1998); Bruce L. Benson, "The Spontaneous Evolution of Commercial Law," *Southern Journal of Economics* 55 (1989): 644, 644–661; Bruce L. Benson, *The Enterprise of Law: Justice Without the State* (1990); Alfred G. Cuzan, "Do We Ever Really Get Out of Anarchy?" *Journal of Libertarian Studies* 3 (1979): 151; Anthony de Jasay, *The State* (1985); Anthony de Jasay, *Against Politics: On Government, Anarchy, and Order* (1997); David Friedman, *The Machinery of Freedom: Guide to a Radical Capitalism* (1989); David Friedman, "Private Creation and Enforcement of Law: A Historical Case,"

Given that government should exist at all, there are three, but only three, legitimate state institutions: armies to keep foreign aggressors from attacking us; police to quell crimes emanating from local evil doers; and courts to distinguish between victims and criminals.[163]

Journal of Legal Studies 8 (1979): 399, 399–415; Hans-Hermann Hoppe, *A Theory of Socialism and Capitalism: Economics, Politics, and Ethics* (1989); Hans-Hermann Hoppe, *The Economics and Ethics of Private Property: Studies in Political Economy and Philosophy* (1993); Hans-Hermann Hoppe, "The Private Production of Defense," *Journal of Libertarian Studies* 14 (1998–99): 27; Jeffrey Rogers Hummel, "National Goods Versus Public Goods: Defense, Disarmament, and Free Riders," *Review of Austrian Economics* 4 (1990): 88; James J. Martin, *Men Against the State: The Expositors of Individualist Anarchism in America 1827–1908* (1970); Andrew P. Morris, "Miners, Vigilantes, and Cattlemen: Overcoming Free Rider Problems in the Private Provision of Law," *Land and Water Law Review* 33 (1998): 581, 581–696; Franz Oppenheimer, *The State* (1914); Murray N. Rothbard, *For A New Liberty* (1978); Murray N. Rothbard, *The Ethics of Liberty* (1982); Murray N. Rothbard, "Society Without a State," in *Anarchism: Nomos XIX* (1978), p. 191; Murray N. Rothbard, *Man, Economy, and State* (1993); Aeon J. Skoble, "The Anarchism Controversy," in *Liberty for the 21st Century: Essays in Contemporary Libertarian Thought* (1995), p. 71; Larry J. Sechrest, "Rand, Anarchy, and Taxes," *Journal of Ayn Rand Studies* 1 (1999): 87, 87–105; Lysander Spooner, *No Treason* (1966); Edward Stringham, "Market Chosen Government," *Journal of Libertarian Studies* 14 (1998): 53, 53–77; Patrick Tinsley, "With Liberty and Justice for All: A Case for Private Police," *Journal of Libertarian Studies* 14 (1998): 95; Tennehill, et al., *The Market for Liberty* (1984); William C. Woolridge, *Uncle Sam the Monopoly Man* (1970).

[163] On limited government libertarianism as defined above, see *The Libertarian Reader* (1982); Tibor Machan, "Against Non-Libertarian Natural Rights," *Journal of Libertarian Studies* 2 (1978): 233; Tibor Machan, *Capitalism and Individualism* (1990); Ludwig von Mises,.*The Anti-Capitalist Mentality* (1972); Ludwig von Mises, *Bureaucracy* (1969); Ludwig von Mises, *Omnipotent Government* (1969); Ludwig von Mises, *Socialism* (1969); Ludwig von Mises, *Theory and History* (1957); Charles Murray, *What It Means to be a Libertarian* (1997); Robert Nozick, *Anarchy, State, and Utopia* (1974); Leonard E. Read, *Awake for Freedom's Sake* (1977); Leonard E. Read, *Anything that's Peaceful* (1964).

There are still other writers who characterize themselves as libertarians but allow greater scope for government than courts, armies, and police. For such styled libertarians see Tom Bethell, *The Noblest Triumph: Property*

B. DISCRIMINATION

Whichever of the two versions of this philosophy is under discussion, both are united on the proposition of free association: all interaction between people shall be voluntary; no one should be forced to deal with another person against his will. Thus, discrimination against certain individuals or groups or segments of society would also be considered a "victimless crime." Since no one has a right to force anyone to interact with him against the will of the latter, it would be no crime under libertarian law to refuse to buy from, sell to, employ, marry, befriend, join, or in any other way whether commercial or personal, interact with people on the basis of race, religion, sex, or, indeed, any other criteria.

This implies that all laws which seek to compel people to engage with one another, such as the so-called Civil Rights Act of 1964, would be invalid under libertarian law.[164] If the authors of this article

---

and Prosperity through the Ages (1998); David Boaz and Edward H. Crane, *Beyond the Status Quo* (1985); David Boaz, *Libertarianism: A Primer* (1997); Richard A. Epstein, *Simple Rules for a Complex World* (1995); Milton Friedman, "Alleviation of Poverty and Social Welfare Measures," in *The Economics of American Poverty: An American Paradox* (1965); Milton Friedman, *Capitalism and Freedom* (1962); Milton Friedman and Rose Friedman, *Free to Choose* (1980); Milton Friedman, *Money Mischief: Episodes in Monetary History* (1992); Milton Friedman, *There's No Such Thing as a Free Lunch* (1975); Milton Friedman and Rose Friedman, *Tyranny of the Status Quo* (1983); James D. Gwartney and Richard L. Stroup, *What Everyone Should Know about Economics and Prosperity* (1993); Richard Pipes, *Property and Freedom* (1999).

[164] For the libertarian case in opposition to the criminalization of discrimination, see Walter Block, "Compromising the Uncompromisable: Discrimination," *American Journal of Economics and Sociology* 57 (1998): 223; Walter Block, "Discrimination: An Interdisciplinary Analysis," *Journal of Business Ethics* 11 (1992): 241; Richard Epstein, *Forbidden Grounds* (1992); Linda Gottfredson, "The Practical Significance of Black-White Differences in Intelligence," *Behavioral and Brain Science* 10 (1987): 510; Linda Gottfredson, "Reconsidering Fairness: A Matter of Social and Ethical Priorities," *Journal of Vocational Behavior* 33 (1988): 293; Richard Hernstein and Charles Murray, *The Bell Curve* (1994); Michael Levin, "Comparable Worth: The

believed that left handers are the spawn of the devil, and placed a sign on the front door of their hotel[165] reading "No dogs or left handed people allowed on the premises," we would not be subjected to any legal penalty under the libertarian code of law.[166]

Private discrimination, however, must be sharply differentiated from the public variety. *Individual citizens*, in this view, have the right to freedom of association. This is so important it deserves to be emphasized. To say that they do not have the freedom to associate with whomever they wish is actually to claim the legitimacy of outright slavery. For the only thing wrong with that "curious institution" was that it violated the rights of freedom of association of the slaves. Forget about the whips and the chains. There is nothing unique about these to slavery; sado-masochists engage in their use every day. The problem with slavery was that its victims had no right to quit; that is, to *disassociate* themselves from their masters. If they but had a right to free association, this would render slavery innocuous. It would reduce it to no worse than the status of voluntary sado-masochism.

But government is not an individual person, with rights to associate with those it wishes to, and to avoid those with whom it wishes to

---

Feminist Road to Socialism," *Commentary* 78 (1984): 13; Michael Levin, *Feminism and Freedom* (1987); Michael Levin, "Why Race Matters: A Preview," *Journal of Libertarian Studies* 12 (1996): 287; Michael Levin, *Why Race Matters: Race Differences and What They Mean* (1997); Charles Murray, "Affirmative Racism," *The New Republic*, Dec. 1984, p. 18; Charles Murray, *What It Means to be a Libertarian* (1997); Jan Narveson, "Have We a Right to Non-Discrimination?" in *Business Ethics in Canada* (1987); Robert Nozick, *Anarchy, State, and Utopia* (1974); Murray N. Rothbard, *For a New Liberty* (1973); J. Philippe Rushton, "Race Differences in Behaviour: A Review and Evolutionary Analysis," *Personality and Individual Difference* 9 (1988): 1009; Daniel Seligman, *A Question of Intelligence: The IQ Debate in America* (1992).

[165] Our critics might think that a good name for this hotel, in view of our last names, would be "Chez Blockhead."

[166] The same goes for Jews, blacks, homosexuals, females, old people, young people, or any other supposedly "victimized" groups.

have no interaction. Very much to the contrary, the state has responsibilities, not rights.

If the limited government and anarchist wings of libertarianism
are united on the claim that private individuals or groups have a
complete and total right to discriminate on any basis they choose,
and against any group or individual they wish, both would also agree
that government, if it is justified at all, should *not* be allowed to do
so.[167] The point here is that the purpose of the state is to protect the
lives, liberties, and fortunes of all of its citizens, and on a basis that
does not distinguish between them. Government, in this philosophy,
is not only to be blind to the race, color, natural or ethnic origin,
religion, sex, disability, age, sexual orientation, or veteran status, the
usual suspects, but is to totally ignore *all* other criteria as well.[168] For
example, the state must not discriminate on the basis of intelligence,
athletic ability, eye color, business acumen, initiative and ambition,
unless these characteristics are somehow related to conducting its
business of protecting personal or property rights.

Let us consider a few examples. First, as mentioned above,[169] the
State of Arkansas provides a full academic scholarship to a state-
approved public or private Arkansas institution of higher education
for graduates of Arkansas secondary schools who demonstrate
"extraordinary academic ability."[170] Previously, we criticized this
policy on the ground that a disproportionately high number of the

---

[167] We shall henceforth consider the views of the minarchists, or limited-
government advocates alone, so as to obviate for argument's sake the point
made by the anarchist libertarians, that government should not exist at all.

[168] There is only one exception to this general rule. If the legitimate function of
the government pertains to any of these distinctions, then that may be taken
into account. For example, if the police must infiltrate the Mafia, it cannot
ask a black cop to do so; for the Bloods or the Crips, a Jewish officer simply
will not do; if the police must send someone in to spy on a gang of criminals
composed of females, or lesbians, a male is counter indicated.

[169] See text accompanying note 1.

[170] See text accompanying note 1.

members of one racial group wins these scholarships, whites, and a disproportionately low number of another, blacks, fail to do so.

We are now in a position to criticize this scholarship plan on a much more radical basis. Even if the *same* proportion of whites and blacks won these scholarships, the program would *still* be contrary to libertarian law, since it would continue to make invidious comparisons between inept and brilliant students, awarding tax money to virtually all of the latter and none to the former.[171]

That is to say, even if the program were not problematic on racial grounds, it would be so on the basis of intelligence. The scholarships would be awarded to smart students of either race, while ignorant students of both races would be victimized by state discrimination. But where is the warrant for governments to divide the population on the basis of intelligence, supporting those who exhibit this characteristic to a great degree and ignoring those who do not?[172] There is no such justification. If it is illegitimate for the government to discriminate on the basis of IQ, then it may not give out scholarships on this basis. If it wishes to award scholarships to students, it must do so in an actuarially "fair" way, for example, by lottery.

The same goes for entrance requirements at public universities. They are also part of the apparatus of government. If the state is prohibited by libertarian law from awarding scholarships on the basis of perspicaciousness, then colleges cannot do this either, nor can they pick and choose among applicants for admission on

---

[171] We abstract from the question of whether or not the testing instrument accurately distinguishes the one group from the other, assuming for the sake of argument that it does.

[172] See Robert B. Reich, "How Selective Colleges Heighten Income Inequality," *Chronicle of Higher Education Review*, http://www.prospect.org/. Mr. Reich criticizes analogous policies (elite universities accepting only very sharp-witted students) because they increase income inequality. This reason should be sharply distinguished from our own: that awarding scholarships to the "best and the brightest" is an instance of statist discrimination. In our view, private citizens, in sharp contrast to governmental agencies, are entirely justified in acting in ways which increase income inequality.

this basis. It cannot be denied that the University of California at Berkeley,[173] for example, would lose its reputation for prestige under these conditions. However, it is no part of libertarian law to preserve or enhance the renown of institutions such as these which are illegitimate in the first place. Short of complete privatization of state colleges, reducing their level of excellence would be entirely acceptable from the perspective of this political philosophy.

The point is, if something is illegitimate at its core, as public education is from the libertarian perspective, but somehow we stipulate that it must exist, then it is a positive benefit for it be run as *inefficiently* as possible. True, it would be the death knell for prestigious public institutions of higher learning to be forced not to discriminate in favor of the highly intelligent. But this is precisely what is required by considerations of justice. If an institution should not exist at all, but somehow persists, then equity entails that it be *ineffective*.[174]

Let us now consider the characteristic of athletic ability. It is a well-known fact[175] that, with the exception of a few sports such as swimming and diving, yachting, hockey, and handball, blacks exceed whites in terms of athleticism.[176] Certainly, in football and basketball, whether at the college or professional level, blacks are vastly over-represented.[177] Therefore, the logic of our case against the

---

[173] What about ostensibly "private" institutions of higher learning such as Harvard, Yale, and Columbia? These, too, would be considered public in that an inordinate percentage of their budgets emanate from coercive tax levies.

[174] For the application of this argument to Nazi concentration camps, and the voluntary army employed to support an unjust war, see Walter Block, "Against the Volunteer Military," *Libertarian Forum*, August 15, 1969, p. 4.

[175] See Thomas Sowell, *The Vision of the Anointed* (1995), p. 35: "No one regards the gross disparity in 'representation' between blacks and whites in professional basketball as proving discrimination against whites in that sport." See also Jon Entine, *Taboo: Why Black Athletes Dominate Sports, and Why We're Afraid to Talk about it* (2000).

[176] See, e.g., *White Men Can't Jump* (20th Century Fox, 1992). Also, "white man's disease" is now common parlance in basketball circles, and refers to the inability of white men to jump high for rebounds, blocks, or slam-dunks.

[177] See below Appendix 1.

Governor's Scholarship Program of Arkansas based on intelligence mitigates against any and all athletic scholarship awards on the part of all state institutions. If the academic scholarships favor whites at the expense of blacks, and must therefore be rescinded, then athletic scholarships that elevate blacks to the detriment of whites must be repealed on the same ground.

Furthermore, just as we were able to offer a more radical critique of the Governor's Scholarship Program in that it disadvantaged the ignorant, so can we criticize all athletic scholarships in that they discriminate against those who are inept in sports. That is, even if it were the case that blacks and whites won athletic scholarships in exact proportion to their overall numbers, these awards would *still* be unjustified in that athletic whites and blacks would be treated better than their more awkward counterparts in both racial groups. The authors of the present paper realize full well that if athletic scholarships were bestowed in a manner unrelated to athleticism, this would spell the death knell for competitiveness. Yet, from a libertarian perspective, promoting competitiveness is certainly not part of the mandate of limited government. If institutions wish to field excellent teams, they would have the option of privatizing. Otherwise, mediocrity would be their (deserved) fate.[178]

C. OBJECTIONS TO THE LIBERTARIAN ANALYSIS

Let us conclude by considering two objections to the foregoing. First, advocates of free enterprise and economic freedom, such as ourselves,[179] typically oppose affirmative action, quotas, and equal

---

[178] See note 155.

[179] See Walter Block and Roy Whitehead, "Human Organ Transplantation: Economic and Legal Issues," *Quinnipiac Health Law Journal* 3 (2000): 87; Walter Block and Roy Whitehead, "Environmental Justice Risks in the Petroleum Industry," *William and Mary Environmental Law and Policy Review* 24 (2000): 67; Walter Block and Roy Whitehead, "Direct Payment of State Scholarship Funds to Church-Related Colleges Offends the Constitution and Title VI," *BYU Journal of Public Law* 14 (2000): 191; Walter Block and Roy Whitehead, "Gender Equity in Athletics: Should We Adopt a Non-Discriminatory Model?" *University of Toledo Law Review* 30 (1999):

proportionality. In the present case, the very opposite is true. Namely, we are on record herein as *supporting* these programs. We consider in some detail scholarships based on intelligence and athletic ability as cases in point, but would generalize to cover any other such criteria. Why the difference?

This is because, while we oppose the imposition of quotas for private individuals or firms, this certainly does not hold true with regard to the minions of the state. Very much to the contrary, in this philosophy, anything to rein in the unjustified use of government power is all to the good. Not only schools, but also libraries, museums, art galleries, opera, and symphony orchestras, for example, discriminate against blacks, *vis-à-vis* whites, since the latter make greater proportional use of them. Moreover, and just as important, expenditures in these directions vitiate against the stupid and those who are, and wish to remain, ignorant. Even if blacks and whites availed themselves of these services strictly according to their proportion to the overall population, this would still be an unwarranted discrimination on the part of the government against various elements of the population. As long as smart people use these resources to a greater degree than their ignorant counterparts, this is an illegitimate incursion of government into the economy. Therefore, government is unjustified in offering these goods and services no matter what the relative utilization of them by blacks and whites.

Further, if government purchases from the private sector the land, labor, and capital necessary to provide those "intellectual" services, then this holds true for things such as desks, pencils, paper, computers, jet planes, pistols, bazookas, battleships, police and soldiers' uniforms, paper clips, rubber bands, and envelopes. These,

---

223; Walter Block and Roy Whitehead, "Mandatory Student Fees: Forcing Some to Pay for the Free Speech of Others," *Whittier Law Review* 20 (1999): 759; Walter Block and Roy Whitehead, "The Unintended Consequences of Environmental Justice," *Forensic Science International* 100 (1999): 57; Walter Block and Roy Whitehead, "Sexual Harassment in the Workplace: A Property Rights Perspective," *University of Utah Journal of Law and Family Studies* 4 (2002): 229; Walter Block and Roy Whitehead, "Crying 'Wolf' in American: Reevaluating Drug Prohibition Policy," (unpublished).

too, discriminate against those on the low end of the bell curve.[180] Thus, if government is prevented from financing the former, this holds for the latter as well. This is obviously an attempt at a *reductio ad absurdum* of the libertarian position in that, were the state not allowed to purchase this latter set of items, it could not fulfill its obligations under minarchism.

The reply is that the provision of armies, courts, and police are part and parcel of the proper scope of government, while competing with industries which do or could provide intellectual services is not. This applies, as well, for the myriad of other services supplied by government (i.e., in health and welfare) which have nothing to do with upholding the rights to personal safety and property mandated by the libertarian vision. It must be conceded that it would be possible for the public sector to provide all sorts of goods and services on a non-discriminatory basis, not only in terms of race, sex, and ethnicity, but also intelligence and other abilities. Each could be supplied on a "fair" basis through lottery selection. However, this would still be inappropriate in the libertarian view, since these concepts are not within the proper scope of a limited government.

CONCLUSION

We will conclude with a word on federal/state relations. Ordinarily, writers such as ourselves who favor markets, private property, and the freedom of association also approve of subsidiaries for government.[181] That is, when there is a conflict between different levels, we advance the cause of the most local (cities *vis-à-vis* states, and the latter when in conflict with the federal government). However, in the present case we are taking the side of the federal government *vis-à-vis* the state of Arkansas.

---

[180] Hernstein and Murray (1994), pp. 556–58. Whites and males are likely to be over-represented in the provision of these goods and services to the government.

[181] For a debate on this issue between two libertarians, see Gene Healy, "Liberty, States' Rights, and the Most Dangerous Amendment," *Liberty*, August 1999, p. 13; Roger Pilon, "In Defense of the Fourteenth Amendment," *Liberty*, February 2000, p. 39; Gene Healy, "Roger and Me," *Liberty*, February 2000, p. 46; Roger Pilon, "I'll Take the 14th," *Liberty*, March 2000, p. 15.

There are three possible theories on this matter which, when taken together, are seemingly exhaustive. First, the federal government always has jurisdiction over the states. Second, the states are supreme *vis-à-vis* the federal government; therefore, the federal government never has jurisdiction over the states. Third, whenever there is a conflict between the two levels of government, the presumption is in favor of the least centralized. Thus, the nod must go to the state when in conflict with the federal and to the town or county when in conflict with the state.

It is our contention, however, that there is a fourth alternative that is superior to any of these three. It is to ignore the level of government which is taking any given position on the ground that it is irrelevant to libertarianism. Instead, take the correct position, regardless of the level from which government it is emanating.

In the present circumstance, this is our story and we are sticking to it. That is, it cannot be denied that the State of Arkansas, with its Governor's Scholarship Program, not only discriminates against black people, but against those on the left side of the bell curve of intelligence as measured by IQ as well. Therefore, it is an unwarranted discrimination on the part of this state government.

APPENDIX 1 | RACIAL AND ETHNIC COMPOSITION OF PROFESSIONAL ATHLETIC EMPLOYMENT (IN PERCENT)[182]

		White	Black	Hispanic	Other
Total Population		73	12	11	4
NBA	Players	20	79	0	0
	General Managers	72	28	0	0
	Coaches	67	33	0	0
	Staff	77	17	2	3
NFL	Players	31	66	1	0
	General Managers	83	17	0	0
	Coaches	75	24	1	0
	Staff	80	15	3	2

[182] See Michael Lynch and Rick Henderson, "Team Colors," *Reason*, July 1998, p. 21 (cited in Walter Block et al., "Gender Equity in Athletics: Should We Adopt a NonDiscriminatory Model?" *Toledo Law Review* 30 (1999): 244.

37. SEXUAL HARASSMENT IN THE WORKPLACE: A PROPERTY RIGHTS PERSPECTIVE

EMPLOYERS OFTEN EXPRESS SUCH AN UNWARRANTED FEAR OF sexual harassment claims that they ignore the problem and hope that it will just go away and never happen in their workplace. This fear results from a lack of understanding of the nature of sexual harassment claims, confusion about the true meaning of untidy terms like "severe," "hostile," and "pervasive," and ignorance of appropriate management steps to both prevent harassment in the workplace and provide for a legitimate defense to sexual harassment claims. This article

- examines the kinds of sexual harassment claims that arise under Title VII of the 1964 Civil Rights Act,[1] as amended by the Civil Rights Act of 1991, the two key federal statutes used to combat sexual harassment in the workplace,

- expresses concern about the First Amendment free speech conflicts that arise in the context of harassment claims,

- discusses practical steps employers may take to reduce the likelihood of both sexual harassment in the workplace and their possible liability, and

Roy Whitehead, Jr. and Walter Block, *Journal of Law and Family Studies* 4, no. 2 (2002): 229–263.

[1] 42 U.S.C. § 2000 (e) to 2000 (e) (17) (1982) (amended by the Act of 1991).

• concludes with a philosophical and economic perspective on the issue based on property rights, free association, contract, and free speech.

THE LAW

Under section 102(a) of the 1991 Civil Rights Act,[2] both punitive and compensatory damages and a jury trial are available to plaintiffs who win a sexual harassment suit. Title VII, administered by the EEOC, prior to the 1991 Act, only provided for recovery of back pay and restoration of job benefits. The amount that may be recovered under the 1991 Act depends on the size of the employer and ranges from $50,000 to $300,000.[3] In addition, state court tort remedies are available for torts resulting from the harassing conduct such as battery, mental anguish, invasion of privacy, outrageous behavior, and wrongful discharge. Such recovery is governed by the law of the various states.

In applying current standards for sexual harassment cases, the courts are becoming more forceful in requiring employers to know about and effectively deal with harassment in the workplace. Employers are accountable for behavior they, "in the exercise of reasonable care," should have known was occurring.[4] Additionally, courts and the EEOC have imposed greater responsibility on management to develop plans to deal quickly and effectively with legitimate sexual harassment claims.[5]

WHAT DOES IT LOOK LIKE

Sexual harassment in the office means unwelcome sexual advances, requests for sexual favors, and other verbal or physical conduct of a sexual nature when:[6]

---

[2] 42 U.S.C.A., § 1981(a)(1) (2001).

[3] 42 U.S.C.A., § 1981 (b)(3) (2001).

[4] *Ellison v. Brady*, 924 F.2d 872, 881 (9th Cir. 1991) and *Jenson v. Eveleth Taconite Co.*, 824 F. Supp. 847 (D. Minn. 1993).

[5] *Faragher v. City of Boca Raton*, 524 U.S. 775, 808 (1998).

[6] 29 C.F.R. § 1604.11(a)(1)(2001).

(a) Submission to such conduct is either explicitly or implicitly made a condition of an individual's employment;[7]

(b) Submission to or rejection of such conduct by an individual is used as a basis for an employment decision effecting such individuals;[8]

(c) Such conduct has a purpose or effect of substantially interfering with an individual's right to work in an environment free of intimidation, hostility, or threats stemming from acts or language of a sexual nature;[9] and/or

(d) the conduct interferes with an employee's ability to focus on the job responsibilities.[10]

The EEOC and some courts have found the following to comport with sexual harassment:

(a) Sexually suggestive or obscene comments, threats, insults, slurs, jokes about gender-based traits of a person, or sexual propositions;[11]

(b) Physical conduct such as intentional touching, pinching, brushing against another's body, suggesting or coercing sexual intercourse, or physical assault;[12]

(c) Non-verbal behavior such as leering or staring at another's body, displaying sexually suggestive photographs, cartoons, or magazines;[13]

---

[7] *Id.* at 1604.11(a)(2).

[8] *Id.* at 1604.11(a)3).11

[9] *Id.*

[10] *Ellison v. Brady*, 924 F.2d 872, 874 (9th Cir. 1991).

[11] *Lipsett v. University of Puerto Rico*, 864 F. 2d 881, 901 (1st Cir. 1988).

[12] *Jones v. Wesco Investments*, 846 F.2d 1154, 1155 (8th Cir. 1988).

[13] *Robinson v. Jacksonville Shipyards*, 760 F. Supp. 1486, 1494 (M.D. Fla. 1991).

(d) Continued expression of sexual or social interest in an individual after being informed that the interest is unwelcome;[14]

(e) Belief that an individual is required to consent to the foregoing behavior as a term or condition of her employment;[15] and

(f) Employer responsibility for acts of non-employees such as customers or service technicians, when the employer knows, or should have known, of the unwelcome conduct and fails to take immediate or appropriate action.[16]

Determination of whether conduct amounts to sexual harassment is generally made on a case-by-case basis after looking at all the circumstances. It is apparent, however, that most definitions of sexual harassment turn on an abuse of power in a relationship of unequal power, for example, teacher and student, or supervisor and employee.[17]

TWO KINDS OF SEXUAL HARASSMENT CLAIMS

The courts and the EEOC recognize sexual harassment claims on two primary theories: *quid pro quo* sexual harassment and hostile environment sexual harassment. *Quid pro quo* sexual harassment occurs when a superior conditions the granting of an economic or job benefit upon submission to sexual conduct or punishes the subordinate employee for refusing to comply with the sexual request.[18] Hostile environment harassment exists when sexual or gender-related conduct "has the purpose or effect of unreasonably interfering with

---

[14] *Ellison v. Brady*, 924 F.2d 872, 874 (9th Cir. 1991).

[15] *Simmons v. Lyons*, 746 F.2d 265, 269 (5th Cir. 1984).

[16] 29 C.F.R. § 1604.11(b)(2001).

[17] See, e.g., Roy Whitehead, Pam Spikes, and Brenda Yelvington, "Sexual Harassment in the Office," *The CPA Journal* (February 1996): 42–45.

[58] *Hall v. Gus Construction Company*, 842 F.2d 1010 (8th Cir. 1988).

an individual's performance or creating an intimidating, hostile, or offensive working environment."[19]

In *quid pro quo* harassment claims, a five-part test has been used by the courts to decide whether the plaintiff has established a *prima facie* case. In *quid pro quo* cases, the plaintiff is required to show:[20]

(a) The employee belongs to a protected group;

(b) The sexual advances were unwelcome;

(c) The harassment complained of was based upon sex;

(d) The individual's reaction to the advances affected a tangible aspect of employment such as compensation, advancement, terms, conditions, or privileges; and,

(e) *Respondeat superior* identity has been established.

Once a *prima facie* case has been established, the burden of going forward shifts to the employer to articulate a nondiscriminatory reason for the employment decision. The employer may show that there is a basis for the same decision even if the harassment had not occurred. To prevail under a *quid pro quo* theory, some courts require that the plaintiff show some economic injury, like a promotion or pay disparity, arising from the employer's denial of the employment benefit.[21] Here, the employer is strictly liable for the conduct of supervisory employees who are acting within the scope of their authority. Knowledge of the supervisor's activities is imputed to the employer under a theory that the supervisor is acting as the employer's agent.[22]

The hostile environment theory has frightened employers because many believe they are liable for harassment cases that

---

[19] *Meritor Savings Bank v. Vinson*, 477 U.S. 57, 65 (1986).

[20] *Jones v. Flagship International*, 793 F.2d 714, 721–22 (5th Cir. 1986).

[21] *Carrero V. N.Y. Housing Authority*, 890 F.2d 569, 579 (2d Cir. 1989).

[22] *Kotcher v. Rosa and Sullivan Appliance*, 957 F.2d 59, 62 (2d Cir. 1992).

have occurred without their actual knowledge. Further, hostile environment cases may, in cases where the harassment has some relation to the work environment, involve off-job conduct by co-workers or supervisors.[23] Under the hostile environment theory, the plaintiff is required to show:

(a) She belonged to a protected group;

(b) She was subjected to unwelcome sexual harassment;

(c) The harassment was based upon sex or gender;

(d) The harassment affected a "term, condition, or privilege, of employment;"

(e) The employer knew or should have known of the harassment in question and failed to take the proper remedial or preventive action.[24]

Another important concern in hostile environment cases is that the sexual harassment claim need not be based on conduct that is solely sexual in nature, since intimidation and hostility toward gender can result from conduct other than explicit sexual advances. For example name calling, urinating in a gas tank, and refusing to service a company truck driven by new female employees were considered relevant in establishing a hostile work environment based on gender even though the conduct was not explicitly sexual in nature.[25] In addition, in a hostile environment case, unlike a *quid pro quo* case, it is not necessary that the plaintiff suffer any economic loss of employment benefits.[26] Finally, sexual or gender stereotyping can contribute to a hostile environment.[27]

---

[23] *Kaufman v. Applied Signal*, 970 F.2d 178, 185 (6th Cir. 1992).

[24] *Jones v. Wesco Investments*, 846 F.2d 11561, 1 166 (8th Cir. 1988).

[25] See *Hall v. Gus Construction Company*, 842 F.2d 1010, 1013–14 (8th Cir. 1988).

[26] *Meritor Savings Bank v. Vinson*, 477 U.S. 57, 67–68 (1986).

[27] *Ellison v. Brady*, 924 F.2d 872, 881 (9th Cir. 1991).

One of the major issues that may arise in a hostile environment case is whether the fact that the alleged victim voluntarily participated in the relevant sexual conduct is a defense to a sexual harassment claim. The question is answered in the leading case of *Meritor Savings Bank v. Vinson*[28] in which the Supreme Court, speaking through Justice Rehnquist, decided that the test is not whether the victim voluntarily participated, in the sense that she was not forced to participate, but whether the sexual advances were unwelcome.[29] In *Meritor*, she was fondled in front of other employees,[30] apparently voluntarily visited motels,[31] and participated in sexual intercourse forty or fifty times with her supervisor.[32] The supervisor also followed her into the restroom during working hours and exposed himself to her.[33] She said she participated because she was afraid of the supervisor[34] and in order to attain job benefits that included unusually rapid promotions.[35]

When she eventually left because of the sexual harassment and filed a federal court action, the bank's defense was that it had no knowledge of the conduct of the supervisor because she didn't file a grievance[36] and that the plaintiff had voluntarily participated in the sexual activity.[37] However, the bank had an employee grievance procedure that did not specifically discuss sexual harassment nor inform an employee how to bypass a guilty superior.[38] The Supreme Court decided that the test is not whether the victim voluntarily participates, but whether the sexual

---

[28] *Meritor Savings Bank v. Vinson*, 477 U.S. 57 (1986).

[29] *Id.* at 68.

[30] *Id.* at 60.

[31] *Id.*

[32] *Id.*

[33] *Id.*

[34] *Id.*

[35] *Id.* at 60.

[36] *Id.* at 72.

[37] *Id.* at 68.

[38] *Id.* at 72.

attention is welcome.[39] Other cases have also said that advances that were initially welcome between individuals can become unwelcome if the victim changes her mind and makes it clear to the man that the advances are no longer welcome.[40]

The Eighth Circuit Court of Appeals has defined unwelcome sexual harassment to mean that "the employee did not solicit or invite it, and the employee regarded the conduct as undesirable or offensive."[41] A woman's consistent failure to respond to suggestive comments or jokes may be sufficient to express to a man that the conduct is unwelcome.[42] On the other hand, the Supreme Court has held that evidence of the plaintiff's sexually provocative speech or dress may be relevant in determining whether the plaintiff found sexual advances unwelcome.[43] In another case, the Eighth Circuit found that nude photographs taken of the plaintiff, and her appearance in a motorcycle publication, were not material to the issue of whether she found the office conduct of other employees hostile.[44] Her private life away from work did not mean she acquiesced to sexual comments and advances on the job.[45] Finally, if the plaintiff voluntarily initiates or participates in a mutual exchange of sexual comments and jokes with co-workers, this may constitute evidence that the plaintiff welcomed that kind of conduct.[46]

In a hostile environment case, the harassing conduct must be sufficiently pervasive to alter the conditions of employment and

---

[39] *Id.* at 68.

[40] *Ellison v. Brady*, 924 F.2d 842, 873–74 (9th Cir. 1991).

[41] *Moylan v. Manes County*, 792 F.2d 746, 749 (8th Cir. 1986). For a discussion of the term "unwelcome" see *Swentek v. U.S. Air, Inc.*, 830 F.2d 552, 557 (4th Cir. 1987).

[42] *Lipsett v. University of Puerto Rico*, 864 F.2d 881 (1st Cir. 1988).

[43] *Meritor*, 477 U.S. at 68–69.

[44] *Bums v. McGregor*, 989 F.2d. 959, 963 (8th Cir. 1993).

[45] *Id.*

[46] *Moylan v. Maries County*, 792 F.2d 746, 749 (8th Cir. 1986).

create an abusive environment. Some authorities believe that conduct that keeps the employee from focusing her attention on her job meets this criterion. The plaintiff must also show a practice or pattern of harassment. Usually a single or isolated incident will not be sufficient to establish a hostile environment. Initially the courts decided whether hostile environment existed based on a reasonable person standard. Recently, at least one court has said in cases involving female plaintiffs that the test is a "reasonable woman" standard.[47] In that case the court stated:

> In order to shield employers from having to accommodate the idio-syncratic concerns of the rare hypersensitive employee, we hold that a female plaintiff states a *prima facie* case of hostile environment when she alleges conduct which a reasonable woman would consider sufficiently severe or pervasive to alter the conditions of employment and create an abusive work environment.[48]

This reasonable person or reasonable woman standard was not uniformly applied, however, in the various federal circuits. The Supreme Court dealt with this problem in *Harris v. Forklift Systems, Inc.*[49] The defendant employer in Harris claimed that the plaintiff, a strong self-reliant woman, should not prevail because she was unable to show psychological damage resulting from the harassment.[50] The company president called Harris "a dumb ass woman,"[51] asked her to visit a motel with him to talk about her raise,[52] asked her to get coins out of his pocket,[53] tossed objects on the floor for her to pick up,[54] said she closed

---

[47] *Ellison v. Brady*, 924 F.2d 872, 879 (9th Cir. 1991).

[48] *Id.*

[49] *Harris v. Forklift Systems, Inc.*, 510 U.S. 17 (1993).

[50] *Id.* at 20.

[51] *Id.* at 19.

[52] *Id.*

[53] *Id.*

[54] *Id.*

a sale by promising sex to the customer,[55] and made sexual innuendos about her clothing.[56] The Supreme Court rejected the employer's psychological harm defense and defined the appropriate standard as (1) whether a reasonable woman would find the harasser's conduct sufficiently severe or pervasive to alter conditions of employment, and (2) whether subjectively the victim perceived the environment as abusive.[57] The majority said that "Title VII comes into play long before the harassing conduct leads to a nervous breakdown."[58] If the environment is hostile and abusive to an employee, there is no additional need for it also to be psychologically injurious.[59]

What are we to make of the requirements that the conduct be "severe" or "pervasive" enough to create a hostile or abusive environment for the plaintiff or a reasonable person? These terms are troubling to a First Amendment student because neither the EEOC nor the courts bother to define them. "Severe," "hostile," and "pervasive" are perplexing terms. Reasonable people, even of the same philosophical perspectives, will differ on what they mean. It is a bit like nailing Jell-O to the wall. We do know that these words have been construed to refer to crude political statements about a member of the congress,[60] a painting,[61] pinups,[62] an explicit

---

[55] *Id.*

[56] *Id.*

[57] *Id.* at 21–22.

[58] *Id.* at 22.

[59] *Id.*

[60] Several Navy officers, concerned about Congresswoman Pat Schroeder's role in the investigation of the "Tail Hook" Sexual Harassment incident, displayed a banner at an on base party that said, "Hickory Dickory Dock, Pat Schroeder can suck my cock." See Eugene Volkh, "Freedom of Speech and Workplace Harassment," *UCLA Law Review* 39 (1992): 1791, 1802 n. 54.

[61] Complaint regarding a painting, hanging in the City Hall of Murfreesboro, Tennessee, that showed a woman with one breast exposed. Jennifer Goode, "It's Art vs. Sexual Harassment," *The Tennessean*, March 1, 1996, at A1.

[62] See *Robinson v. Jacksonville Shipyards Inc.*, 760 F.Supp. 1486, 1493 (M.D. Fla. 1991), a case that imposed liability for centerfolds.

card,[63] and a telephone call.[64] Given the "Jell-O-ness" of the rule, it is difficult to judge how others will apply it. There is a real danger that some fact finders, or more likely regulators, will conclude that various religious or political statements, vulgar jokes,[65] or indecent art can be severe and pervasive enough to create a hostile environment. More so when the regulators find the expression personally disagreeable or politically incorrect. So, there is a real potential that sexual harassment law can be used to suppress protected speech. It is the nature of the employment context.

The employer's natural response, given that he does not even know exactly what the terms mean, is to avoid possible liability, and will likely cause him to "shut the employees up."[66] After all, that is the safe approach! An employer concerned about sexual harassment liability can't profit from the employee's speech, he can only lose from it.[67] This is precisely the chilling effect on protected speech that vague laws and regulations that use untidy words like "pervasive," "severe," and "abusive" have.[68] Vagueness leads people to steer far wider from the forbidden zone of actual harassment than if the boundaries are clearly marked.[69] The employer's only safe recourse is a zero-tolerance policy. In any case, harassment law poses First Amendment problems regardless of how it is handled because speech that "stigmatizes" or "victimizes" someone does not always strip aside the speaker's First Amendment protections. Despite these

---

[63] *Bartlett v. United States*, 835 F.Supp. 1246, 1256 (E.D. Wash. 1993).

[64] *Intlekofer v. Turnage*, 973 F.2d 773, 775 (9th Cir. 1992) (relying in part on a telephone call at home from a co-worker to support a hostile environment claim).

[65] *Morgan v. Hertz Corp.*,542F. Supp. 123, 128 (W.D. Tenn. 1981), aff'd 725 F.2d 1070 (6th Cir. 1984) (condemning remarks like, "Did you get any over the weekend").

[66] See, e.g., Eugene Volokh, "What Speech Does 'Hostile Work Environment' Harassment Restrict?" *Georgetown Law Journal* 85 (1997): 627, 635.

[67] See, e.g., Mark I. Schickman, "Sexual Harassment: The Employer Role In Prevention," *Compleat Lawyer* 13 (1996): 24, 24–25.

[68] See Volokh, note 68.

[69] See Volokh, note 62.

troubling problems, the courts plow on in their quest to cleanse the workplace of "severe" and "pervasive" conduct and speech, whatever the terms mean. The next sexual harassment venture of the Supreme Court was to try to lay down some boundaries for alleged "supervisor" harassment.

LAYING DOWN THE LAW FOR SUPERVISOR HARASSMENT

In two precedent-setting cases,[70] the Supreme Court attempted to clarify the liability tests for employers when a supervisor is alleged to have sexually harassed an employee. They provide a roadmap for employer liability and possible defenses in two relatively common instances. First, when an employee is victimized by a supervisor with immediate (or higher) authority over the employee. And, secondly, in situations when a supervisor creates a hostile work environment by making explicit threats to alter a subordinate's terms or conditions of employment, based on sex, but when rebuffed, does not act to fulfill the threat.

A. FARAGHER[71]

After resigning as a lifeguard for the city of Boca Raton, Florida, Beth Faragher sued the city and her two immediate supervisors, alleging that the male supervisors had created a "sexually hostile atmosphere"[72] by repeatedly subjecting her and other female employees to "uninvited and offensive touching,"[73] by making lewd remarks, and by speaking of women in offensive terms.[74] She claimed this conduct constituted discrimination in the "terms, conditions,

---

[70] *Faragher v. City of Boca Raton*, 524 U.S. 775 (1998); *Burlington Industries v. Ellerth*, 524 U.S. 742 (1998).

[71] 524 U.S. 775 (1998).

[72] *Id*. at 780.

[73] *Id*.

[74] *Id*.

and privileges of her employment"[75] in violation of Title VII of the Civil Rights Act.[76] Faragher never complained to higher city officials about the treatment.[77] Another supervisor once told another female employee, "the city just doesn't care."[78] There was no showing that higher-echelon officials of the city (employer) had actual knowledge of the two supervisors' conduct.[79] The city had a sexual harassment policy but failed to provide it to the beach employees.[80] It made no effort to keep track of the conduct of the two beach supervisors,[81] and the city's policy failed to provide for a procedure to bypass harassing supervisors in filing a complaint.[82] The lower courts split on the issue of the city's liability.

The Supreme Court decided that "[an] employer is subject to vicarious liability to a victimized employee for an actionable hostile sexually environment [claim] created by a supervisor with immediate (or successively higher) authority over the employee."[83] The term "vicarious" generally means performed, exercised, received, or suffered in place of another.[84] When the supervisor's harassment culminates in a tangible employment action, such as discharge, demotion, firing, failure to promote, reassignment with different responsibilities, undesirable working conditions, or a decision resulting in a significant reduction in benefits, the liability is absolute.[85] This is so because tangible employment

---

[75] *Id.* at 780.

[76] *Id.*

[77] *Id.* at 782.

[78] *Id.* at 783.

[79] *Id.* at 784.

[80] *Id.* at 808.

[81] *Id.*

[82] *Id.*

[83] *Id.* at 807.

[84] *Webster's College Dictionary* (1973).

[85] 524 U.S. at 790.

decisions are the means by which the supervisor brings the official power of the enterprise (employer) to bear on the employee.[86] A tangible employment decision, such as a retaliatory discharge for rebuffing sexual advances, requires an official act of the enterprise, a company act.[87] For these reasons, a tangible employment action taken by the supervisor becomes, for Title VII purposes, an act of the employer.[88]

The next question is whether there is employer liability when the commission of supervisor sexual harassment does not result in a tangible employment action.[89] Here, the answer is less obvious. However, the Court did provide important guidance for management on steps that may be taken to avoid liability.[90] The Court did so by establishing two affirmative defenses that may be raised when no retaliation or loss of tangible job benefits has occurred.[91]

THE EMPLOYER DEFENSES

In *Faragher*, the Court said that when no tangible job action is taken against the employee, the employer may raise two affirmative defenses to liability or the award of damages:[92]

> (a) [T]hat the employer exercised reasonable care to prevent and correct promptly any sexually harassing behavior, and

> (b) [T]hat the plaintiff employee unreasonably failed to take advantage of any preventive or corrective opportunities provided by the employer or to avoid harm.

---

[86] *Id.* at 790–91.

[87] *Id.* at 804–5.

[88] *Id.* at 802.

[89] *Id.* at 807.

[90] *Id.*

[91] *Id.*

[92] *Id.*

Justice Souter wrote that the need for a stated sexual harassment policy and grievance procedure suitable to the employment circumstances may be addressed in litigating the first element of the defense,[93] and that a demonstration that the complaining employee unreasonably failed to use the established complaint procedure will normally suffice to satisfy the second element.[94] Applying the two affirmative defenses to the facts of *Faragher*, the court found as a matter of law that the city could not have exercised reasonable care because it failed to provide its sexual harassment policy to beach employees, made no attempt to keep track of the two beach supervisors' conduct, and its policy failed to provide a procedure to bypass harassing supervisors.[95]

B. BURLINGTON V. ELLERTH[96]

Kimberly Ellerth quit her job after 15 months as a salesperson with Burlington Industries, alleging she had been subjected to sexual harassment by a mid-level supervisor, Ted Slowik.[97] Slowik had authority to hire and promote employees, subject to higher approval: he was not a policy maker.[98] Ellerth claimed to have been subjected to repeated boorish and offensive sexual remarks and gestures and was threatened with a loss of job benefits.[99] On one occasion when she failed to respond to remarks Slowik made about her breasts, he told her, "you know Kim, I could make your life very hard or very easy at Burlington."[100] Ellerth rebuffed all of Slowik' s advances, yet

---

[93] *Id.*

[94] *Id.* at 807–8.

[95] *Id.* at 808.

[96] *Burlington Industries v. Ellerth*, 524 U.S. 742 (1998).

[97] *Id.* at 747.

[98] *Id.*

[99] *Id.* at 747–48.

[100] *Id.* at 748.

suffered no retaliation and was, in fact, promoted once.[101] Moreover, she never informed anyone in authority of Slowik's conduct despite knowing about Burlington's sexual harassment policy.[102]

Justice Kennedy again held that an employer is subject to vicarious liability to a victimized employee for an actionable hostile environment created by a supervisor with immediate, or successively higher, authority over an employee.[103] The liability is absolute when the employee has suffered the loss of a tangible job benefit, like a promotion, for rebuffing the sexual harassment.[104] Again, the Court maintained that when no tangible job action has been taken against the employee, the employer may raise the two affirmative defenses of reasonable care to prevent and promptly correct sexually harassing behavior and the unreasonable failure of the employee to take advantage of preventative or corrective opportunities provided by the employer's sexual harassment policy.[105] The Court remanded the case to the trial court for a determination of whether Ellerth had a claim for vicarious liability and whether the affirmative defenses applied.[106]

PUBLIC POLICY GOALS OF THE COURT

The decisions in *Faragher* and *Burlington* clearly illustrate several public policy goals of the Supreme Court. First, the Court is clearly sending a signal to employers that the actions of a supervisor, which affect a tangible job benefit of the harassed employee, will trigger absolute employer liability because they are company acts.[107] Secondly, the primary purpose of Title VII is to "make whole

---

[101] *Id.*

[102] *Id.*

[103] *Id.* at 765.

[104] *Id.*

[105] *Id.*

[106] *Id.* at 766.

[107] *Faragher*, 524 U.S. at 807.

persons who suffer discrimination."[108] The Court is advancing this primary purpose by demanding that employers publish, educate employees and supervisors about, and enforce sexual harassment grievance procedures. Finally, the Court is encouraging employees to mitigate any damage to their employment by requiring them to take advantage of those employer-promulgated sexual harassment grievance procedures in order to prevent a hostile environment. It apparently seeks to promote these goals by providing a reward in the form of an affirmative defense to employers who comply and to deny recourse to employees who refuse to follow properly drafted employer sexual harassment grievance procedures. Thus, the next important question is what kind of employer action is necessary to comply and avoid liability for supervisor harassment?

MANAGING SUPERVISOR SEXUAL HARASSMENT LIABILITY

There are several steps the astute employer may take to limit liability for supervisor sexual harassment claims. First, all supervisors should be informed, in writing, that sexual harassment of a subordinate that affects a tangible job benefit, as previously defined, will result in absolute employer liability. This is so because the denial of a tangible job benefit, for the purposes of Title VII, becomes a company act.[109] There are, in addition, several preventive steps that must be taken in regard to all employees.[110] They are:

(1) The employer should publish a strong, well-articulated policy concerning sexual harassment;

(2) All employees should be informed of, and provided a copy of, the policy;

---

[108] *Albemarle Paper Co. v. Moody*, 422 U.S. 405, 418 (1975).

[109] See generally *Faragher v. City of Boca Raton*, 524 U.S. 775 (1998).

[110] Roy Whitehead and Kenneth Griffin, "The Supreme Court Finally Lays Down The Law On Employer Liability For Sexual Harassment," *The CPA Journal* (November 1998): 70–71.

(3 The CEO should clearly and forcefully advise all employees that sexual harassment will not be tolerated.

(4) The complaint procedure should allow employees to report sexual harassment to someone other than the harassing supervisor;

(5) Supervisors should be informed, in writing, that the employer is absolutely liable for a supervisor's sexual harassment involving the loss of an employee's tangible job benefits; and

(6) The employer should swiftly take appropriate remedial action by fairly investigating, taking effective action, protecting the victim from retaliation, and restoring any lost tangible job benefits in a timely manner.

Many astute employers have already taken some or all of these preventive steps. A careful reading of some previous sexual harassment decisions reveals that the courts, as a matter of policy, are requiring employers to educate their employees, adopt effective and fair complaint procedures, guard against retaliation, and effectively deal with sexual harassment complaints. For example, the courts will consider a policy that specifically addresses and effectively deals with sexual harassment when reviewing liability issues.[111] Those employers whose sexual harassment policies and procedures do not comport with these decisions are well advised to adopt the appropriate policies forthwith.

As previously stated, employers are very concerned about strict liability under the so-called hostile environment theory, correctly contending that the conduct complained of may have occurred without their knowledge. Given *Faragher* and *Ellerth*, what kind of action can the employer take that will constitute a legitimate

---

[111] See, e.g., *Meritor Savings Bank v. Vinson*, 447 U.S. 57, 72–73 (1986), *Barrett v. Omaha National Bank*, 26 F.2d 424, 427 (8th Cir. 1984), and Roy Whitehead, Pam Spikes, and Brenda Yelvington, "Sexual Harassment In The Office," *The CPA Journal* (February 1996): 45–49.

defense against both *quid pro quo* and hostile environment sexual harassment claims? The law in this area is still developing, but some commentators say that there are several key steps that employers can take to protect against liability.[112] In fact, the EEOC, by regulation, mandates that the existence of a sexual harassment policy and complaint procedure is relevant and will directly affect the employer's liability.[113] Thus, the failure to provide a reasonable policy and complaint procedure for employees is convincing evidence that the employer has ignored the problem, and will likely lead to employer liability for sexual harassment claims.

A careful reading of *Meritor* also shows that the Supreme Court will consider effective a policy that specifically addresses sexual harassment, rather than merely discrimination, when reviewing liability issues. We also know from *Meritor* that a procedure requiring the employee to complain to or through the person who is the harasser is an inadequate defense because it violates EEOC guidelines.[114] The EEOC guidelines recommend that the employer's remedy should be "immediate and appropriate."[115]

Perhaps the most instructive case for employers is *Barrett v. Omaha National Bank*.[116] Here, the Eighth Circuit held that an employer properly remedied a hostile working environment by fully investigating, reprimanding a harasser for grossly inappropriate conduct, placing the offender on probation for ninety days, and warning the offender that any further misconduct would result in discharge.[117] One court says the remedy should be "reasonably calculated to end the harassment."[118] One can convincingly argue that the failure of an

---

[112] See Roy Whitehead, Kenneth Griffin, and Pam Spikes, "Preparing For Same Sex Sexual Harassment," *The CPA Journal* (June 1998): 54–55.

[113] 29 C.F.R. 1604.11(0) (2001).

[114] See *Meritor*, 477 U.S. at 73.

[115] 29 C.F.R. 1604.11(d) (2001).

[116] 726 F.2d 424, 427; see also *Nash v. Electrospace System*, 9 F.3d 401, 404 (5th Cir. 1993).

[118] *Katz v. Dole*, 709 F.2d 251, 256 (4th Cir. 1983).

employer to provide a grievance procedure for sexual harassment is evidence of employer contribution to a hostile sexual environment and would result in liability.

One of the distressing traps that employers have fallen into in the past is, despite their good motives, appearing to be insensitive to the victim of harassment. In one case, the Internal Revenue Service allowed the harasser to continue to send bizarre letters to the victim after he had been told by his superiors to stop. Then, when they failed to stop the harassing conduct, they actually transferred the victim, rather than the harasser, to another city.[119] The bottom line is that an employer has an affirmative duty to take immediate action in sexual harassment matters, and that an honest effort to comply with that affirmative duty is often going to be a satisfactory employer defense.

What responsibility, if any, does a victim of sexual harassment have, and how can the victim protect herself?[120] Many victims tolerate harassing behavior for a considerable period of time because they believe that if they do not say anything the problem will just disappear. This is probably the worst approach to follow because the harassment may be motivated as much by the exercise of power over the victim as by sexual interest. Generally, the victim should speak up and make quite clear to the harasser that the unwelcome conduct will not be tolerated. The victim should keep careful records of what is happening, including times, dates, and locations. The victim should also create a record by writing a letter to the perpetrator or to a trusted friend carefully outlining what has occurred.[121]

---

[119] *Ellison v. Brady*, 924 F.2d 872, 882 (9th Cir. 1991).

[120] For simplicity, we have been speaking as if all victims are female and all harassers male. Actually both roles can be filled by either gender. See generally *Oncale v. Sundowner Offshore Services*, 523 U.S. 75 (1998) (male victim) and *Kinman v. Omaha Public School District*, 94 F.3d 463 (8th Cir. 1996) (female harasser).

[121] See Jean O. Hughes and Bernie R. Sandler, "In Case of Sexual Harassment, A Guide for Women Students," in *The Project on the Status and Education of Women* (Washington, D.C.: Association of American Colleges, 1986).

Employers clearly have a responsibility to develop effective policies to deal with sexual harassment in the workplace. Those employers who have not already developed separate and effective sexual harassment policies are placing their financial assets at risk. The successful sexual harassment policy will be supported by the chief executive officer,[122] offer a clear and convenient, separate method of complaining about sexual harassment,[123] provide for an immediate and fair investigation,[124] and demonstrate to employees that sexual harassment will not be tolerated and that disciplinary action will be taken swiftly.[125] Employers who establish and follow an appropriate sexual harassment policy will benefit from a lessened risk of employer liability. The employer who heeds Justice Ginsberg's admonition that "[i]t suffices to prove that a reasonable person subjected to discriminatory conduct would find ... that the harassment so altered the working conditions as to make it more difficult to do the job"[126] will have little concern about sexual harassment in the workplace. What rational employer wants employees not to focus on the job at hand? But, is this the best way? We now turn to a philosophical, property-rights approach to escaping government coercion.

PHILOSOPHY

We have set the stage for our consideration of sexual harassment law by describing it, giving its rationale, citing cases, and offering advice to employees and employers as to how they can most likely avoid becoming enmeshed in lawsuits concerning this offense. We have in this way, to the best of our ability, analyzed it from a positive perspective. But to do so is only to set the stage for examining these legislative and judicial enactments from the normative point of view. We now leave off our description of these laws and how they work

---

[122] See generally *Barrett v. Omaha National Bank*, 726 F.2d 424 (8th Cir. 184).

[123] See generally *Faragher v. City of Boca Raton*, 524 U.S. 775 (1998).

[124] See generally *Ellison*, 924 F.2d 872.

[125] *Id.*

[126] *Harris v. Forklift Systems*, 510 U.S. 17, 25 (1993) (Ginsburg, J., concurring) (internal quotation marks omitted).

and take up a discussion of whether or not these laws are just and, even, logically coherent. In a word, the answer we offer is, "No."

It is now time to cast a baleful, philosophical eye on the entire enterprise of sexual harassment legislation, prohibition of *quid pro quo* agreements, and legal opposition to hostile environments. We do so from the classical liberal perspective, one based on private property, contract, freedom of association, and free-speech rights.[127] In this view, all human interaction should be voluntary. The law should prohibit only those acts that violate the rights of people to the sanctity of their persons and justly owned property. To relate this to the issue at hand, the law against rape is certainly a legitimate one. For when this act occurs, a man exerts physical force against a woman[128] in opposition to her own will; this is an invasive act, one which attacks a woman's most important private property right, that

---

[127] See generally Murray N. Rothbard, *For a New Liberty* (New York: Macmillan, 1973); Murray N. Rothbard, *The Ethics of Liberty* (New York: New York University Press, 1998); Hans-Hermann Hoppe, *A Theory of Socialism and Capitalism: Economics, Politics, and Ethics* (Dordrect, Holland: Kluwer Academic Publishers, 1989); Hans-Hermann Hoppe, *The Economics and Ethics of Private Property: Studies in Political Economy and Philosophy* (Dordrect, Holland: Kluwer Academic Publishers, 1993); Robert Nozick, *Anarchy, State, and Utopia* (New York: Basic Books, 1974); Walter Block, *Defending the Undefendable* (San Francisco, Calif.: Fox and Wilkes, 1991); Walter Block, "Libertarianism vs. Libertinism," *Journal of Libertarian Studies* 11 (1994): 117; Charles Murray, *What it Means to be a Libertarian* (New York: Broadway Books, 1997); Jan Narveson, *The Libertarian Idea* (Philadelphia, Penn.:Temple University Press, 1988); J. Patrick O'Brien and Dennis O. Olson, "The Great Alaskan Money Give Away Program," *Economic Inquiry* 18 (1990): 604; Jerry W. Dauterive, William Barnett, and Everett White, "A Taxonomy of Government Intervention," *Journal of Southwest Society of Economics* 12 (1985).

[128] We will continue to speak as if only males can commit such acts, and only women can be victimized by them. Obviously, while these two categories may be the most statistically significant, they certainly do not exhaust the four different possibilities.

in her own person.[129] This holds, too, for assault and battery, which encompasses even the slightest of unwanted touching.[130]

Let us now consider how a hostile environment stacks up in this regard. We argue that it is not a *per se* violation of human rights. One can readily imagine a scenario in which women are subjected to the most hostile of sexually tinged environments, where they are paid to accept such treatment, and do so willingly—for example, a strip bar. There, men taunt women; they ask them to disrobe; they make lewd and suggestive remarks about their figures, their clothes, their makeup; they tell off-color jokes, etc. It is hard to imagine an environment more sexually hostile than that. If we are to take seriously laws prohibiting a hostile environment, all such establishments should be shut down, forthwith. From the fact that they are not, that is, that firms which provide such services are allowed to operate with legal impunity, we may deduce that the prohibition of a sexually hostile environment is honored more in the breach than in the fact. Further, we may also conclude that there is something philosophically suspect about legislatively proscribing hostile environments. It is as if rape or murder were declared illegitimate, except when it occurs legally. We have here, in other words, a legal system with no less than an inner contradiction.[131] We as a society

---

[129] For the implications of this viewpoint on abortion law, see generally Walter Block, "Abortion, Woman and Fetus: Rights in Conflict?" *Reason* (April 1978), pp. 18–25; Walter Block, *Compromising the Uncompromisable: A Private Property Rights Theory of Abortion* (manuscript on file with author); Walter Block, *Libertarianism, Positive Obligations, and Property Abandonment: Children's Rights* (manuscript on file with author).

[130] On this point, esteemed legal scholars Professors Prosser and Keeton explain that "the plaintiff is entitled to demand that the defendant refrain from the offensive touching, although the contact results in no visible injury," and "the defendant may be liable when intending only a joke, or even a compliment, as where an unappreciated kiss is bestowed without consent (citations omitted)." See W.P. Prosser et al., *Prosser and Keaton on the Law of Torts*, Section 9 (Los Angeles: West Group, 1984).

[131] Suppose there were a private amusement facility called "Murder Park." Here, each customer would be issued a revolver with six bullets, and told to have at

have not banned strip clubs, nor should we, since they are instances of "capitalist acts between consenting adults."[132] But strip clubs are a paradigmatic case of sexual harassment. Therefore, logical consistency requires that since strip clubs are legal, then so should sexual harassment be, for the latter is precisely and exactly what takes place in the former.

And no less is true of *quid pro quo*, the *bête noir* of the feminists. The essence of this sort of agreement is voluntary mutually beneficial trade, barter or exchange: you give us this, and we will give you that. As such, *quid pro quo* is the very basis of the free enterprise system and, indeed, of the entire western cultural vision of society. There are, after all, only two possible ways for human beings to interact with one another: through seizing each other's person and property, or receiving them (or the use of them) only with the agreement of the other party, typically in return for something of one's own. Norman Rockwell drew a very famous *Saturday Evening Post* magazine cover, depicting a milk deliveryman and pie deliveryman, each one sitting in his own truck and partaking of both food items. Nothing can better illustrate *quid pro quo* than the sort of peaceful trade that occurred immediately prior to this artistic rendering. We are certainly not ready to rule out all purchases and sales on the ground that they are living illustrations of *quid pro quo* in action. Given this, there are no logical grounds on the basis of which we can insist that they not be allowed in this one aspect of the law.

---

anyone else in the arena (surrounded by tall, thick walls so that the mayhem would be confined to the premises) who was there for that purpose. There would be a ceasefire for 10 minutes every hour so that the dead bodies could be hauled away, and the remaining combatants issued new ammunition. Such an establishment would not at all violate laws against murder, for that crime is the killing of people against their will. Here, on the contrary, all customers by purchasing a ticket demonstrate that they are engaging in the otherwise murderous interaction on a voluntary basis.

[132] This is the very felicitous phrase of Robert Nozick. See Nozick, *Anarchy, State, and Utopia*.

Consider the fact that prostitution is legal in some parts of Nevada.[133] The implication is that, at least in these areas, it is licit to offer consideration for sexual services. But if so, then it is well within the law to make what would otherwise be considered lewd and lascivious offers to women—namely, money for sex.

Suppose that we, the authors of the present paper, set ourselves up as the Blockhead Corporation, located in Reno, Nevada, and wish to hire a female who would function half time as a secretary and half time as a prostitute. We advertise for the usual secretarial skills (typing, filing, correspondence, etc.), and also for those suitable to the other half of the job as well. After she is hired, we avail ourselves of both types of her accomplishments. We have now probably violated, and with a vengeance, every injunction in the panoply of the genus sexual harassment, species *quid pro quo* and hostile environment. Nevertheless, we should not be considered law violators.[134] Prostitution is legal. And this applies too, to secretarial services. Yet, it should not be the case that when we combine two perfectly legal, contractual, employment interactions, the sum total of them should be considered illegal. It is difficult for the logical mind to come to any such conclusion.[135] Nor is it any proper objection to

---

[133] This applies to every county in the state of Nevada apart from Clark County. See Nev. Rev. Stat. 201.300 (1998).

[134] Of course, if this is to be a licit commercial arrangement, there can be no fraud. That is, the employer must be crystal clear as to the contents of the contract. Without a meeting of the minds over the specifics, any demands for sex as part of the job description would be fraudulent.

[135] For a critique of the *status quo ante* on blackmail, see Eric Mack, "In Defense of Blackmail," *Philosophical Studies* 41 (1982): 274; Murray N. Rothbard, *Man, Economy, and State* (Auburn, Ala.: The Mises Institute, 1993), p. 443, n.49; Walter Block, "The Blackmailer as Hero," *The Libertarian Forum* 4, no. 12 (December 1972): 1; Walter Block, *Defending the Undefendable* (San Francisco, Calif.: Fox and Wilkes, 1999), p. 44–49; Walter Block and David Gordon, "Extortion and the Exercise of Free Speech Rights: A Reply to Posner, Epstein, Nozick, and Lindgren," *Loyola Los Angeles Law Review* 19, no. 1 (1985): 37; Walter Block, "Trading Money for Silence," *University of Hawaii Law Review* 8 (1986): 57; Walter Block, "The Case

our thesis to claim that prostitution is legal in only a small part of the country.[136] There are two possible rejoinders to this. First, if *quid pro quo* contracts with females and the imposition of an environment hostile to them can be demonstrated as behavior which violates no law (even if only in most of Nevada), then we have shown that there is nothing *per se* problematic about sexual harassment. If so, it should not be proscribed anywhere else, either. Second, a case on libertarian grounds can easily be made on behalf of legalizing prostitution in all other jurisdictions. After all, if a woman really owns her own body, an oft-made contention of the feminist and pro-choice forces,[137] then she can decide for herself to use it to provide sexual services

---

for De-Criminalizing Blackmail: A Reply to Lindgren and Campbell," *Washington University of St. Louis Law Review* 24 (1997): 225; Walter Block, "A Libertarian Theory of Blackmail," *Irish Jurist* 33 (1998): 280; Walter Block and Robert W. McGee, "Blackmail from A to Z," *Mercer Law Review* 50 (1999): 569.

[136] There is a parallel between this phenomenon and blackmail, which also combines two acts, each of which is legal in isolation (e.g., asking for money, threatening to tell about an embarrassing secret) but prohibited by law when combined. For support of the *status quo* on this law, see Peter Alldridge, "Attempted Murder of the Soul: Blackmail, Privacy, and Secrets," *Oxford Journal of Legal Studies* 13 (1993): 368; Scott Altman, "A Patchwork Theory of Blackmail," *University of Pennsylvania Law Review* 141, no. 5 (May 1993): 1639; James Boyle, "A Theory of Law and Information: Copyright, Spleens, Blackmail, and Insider Trading," *California Law Review* 80 (1992): 1413; Jennifer Gerarda Brown, "Blackmail as Private Justice," *University of Pennsylvania Law Review* 141, no. 5 (May 1993): 1935; Debra J. Campbell, "Why Blackmail Should be Criminalized: A Reply to Walter Block and David Gordon," *Loyola Los Angeles Law Review* 21 (1988): 883; Ronald Coase, "The 1987 McCorkle Lecture: Blackmail," *Virginia Law Review* 74 (1988): 655; George Daly and J. Fred Giertz, "Externalities, Extortion, and Efficiency: Reply," *American Economics Review* 68, no. 4 (September 1978): 736; Sidney W. DeLong, "Blackmailers, Bribe Takers, and the Second Paradox," *University of Pennsylvania Law Review* 141, no. 5 (May 1993): 1663.

[137] But only as regards abortion. For a libertarian perspective on this issue, see note 130.

to men for a fee. Denying this is to turn back the clock to an era in the U.S. when the signature of an adult woman on a contract would be considered null and void.

Suppose, however, that a foreman of the Blockhead Corporation, unbeknownst to us, makes a *quid pro quo* offer to a female employee: either go to bed with him and get a raise, or refuse and be fired. Now, it has already been established that we, the owners of the corporation, have a right to do this, provided no physical threat or fraud occurs. And, if it is licit for us to engage in such activities, it is also legitimate for us to pass on to our foreman the right to operate in this manner. We might do so, for example, in lieu of paying a higher salary.

But suppose our policy is not to allow *quid pro quo* (sex for money) contracts in our corporation on the part of our employees, but our foreman does this on his own initiative. Let us consider the libertarian analysis that applies in this case. Our answer is that while this man did not violate the rights of the woman (after all she, is an adult, a free agent, able to make up her own mind about offers of this sort), he did transgress against us, the owners of the firm. Rothbard's analysis of the analogous case of payola is worthy of quotation at length:

> In a typical payola scandal, a record company bribes a disc jockey to play Record A. Presumably, the disc jockey would either not have played the record at all, or would have played Record A fewer times; therefore, Record A is being played at the expense of Records B, C, and D which would have been played more frequently. ... Surely, in a moral sense, the public is being betrayed in its trust in the disc jockey's sincerity. ... But the public has no property right in the radio program, and so they have no legal complaint in the matter. ... The other record companies, the producers of Records B, C, and D, were also injured since their products were not played as frequently, but they, too, have no property rights in the program. ...
>
> Was anyone's property rights aggressed against by the disc jockey's taking of a bribe? Yes, ... the disc jockey violated his contractual obligation to his employer ... to play those records

which in his view will most suit the public. Hence, the disc jockey violated the property of the station owner or sponsor. ... [I]t is the disc jockey who accepts payola who has done something criminal and deserves to be prosecuted, but not the record company who paid the bribe.

Furthermore, if the record company had bribed the employer directly ... then there would have been no violation of anyone's property right and therefore properly no question of illegality. Of course, the public could easily feel cheated if the truth came out, and would then be likely to change their listening custom to another station or sponsor.[138]

As for the payola-accepting jockey, so for the foreman of Blockhead who uses this firm for his own advantage, against his employers' interest. The woman in the case no more has her rights violated than do the producers of Records B, C, and D, nor the listening public. Further, were the radio station to allow the disk jockey to accept payola from Record Company A, in lieu of a higher wage, it would be entirely within its rights, since the radio station and only the radio station owns the right to play what it wishes. Similarly, if Blockhead pays the foreman with lower wages, but allows him the right to engage in *quid pro quo* contracts with the female employee, then again no one's rights are violated.

There is an obvious point to be made here—the owners of the firm own the right to engage in *quid pro quo* contracts with female employees. If they cede it to a foreman, for mutually agreeable consideration, well and good. But if he seizes this on his own, he is stealing from the firm. The kernel of truth behind legal prohibitions of *quid pro quo* dealings on the part of employees is this: without the express permission of the employer, it amounts to theft from the employer. Thus, *quid pro quo* may be legitimately precluded from the workplace in certain circumstances. This arises not due to any intrinsic impropriety, but because it is a prerogative of the firm, and the firm's owners object to the use of *quid pro quo* on the part of their male subordinates without permission.

---

[138] Rothbard (1998), pp. 129–30.

There is a bottom line in all of this: hostility is in the eye of the beholder. There is no such thing as an objectively defined hostile environment. The reasonable woman standard is an exercise in logical futility, for female tastes in this (as in so much more) vary widely. One woman's hostile environment is another's ideal employment situation. The female who is comfortable working in Hooters might be very unhappy employed by a nunnery; one who can prosper in the milieu of a house of prostitution might feel out of place in a kindergarten. Similarly, those who yearn to work in a library, bank, elementary school, or law office might not find a safe and happy harbor as a waitress in a topless restaurant.[139]

CRITIQUE OF THE LAW

Let us now consider in detail some of the specifics of this law discussed above in a purely descriptive manner. We shall intersperse commentary into the citation of the law. As we state above:[140]

> Sexual harassment in the office means unwelcome sexual advances, requests for sexual favors, and other verbal or physical conduct of a sexual nature when:
>
> (a) Submission to such conduct is either explicitly or implicitly made a condition of an individual's employment.[141]

This may be disregarded. If it is agreed to by consenting adults, there is no warrant for setting such a contract aside, any more than there is for any other such agreement.

> (b) Submission to or rejection of such conduct by an individual is used as a basis for an employment decision effecting such individuals.[142]

---

[139] Or maybe not. The point is, no one can say anything for sure on this matter apart from noting that tastes will differ.

[140] See note 2 and accompanying text.

[141] 29 C.F.R. §1604.11(a)(l) (2001).

[142] *Id.* at §1604.11(a)(2).

There is no other rational way in which the bordello employer can
decide whom to employ.

> (c) Such conduct has a purpose or effect of substantially
>   interfering with an individual's right to work in an
>   environment free of intimidation, hostility, or threats
>   stemming from acts or language of a sexual nature.[143]

A woman may indeed have such a right.[144] But if she does, she
also has a right to renounce it, for a fee, if she so wishes. To deny
the latter is to deny the former. That is, if the EEOC maintains that a
female does not have the right to relinquish what would otherwise be
her right not to be continually approached in a sexual manner, then
she cannot have that right in the first place, contrary to the views of
this regulatory body.

> (d) The conduct interferes with an employee's ability to
>   focus on the job responsibilities.[145]

Consider again the Blockhead firm located in Reno, Nevada
(or anywhere else where prostitution is legal). None of our sexual
advances can be considered unwelcome since the woman we hire
will contractually agree to accept these overtures. It is an explicit part
of the contract; by signing it, she obligates herself to perform these
duties. We may indeed legitimately threaten her if she withholds
sexual services because in such a case she is guilty of contract
violation. Our threat would be similar to that of any (ordinary)
employer whose secretary refuses to type and file, or whose bordello
prostitute refuses to entertain men in bed: she will be fired and her
salary go unpaid. It is impossible, moreover, for our conduct to
interfere with the employee's ability to focus on job responsibilities

---

[143] *Id.* at §1604.11(a)(3).

[144] If so, then so does a man; men and women have equal rights in the
libertarian society.

[145] *Ellison v. Brady*, 924 F.2d 872, 877 (9th Cir. 1991).

because these are precisely her job responsibilities. We continue to cite from our previous description of the law:

> Some behaviors found by the EEOC and the courts to constitute sexual harassment are:
>
> (a) Sexually suggestive or obscene comments, threats, insults, slurs, jokes about gender-based traits of a person, or sexual propositions.[146]

But it is obvious, the politicians responsible for these laws notwithstanding, that this is precisely what occurs in a peep show emporium, or with regard to a Victoria's Secret catalogue. If the law does not prohibit these activities, and it does not, then it is intellectually incoherent for it to proscribe so-called sexual harassment.

> (b) Physical conduct such as intentional touching, pinching, brushing against another's body, suggesting or coercing sexual intercourse, or physical assault.[147]

Coercing sexual intercourse is rape. Intentional unwanted touching and pinching and brushing constitute battery. No responsible legal commentator opposes the prohibition of such *per se* criminal behavior. But *suggesting* sexual intercourse is surely an entirely different matter. If the EEOC and the courts ever succeeded in eliminating such suggestions, this would sound the death knell for the human race. That the dating and mating game should be played out only, perhaps, at least so far, in bars, while legally prohibited from churches, universities, and the workplace, is certainly not mandated by the idea that coercion should be banned from human interaction.

The point is, suggesting sexual intercourse has widely been interpreted as promoting a hostile environment, or constituting sexual harassment, when it occurs on a college campus, especially if the

---

[146] *Lipsett v. University of Puerto Rico*, 864 F.2d 881, 906 (1st Cir. 1988).

[147] *Jones v. Wesco Investments*, 846 F.2d 1154, 1155 (8th Cir. 1988).

suggestor is a male professor and the suggestee is a female student. Similar findings have been made for the business firm, particularly if the initiator of this suggestion is a male boss, and it is made to a female subordinate. And yet, as we have seen, suggesting sexual intercourse is the paradigmatic action at the Blockhead company. We have already established the legal validity of this firm's practices (at least in most parts of Nevada). Legal consistency requires that, at the very least, suggesting sexual intercourse be allowed in these domains. Suggesting sexual intercourse, at least at some point in the heterosexual relationship, is the primary vehicle for the perpetuation of the human race. If this is deemed *per se* illegal harassment, it can only serve the interests of those who oppose heterosexuality.

> (c) Non-verbal behavior such as leering or staring at another's body, displaying sexually suggestive photographs, cartoons, or magazines.[148]

Movies, television, and Broadway shows are nowadays replete with partial, frontal, and total nudity; it is unreasonable to expect that viewers would resist leering or staring at another's body. Were such a law to be carried out in a logically consistent manner, not only could there be no such industries, women would be confined to wearing chadors, as is the practice of the Taliban in Afghanistan and in many of the Islamic countries. This is hardly the direction in which we really want to go.

> (d) Continued expression of sexual or social interest in an individual after being informed that the interest is unwelcome.[149]

There are many thousands and thousands of cases on record of successful marriages of several decades and more duration where

---

[148] *Robinson v. Jacksonville Shipyards*, 760 F. Supp. 1486, 1494 (M.D. Fla. 1991).

[149] *Ellison v. Brady*, 924 F.2d 872, 874–75 (9th Cir. 1991) at 151.

the husband's initial overtures to the wife were at first rebuffed. But the male, as was his wont,[150] persevered. He was pressing and persistent. This might not please the feminists in the courts and in the EEOC, but this is part and parcel of male human nature.[151] According to what might be called the heterosexual norm, or ethic, the man is the pursuer, the woman the pursued. She sets up roadblocks, he overcomes them. The female, not the male, is the coy one. But this model does not resonate well in these modern, politically correct

---

[150] See on this Jerome H. Barkow, Leda Cosmides, and John Tooby, *The Adapted Mend: Evolutionary Psychology and the Generation of Culture* (Oxford: Oxford University Press, 1992); David M. Buss, *The Evolution of Desire* (New York: Basic Books, 1994); Richard Dawkins, *The Selfish Gene* (Oxford: Oxford University Press 1989); Robert H. Frank, *Passion Within Reason: The Strategic Role of the Emotions* (London: W.W. Norton, 1988); Mark Ridley, *The Red Queen: Sex and the Evolution of Human Nature* (New York: MacMillan, 1993); Donald Symons, *The Evolution of Human Sexuality* (Oxford: Oxford University Press, 1979); R. Trivers, *Social Evolution Reading* (Menlo Park, Calif.: Benjamin/Cummings Publishing, 1985); E. O. Wilson, *Sociobiology: A New Synthesis* (Cambridge, Mass.: Harvard University Press, 1975); Robert Wright, "Feminists, Meet Mr. Darwin," *New Republic* 211 (1994): 34. Sociobiologically speaking, females are supposed to be flirtatious—males, pressing and persistent.

[151] There is a wealth of anecdotal evidence attesting to male assertiveness and female reticence. Some of it is in the form of humor. According to one joke:

If a general says "yes," he means "yes." If he says "no," he means "no." If he says "maybe," he is not a general. If a diplomat says "yes," he means "maybe." If he says "maybe," he means "no." If he says "no," he is not a diplomat. If a girl (virgin) says "no," it means "maybe." If she says maybe, it means "yes." If she says "yes," she is not a girl (virgin).

And according to another bit of folk wisdom, when a woman says "No," it means "Maybe"; when she says "Maybe," it means "Yes."

In sharp contrast, the feminists have launched a campaign around the motto "No means no." We wonder what planet they are from, in terms of an understanding of human nature. Anyone who believes that every time a woman declines a man's advances she is serious about it only evidences his ignorance of the human condition.

times. Here, the sexes are supposed to be equal. The woman has as much right to initiate contact as the man.[152]

Of course, it is possible to go too far in this direction. There is, after all, such a thing as harassment, in contrast to rape. Even if the male expression of interest is limited to sending flowers, notes by mail, and leaving telephone messages (as opposed to physical invasion), it is possible for enough to be more than enough. But, for such cases, we already have remedies on the books (obtaining a protective order and anti-stalking statutes) and hardly need the minions of politically correct EEOC feminists to improve matters.

To anticipate the burden of the next section, on how a free market can alleviate legitimate harassment problems, reflect on the following: mail sent by an unrequited suitor is now delivered by the public postal monopoly; were this industry fully privatized,[153] there is little doubt that firms would deal with junk mail far more efficaciously than at present. Telephone messages come courtesy of one of the most highly government regulated of industries. A bit more economic freedom here, too, might well eventuate in the more

---

[152] For a recent critique of the modem mores, and a defense of the more traditional ones, see Danielle Crittenden, *What our Mothers Didn't Tell Us* (New York: Simon and Schuster, 1998); Richard Dooling, *Blue Streak: Swearing, Free Speech, and Sexual Harassment* (New York: Random House 1996); Ellen Fein and Sherrie Schneider, *The Rules: Time-Tested Secrets for Capturing the Heart of Mr. Right* (New York: Warner Books, 1996).

[153] The case for privatizing the post office is offered by Douglas K. Adie, *The Mail Monopoly: Analyzing Canadian Postal Service* (Vancouver, British Columbia: The Fraser Institute, 1990); Douglas K. Adie, *Monopoly Mail: Privatizing the United States Postal Service* (New Brunswick, N.J.: Transaction Publishers, 1988); Douglas K. Adie, "Why Marginal Reform of the US. Postal Service Won't Succeed," in *Free the Mail: Ending the Postal Monopoly*, Peter J. Ferrara ed., (Washington, D.C.: The Cato Institute,1990); Thomas G. Moore, "The Federal Postal Monopoly: History, Rationale, and Future" in *Free the Mail: Ending the Postal Monopoly*; Stuart M. Butler, "Privatizing Parcel Mail," *Management* 6 (1986); Stephen Moore, "Privatizing the US. Postal Service," in *Privatization: A Strategy for Taming the Federal Budget Fiscal Year 1988* (Washington, D.C.: Heritage Foundation, 1988).

efficient elimination of junk phone calls. Flowers are commonly delivered on public streets. Under full free enterprise for this industry, there is little doubt that unwanted flower deliveries, too, would be better squelched.[154]

> (e) Belief that an individual required to consent to the foregoing behavior as a term or condition of her employment.[155]

Sexually suggestive comments are precisely what the secretary-prostitute of Blockhead signed up to tolerate. Nor were her duties limited just to tolerating off-color comments either. There is no way that sexual intercourse can be coerced here any more than in a house of prostitution. Nor need one resort to the Blockhead case to deal with leering or staring at another's body. Such behavior occurs in every Hooters, every Playboy Club, in every topless establishment, in every restaurant where women wear micro miniskirts and other

---

[154] See on this Walter Block, "Public Goods and Externalities: The Case of Roads," *Journal of Libertarian Studies* 7 (1983): 1, 34; Walter Block, "Road Socialism," *International Journal of Value-Based Management* 9 (1996): 195–207; Walter Block, "Theories of Highway Safety," *Transportation Research Record* 912 (1983): 4; Walter Block, "Congestion and Road Pricing," *Journal of Libertarian Studies* 4 (1980): 299; Walter Block, "Free Market Transportation: Denationalizing the Roads," *Journal of Libertarian Studies* 3 (1979); 209; Michelle S. Cadin and Walter Block, "Privatize the Public Highway System," *The Freeman* 47 (1977): 96; Gerald Gunderson, "Privatization and the 19th-Century Turnpike," *Cato Journal* 9 (1989): 191; Daniel B. Klein, John Majewski, and Christopher Baer, "Responding to Relative Decline: The Plank Road Boom of Antebellum New York" *Journal of Economic History* 53 (1993): 106; Daniel B. Klein and G.J. Fielding, "Private Toll Roads: Learning from the Nineteenth Century," *Transportation Quarterly* 46 (1992): 321; Daniel Klein and G.J. Fielding, "How to Franchise Highways," *Journal of Transport Economics and Policy* 62 (1993): 113; Gabriel Roth, *The Private Provision of Public Services in Developing Countries* (Oxford University Press, 1987); Gabriel Roth, *Paying for Roads: The Economics of Traffic Congestion* (Harmondsworth, England: Penguin 1967); Murray N. Rothbard, *For a New Liberty*; William C. Woolridge, *Uncle Sam, the Monopoly Man* (New Rochelle, N.Y.: Arlington House, 1970).

[155] *Simmons v. Lyons*, 746 F.2d 265, 269 (5th Cir. 1984).

revealing costume. They are hired for the express purpose of being leered at, with their own consent. Were they not the sort of people to call forth this type of male behavior, they would be fired, or not hired in the first place.

THE ECONOMICS OF HARASSMENT

So far, we have been arguing that sexual harassment law is illogical, insofar as it involves voluntary, mutually agreeable behavior between consenting adults. That is, unless there is a fraudulent promise that normal heterosexual overtures will not take place in given premises, any woman who is on the receiving end of such behavior is free to take a different job; that she stays in her present position, where such overtures occur, is an indication that she values the package of work plus being "victimized" more highly than her next best alternative. Laws attempting to prohibit such occurrences thus constitute an ill-conceived response to what is a non-problem: ordinary hetero-sexual male-female, water-cooler-type interaction. This does not at all mean that, in this view, modesty and decorum and non-aggressive male behavior are out of reach for the women who do not yearn to be artists, models, actresses, prostitutes, or topless waitresses. The solution, in this perspective, may not emanate from the courts and the EEOC, but it nonetheless plays an important role in our society.

Very much to the contrary of the usual supposition on these matters, the answer is provided by the free enterprise system. In order to see this, we must discuss some concepts in labor economics. Heterosexual males vary in their presentations of themselves to heterosexual females, all the way from courtly behavior suitable to the Knights of the Round Table to that of the boor and lout.[156] Consider the position of a manager of a firm with a large number of females on staff, who is called upon to deal with one of the latter.

---

[156] For the purpose of this analysis, we assume that anything worse, e.g., from slight to heavy physical abuse to actual rape, does not exist; such acts are dealt with by the forces of law and order, not by ordinary businesses on the shop floor.

As is well known in economics, wages tend to equal the marginal revenue productivity of the worker.[157] But this includes not only the amount that the employee himself can add to the bottom line, but his effect on the contribution of others.[158] Let loose a few churls in the establishment, even those who full well know their job, and the productivity of most if not all of the females will plummet. Thus, as an employer, you would either not hire the barbarian, or you would only be willing to pay him a very low wage (perhaps, even, a large, negative one) which is but another way of saying you would not hire him at all. A firm which also employed a large number of females, particularly ones sensitive to crude male behavior, and insisted upon hiring such men, would be consigned to the dust bin of economics, i.e., bankruptcy.

The market, then, is a woman's best protector against untoward male behavior. The scalpel of the free enterprise system will better rid women of unwanted attention than the bludgeon of government law. For if the government errs (as we have been arguing) there is no automatic feedback mechanism which forces it to mend its ways. If it loses money, it can always make up for this shortfall by increasing taxes, or reducing other expenditures. In the private sector, in contrast, a loss of profit is absolutely crucial. The market is a better supplier not only of women's rights,[159] but of comfort in social settings than is the law (which can legitimately be used only to quell assault, battery, and rape).

Yet another example of business coming to the rescue of female sensibilities concerns restaurants and other such establishments that

---

[157] See, e.g., Morgan O. Reynolds, *Economics of Labor* (Cincinnati, Ohio: South-Western, 1995).

[158] A significant part of the reason a Michael Jordan or a Kobe Bryant is so productive in basketball is not due entirely to their own points, rebounds, or steals total, but because they also made their teammates into better players. This phenomenon is hardly confined to that particular sport, or, indeed, to the realm of athletics in general.

[159] This is because we have argued that women have a right not to niceness but only to security of their persons.

are open to the public and earn profit only from satisfied customers. Bouncers in a bar put a damper on verbiage that borders on abuse. The last thing an owner wants is for women to be made uncomfortable in his emporium. The search for profits leads the proprietor, as if by an invisible hand,[160] to do that which is in the interests of his female customers.

However, consider wolf whistles that typically occur on sidewalks. Feminists, and even others, take sharp exception to these outbursts. To them, this type of behavior shows male contempt for females; the interpretation is that the former see the latter only as a form of meat or sexual object.[161] But there is a reason why this objectionable behavior still occurs; nowhere is it written in stone that the market is supposed to come to the rescue of all maidenly sensibilities.

These wolf whistles are predominantly launched by construction workers and their ilk. The economic analysis we have offered does not apply to such situations because of externalities: the victimized women and the victimizing men are not employed by the same firm. If they were, the arguments mentioned above would provide sufficient incentive for the employer to bring them to a quick halt. Most economists would characterize this as a market failure.[162] But it is no

---

[160] See Adam Smith, *An Inquiry into the Nature and Causes of the Wealth of Nations*, Kathryn Sutherland, ed. (Oxford: Oxford University Press,1993). For a critique from the free-enterprise perspective, see Murray N. Rothbard, *The Logic of Action: Method, Money, and the Austrian School* (Cheltenham, U.K.: Edward Elgar, 1997).

[161] We assume away, for argument's sake, the claim that, although crude and unwelcome, wolf whistles are not *per se* rights violative, and do sometimes serve their purpose of allowing men to introduce themselves to women. That is, we temporarily adopt the leftist perspective that to see a woman as a sexual object is to commit in effect an assault upon her.

[162] See Gene Callahan, *Economics for Real People* (Auburn, Ala.: Ludwig von Mises Institute, 2001) or any other introduction to microeconomics or public finance on this matter. That is, in the view of most practitioners of the dismal science, the economics of discrimination as depicted above accurately describes intra-firm activity, but not that which occurs inter-firm.

such thing.[163] It is due not to a market failure, but to a failure to allow markets to operate in the first place. For example, if the streets were privately owned,[164] the proprietor of the sidewalk would have exactly the same financial incentive we have attributed to the owner of the bar and restaurant. Women who were annoyed by wolf whistles would not frequent his street establishment; since his profits depend upon the number of satisfied customers, he would have every inducement to deal with street whistlers as with offensive lounge lizards.

Consider the kinds of establishments for which boorish men typically work, if not in organizations that employ numerous women. After all, there are an awful lot of men who act in this manner, and they have to work somewhere.

Traditionally, the market solution is segregation. Boorish men tend to be diverted to places where they will do the least harm to the fairer sex: in the forests, deep sea fishing, merchant seamen, steel mills, putting out fires, etc. The problem with affirmative action[165] is that it breaks down such answers to the problem; such firms are forced to hire females. It is as if there were two groups of people who hated each other on sight (e.g., boorish men, and women who view their treatment of women as very harmful). The market, naturally enough, would tend to segregate them, so that they would not be continually at war with one another. Along comes government, not able to refrain from interfering, and pursues policies that put these

---

[163] For a critique of the "externalities as market failure" literature, see Hans-Hermann Hoppe, "Fallacies of the Public Goods Theory and the Production of Security," *Economics and Ethics of Private Property*; Jeffrey Hummel, "National Goods vs. Public Goods: Defense, Disarmament, and Free Riders," *Review of Austrian Economics* 4 (1990): 88; Walter Block, "Public Goods and Externalities: The Case of Roads," *Journal of Libertarian Studies* 4 (1983): 1.

[164] See note 155.

[165] For critiques, see Walter E. Williams and Walter Block, "Male-Female Earnings Differentials: A Critical Reappraisal," *Journal of Labor Research* 2, no. 2 (1981): 385; *Discrimination, Affirmative Action, and Equal Opportunity* (Vancouver, British Columbia: The Fraser Institute, 1982).

two groups into close and unwelcome proximity with one another. The result, of course, is chaos.[166]

The same economic analysis that applies to cigarette smoking can be utilized in the present context. Perhaps this furnishes a better analogy. Here, there is one group of people (the smokers) that create a nuisance (second-hand smoke), and another group that feels victimized. The government, in its infinite wisdom, bludgeons all establishments into adopting the same rules: previously, to set up smoking sections; but now, more and more, to ban indoor smoking entirely.[167] In sharp contrast, the market, driven by profit consider-ations (e.g. customer satisfaction), wields a scalpel. Some shops, such as those which supply health foods, ban smoking entirely. Others, such as pool halls, billiard rooms, bowling lanes, bars and

---

[166] There is a slight misanalogy here, in that in the case described in the text, there is mutual hatred and abuse emanating from both groups, while in sexual harassment one category of people are the harassors, and the other, the harassees. For Ronald H. Coase, however, this would be a valid analogy, in that in order to stop the harassors from victimizing the harassees, one would have to bring discomfort to the former. See "The Problem of Social Cost," *Journal of Labor Economics* 3 (1960): 1. That is, for Coase, there can be no such thing as harassment: all such interactions are reciprocal.

For critics of Coase, see Walter Block, "Ethics, Efficiency, Coasian Property Rights, and Psychic Income: A Reply to Harold Demsetz," *Review of Austrian Economics* 8 (1995): 61; Walter Block, "O.J.'s Defense: A *Reductio Ad Absurdum* of the Economics of Ronald Coase and Richard Posner," *European Journal of Law and Economics* 3 (1996): 265–86; Roy E. Cordato, "Subjective Value, Time Passage, and the Economics of Harmful Effects," *Hamline Law Review* 12 (1989): 229; Elisabeth Krecke, "Law and the Market Order: An Austrian Critique of the Economic Analysis of Law," in *Commentaries on Law and Economics*, Robert W. McGee, ed. (South Orange, NJ: Dumont Institute for Public Policy Research, 1977), p. 86; Gary North, *The Coase Theorem* (Stone Mountain, Georgia: Publisher Services, 1992); Murray N. Rothbard, "Law, Property Rights, and Air Pollution," in *Economics and the Environment: A Reconciliation*, Walter E. Block ed. (Vancouver, British Columbia: The Fraser Institute, 1990), p. 233.

[167] Since January 1, 1998, California has banned smoking in virtually all indoor public places including bars. See Ted Reuter, "California Living: Snuff Out that Cigarette, Please," *Christian Science Monitor*, January 12, 1998.

grills, place no rules whatsoever against this practice. And then, in the vast middle ground, there are a plethora of rules stipulating smoking times, days, sections, etc., all in an attempt to tailor their response to consumer demands.[168]

So far, we have analyzed male-female interaction from the former vantage point. Let us now consider the latter perspective. Suppose, now, that most females, as contended by those responsible for the repression of sexual harassment, are very reticent and shy. For them, the ordinary behavior of robust, heterosexual males is odious. Apart from refusing to pollute the work premises by hiring males, as we have just discussed, let us now discuss how the market will protect women from male overtures.

Again, the system works through competition. Not only are firms in competition with each other in the product or final goods markets which is well known, they also compete with one another when it comes to hiring workers. The preeminent form of rivalry is, of course, the wage paid. But employers also contend with each other over employees through the provision of working conditions.

Consider, as an analogy to our case in point, the question of air conditioning. The employer faces the choice of whether or not he should install this amenity on his premises for the enjoyment of his workers. If he does, he will undergo a cost. On the other hand, he will more likely satisfy, attract, and retain employees. The profit-maximizing firm will engage in this expense if he can thereby recoup these costs in the form of lower wages paid. Most employees would accept a reduced wage in an air-conditioned factory in preference to the otherwise identical job lacking such favorable working conditions. Those firms which do not install air conditioning have to pay higher wages. Workers tend to sort themselves out based on their tastes for air conditioning. Those who spurn it tend to gravitate to old-fashioned types of surroundings, where they are paid more, and have to forego the benefits of cooler air. Those who like it, but only slightly, can be found in premises of either type. And those

---

[168] See Walter Block, "Tobacco Advertising," *International Journal of Value-Based Management* 10 (1997): 3, 221–35.

who cannot get along without it tend to aggregate in air-conditioned facilities, even at the cost of a wage cut.

Women, too, differ in their taste[169] or distaste for assertive/ aggressive male behavior (e.g., for what is considered by some to be a hostile environment). There are some, call them Ls, who have a marked aversion to all such goings on. They tend to gravitate to work environments which preclude males altogether (e.g., a nunnery, a kindergarten). Others, at the opposite end of the continuum, call them Ps, relish these sorts of hostile environments. In the middle, the category of probably most females, call them Hs, are those who take an intermediate stance on this issue.

Assume that, apart from this issue, the marketable skills of all three groups are equal. Then, with equal productivity, we would expect money wages not to differ between them. Now, let us introduce the issue of hostility of environment. Under the economic system of *laissez faire* capitalism, firms are free to institute a policy proscribing a hostile environment or not. That is, completely as a private matter, they can offer contracts to males,[170] positing that if they are found guilty of sexual harassment, they will have to pay a penalty, for example, forego a bond they have to post upon being hired. This will undoubtedly imply a cost, as in the air conditioning case, for there will be the additional disbursements in order to monitor the system, hiring hearing officers to determine guilt or innocence, to say nothing of the extra monetary and psychic costs imposed on males.

Let us now consider employer incentives to introduce such a system, given that he is "free to choose."[171] He would do so if he could thereby reduce his costs in the form of lower wages, which he could thereby pay to appreciative females. There are those, of course,

---

[169] See Gary Becker, *Human Capital* (Washington, D.C.: The National Bureau of Economic Research, 1964).

[170] See Gary Becker, *The Economics of Discrimination* (Chicago: The University of Chicago Press, 1957).

[171] This is the felicitous title of a book by Milton and Rose Friedman. See Milton and Rose Friedman, *Free to Choose* (New York: Harcourt Brace Jovanovich, 1980).

who would object to the fact that women have to pay a compensating differential in the form of lower wages. After all, they are the victims, not the aggressors. If this is market fairness, we want less of it, not more, they might say. This objection misses the point, however. Here, we are discussing not the first case where there was a large majority of women, and males were made by the market to either toe the line or not be hired at all. Rather, we are now considering the case of a male-dominated industry or firm (e.g. oil refinery, lumberjack, steel mill, coal mine) where the sensibilities of women work, mainly, to reduce the productivity of men. Under these circumstances, of course, women will have to lose out financially in the market, compared to the situation where they had no such negative effects on the productivity of men. It is the same with all statistical outliers. Men who are over seven feet tall and weigh more than 300 pounds, or who are less than five feet tall and weigh in at under 100 pounds, cannot buy off-the-rack clothes. They must purchase tailor-made products, and these cost more. Similarly, it is costly to tailor the reactions of hordes of men to female sensibilities.

RESPONSIBILITY

> (f) Employer responsibility for acts of non-employees such
> as customers or service technicians, when the employer
> knows, or should have known, of the unwelcome conduct
> and fails to take immediate or appropriate action.[172]

Perhaps the most evil and insidious aspect of this whole episode is the requirement that one person be held accountable for the actions of another. Let us here accept, if only for the sake of argument, that there is indeed a crime of sexual harassment. Placing responsibility for such acts on those who have not committed them is highly improper. Whether it is employees of the firm, customers, suppliers, their employees, it matters not one whit—under this law, the employer will be found guilty even though he had no part whatsoever in the harassment.

---

[172] C.F.R. §1604.11(d) (2001).

That alone ought to be enough to establish the illegitimacy of vicarious liability, for the entire corpus of law is built on the bedrock that the guilty party, not anyone else, shall pay for his crime. Suppose a transportation firm hires a driver to convey passengers in its bus from one city to another in a safe and law-abiding manner. Instead, this employee drives recklessly, and hits another vehicle. In justice, only this negligent chauffeur should be forced to compensate the victims. In actual point of fact, however, it is likely that the firm itself will be made liable.[173] This stems from an unjustified search for "deep pockets." Just because the malfeasant driver does not have enough money to fully compensate the victims does not render it appropriate to attack the bank account of a totally innocent person, the owner of the firm.[174]

The view underlying sexual harassment law, in contrast, is predicated upon vicarious liability or *respondeat superior*. Here, one person, the employer, can be held liable for the crimes or torts of another, even though the party of the first part did not ask the party of the second to commit the act. No greater injustice can be imagined.

Rothbard goes so far as to characterize this as the "notorious theory of vicarious liability."[175] States Thomas Baty: "In hard fact, the reason for the employer's liability is the damages are taken from a deep pocket."[176] And in the view of Prosser,

---

[173] Assume there is no insurance policy in effect.

[174] A counter argument is that the employer was causally related to the accident, and therefore at least in part responsible for it, in that had he not hired this particular driver, it would not have occurred. This is subject to the *reductio ad absurdum* response that there are many other people also causally responsible for the accident, and it would be highly unjust to make them pay for it. For example, the accident would not have occurred had not the driver been able to buy clothes, and food; had the car or road not been built in the first place. Thus, we can also implicate in this accident those who mined the iron necessary to construct the bus.

[175] Murray N. Rothbard, "Law, Property Rights, and Air Pollution."

[176] *Id.* at 247.

most courts have made little or no effort to explain the result, and have taken refuge in rather empty phrases, such as ... the endlessly repeated formula of "respondeat superior," which in itself means nothing more than look to the man higher up.[177]

In our own rendition of this aspect of the law, we state, "the employer is strictly liable for the conduct of supervisory employees who are acting within the scope of their authority."[178] (This, of course, was reportorial, not advocated by us.) And, indeed, there is a certain coherence to this way of putting the matter. For if the "employees ... are acting within the scope of their authority" in their malfeasance, then, and to that extent, the employer should be responsible for their acts, in that he in effect ordered them to commit the tort. But that is not at all what the EEOC is mandating. Here, there is the far lesser requirement only that the employer "knows, or should have known, of the unwelcome conduct and fails to take immediate or appropriate action."

But this should not even be relevant. If A knows that B is about to rob a grocer, it is clear who should go to jail when this nefarious activity actually occurs. Obviously B is the guilty party, and A a total innocent.

If the law is going to hold employers responsible for acts of employees, all in the search for deep pockets, there is no rational end to this process. Suppose an employee commits an actual rape of a co-worker. It is clear that, in a just society, only the rapist should go to jail. To incarcerate the employer would be an injustice. Obviously, only the rapist is guilty of the crime, and should do the time, and this holds true whether the rape occurs on the business premises or somewhere else.

But there are other anomalies in this situation. It is unreasonable to hold employers responsible for employees, since the latter are in effect agents of the former; but if we do, then logical consistency

---

[177] *Id.*

[178] See note 20.

requires that we should hold all principals responsible for the acts of their agents. For example, following this line of reasoning, we would hold the tenant or landlord responsible for the acts of the real estate broker; the investor for the acts of the stockbroker; business partners, or spouses, for that matter, for the acts of each other. Alternatively, if the reason we are holding the employer responsible for the acts of the employee is that the former is higher up in the sociological hierarchy than the latter, we might consider generalizing this relationship, too. If we did, we would then jail landlords for the acts of their tenants. But it is merely Marxist drivel to think that employers have more power than employees (tell that to Michael Jordan and Jerry Reinsdorf) or landlords than tenants (tell that to the landlord of Bill Gates or Donald Trump). This being the case, then, we might with equal illogic hold employees responsible for the acts of employers, or tenants responsible for those of their landlords.

Vicarious liability and *respondeat superior* are a search for deep pockets, not justice.

CUI BONO?

If sexual harassment laws are the unmitigated disaster we have made them out to be, we must now attempt to explain why we have them on the books.

One way to answer this question is to ask, "Who benefits from this legislation?" The underlying theory is that those who gain from these enactments were likely instrumental in their passage in the first place, and in their subsequent support.[179]

The point is, it is difficult to avoid the conclusion that sexual harassment law in general, and the idiosyncratic definition and interpretation of hostile environments, are aimed at interfering, as much as possible, with normal male-female interaction. As we have seen, it

---

[179] This is the methodology employed by Elvis Cole and all other great detectives. See Robert Crais, *Sunset Express* (New York: Hyperion, 1996). Apart from means and opportunity, the motive for the crime is often the best way to discern the identity of the criminal.

is entirely unremarkable for heterosexual males to take the initiative in setting up relationships with heterosexual females. If they are to do so, they must necessarily at least sometimes make overtures which are unwelcome. There is no way that they can possibly know, for sure, before the fact, whether their suits shall be welcome or not, even apart from the traditional coyness of heterosexual females. To penalize heterosexual males for such behavior is surely an attempt to reduce it.

When looked at in this way, there are some obvious candidates to play the role of beneficiary of these laws: all those who gain from making it more difficult for heterosexual men and women to interact with one another in traditional courtship patterns. This would include lesbians, since if men were kept apart from women, some of the latter might become attached to female homosexuals, whom they previously spurned; also female man-haters, on ideological grounds. Homosexual men would gain in a similar manner, if heterosexual men are cut off from heterosexual women. The point is, there are always people on the margin of homo- and hetero-sexuality; make things more difficult in one of these directions, and at least some of these will become inclined to the other direction.

As well, there are the feminists who oppose [male] freedom almost for the sake of opposing freedom.[180] The idea that men, mostly assertive, often boorish, should be able to approach women with impunity for the ultimate purpose of heterosexual intercourse must be anathema to them. To this rogues gallery we must add the over-populationists[181] and other radical-wing environmentalists for whom the ideal of fewer people figures heavily in their solution to the

---

[180] See Michael Levin, *Feminism and Freedom* (New York: Transaction Books, 1987); Michael Levin, "Comparable Worth: The Feminist Road to Socialism," *Commentary* (September 1984): 39.

[181] See Paul R. Ehrlich, *The Population Bomb* (New York: Ballantine, 1968); Paul R. Herlich and Anne H. Ehrlich, *The Population Explosion* (New York: Simon and Schuster, 1990); David Foreman, "Only Man's Presence Can Save Nature," *Harpers* (April 1990); Al Gore, *Earth in the Balance: Ecology and the Human Spirit* (Boston: Houghton-Mifflin, 1992).

earth's supposed problems. If men and women cannot get together as easily as before, they are likely to breed fewer children, something fervently to be wished for, at least in this quarter.

We do not at this time contend that these groups have been active in promoting the anti-sexual-harassment agenda. This may indeed be the case. We only maintain that this is a likely avenue for future research into the question of who supports such legislation.

CONCLUSION

We conclude, given the foregoing, that sexual harassment law is unjust, and ought to be repealed. We maintain that *quid pro quo* is part and parcel of economic freedom, and that this has value both instrumentally in creating a prosperous economy, and intrinsically, for its own sake.[182] In our view, the market can eliminate a hostile work environment—where there is an economic need for this—far more effectively and justly than can government.

For rejoinders, see Daniel Coffey and Walter Block, "Postponing Armageddon: Why Population Growth Isn't Out of Control," *Humanomics* 15 (1999): 66; Julian Simon, *The Ultimate Resource* (Princeton, N.J.: Princeton University Press 1981); David Friedman, *Laissez faire in Population: The Least Bad Solution* (Population Council 1972); Peter T. Bauer, "Population Scares," *Commentary*, (November 1987): 39.

[182] See James Gwartney, Robert Lawson, and Walter Block, *Economic Freedom of the World, 1975–1995* (Vancouver, British Columbia: The Fraser Institute, 1996).

38. THE BOY SCOUTS, FREEDOM OF ASSOCIATION, AND THE RIGHT TO DISCRIMINATE: A LEGAL, PHILOSOPHICAL, AND ECONOMIC ANALYSIS

IN *BOY SCOUTS OF AMERICA V. DALE*,[1] THE SUPREME COURT WAS faced with one of the most contentious questions facing today's society. That is whether an organization like the Boy Scouts can determine with whom it associates, or whether there is some over-riding public interest in compelling associational acceptance of, as in this case, an avowed homosexual. Are the Boy Scouts to be regarded by some as heroic defenders of James Madison's treasured idea of freedom of association? Or are they to be seen, as they are in many quarters, as evil discriminators against individuals who have a privacy right to their sexual orientation? This controversy commenced when the complainant James Dale became a scout in 1978 at the age of eight.[2] He remained one until he turned eighteen.[3] Dale was an exceptional scout and achieved its highest honor, the

---

Roy Whitehead, Jr. and Walter Block, *Oklahoma City University Law Review* 29 no. 3 (Fall 2004).

[1] *Boy Scouts of America v. Dale*, 530 U.S. 640 (2000).

[2] *Id.* at 644.

[3] *Id.*

rank of Eagle Scout.[4] About the time he left home to attend Rutgers University, the Boy Scouts approved his application for the adult position of assistant scout master in Troop Seventy-Three.[5] When Dale arrived at Rutgers University, he acknowledged that he was gay and eventually became the co-president of the Rutgers Lesbian/Gay Alliance.[6] Later, Dale was interviewed by a newspaper reporter writing about the psychological and health needs of lesbian and gay teenagers.[7] "[T]he newspaper published the interview and Dale's photograph over a caption identifying him as the co-president of the Lesbian/Gay Alliance."[8]

Not surprisingly, Dale then received a letter from the Monmouth council executive revoking his adult membership.[9] In response to Dale's inquiry about his revocation, the executive responded by letter indicating that the Boy Scouts "specifically forbid membership to homosexuals."[10]

Thereafter, Dale responded by filing a complaint against the Boy Scouts in New Jersey Superior Court.[11] He alleged that the Boy Scouts had violated New Jersey's public accommodations statute and its common law by revoking his membership based solely on his sexual orientation.[12] "New Jersey's public accommodations statute prohibits, among [many] things, discrimination on the basis of sexual

---

[4] *Id.*

[5] *Id.*

[6] *Id.* at 645.

[7] *Id.*

[8] *Id.*

[9] *Id.*

[10] *Id.* (citations omitted).

[11] *Id.*

[12] *Id.*

orientation in places of public accommodation."[13] Some of the places listed in the statute do not appear to be physical "places" in the traditional meaning of the word.

Nevertheless "[t]he New Jersey Superior Court's Chancery Division granted summary judgment in favor of the Boy Scouts."[14] The superior court decided that the Boy Scouts was not a place of public accommodation but rather was a distinct private group exempt

---

[13] Id. see N.J. Stat. Ann. §10:5-5 (West Supp. 2004), stating:

> A place of public accommodation shall include, but not be limited to: any tavern, roadhouse, hotel, motel, trailer camp, summer camp, day camp, or resort camp, whether for entertainment of transient guests or accommodation of those seeking health, recreation or rest; any producer, manufacturer, wholesaler, distributor, retail shop, store, establishment, or concession dealing with goods or services of any kind; any restaurant, eating house, or place where food is sold for consumption on the premises; any place maintained for the sale of ice cream, ice and fruit preparations or their derivatives, soda water or confections, or where any beverages of any kind are retailed for consumption on the premises; any garage, any public conveyance operated on land or water, or in the air, any stations and terminals thereof; any bathhouse, boardwalk, or seashore accommodation; any auditorium, meeting place, or hall; any theatre, motion-picture house, music hall, roof garden, skating rink, swimming pool, amusement and recreation park, fair, bowling alley, gymnasium, shooting gallery, billiard and pool parlor, or other place of amusement; any comfort station; any dispensary, clinic or hospital; any public library; any kindergarten, primary and secondary school, trade or business school, high school, academy, college and university, or any educational institution under the supervision of the State Board of Education, or the Commissioner of Education of the State of New Jersey. Nothing herein contained shall be construed to include or to apply to any institution, bona fide club, or place of accommodation, which is in its nature distinctly private; nor shall anything herein contained apply to any educational facility operated or maintained by a bona fide religious or sectarian institution, and the right of a natural parent or one in loco parentis to direct the education and upbringing of a child under his control is hereby affirmed; nor shall anything herein contained be constructed to bar any private secondary or post secondary school from using in good faith criteria other than race, creed, color, national origin, ancestry or affectional or sexual orientation in the admission of students.

[14] *Boy Scouts of America v. Dale*, 530 U.S. at 645.

from coverage under New Jersey's accommodation law.[15] The court also decided that the Boy Scouts' beliefs about homosexuality were unmistakable and that the First Amendment freedom of "expressive association"[16] prevented the state from compelling the organization to associate with Mr. Dale as an adult leader.[17]

On appeal, the New Jersey Superior Court's Appellate Division reversed and remanded Dale's claim holding that the state's public accommodations law applied to the Boy Scouts.[18] Thus, the court rejected the Boy Scouts' federal constitutional claim of freedom of association.[19]

The Boy Scouts appealed to the New Jersey Supreme Court.[20] The Scouts argued that the application of New Jersey's public accommodations law violated their constitutional rights "to enter into and maintain ... intimate or private relationships ... [and] to associate for the purpose of engaging in protected speech."[21] However, the New Jersey Supreme Court concluded that the Boy Scouts' "large size, nonselectivity, inclusive rather than exclusive purpose, and practice of inviting or allowing nonmembers to attend meetings, establish that the organization is not 'sufficiently personal or private to warrant constitutional protection' under the freedom of intimate association."[22] In regard to the Boy Scouts' claimed right of expressive association, the New Jersey Supreme Court "agree[d] that Boy Scouts expresses a belief in moral values and uses its activities

---

[15] *Id.*

[16] *Id.* at 648.

[17] *Id.* at 645–46.

[18] *Id.* at 646.

[19] *Id.*

[20] *Dale v. Boy Scouts of America*, 734 A.2d 1196, 1219 (N.J. 1999), *rev'd*, 530 U.S. 640 (2000).

[21] See *id.* (quoting *Board of Directors of Rotary International v. Rotary Club of Duarte*, 481 U.S. 537, 544 (1987)).

[22] *Id.* at 1221.

to encourage the moral development of its members."[23] However, the court noted that it was "not persuaded … that a 'shared goal[ ]' of Boy Scout members is to associate in order to preserve the view that homosexuality is immoral."[24] Therefore, the court held that "Dale's membership does not violate Boy Scouts' right of expressive association because his inclusion would not 'affect in any significant way' [Boy Scouts] existing members' ability to carry out their various purposes."[25] The New Jersey court also determined that the State had a compelling interest in eliminating "the destructive consequences of discrimination from our society,"[26] and that the State's public accommodations law does no more than necessary to accomplish its purpose of stamping out such "destructive discrimination."[27]

The Boy Scouts relied on *Hurley v. Irish-American Gay, Lesbian, & Bi-sexual Group of Boston*[28] to support its First Amendment right to exclude Dale from the organization.[29] The New Jersey Supreme Court decided that *Hurley* was not definitive. In the court's view, *Hurley* was distinguishable because "the reinstatement of Dale [did] not compel [the] Boy Scouts to express any message."[30]

---

[23] *Id.*

[24] *Id.* 1223–24 (alteration in original) (citing *Roberts v. United States Jaycees*, 468 U.S. 609, 636 (1984)).

[25] *Id.* at 1225 (alteration in original) (citations omitted).

[26] *Id.* at 1227.

[27] *Id.*

[28] *Hurley v. Irish-American Gay, Lesbian, and Bisexual Group*, 515 U.S. 557 (1995). Here, as we will explore in greater detail later, the Supreme Court held that a gay group did not have a First Amendment right to march in a St. Patrick's Day parade. The Court decided that inclusion of the gay group would interfere with the parade organization's First Amendment rights by giving the impression that they sponsored the views of the gay group. See *id.* at 572–73. The Court determined that the parade is an inherently expressive undertaking. *Id.* at 573–78.

[29] *Dale v. Boy Scouts of America*, 734 A.2d at 1228.

[30] *Id.* at 1229.

THE MAJORITY

In *Boy Scouts of America v. Dale*,[31] Chief Justice Rehnquist commenced his analysis of the issue by citing *Roberts v. United States Jaycees*[32] for the proposition that "implicit in the right to engage in activities protected by the First Amendment" is "a corresponding right to associate with others in pursuit of a wide variety of political, social, economic, educational, religious, and cultural ends."[33] He pointed out that government actions may constitutionally burden this freedom in many ways.[34] A prime example includes "intrusion into the internal structure or affairs of an association"[35] like imposing a "regulation that forces the group to accept members it does not desire."[36] Obviously, forcing a group to accept members it does not desire may impair the ability of the group to express the views that it wants to articulate. Relying on *Roberts*, Rehnquist explained, "freedom of association ... plainly presupposes a freedom not to associate."[37] Consequently, he said "the forced inclusion of an unwanted person in a group infringes the group's freedom of

---

[31] *Boy Scouts of America v. Dale*, 530 U.S. 640 (2000).

[32] *Roberts*, 468 U.S. 609 (1984). The Jaycees brought an action contending that Minnesota's public accommodations law requiring them to admit women violated the male members' intimate association rights. The Supreme Court concluded that "Jaycees chapters lack[ed] the distinctive characteristics that might afford constitutional protection to the decision ... to exclude women." *Id.* at 621. The Court emphasized that the local chapters "are neither small nor selective[,]" and that "much of the activity central to the formation and maintenance of the association involves the participation of strangers to that relationship." *Id.*

[33] *Id.* at 622.

[34] *Boy Scouts of America v. Dale*, 530 U.S. at 648.

[35] *Id.* (quoting *Roberts*, 468 U.S. at 623).

[36] *Roberts*, 468 U.S. at 623.

[37] *Boy Scouts of America v. Dale.*, 530 U.S. at 648 (quoting *Roberts*, 468 U.S. at 623).

expressive association"[38] when his presence has an effect on the group's ability to advocate their views.[39]

The freedom of expressive association, however, is not always absolute.[40] For instance, the Supreme Court ruled that this freedom may be impacted "by regulations adopted to serve compelling state interests, unrelated to the suppression of ideas, that cannot be achieved through means significantly less restrictive of associational freedoms."[41] The Chief Justice then turned to a determination of whether or not the Boy Scouts are entitled to protection because they engage in "expressive association."[42] His inquiry led to an examination of the Boy Scouts' mission statement. The gist of this document is essentially that the Boy Scouts seek to instill values in young people that will lead them to make ethical choices in their life experiences.[43]

Relying on the Boy Scouts' mission statement, the Chief Justice noted that it seems indisputable that the Boy Scouts were seeking to transmit a system of values by engaging in expressive activity.[44]

---

[38] *Id.*; see also *New York State Club Association v. City of New York*, 487 U.S. 1, 13 (1988).

[39] *Boy Scouts of America v. Dale.*, 530 U.S. at 648.

[40] *Roberts*, 468 U.S. at 623.

[41] *Id.*

[42] *Boy Scouts of America v. Dale.*, 530 U.S. at 648.

[43] "It is the mission of the Boy Scouts of America to serve others by helping to instill values in young people and, in other ways, to prepare them to make ethical choices over their lifetime in achieving their full potential." *Id.* at 649. These values are based on both the Scout Oath and the Scout Law which state:

Scout Oath: On my honor I will do my best [t]o do my duty to God and my country and to obey the Scout Law; [t]o help other people at all times; [t]o keep myself physically strong, mentally awake, and morally straight.

Scout Law: A Scout is: [t]rustworthy [o]bedient [l]oyal [c]heerful [h]elpful [t]hrifty [f]riendly [b]rave [c]ourteous [c]lean [k]ind (and) [r]everent.

Id. at 649.

[44] *Id.* at 650 (citing *Roberts*, 468 U.S. at 636 (O'Connor, J., concurring) ("Even the training of outdoor survival skills or participation in community service

Having decided that the Boy Scouts' stated mission denotes expressive activity, the next inquiry was "whether the forced inclusion of Dale as an assistant scout master would significantly affect [their] ability to advocate public or private viewpoints."[45] This inquiry required the Court to briefly examine the Boy Scouts' views on homosexuality.[46] A careful reading of the mission statement clearly reveals that the Boy Scouts do not expressly mention sexual orientation in their Scout Oath or Scout Law.[47] However, according to the Boy Scouts, homosexual conduct is inconsistent with the important life values found in the Scout Oath and Scout Law.[48] Accordingly, the values that the Scouts claim to instill in their members are based on the same Oath and Law.[49] So from where do these values arise? In the view of the organization, the values it seeks to instill are represented by the terms "morally straight" and "clean."[50] Hence, such terms are incompatible with homosexuality."[51]

Certainly, reasonable people can derive different meanings of the terms "morally straight" and "clean."[52] Many people might believe that homosexual conduct falls within these parameters. Further, others may maintain that sexual orientation is no one else's business. Still others, apparently including the Boy Scouts, believe that homosexuality is incompatible with living a morally straight and clean life.[53]

---

might become expressive when the activity is intended to develop good morals, reverence, patriotism, and a desire for self-improvement").

[45] *Id.*

[46] *Id.*

[47] *Id.*

[48] *Id.*

[49] *Id.*

[50] *Id.*

[51] *Id.*

[52] *Id.*

[53] *Id.*

The Supreme Court observed the New Jersey Supreme Court's conclusion that "exclusion of members solely on the basis of their sexual orientation is inconsistent with Boy Scouts' commitment to a diverse and 'representative' membership ... [and] contradicts Boy Scouts' overarching objective to reach 'all eligible youth.'"[54] The New Jersey court concluded that the Boy Scouts violated the State's discrimination law, in part, because the exclusion of homosexual members "appears antithetical to the organization's goals and philosophy."[55]

Chief Justice Rehnquist would have none of this. His ringing response was to reject the entire notion that a court could rebuff a private organization's philosophy.[56] He said that "it is not the role of the courts to reject a group's expressed values because they disagree with those values or find them internally inconsistent."[57] Further, "[a]s is true of all expressions of First Amendment freedoms, the courts may not interfere on the ground that they view a particular expression as unwise or irrational."[58] He continued, "[r]eligious beliefs need not be acceptable, logical, consistent, or comprehensible to others in order to merit First Amendment protection."[59] In their appellate briefs, the Boy Scouts claimed they taught their members that homosexual conduct is not morally straight.[60] The Court accepted that assertion as true.[61] For that reason, there was no need

---

[54] *Id.* at 650–51 (quoting *Dale v. Boy Scouts of America*, 734 A.2d 1196, 1226 (1999), *rev'd*, 530 U.S. 640 (2000)).

[55] *Dale*, 734 A.2d at 1226.

[56] *Boy Scouts of America v. Dale*, 530 U.S. at 651.

[57] *Id.*

[58] *Id.* (quoting *Democratic Party of the United States v. Wisconsin ex rel La Follette*, 450 U.S. 107, 124 (1981)).

[59] *Id.* (quoting *Thomas v. Review Board of Indiana Employment Security Division*, 450 U.S. 707, 714 (1981)).

[60] *Id.*

[61] *Id.*

to inquire further.[62] Why? Because it is not the business of the Court to determine if a particular view is unwise or irrational, and the record clearly establishes the Boy Scouts' view on homosexuality.[63] The Court concluded that the Boy Scouts' professed beliefs about homosexual conduct were sincere.[64] Finally, the majority noted the fact that the Boy Scouts had publicly and consistently expressed the same views with respect to homosexual conduct by its pleadings in prior litigation.[65]

The next question faced by the Court was "whether Dale's presence as an assistant scout-master [would place a significant burden on] the Boy Scouts' desire to 'not promote homosexual conduct as a legitimate form of behavior.'"[66] The Chief Justice noted, "[a]s we give deference to an association's assertions regarding the nature of its expression, we must also give deference to an association's view of what would impair its expression."[67] Collectively, given Dale's publicized interview about his sexual orientation, his co-presidency of the gay and lesbian organization in college, and his continued gay rights activities, it is obvious that his presence would force the Boy Scouts to send a message, against their will, that they accept

---

[62] *Id.* at 651–52.

[63] *Id.* at 652. The Boy Scouts' 1993 position statement reads:

> The Boy Scouts of America has always reflected the expectations that Scouting families have had for the organization. We do not believe that homosexuals provide a role model consistent with these expectations. Accordingly, we do not allow for the registration of avowed homosexuals as members or as leaders of the BSA.

> *Id.* (citations omitted).

[64] *Id.* at 652–53; see *Curran v. Mount Diablo Council of Boy Scouts of America*, 952 P.2d 218 (Cal. 1998).

[65] *Boy Scouts of America v. Dale*, 530 U.S. at 653 (quoting Reply Brief for Petitioners at 5, *Boy Scouts of America v. Dale*, 530 U.S. 640 (2000) (No. 99-699)).

[66] *Id.*

[67] *Id.*

and even highly regard homosexual conduct as a legitimate form of behavior.[68]

The Court turned to the holding in *Hurley* as a basis for its belief that Dale's presence would force the Boy Scouts to send a message that they condone homosexual conduct.[69] Recall that *Hurley* involved the question of whether Massachusetts' public accommodations law would require the organizers of a private St. Patrick's Day parade to include among the marchers an Irish-American gay, lesbian, and bi-sexual group called GLIB.[70] GLIB contended that the parade organizers violated their First Amendment rights by denying them the opportunity to march.[71] In that case, the Court observed "that the parade organizers did not wish to exclude the GLIB members because of their sexual orientations, but because they wanted to march behind a GLIB banner."[72] The Court stated:

> [A] contingent marching behind the organization's banner would at least bear witness to the fact that some Irish are gay, lesbian, or bi-sexual, and the presence of the organized marchers would suggest their view that people of their sexual orientations have as much claim to unqualified social acceptance as heterosexuals. ... The parade's organizers may not believe these facts about Irish sexuality to be so, or they may object to unqualified social acceptance of gays and lesbians or have some other reason for wishing to keep GLIB's message out of the parade. But whatever the reason, it boils down to the choice of a speaker not to propound a particular point of view, and that choice is presumed to lie beyond the government's power to control.[73]

---

[68] *Id.*

[69] *Id.*

[70] *Id.*

[71] *Id.*

[72] *Id.*

[73] *Id.* at 654 (alteration in original) (quoting *Hurley*, 515 U.S. 557, 574–75 (1995)).

Here, the Court found that the Boy Scouts legitimately believe "that homosexual conduct is inconsistent with the values it seeks to instill in its ... members."[74] That is so, just "[a]s the presence of GLIB in Boston's St. Patrick's Day parade would have interfered with the parade organizers' [First Amendment rights not to be forced] to propound a particular point of view."[75] Dale's presence as an assistant scout master in a Boy Scout troop would just as surely interfere with the Boy Scouts' choice not to suggest a view on homosexuality contrary to its own beliefs.[76]

Next, the Court turned to the New Jersey court's "determination that the Boy Scouts' ability to disseminate its message was not significantly affected by the forced inclusion of Dale as an assistant scoutmaster."[77] The New Jersey Court found that "Boy Scout members do not associate for the purpose of disseminating the belief that homosexuality is immoral; Boy Scouts discourages its leaders from disseminating *any* views on sexual issues; and Boy Scouts include sponsors and members who subscribe to different views in respect of homosexuality."[78]

Chief Justice Rehnquist wholly disagreed with the New Jersey Supreme Court's conclusion for three reasons. First, he fiercely stated that associations did not have to associate "for the 'purpose' of disseminating a certain message in order to be entitled to the protections of the First Amendment."[79] It is enough that an association may engage in expressive activity that could be impaired by Dale's presence in order to be entitled to protection.[80] Rehnquist

---

[74] *Id.*

[75] *Id.*

[76] *Id.*

[77] *Id.*

[78] *Id.* at 654–55 (emphasis in original) (quoting *Dale v. Boy Scouts of America*, 734 A.2d 1 196, 1223 (N.J. 1999), *rev'd*, 530 U.S. 640 (2000)).

[79] *Id.*

[80] *Id.*

cited *Hurley* for the proposition that a gay group could be excluded from marching in a parade even when the purpose of the parade was not to espouse any views whatsoever about sexual orientation.[81]

Second, Chief Justice Rehnquist said that even if the Boy Scouts discouraged leaders from disseminating views on sexual issues, "the First Amendment protects the Boy Scouts' method of expression."[82] Even if Boy Scout leaders try to dodge questions of sexuality and teach only by example, their approach does not impeach the sincerity of their beliefs concerning homosexuality.[83]

Third, Rehnquist found that "the First Amendment ... does not require ... every member of a group agree on every issue in order for the group's policy to be 'expressive association.'"[84] Dale argued that the Boy Scouts do "not revoke the membership of heterosexual Scout leaders that openly disagree with the Boy Scouts' policy on sexual orientation."[85] The Court decided that even if true, this statement is irrelevant.[86] The fact that the Boy Scouts take an official position with respect to homosexual conduct is in itself sufficient for First Amendment purposes.[87] The Chief Justice opined that "[t]he presence of an avowed homosexual and gay rights activist [like Mr. Dale] in an assistant scoutmaster's uniform sends a distinctly different message from the presence of a heterosexual assistant scoutmaster who is on record as disagreeing with Boy Scouts policy."[88] The Boy

---

[81] *Id.*

[82] *Id.*

[83] *Id.*

[84] *Id.*

[85] *Id.*

[86] *Id.* In the view of the Court, the record shed some doubt on Dale's claim. "For example, the National Director of the Boy Scouts certified that '*any* persons who advocate to Scouting youth that homosexual conduct is' consistent with Scouting values will not be registered as adult leaders." *Id.* at 655 n.1 (citations omitted).

[87] *Id.* at 655.

[88] *Id.* at 655–56.

Scouts clearly have a First Amendment right to choose one message and not the other.[89] The fact that this organization tolerates dissent within its ranks does not mean that its views are stripped of their First Amendment protection.[90]

The next question that the Court faced was whether the imposition of New Jersey's public accommodations law requiring the Boy Scouts to accept Dale violates the Boy Scouts' freedom of expression.[91] The Court was very concerned about the broad parameters of New Jersey's public accommodations law.[92] The Statute lists over fifty different types of places in its definition of a place of public accommodation.[93] The Court pointed out that the New Jersey Supreme Court "applied its public accommodations law to a private entity without even attempting to tie the term 'place' to a physical location."[94] The law covers traditional places like taverns, hotels, shops, and libraries.[95] However, the law also sweeps within its grasp more imprecise locations such as summer camps and playing fields.[96]

The Court declared in cases such as *Roberts* and *Board of Directors of Rotary International v. Rotary Club of Duarte*[97] that the "states have a compelling interest in eliminating discrimination against

---

[89] *Id.* at 656.

[90] *Id.*

[91] *Id.*

[92] *Id.* at 656–57. The majority stated, "Over time, the public accommodations laws have expanded to cover more places. New Jersey's statutory definition of '[a] place of public accommodation' is extremely broad. The term is said to 'include but not limited to,' a list of over [fifty] types of places." *Id.*

[93] *Boy Scouts of America v. Dale*, 530 U.S. at 657.

[94] *Id.*

[95] *Id.*

[96] *Id.*

[97] *Duarte*, 481 U.S. 537 (1987).

women in public accommodations."[98] Nevertheless, the Court declared that in each of those cases enforcement of the public accommodations statutes "would not materially interfere with the ideas that the organization[s] sought to express."[99] In *Roberts*, the Court said that the "Jaycees [had] failed to demonstrate ... any serious burdens on the male members' freedom of expressive association."[100] In *Duarte*,[101] the Court wrote:

> [I]mpediments to the exercise of one's right to choose one's associates can violate the right of association protected by the First Amendment. In this case, however, the evidence fails to demonstrate that admitting women to Rotary Clubs will affect in any significant way the existing members' ability to carry out their various purposes.[102]

In contrast, New Jersey's public accommodations law directly impacts associational rights that enjoy First Amendment protection by compelling the Boy Scouts to accept Dale.[103] Accordingly, Dale's presence places an intolerable burden on the Boy Scouts' freedom of expressive association. Why? Because his presence

---

[98] *Boy Scouts of America v. Dale*, 530 U.S. at 657.

[99] *Id.*

[100] *Id.* at 657–58 (quoting *Roberts*, 468 U.S. 609, 626 (1984)).

[101] In *Duarte*, 481 U.S. 537 (1987), the Court considered a situation in which the charter of a local chapter of Rotary International was revoked by the national organization, because it admitted female members. Here, the Court concluded "the relationship among Rotary Club members is not the kind of intimate or private relation that warrants constitutional protection." *Id.* at 546. It emphasized the Rotary Club's inclusive membership policy, pointing to its own declaration that "[t]he purpose of Rotary 'is to produce an inclusive, not exclusive, membership." *Id.* Importantly, Rotary's membership policy was designed to be inclusive in order to enable "the club to be a true cross section of the business and professional life of the community." *Id.* (citations omitted).

[102] *Boy Scouts of America v. Dale*, 530 U.S. at 658 (quoting *Duarte*, 481 U.S. at 548).

[103] *Id.* at 659.

implies acceptance of homosexual conduct. The Court stated that New Jersey's public accommodations law does "not justify such a severe intrusion on the Boy Scouts' rights to freedom of expressive association."[104] The dissent berates the majority, because the latter fails to recognize that gayness is regarded by many citizens as compatible with a clean and morally straight lifestyle.[105] However, the Chief Justice's retort was that the First Amendment protects expression, popular or unpopular, by citing decisions of unpopular cases involving flag burning and the Ku Klux Klan.[106] Rehnquist also mentioned that the Court's personal views must not influence its decision regarding the Boy Scouts' treatment of gays, regardless whether such treatment is right or wrong.[107] The Court held by a close 5–4 vote that the First Amendment prohibits the State from imposing a requirement that Dale be made an assistant scoutmaster.[108]

THE DISSENT

Justice Stevens authored a ringing dissent in response to the majority's determination that Dale's presence intrudes on the Boy Scouts' freedom of association. First, in perhaps a gentle jab at the majority (who are normally strong supporters of federalism), Stevens said that New Jersey should be commended for its attempts to eradicate the cancer of discrimination from society.[109] The Court,

---

[104] *Id.*

[105] See *id.* at 699–700.

[106] *Id.* at 660 (citing *Texas v. Johnson*, 491 U.S. 397 (1989) (holding that there is a right to burn one's American flag); citing also *Brandenburg v. Ohio*, 395 U.S. 444 (1969) (holding that Ku Klux Klan leaders had a First Amendment right to advocate unlawfulness).

[107] *Id.* at 661.

[108] See *id.*

[109] *Id.* at 663 (citing Justice Brandeis' comment in *New State Ice Co. v. Liebmann*, 285 U.S. 262, 311 (1932) (dissenting opinion),

> To stay experimentation in things social and economic is a grave responsibility. ... It is one of the happy incidents of the federal system that a single courageous State may, if its citizens choose, serve as a laboratory;

Stevens noted, simply failed to accord that State the respect it is due in our federal system.[110] Next, the dissent claims "[i]t is plain as the light of day" that the terms "morally straight" and "clean" have nothing to do with homosexuality.[111] Further, it is just as clear that scoutmasters neither give information nor advice about sexual matters, but rather leave that to the parents.[112] Finally, the Boy Scouts' pronouncements simply declare that homosexuality is not "appropriate."[113] Consequently, this idea or principle of excluding gays does not appear to be a part of the Boy Scouts' publicly taught values and creeds.[114] The dissent maintained that there was no connection between these essentially private policy statements and the Boy Scouts' expressive interests[115] that justify the majority's decision. The dissent seemed to think that the Boy Scouts' failure to forcefully and publicly advocate their concern with gayness was somehow evidence of an acceptance of homosexuality or the lack of an expressive objection to the practice of that lifestyle.[116] Perhaps

---

and try novel social and economic experiments without risk to the rest of the country.

The Chief Justice's response to Brandeis' comment was that in *New State Ice*, he was speaking of experimentation regarding economic matters during the depression years. *Boy Scouts of America v. Dale*, 530 U.S. at 660. Rehnquist implies that Brandeis was a champion of free speech in matters of expression. *Id.* Brandeis thought that the founders "believed that freedom to think as you will and to speak as you think are means indispensable to the discovery and spread of political truth." *Id.* at 660–61 (citing *Whitney v. California*, 274 U.S. 357, 375 (1927) (Brandeis, J., 395 U.S. 444 concurring), *overruled in part* by *Brandenburg v. Ohio*, (1969)).

[110] *Boy Scouts of America v. Dale*, 530 U.S. at 664.

[111] *Id.* at 668.

[112] See *id.*

[113] *Id.* at 673.

[114] *Id.* "Rather, the 1978 policy appears to be no more than a private statement of a few BSA executives." *Id.*

[115] *Id.* at 676.

[116] See *id.* at 677–78.

the question for the Boy Scouts is whether they should have been more outspoken or bigoted toward gays?[117]

Next, the minority opinion maintained that in order to win an expressive association claim, the Boy Scouts must show *more* than merely some expressive activity.[118] They must also establish a serious burden on the group's collective effort.[119] But in the minority's view, Dale's presence was not a serious burden on the Boy Scouts. This was so because the Boy Scouts never demonstrated that Dale would in any way advocate his beliefs to the youngsters in his charge.[120]

Justice Stevens recognized that the Boy Scouts had a First Amendment right not to talk about homosexuality to its youthful members.[121] However, that interest could be accomplished by directing adult leaders not to discuss matters relating to sex and religion.[122] According to Stevens, the Boy Scouts' concern that Dale would use his position as a "bully pulpit"[123] to convey his ideas on homosexuality has no basis in fact.[124] In addition, there is no indication that Dale would disobey Boy Scout policies.

Next, Justice Stevens took great issue with the majority's conclusion that Dale's presence would send a message that the Boy

---

[117] At least that was the opinion of one writer. Writing about the New Jersey Supreme Court decision he said, "By the perverse logic of this decision, the Boy Scouts erred not in the direction of bigotry but rather in not being bigoted enough." Terence Pell, *Not Bigoted Enough*, Wash. Post, Aug. 23, 1999, at A17, available at 1999 WL 23299503.

[118] *Boy Scouts of America v. Dale*, 530 U.S. at 682.

[119] See *id.* at 683; see also *Roberts*, 468 U.S. 609, 626–27 (1984).

[120] *Boy Scouts of America v. Dale*, 530 U.S. at 689.

[121] *Id.* at 688.

[122] *Id.*

[123] *Id.* at 689.

[124] *Id.* "BSA has not contended, nor does the record support, that Dale had ever advocated a view on homosexuality to his troop before his membership was revoked." *Id.*

Scouts endorsed a gay life style.[125] He argued that the majority's reliance on *Hurley* was misplaced.[126] Recall in *Hurley* that a gay group wished to march in a private organization's St. Patrick's Day parade with a large banner to express their gay pride.[127] The Court concluded that the parade organizers, a private group, could not be compelled to proclaim a belief with which it disagreed.[128]

Here, Justice Stevens said that Dale's presence at a scout meeting was nothing like marching in a parade with a banner.[129] Contrary to *Hurley*, Dale neither carries a banner nor openly advocates his views at troop meetings.[130] Mere attendance at a meeting is not enough to rise to the level of expression.[131] Usually, an expressive association claim involves at least the "avowal and advocacy of a consistent position on some issue over time."[132] The fact that a gay man participates in an organization no more conveys a support for the lifestyle than does a gay person participating in baseball, tennis, or golf.[133]

Finally, the dissenters reminded us that "[u]nfavorable opinions about homosexuals 'have ancient roots.'"[134] As a result of free interaction between people, these ancient and unfavorable opinions have

---

[125] See *id.* at 692–97. Stevens forcefully argued that the majority's reliance on the simple fact that Dale is gay somehow sent a message endorsing homosexuality was wrong. Such a presumed message is the same as a "constitutionally prescribed symbol of inferiority." *Id.* at 696.

[126] *Id.* at 693–95.

[127] *Hurley*, 515 U.S. 557, 561 (1995).

[128] See *id.* at 573.

[129] *Boy Scouts of America v. Dale*, 530 U.S. at 694–95.

[130] *Id.* at 695.

[131] *Id.*

[132] *Id.* at 696.

[133] See *id.* at 697.

[134] *Id.* at 699 (quoting *Bowers v. Hardwick*, 478 U.S. 186, 192 (1986), *overruled by Lawrence v. Texas*, 539 U.S. 558 (2003)).

consistently been modified.[135] The minority opinion cited examples of domestic partner legislation, greater understanding in religious faiths, and removal of homosexuality from a list of mental disorders to support this idea of modification.[136] Indeed, it is apparent that the publicly avowed view toward gays is heavily tilted toward acceptance. (In contrast, the authors of this article take the position that sexual conduct between consenting adults is absolutely none of the State's concern.) Of course, the majority's response to this was that the Boy Scouts' position on homosexuality did not have to be rational or reasonable to fall under First Amendment protection.[137]

But what relevance does any of the foregoing have to do with voluntary association? Let us stipulate that Dale is a very honest, upright, religious, witty, and moral person whom we would trust to care for and educate our children. And we further posit that his sexual orientation has absolutely no effect on his abilities to be a wonderful scoutmaster. These provisos notwithstanding, it is still illicit for the government to compel one person to associate with another just because the latter is of good moral character. Perhaps one prefers associating with his or her friends who smoke cigarettes, drink beer, play poker, eat fatty steaks, tell dirty jokes, and watch pornographic movies. Could the government legitimately compel that person to shun his or her disreputable friends and instead go camping with the sainted Mother Theresa, or even Dale, just because they are of good moral character? We think not; the whole idea is preposterous in a free society. In the end, whether gay leaders are compatible with family values is not the fundamental issue. Rather, it is whether an organization has the right to set its own membership rules. These specifications for joining may not fit with some of today's politically correct social norms. They might be hurtful to an individual's feelings. But at the end of the day, the alternative to the right of exclusion is total state control of private association. We need not succumb to the tyranny of the supposed good intentions

---

[135] *Id.*

[136] *Id.* at 699–700.

[137] See *id.* at 660.

of the state of New Jersey. We think that James Madison would appreciate the Boy Scouts' moral courage in standing up for his First Amendment.[138]

PHILOSOPHY

According to the New Jersey Supreme Court, the Boy Scouts are guilty of an egregious offense against morality, propriety, and most importantly, the law, in their decision to exclude gays as scoutmasters. This philosophical position taken on by the court in this decision is that discrimination, on the basis of an entire litany of criteria, is wrong and should be proscribed by law. The finding of this court, however, is philosophically flawed. Indeed, it is so dead from the neck up that even the adherents of this perspective are unable to carry through on their own principles and apply them widely.

For example, while employers may not exclude or discriminate against employees on the basis of race, gender, national origin, sexual preference, etc., the latter are not at all proscribed by law from doing just that with regard to the former. That is, if a prospective employee declines to take a job with Brigham Young, Loyola, or Yeshiva Universities on the grounds that their religious mission offends him, that person is still in full compliance with the law. But let any one of them apply a similar criterion in their hiring of professors, and all hell breaks loose, legally speaking. Needless to say, it would be a matter of outlawry for them to refuse to employ scholars for these reasons.

---

[138] See note 109. According to James Madison, "[t]o compel a man to furnish contributions of money for the propagation of opinions which he disbelieves, is sinful and tyrannical" (citations omitted). For more on this question of the government practice of compelling people to support opinions with which they disagree, see Roy Whitehead and Walter Block, "Mandatory Student Fees: Forcing Some to Pay for the Free Speech of Others," *Whittier Law Review* 20 (1999): 759, 772.

Suppose people decide to go out to dinner together but eschew all Chinese, black,[139] Jewish, and Italian restaurants, not on the ground that their culinary offerings do not appeal to them, but rather because they loathe the nationalities thereby represented. Are they thereby guilty of law breaking? They are not. But were any of these establishments to make similar choices with regard to employees or customers (e.g., by posting a sign on their premises stating "no Chinese, blacks, Jews, or Italians will be allowed entry either as patrons or workers") then it would be a paradigmatic case of law violation.

This fact, that the burden of non-discrimination is uneven, has further interesting ramifications. For example, sellers are typically forbidden to discriminate, but not buyers; but even this is by no means the end of the story. A diner can patronize an Italian restaurant, avoiding one offering Chinese food, even if this is motivated by racial or ethnic hatred. However, a Greek eating

---

[139] (The non-politically correct language in this article has been left unedited due to one of the authors' heartfelt insistence.) I (one of the authors) like to treat blacks and whites exactly alike, both personally, professionally, and, of relevance here, linguistically. To call blacks African Americans violates this, unless we also call whites European Americans, and I am not willing to employ this latter language; one, because it seems silly to my ear; and two, because it is simply not in common use and would needlessly raise eyebrows. I certainly would not capitalize white and use lower case for black, or vice versa. And of course, I do no such thing in this paper. Another reason: "African American" is not at all precise. For example, what do you call a man now living in the U.S. with very white skin, blue eyes, blond hair and whose parents have lived in South Africa or Zimbabwe (formerly Rhodesia) for centuries and originally immigrated there from England or Holland? If anyone is an "African American," this guy surely is. But that would just spread confusion, for this guy looks white to everyone, is white, considers himself white, and would certainly not be eligible for any sort of U.S. affirmative action program reserved for blacks. Yet another reason for my choice of words is that people on the left use "African American." People on the right do not. I do not consider myself a member of either of these two groups; I am a libertarian. A push in either direction is a violation of my free speech rights. It is an attempt to impose upon me a political stance that I do not wish to embrace.

establishment may not ban Turkish diners even when this decision is precipitated by similar emotions. On the other hand, were any of these restaurants to decide not to hire (e.g., *purchase* the services of) Jews or blacks,[140] they would quickly be found to be in violation of anti-discrimination law.

If the same establishments were to avoid purchasing meats or vegetables from gays, females, or Spaniards, their (legal) guilt would turn on the issue of whether they shop for these things in a supermarket (in which case they could discriminate to their heart's content) or let these things out to competitive bidding contracts (in which case they could not discriminate on race, sex, gender, or ethnicity; however, it would be legal for them to discriminate on the basis of price, e.g., accept the lowest bid). One of the criteria of good law is surely intellectual coherence, something under which such legislation does not pass muster.

Moreover, if it is really true that discrimination is a cancer[141] which must presumably be wiped out entirely, then why do we countenance it in personal relations? For example, dating. Why does the law not force all of those who wish to engage in this practice, whether gay or straight, *not* to discriminate on the basis of race? If blacks[142] are fourteen percent of the overall population, then every seventh date of a white person would have to be with a member of this community. Marriage and friendship patterns, too, would have to come under the eagle eye of the discrimination police. Present intermarriage rates are evidence of the fact that blatant discrimination takes place in this arena.

And, as it happens, *both* heterosexuals and homosexuals are "guilty" of sexual discrimination. Male homosexuals, for example, abjure women as bed partners, as do female heterosexuals. Female

---

[140] See text accompanying note 139.

[141] The New Jersey Supreme Court says that the goal of LAD is to remove the cancer of discrimination. Specifically, the court stated, "[T]he overarching goal on the [LAD] is nothing less than the eradication 'of the cancer of discrimination.'" *Dale v. Boy Scouts of America*, 734 A.2d 1196, 1208 (N.J. 1999) (quoting *Jackson v. Concord Co.*, 253 A.2d 793 (N.J. 1969)).

[142] See text accompanying note 139.

homosexuals forswear men which is the same practice of male heterosexuals. If discrimination must be eliminated then all of this "evil" behavior should be proscribed, forthwith. Only bisexuals would be acting lawfully. The logical implication of the court in *Dale v. Boy Scouts of America* is that of compulsory bisexuality for everyone. Until and unless they are willing to embrace this consistent application of their own philosophy, they are forced by the laws of logic to change their verdict.

Furthermore, "[a]ll-boys schools are attacked for discrimination, but all-girls schools are consistent with the needs of diversity. All-white clubs are *verboten*, but all-black clubs are a healthy reflection of racial pride. All-Christian schools are pockets of bigotry, but all-atheist schools are essential to pluralism."[143] The law mandates that girls be accepted for boys' sports teams, but the reverse does not apply. Were girls' sports teams forced to allow male participation and if ability were still the determining factor for inclusion, this would pretty much spell the death knell for all female participation in athletics, with the possible exception of such activities as golf, and "ballet sports" such as gymnastics, diving, and synchronized swimming.[144] Certainly, it would be the rare female who could hold her own *vis-à-vis* males in football, baseball, basketball, etc.

Consider the fact that the Black Muslim group of Malcolm X was not forced to admit whites; that religious groups such as Mormons, Jews, Catholics, etc., may legally exclude non-members from (certain aspects of) their services. There is also the fact that there is a strict enforcement of male-only and female-only rest rooms: neither may "poach" upon the preserves of the other; each, that is, may exclude the other.

---

[143] Llewellyn H. Rockwell, Jr., "The Right to Exclude," Mises Institute, at http://www.mises.org/fullstory.aspx?control=282andid=76.

[144] See Roy Whitehead et al., "Gender Equity in Athletics: Should We Adopt a Non-Discriminatory Model?" *University of Toledo Law Review* 30 (1999): 223; Roy Whitehead and Walter Block, "Christian Landlords and the Free Exercise Clause: Sinners Need Not Apply," *Oklahoma City University Law Review* 33, no. 1 (Spring): 115–50

Conceivably, all of these decisions may be "justified." Perhaps employers are more powerful or have better bargaining power than employees.[145] Even if this is so, this is unrelated to racial or gender discrimination. If this is legally offensive, *per se*, then mere wealth should be irrelevant. After all, the rapist cannot defend his actions on the ground that his victim is richer than himself. In any case, it is the customer, not the owner of the restaurant, "who is always right." If there is any imbalance of power in that scenario, it presumably cuts in precisely the opposite direction. For example, since the patron of an eating establishment holds a thumbs up or thumbs down vote, then it should be, if anyone, the owner and not the customer who would have the right to freely pick and choose.

This court's finding is also philosophically flawed in that it ignores the fact that private property rights are in effect a license to exclude. The entire point of such rights is to draw a line between "mine" and "thine." If a man cannot exclude others from his premises, then there is a strong sense in which they are not *his* premises at all.

Llewellyn Rockwell states:

> But liberty also means the right to exclude because property owners decide questions of access. There is no right to crash a private dinner party, for example. The owners of the house have the right to invite or not invite on any grounds. Similarly, there is no right to invade a private organization.[146]

If private, male-only golf courses cannot be forced to admit women, it would appear to be a legal stretch to compel the Boy Scouts to welcome gays in their senior ranks.

The New Jersey Supreme Court attempted to argue its way out of this conundrum by defining the Boy Scouts as a "public accommodation."[147] But this is a philosophical howler of the first

---

[145] This will come as a surprise to the employers of Michael Jordan or of marginal farmers during harvest when they are desperate for workers.

[146] Rockwell, see note 143.

[147] *Id.*

magnitude. For this organization is not at all "open to the entire public." Rather, it is receptive *only* to those members of the public who meet its membership criteria and this most certainly does not include gay scoutmasters. Moreover, were the "public accommodation" doctrine pushed to its logical conclusion, it would spell the death knell of private property. *Any* property, without exception, is open to *some* members of the public, even private homes and clubs. To infer that if an owner is willing to engage his property with some people then he, therefore, must be forced to do so with all people is logically invalid.

If the real reason for this attack on the liberties of Americans is not and cannot be a concern with discrimination (as shown by the fact that the court will not consistently apply this tyrannical principle), nor yet is it "public accommodation" (because this mischievous doctrine undermines all property rights), what then is the true explanation for this loss of our liberties?[148] In a word, it is concern with victims (but only with some victims) who are embraced by the forces of political correctness. Rockwell asks in this regard:

> What if the Boy Scouts had decided to exclude, say, racists as Scout masters. Would the courts have intervened on behalf of, for example, a Klan member's right to join? Not on your life. This is not an equal application of the law, but one that favors interest groups approved by government.[149]

In this regard, it is more than passing curiosity that gays, who have long been associated with the view that they should be allowed a sphere of privacy in the bedroom or in the bathhouse for acts between consenting adults, are now intent upon violating the private spaces of those who do not welcome them.

---

[148] It is surely a paradox that at a time when the United States armed forces are conducting an expedition ostensibly to promote the liberties of the Iraqis, liberties at home are in great danger.

[149] Rockwell, see note 143.

The legal precedent for the present diminution of property rights is the 1948 Supreme Court decision abrogating restrictive covenants that mentioned race.[150] *Shelley v. Kraemer*[151] mandated restrictive covenants not be enforced.[152] But if property rights and contracts are undermined by judicial decisions, the rot infects our entire society.[153] If civilization is built upon these twin pillars, to the extent they are diluted, our entire social order is put at risk.

In sharp contrast to *Shelley* is the following ringing endorsement of contractual and private property rights mandating that the state not

> limit or abridge, directly or indirectly, the right of any person, who is willing or desires to sell, lease, or rent any part or all of his real property, to decline to sell, lease or rent such property to such person or persons as he, in his absolute discretion, chooses.[154]

"But in 1967, the U.S. Supreme Court struck that amendment down —on the same grounds that the New Jersey court ruled against the Boy Scouts."[155]

In Rockwell's view:

> Since then the right of free association has experienced many blows, from the 1964 Civil Rights Act, which defined any business enterprise as a public accommodation to be controlled by government, straight to this New Jersey decision. If a group is

---

[150] *Id.*

[151] *Shelley v. Kraemer*, 334 U.S. 1 (1948).

[152] *Id.*

[153] Rockwell, see note 143.

[154] *Id.* These words appear in a 1964 amendment to the California Constitution. Cal. Const. art. I, §26 (repealed 1974).

[155] Rockwell, see note 143; see generally *Reitman v. Mulkey*, 387 US. 369 (1967).

politically powerful enough, it can have the tyrants in black robes override anyone's property rights.[156]

Libertarians[157] oppose not only this attack by a gay man on that venerable institution, the Boy Scouts, they also dispute the entire philosophy upon which such a lawsuit rests. Nor is it only a matter of a "slippery slope;" the iceberg is already upon us, not just its tip. If an organization such as the Boy Scouts can be successfully assaulted in the courts by a gay person then *reductio ad absurdum* are all but impossible.

ECONOMICS

Why is it that we have run so far off the rails in terms of antidiscrimination law? How is it that we have arrived at a point where compulsory bisexuality is the only practice consistent with legislation in this area? Can it really be required by law that parents be forced to send their impressionable adolescent boys to an organization featuring gay scoutmasters?

There are many plausible explanations for this sorry state of affairs: a failure of the will, rampant immorality, sheer bloody-minded

---

[156] *Id.* For a philosophical view on the right to discriminate see Jan Narveson, "Have We a Right to Non-Discrimination?" in *Business Ethics in Canada* (Scarborough, Ont: Prentice-Hall Canada, 1987), pp. 183, 183–98; Walter Block, "Discrimination: An Interdisciplinary Analysis," *Journal of Business Ethics* 11 (1992): 241, 241–54; Walter Block, "Compromising the Uncompromisable: Discrimination," *American Journal of Economics and Sociology* 57 (1998): 223, 223–37.

[157] For the libertarian philosophy which underscores the underlying intellectual basis of this section, indeed of the entire paper, see Murray N. Rothbard, *For A New Liberty*; Murray N. Rothbard, *The Ethics of Liberty*; Hans-Hermann Hoppe, *A Theory of Socialism and Capitalism: Economics, Politics, and Ethics*; Hans-Hermann Hoppe, *The Economics and Ethics of Private Property: Studies in Political Economy and Philosophy*; Robert Nozick, *Anarchy, State, and Utopia*; Walter Block, *Defending the Undefendable*; Walter Block, "Libertarianism vs. Libertinism"; Charles Murray, *What it Means to be a Libertarian*; Jan Narveson, *The Libertarian Idea*; Anthony de Jasay, *The State*.

busybody-ness, an altogether perverse interpretation of the otherwise reasonable desire to help the underdog, philosophical confusion, and "bloody cheek" in the British expression. But we must not, in casting around for blame on this matter, neglect the dismal science. Economic illiteracy also goes a long way toward explaining why so many segments of our society should either have embraced the anti-discrimination idea with alacrity or at least accorded it passive acceptance.

The major fallacy underlying the so-called civil rights movement is the idea that discrimination, particularly on the part of the rich and powerful,[158] is economically deleterious to the downtrodden. Indeed, this is an important source of poverty, if not the major explanation for this state of affairs.[159] Visions of employers turning away

---

[158] There are three main sources of economic discrimination: on the part of employers, fellow employees, and customers. In keeping with popular sentiment on this matter, we shall confine our remarks to the discrimination on the part of employers where such discrimination, as we shall show, is powerless to harm the economically weak.

[159] On the economics of discrimination see Gary S. Becker, *The Economics of Discrimination*; Walter Block, "Economic Intervention, Discrimination, and Unforseen Consequences," in *Discrimination, Affirmative Action, and Equal Opportunity*, Walter E. Block and Michael A. Walker, eds. (Vancouver, British Columbia: The Fraser Institute, 1982): 103–24; Walter Block and Walter Williams, "Male-Female Earning Differentials: A Critical Reappraisal," *Journal or Labor Research* 2, pt. 2 (1981): 383–88; Walter Block and Michael A. Walker, *Focus on Employment Equity: A Critique of the Abella Royal Commission on Equality in Employment* (Vancouver, British Columbia: The Fraser Institute, 1985); Harold Demsetz, "Minorities in the Market Place," *North Carolina Law Review* 43 (1965): 271, 271–97; Richard Epstein, *Forbidden Grounds: The Case against Employment Discrimination Laws* (Cambridge, Mass.: Harvard University Press, 1992); Carl Hoffman and John Reed, "When is Imbalance Not Discrimination," in *Discrimination, Affirmative Action, and Equal Opportunity*; W.H. Hutt, *The Economics of the Colour Bar: A Study of the Economic Origins and Consequences of Racial Segregation in South Africa* (London: Andre Deutsch, 1964); Ellen Frankel Paul, *Equity and Gender: The Comparable Worth Debate* (New Brunswick, N.J.: Transaction, 1989); Thomas Sowell, Ethnic America (New York: Basic Books, 1981); Thomas Sowell, "Weber and Bakke, and the Presuppositions

blacks[160] from the factory door or enforcing sweatshop conditions
on economically powerless women dance in the minds of those
determined that discrimination shall not legally take place on the
basis of race, sex, ethnicity, sexual preference, or any of a continually
increasing number of considerations.

The only difficulty with this perspective is that it happens not
to be true. For instance, compare the wage "gap" between male
and female workers. According to the most popular hypothesis,
the fact that females earn only some seventy cents for every dollar
garnered by a male is *per se* proof of male, chauvinist employer
exploitation.[161] The implicit claim is that, now acknowledged male
advantages over females in upper body strength are less and less
economically relevant, there are no differences in productivity levels
on average between the two genders. This is also, as it happens, a
not unreasonable surmise. (If it were conceded that females were
less productive in the market place than males, this would furnish
an alternative explanation for the wage gap.) This situation gives
rise to the following two-by-two matrix:

	Male	Female
Wages	$10	$7
Productivity	$10	$10

Here, males and females have equal productivity at $10 per hour
respectively. However, based on a wage gap of 30 percent, the

---

of 'Affirmative Action'," in *Discrimination, Affirmative Action, and Equal
Opportunity*; Thomas Sowell, *The Economics and Politics of Race: An Inter-
national Perspective* (New York: William Morrow, 1983); Thomas Sowell,
Civil Rights: Rhetoric or Reality (New York: William Morrow, 1984);
Thomas Sowell, *Race and Economics* (New York: Longman, 1975); Walter
Williams, *The State Against Blacks* (New York: McGraw-Hill, 1982); Walter
Williams, "On Discrimination, Prejudice, Racial Income Differentials, and
Affirmative Action," in *Discrimination, Affirmative Action, and Equal
Opportunity*, pp. 66–99.

[160] See text accompanying note 139.

[161] These numbers are for illustrative purposes only.

former earn $10 per hour while the latter suffer under wages of only $7 per hour.

There are grave difficulties with such a scenario. Were the scenario true, it could not long endure. For it implies that any employer who hires a woman will earn $3 per hour more in profits than were he to hire a man. Surely, under the conditions specified above, the firm dominated by female employees will be able to underbid, and price out of the market, all competitors with a different make-up in their work forces. Surely, under these conditions, any but the most warped employer would prefer to hire a woman (thus raising her salary) to a man and would continue doing so until the wages of each came to conform to the other. (Given our numerical example, wages in equilibrium would reach $10 for both genders; at this point, there would be no additional profits earned by the entrepreneur for hiring women that would not be available to him were he to hire men.)

What, then, is the true explanation for the undeniable fact that women's earnings are appreciably below that of their male counterparts? If the discrimination hypothesis must be consigned to the dust bin of economic history, what can take its place? In large part, it is the marital asymmetry hypothesis: men earn more money in the market place than women, because marriage has asymmetrical effects on pay; it enhances that of the husband and reduces that of the wife. Since most people are married for at least some years of their adult lives, this biases the statistical differentials upon which the feminists[162] have pegged their misbegotten "wage gap" complaints.

Why the asymmetry? This is because husbands and wives do not equally divide housekeeping and child-rearing responsibilities. Very much to the contrary, the wife assumes the lion's share of these tasks and the husband assumes a very small proportion, even including

---

[162] For a critique of feminism see Michael Levin, "Comparable Worth: The Feminist Road to Socialism," *Commentary* 78, no. 3 (September 1984); Michael Levin, *Feminism and Freedom* (New York: Transaction Books,1987); Christina Hoff Sommers, *Who Stole Feminism? How Women have Betrayed Women* (New York: Simon & Schuster, 1994).

repairs and garbage removal. In virtually all marriages, the shopping, cooking, cleaning, sewing, bed making, vacuuming, and dishwashing are almost entirely monopolized by the distaff side. This goes in spades for diapering, PTA meetings, caring for sick children, etc. Also, this is to say nothing of getting up in the middle of the night and being on call every few hours during the day in order to breast feed, a biological impossibility for men.

What is the implication of such a state of affairs? It is what economists call the doctrine of alternative costs. If you want to be a concert pianist and practice your instrument eight hours a day, you probably will not be very good at golf, chess, computers, or hundreds of other things; you certainly will not be as productive in these other tasks but for your tie to the piano. If you load yourself up with house and child-care, compared to your otherwise equally-productive-in-the-marketplace husband, he will gain a march on you in the latter direction. Moreover, if a woman expects to seriously or totally reduce her labor force attachment from the time her first child is born until her last child is in high school and thus relatively independent, she is likely to invest her human capital in less well paid, but presumably more secure arenas, such as secretary, nurse, or school teacher; rather than invest in the more remunerative chemistry, computers, or engineering lest the natural atrophy of her skills during her time of zero or lesser labor force participation hurt her financially. Given that her husband is the primary bread winner for these years, she is far more likely to agree to be the "trailing spouse" in the job market than the reverse, in order to maximize total family income.

What are the results of these considerations? It is that while *on average* women should earn just as much as men, given that the average woman is just as productive as the average man, matters are quite different when we take into account marital status. If wage ratio of all females to all males is seventy percent to one hundred percent, it drops precipitously for those who have ever been *married* and rises to virtual equality for those who have *never* benefited from the institution of marriage. Indeed in many cases, the wage "gap" for those who have never married vanishes almost entirely![163]

The same analysis applies to discrimination against any other group, such as blacks,[164] homosexuals, or members of the various ethnicities. Discrimination is not the economic bugaboo that it is commonly supposed to be. Much discrimination was aimed at Jews and Orientals[165] and yet they had higher than average incomes; discrimination did not reduce their economic viability. Given that blacks[166] and Hispanics are also the objects of discrimination, this cannot account for their relative poverty.

If a restaurant does not wish to serve an Oriental[167] person, there will be competitors anxious to do just that. They will earn greater profits, other things equal, since they can "monopolize" customers from this sector of society. If a firm does not to choose to employ a gay person, he will find a job elsewhere. His new employer, more likely than not, will be able to undersell and drive into bankruptcy the first one. No, there is nothing to fear from discriminators. They are a paper tiger. Fear of them is certainly not a justification for riding roughshod over the rights of the citizenry to do exactly as they wish, to choose their friends, business associations, and personal

---

[163] Block, "Discrimination: An Interdisciplinary Analysis," pp. 246–48; Block, "Compromising the Uncompromisable: Discrimination," pp. 223–37.

[164] See text accompanying note 139.

[165] (The non-politically correct language in this article has been left unedited due to one of the author's heartfelt insistence.) A similar argument stated previously in note 139 applies to Orientals–Asians. To be fair to both races, if we use "Asian" to describe an Oriental then we would have to (if we are to be logically consistent) use "European" or "American" to describe an Occidental. That would spread confusion. Then, too, to characterize a person whose family has lived in the U.S. for several centuries, but who originally migrated to the U.S. from Korea, Japan, or China, as an "Asian" isn't just plain silly. Worse, it is confusing.

[166] See text accompanying note 139.

[167] See text accompanying note 165.

relationships, provided only that they keep their mitts off of other people and their property.

STATISTICAL EVIDENCE

What are the facts of the matter? In table one, the ratios of female-to-male median incomes are listed[168] [(in 1997 dollars)] for the years

---

168 Table One:
Annual Median Income, Entire Population

Year	Males$	Females$	Ratio
1997	25,936	14,281	55.1
1996	25,375	13,686	53.9
1995	24,774	13,233	53.4
1994	24,174	12,787	52.9
1993	24,097	12,645	52.5
1992	24,148	12,664	52.4
1991	24,847	12,756	51.3
1990	25,705	12,849	50.0
1989	26,613	12,978	48.8
1988	26,783	12,641	47.2
1987	26,416	12,331	46.7

Annual Median Income, Never Married

Year	Males$	Females$	Ratio
1997	15,076	12,208	81.0
1996	14,508	11,820	81.5
1995	14,201	11,523	81.1
1994	13,844	11,295	81.6
1993	13,572	11,040	81.3
1992	13,239	11,341	85.7
1991	13,765	11,732	85.2
1990	14,382	12,052	83.8
1989	15,056	12,131	80.6
1988	15,206	11,855	78.0
1987	14,520	11,614	80.0

1987–1997.[169] As can be seen, the ratio for all males and females ranges from a low of 46.7 percent in 1987 to 55.1 percent in 1997; from 77.9 percent to 81.0 percent for the single, never married during these years; and from a low of 36.9 percent in 1987 to a high of 47.1 percent in 1997 for those who were married, widowed, separated, or divorced. The point at issue is not the slight rise in all these figures over this eleven year period, but rather the fact that the reason female wages lag behind male wages for the total population is that those who had ever married pull down the average for them. That is, the female-to-male wage ratio for this period of 51.3 percent was so low because the ever-married ratio of 41.7 percent pulled it down. Had no one been touched by the institution of marriage, and nothing else changed, the presumption is that the female-male wage ratio would have been 81.8 percent for this roughly decade-long period.

(Table cont.)
Annual Median Income, Ever Married

Year	Males$	Females$	Ratio
1997	31,517	14,833	47.1
1996	31,140	14,187	45.6
1995	30,648	13,327	43.5
1994	29,845	12,746	42.7
1993	29,584	12,709	43.0
1992	29,942	12,632	42.2
1991	30,474	12,488	41.0
1990	31,296	12,501	39.9
1989	32,281	12,497	38.7
1988	32,285	12,486	37.7
1987	31,949	11,792	36.9

This table is based on one of the author's calculations, using the following source: U.S. Census Bureau, *Historical Income Tables—People*, table P-11, Marital Status —People [Eighteen] Years Old and Over by Median Income and Gender: 1974 to 1997, at http:www.census.gov/hhes/income/histinc/p11.html (last visited November 2, 1999) (on file with *Oklahoma City University Law Review*) [hereinafter *Income Tables*].

[169] *Id.*

These facts are certainly compatible with the marital asymmetry hypothesis that married, separated, divorced, or widowed females would earn far less than their male counterparts and that this effect would be much weaker for those who were never married. These facts are not at all consistent with the discrimination model, for here, the market, or capitalism, for some reason[170] gives *all* females the "short end of the stick." If anything, the male, chauvinist pig might, on this hypothesis, be presumed to have greater animus against unmarried females than married ones since his motto is that all women should be "barefoot, pregnant, and in the kitchen" and this ideal is more nearly approached by the latter than the former. Accordingly, we would expect that if sexism were a strong explanatory variable, the very opposite; namely, that those females who have never married would have lower wages relative to their male counterparts than would obtain in the case of those who have ever married. However, any such contention is flat out contradicted by the empirical evidence.

Table two[171] tells much the same marital asymmetry story as does table one, only in a different and complementary manner.[172] The reason that the female-to-male median income ratio is so high for

---

[170] Presumably this is due to sheer nastiness and perversity.

[171] Table Two:

Age Group Ratio (Female/Male Median Income)	
Total	53.87
15–24 yrs	84.50
25–34 yrs	65.07
35–44 yrs	57.35
45–54 yrs	52.57
55–65 yrs	45.10
65+	57.70

This table is also based on one of the author's calculations. The sources for table two are the U.S. Census Bureau, "Money Incomes of Persons – Selected Characteristics, by Income Level: 1995," in *Statistical Abstract of the United States, 1998: The National Data Book* (118th ed. 1998), p. 475 and *Income Tables*, note 171.

[172] *Id.*

those aged fifteen to twenty-four is because relatively few people in this age cohort are married. This ratio tends to decline as we move up the age ranges because more and more people have ever been married (this includes the separated, divorced, married, and widowed) as they become older. The facts are perfectly congruent with the marital asymmetry hypothesis of the wage gap but not at all with the discrimination hypothesis. Again, posit malevolent, male, chauvinist pigs who are in a position to impose their will on society, wage-wise; they hate females with a passion and wish above all else to do them ill in this regard. Why would they be so *variable* in their detestation? Why not penalize all women *equally* for the "crime" of being female? Why pass over young women or women who have never married? The facts of the matter simply make no sense when perused through these particular eyeglasses.

Economic theory is universal; it applies to all epochs as well as to all geographical areas and political jurisdictions. Let us, then, range more widely and peruse the evidence supplied by a different country, Canada, going back over several decades. We shall consider female/male wage ratios based on income averages, or means, not medians, as has been shown so far. According to one report, the female/male earnings ratio in Canada in 1971 for those never married was 99.2 percent; for those ever married, it was 33.2 percent; and for both, together, it was 37.4 percent.[173] According to another report, the never-married female-to-male average annual earnings for full-time workers in Canada with a university degree was 109.8 percent in 1971;[174] that is, females actually earned almost 10 percent more than their male counterparts.[175] In very sharp contrast, the equivalent figure for ever-marrieds with these qualifications was 56.8 percent[176] and for the entire sample 61.2 percent.[177] And in 1982, Canadian

---

[173] Block, "Unforeseen Consequences," p. 112.

[174] Block and Walker, *Focus on Employment Equity*, p. 51.

[175] *Id.*

[176] *Id.* at 50.

[177] *Id.* at 48.

women with these educational attainments who were never married earned 91.3 percent of their male counterparts,[178] while their ever-married sisters registered only 64.4 percent in this regard.[179] The ratio for the entire sample was 67.2 percent.[180]

CONCLUSION

In the free society, James Dale would no more be free to impose his presence upon the unwilling Boy Scouts than an avowed and militant heterosexual would be able to join the Rutgers University Lesbian/ Gay Alliance; or than the Black Muslim organization would be forced to accept a white person as a member; or than a religious-affiliated university would be compelled to allow an atheistic professor to join its theology faculty. Freedom of association is a necessary condition of a civilized order; laws prohibiting discrimination violate this freedom and must be repealed. All of them.

---

[178] *Id.* at 51.

[179] *Id.* at 50.

[180] *Id.* at 48.

BIBLIOGRAPHY

Abbott Labs. v. Gardner, 387 U.S. 136 (1967).

Abedian, I. and Standish, B. 1985. "Poor Whites and the Role of the State: The Evidence." *South Africa Journal of Economics* 52, no. 2 (June).

Adie, Douglas K. 1973. "Teen-Age Unemployment and Real Federal Minimum Wages." *Journal of Political Economy* 81, no. 2, part 2 (March–April).

———. 1988. *Monopoly Mail: Privatizing the United States Postal Service*. New York: Transaction Publishers.

———. 1990. *The Mail Monopoly: Analyzing Canadian Postal Service*. Vancouver, British Columbia: The Fraser Institute.

———. 1990b. "Why Marginal Reform of the U.S. Postal Service Won't Succeed." In Ferrara (1990).

Adie, Douglas K., and Lowell Gallaway. 1973. "The Minimum Wage and Teenage Unemployment: A Comment." *Western Economic Journal* 11, no. 4 (December).

Agostini v. Felton, 521 U.S. 203 (1997).

Albemarle Paper Co. v. Moody, 422 U.S. 405 (1975).

Alexander, Judith A. 1984. "Equal-Pay-for-Equal-Work Legislation in Canada." Discussion Paper 252. Economic Council of Canada. Ottawa.

Alexander v. Choate, 469 U.S. 287 (1985).

Alexander v. Sandoval, 121 S.Ct. 1511 (2001).

Alldridge, Peter. 1983. "Attempted Murder of the Soul: Blackmail, Privacy, and Secrets." *Oxford Journal of Legal Studies* 13, no. 3.

Altman, Scott. 1993. "A Patchwork Theory of Blackmail." *University of Pennsylvania Law Review* 141, no. 5 (May): 1639–61.

Altschiller, Donald, ed.1991. *Affirmative Action*. New York: H.W. Wilson.

Anderson, A., and D. L. Bark, eds. *Thinking About America: The United States in the 1990s*. Stanford, Calif.: Hoover Institution Press.

Anderson, Terry L., and P.J. Hill. 1979. "An American Experiment in Anarcho-Capitalism: The Not So Wild, Wild West." *Journal of Libertarian Studies* 3, no. 1: 9.

"Anyway You Want Me." 1984. *Toronto Globe and Mail*, 12 October.

Arkansas Department of Higher Eduation. 2000. Student Enrollments, Table III, State Appropriations Per Student for Arkansas Governor's Distinguished Scholars for 1999–00 Fiscal Year (May).

Arkansas Department of Higher Eduation. 2001. Revised Rules and Regulations for the Arkansas Governor's Scholarship Program. DHE Rule 5.1.H.

Arkansas Department of Higher Eduation. NDa. Program Rules and Procedures, Rule 5.

Arkansas Department of Higher Eduation. NDb. Student Enrollments, Table 1, Comparison of The Number of Arkansas Governor's Distinguished Scholarship Awards by Institution for the 1997–98 Through 1999–00 Academic Years.

Arkansas Department of Higher Eduation. NDc. Table II, Amount of Arkansas Governor's Distinguished Scholarship Awards by Institution.

Armentano, Dominick T. 1991. *Antitrust Policy: The Case for Repeal*, Washington, D.C.: The Cato Institute.

Armstrong, Donald. 1982. *Competition versus Monopoly: Combines Policy in Perspective*, Vancouver, British Columbia: The Fraser Institute.

Astin, Helen S. 1973. "Career Profiles of Women." In Rossi and Calderwood (1973).

Atascadero State Hospital v. Scanlon, 473 U.S. 234 (1985).

Axelrod, Robert M. 1984. *The Evolution of Cooperation*. New York: Basic Books.

Axelrod, R., and W.D. Hamilton. 1981. "The Evolution of Cooperation." *Science* 211.

Bardwick, J.M., et al., eds. 1970. *Feminine Personality and Conflict*. Belmont, Calif.: Wadsworth.

Bardwick, Judith M., and Elizabeth Douvan. 1971. "Ambivalence: The Socialization of Women." In Gornick and Moran (1971).

Barkow, Jerome H., Leda Cosmides, and John Tooby. 1992. *The Adapted Mind: Evolutionary Psychology and the Generation of Culture*. Oxford: Oxford University Press.

Barnett, Randy E. 1988. *The Structure of Liberty: Justice and the Rule of Law*. Oxford: Clarendon Press.

Barrett v. Omaha National Bank, 726 F.2d 424 (8th Cir. 184)

"Barring White in Native Class Is Ruled Illegal." 1980. *Toronto Globe & Mail*, 13 February.

Bartz, Wayne R., and Richard A. Rasor. 1978. *Surviving With Kids*. San Luis Obispo, Calif.: Impact.

Baruch, Grace K., and Rosalind C. Barnett. *Implications and Applications of Recent Research on Feminine Development*. Cambridge, Mass.: Institute for Independent Study.

Bauer, Peter T. 1987. "Population Scares." *Commentary* (November).

Bayer, Alan E. 1969. "Marriage Plans and Educational Aspirations." *American Journal of Sociology* 75.

Bebel, August. 1910. *Women and Socialism*. New York: Socialist Literature.

Becker, Gary. 1957. *The Economics of Discrimination*. Chicago: University of Chicago Press.

———. 1964. *Human Capital*. Washington, D.C.: National Bureau of Economic Research.

———. 1971. *The Economics of Discrimination*. 2nd ed. Chicago: University of Chicago Press.

———. Unpublished. "The Case Against Blackmail."

Bennett, James E., and Pierre M. Loewe. 1975. *Women in Business*. Toronto: Financial Post Books.

Benson, Bruce L. 1989. "Enforcement of Private Property Rights in Primitive Societies: Law without Government." *Journal of Libertarian Studies* 9, no. 1 (Winter).

———. 1989b. "The Spontaneous Evolution of Commercial Law." *Southern Journal of Economics* 55, no. 3 (January).

———. 1998. *To Serve and Protect*. New York: New York University Press.

———. 1990. *The Enterprise of Law: Justice Without the State*. San Francisco, Calif.: Pacific Research Institute for Public Policy.

———. 1993. "The Impetus for Recognizing Private Property and Adopting Ethical Behavior in a Market Economy: Natural Law, Government Law, or Evolving Self-Interest?" *Review of Austrian Economics* 6, no. 2.

Bernard, Jesse. 1964. *Academic Women*. University Park: Pennsylvania State University Press.

———. 1974. *The Future of Motherhood*. New York: Penguin Books.

Bethell, Tom. 1998. *The Noblest Triumph: Property and Prosperity Through the Ages*. New York: St. Martin's Press.

Bird, Roger C., ed. 1998. *The Frank M. Engle Lectures, 1978–1997*. Bryn Mawr, Penn.: American College.

Blessing v. Freestone, 520 U.S. 329 (1997).

"Blind Woman and Guide Dog Win Rights Fight." 1980. *Vancouver Sun*, 18 August.

Blinder, Alan S. 1973. "Wage Discrimination: Reduced Form and Structural Estimates." *Journal of Human Resources* 8 (Fall).

Block, Walter. 1969. "Against the Volunteer Military." *Libertarian Forum* 1, no 10 (August).

———. 1972. "The Blackmailer as Hero." *Libertarian Forum* 4, no. 12 (December).

———. 1976. *Defending the Undefendable*. New York: Fleet Press.

———. 1978. "Abortion, Woman and Fetus: Rights in Conflict?" *Reason*, April.

———. 1979. "Free Market Transportation: Denationalizing the Roads." *Journal of Libertarian Studies* 3, no. 2 (Summer).

———. 1980. *Zoning: Its Costs and Relevance for the 1980s*. Vancouver, British Columbia: The Fraser Institute.

———. 1980b. "Congestion and Road Pricing." *Journal of Libertarian Studies* 4, no. 3 (Fall).

———. 1981. "Economic Intervention, Discrimination, and Unforeseen Consequences." In Block and Walker (1981).

———. 1982a. "Economic Intervention, Discrimination, and Unforeseen Consequences." In Block and Walker (1982).

———. 1983. *Focus on Economics and the Canadian Bishops*. Vancouver, British Columbia: The Fraser Institute.

———. 1983b. "Theories of Highway Safety." *Transportation Research Record*, no. 912.

———. 1983c. "Public Goods and Externalities: The Case of Roads." *Journal of Libertarian Studies* 7, no. 1 (Spring).

———. 1985. *Defending the Undefendable*. San Francisco, Calif.: Fox and Wilkes.

———. 1986. *The U.S. Bishops and Their Critics*. British Columbia, Vancouver: The Fraser Institute.

———. 1986b. "Trading Money for Silence." *University of Hawaii Law Review* 8, no. 1 (Spring).

———. 1989. "Population Growth: Is It a Problem?" In Ross, Riordan, and MacArtney (1989).

———. 1991. *Defending the Undefendable*. San Francisco, Calif.: Fox and Wilkes.

———. 1992. "The Economics of Discrimination." *Journal of Business Ethics* 11.

———. 1992b. "Discrimination: An Interdisciplinary Analysis." *Journal of Business Ethics* 11.

———. 1994. "Total Repeal of Anti-trust Legislation: A Critique of Bork, Brozen and Posner." *Review of Austrian Economics* 8, no. 1.

———. 1994b. "Libertarianism vs. Libertinism." *Journal of Libertarian Studies* 11, no. 1.

———. 1995. "Ethics, Efficiency, Coasian Property Rights, and Psychic Income: A Reply to Harold Demsetz." *Review of Austrian Economics* 8, no. 2.

———. 1996. "The Mishnah and Jewish Dirigisme." *International Journal of Social Economics* 23, no. 2.

———. 1996b. "Road Socialism." *International Journal of Value-Based Management* 9.

———. 1996c. "O.J.'s Defense: A Reductio Ad Absurdum of the Economics of Ronald Coase and Richard Posner." *European Journal of Law and Economics* 3.

———. 1997. "The Case for De-Criminalizing Blackmail: A Reply to Lindgren and Campbell." *Western St. Louis University Law Review* 24, no. 2 (Spring).

———. 1997b. "Tobacco Advertising." *International Journal of Value-Based Management* 10, no. 3.

———. 1998. "Compromising the Uncompromisable: Discrimination." *American Journal of Economics and Sociology* 57, no. 2 (April).

———. 1998. "A Libertarian Theory of Blackmail." *Irish Jurist* 33.

———. 1999. *Defending the Undefendable*. San Francisco, Calif.: Fox and Wilkes.

———. 1999b. "Blackmail and Economic Analysis." *Thomas Jefferson Law Review* 21, no. 2 (October).

———. 1999c. "Blackmailing for Mutual Good: A Reply to Russell Hardin." *Vermont Law Review* 24, no. 1 (Fall).

———. 1999d. "The Crime of Blackmail: A Libertarian Critique." *Criminal Justice Ethics* 18, no. 2 (Summer/Fall).

———. 1999e. "Replies to Levin and Kipnis on Blackmail." *Criminal Justice Ethics* 18, no. 2 (Summer/Fall).

———. 2000. "The Legalization of Blackmail: A Reply to Professor Gordon." *Seton Hall Law Review* 30, no. 4.

———. 2000b. "Threats, Blackmail, Extortion, and Robbery, and Other Bad Things." *University of Tulsa Law Journal* 35, no. 2 (Winter).

———. 2000c. "Blackmail is Private Justice." *University of British Columbia Law Review* 34, no. 1.

————. 2000d. "Reply to Weder: Libertarianism, Blackmail, and Decency." *University of British Columbia Law Review* 34, no. 1.

————. 2001. "Toward a Libertarian Theory of Blackmail." *Journal of Libertarian Studies* 15, no. 2 (Winter).

————. Unpub a. "Compromising the Uncompromisable: A Private Property Rights Theory of Abortion."

————. Unpub b. "Libertarianism, Positive Obligations, and Property Abandonment: Children's Rights."

Block, Walter, ed. 1990. *Economics and the Environment: A Reconciliation.* Vancouver, British Columbia: The Fraser Institute.

Block, Walter, and Christopher E. Kent. 1999. "Blackmail." *Magill's Legal Guide.* Pasadena, Calif.: Salem Press.

Block, Walter, and Tom DiLorenzo. 2001. "The Calculus of Consent Revisited." *Public Finance and Management* 1, no. 3.

————. 2001. "Is Voluntary Government Possible? A Critique of Constitutional Economics." *Journal of Institutional and Theoretical Economics* 156, no. 4 (December).

Block, Walter, and David Gordon. 1985. "Extortion and the Exercise of Free Speech Rights: A Reply to Professors Posner, Epstein, Nozick, and Lindgren." *Loyola of Los Angeles Law Review* 19, no. 1 (November).

Block, Walter, and Robert W. McGee. 1999. "Blackmail from A to Z." *Mercer Law Review* 50, no. 2 (Winter).

————. 1999b. "Blackmail as a Victimless Crime." *Bracton Law Journal* 31.

Block, Walter, and Michael A. Walker, eds. 1981. *Discrimination, Affirmative Action, and Equal Opportunity: An Economic and Social Perspective.* Vancouver, British Columbia: The Fraser Institute.

————. 1985. *Focus on Employment Equity: A Critique of the Abella Royal Commission Report on Equality in Employment.* Vancouver, British Columbia: The Fraser Institute.

Block, Walter, and Roy Whitehead. 1999. "Gender Equity in Athletics: Should We Adopt a Non-Discriminatory Model?" *University of Toledo Law Review* 30, no. 2 (Winter).

————. 1999b. "Mandatory Student Fees: Forcing Some to Pay for the Free Speech of Others." *Whittier Law Review* 20, no. 4 (June).

————. 1999c. "The Unintended Consequences of Environmental Justice." *Forensic Science International* 100, nos. 1–2 (March).

————. 2000. "Human Organ Transplantation: Economic and Legal Issues." *Quinnipiac Health Law Journal* 3.

———. 2000b. "Environmental Justice Risks in the Petroleum Industry." *William and Mary Environmental Law and Policy Review* 24, no. 1 (Winter).

———. 2000c. "Direct Payment of State Scholarship Funds to Church-Related Colleges Offends the Constitution and Title VI." *Brigham Young University Journal of Public Law* 14, no. 2.

———. 2001. "Crying 'Wolf' In American: Re-evaluating Drug Prohibition Policy." Unpublished.

———. 2002. "Sexual Harassment in the Workplace: A Property Rights Perspective." *University of Utah Journal of Law and Family Studies* 4.

Block, Walter, and Walter Williams. 1981. "Male-Female Earnings Differentials: A Critical Reappraisal." *Journal of Labor Research* 2, no. 2.

———. 1982a. "Discrimination Helps the Under-Privileged." *Journal of Economic Affairs* 2, no. 4 (May).

———. 1982b. "Economic Intervention, Discrimination, and Unforeseen Consequences." In Block and Walker (1982).

———. 1985. "Discussion." In Block, Brennan, and Elzinga (1985).

Block, Walter, Geoffrey Brennan, and Kenneth Elzinga, eds. 1985. *Morality of the Market: Religious and Economic Perspectives*. Vancouver, British Columbia: The Fraser Institute.

Block, Walter, Stephen Kinsella, and Hans-Hermann Hoppe. 2000. "Second Paradox of Blackmail." *Business Ethics Quarterly* 10, no. 3 (July).

Board of Directors of Rotary International v. Rotary Club of Duarte, 481 U.S. 537 (1987)

Boaz, David. 1997. *Libertarianism: A Primer*. New York: Free Press.

Boaz, David, and Edward H. Crane. 1985. *Beyond the Status Quo*. Washington, D.C.: The Cato Institute.

Boettke, Peter J. 1991. "The Austrian Critique and the Demise of Socialism: The Soviet Case." In Ebeling (1991).

Boettke, Peter J., ed. 1994. *The Elgar Companion to Austrian Economics*. Aldershot, U.K.: Edward Elgar.

Böhm-Bawerk, Eugen von. 1959. "Value and Price." *Capital and Interest*, Book 3, Vol. 2. South Holland, Ill.: Libertarian Press.

Bolick, Clint. 1996. *The Affirmative Action Fraud: Can We Restore the American Civil Rights Vision?* Washington, D.C.: The Cato Institute.

Bonnette, Valeria, and Lamar Daniel. 1990. *Title IX Athletics Investogator's Manual*. Washington, D.C.: U.S. Department of Education.

Boudreaux, Donald J., and Thomas J. DiLorenzo. 1992. "The Protectionist Roots of Antitrust." *Review of Austrian Economics* 6, no. 2 (Spring).

Bowers v. Hardwick, 478 U.S. 186 (1986)

Boy Scouts of America v. Dale, 530 U.S. 694 (2000).

Boyle, James. 1992. "A Theory of Law and Information: Copyright, Spleens, Blackmail, and Insider Trading." *California Law Review* 80, no. 6.

Brandenburg v. Ohio, 395 U.S. 444 (1969).

Breitman, G., ed. 1965. *Malcolm X Speaks: Selected Speeches*. New York: Grove Press.

Brown, Claude. 1965. *Manchild in the Promised Land*. New York: New American Library.

Brown, Jennifer Gerarda. 1993. "Blackmail as Private Justice." *University of Pennsylvania Law Review* 141, no 5 (May).

Bryan and Boring. 1947. "Women in American Psychology: Factors Affecting their Professional Careers." *American Psychologist* 2 (January).

Buchanan, James. 1969. *Cost & Choice*. Chicago: Markham Publishing.

Buchanan, James M., and Gordon Tullock. 1971. *The Calculus of Consent: Logical Foundations of Constitutional Democracy*. Ann Arbor: University of Michigan Press.

Buchanan, James M., Robert D. Tollison, and Gordon Tullock, eds. 1980. *Toward a Theory of the Rent-Seeking Society*. College Station: Texas A&M University.

Buckmaster, Henrietta. 1969. *Let My People Go*. Boston: Beacon Press.

Burgess, E.W., and Paul Wallin. 1953. *Engagement and Marriage*. New York: Lippincott.

Burlington Industries v. Ellerth, 524 U.S. 742 (1998).

Bums v. McGregor, 989 F.2d. 959 (8th Cir. 1993).

Buss, David M. 1994. *The Evolution of Desire: Strategies of Human Mating*. New York: Basic Books.

Cadin, Michelle S., and Walter Block. 1997. "Privatize the Public Highway System." *The Freeman* 47, no. 2 (June/September).

Cahn, Steven M., ed. 1995. *The Affirmative Action Debate*. New York: Routledge.

"California Living: Snuff Out that Cigarette, Please." 1998. *Christian Science Monitor*, 12 January.

Callahan, Gene. 2001. *Economics for Real People*. Auburn, Ala.: Ludwig von Mises Institute.

Camden Citizens in Action v. N.J. Department of Environmental Protection, 145 F. Supp. 2d 505 (D.N.J. 2001).

Campbell, Debra J. 1988. "Why Blackmail Should be Criminalized: A Reply to Walter Block and David Gordon." *Loyola Louisiana Law Review* 21.

Canadian Council of Professional Engineers. Unpub.

Cannon v. University of Chicago, 648 F.2d 1104 (7th Cir. 1981), *cert. denied*, 454 U.S. 1128 (1981).

Cantu, Norma. 1995a. Letter. Assistant Secretary for Civil Rights, U.S. Dep't of Education, to Colleges and Universities (Sept. 20). (On file with author).

Cantu, Norma. 1995b. "Clarification of Intercollegiate Athletics Policy Guidance: The Three-Part Test." Washington, D.C.: U.S. Department of Education.

Cantwell v. Connecticut, 310 U.S. 296 (1940).

Carrero v. N.Y. Housing Authority, 890 F.2d 569 (2d Cir. 1989).

Castaneda v. Partida, 430 U.S. 482 (1977).

Census Bureau. 1998. *Statistical Abstract of the United States, 1998*. Washington, D.C.: U.S. Government Printing Office.

Chodorow, Nancy. 1971. "Being and Doing: A Cross Cultural Examination of the Socialization of Males and Females." *In Gornick and Moran* (1971).

"Choosey Landlords Targets of Council." 1980. *Vancouver Sun*, 24 September.

City of Richmond v. J.A. Croson Co., 488 U.S. 469,501 (1989).

Coase, Ronald. 1960. "The Problem of Social Cost." *Journal of Law and Economics* 3 (October).

———. 1988. "The 1987 McCorkle Lecture: Blackmail." *Virginia Law Review* 74, no. 4 (May).

Coffey, Daniel, and Walter Block. 1999. "Postponing Armageddon: Why Population Growth Isn't Out of Control." *Humanomics* 15, no. 4.

Cohen v. Brown University, 809 F. Supp. 978 (D.R.I. 1992) (*Brown University I*).

Cohen v. Brown University, 991 F.2d 888 (1st Cir. 1993) (*Brown University II*).

Cohen v. Brown University, 879 F. Supp. 185 (D.R.I. 1995) (*Brown University III*).

Coleman, Jules. 1987. "Competition and Cooperation." *Ethics* 98, no. 1.

College Savings Bank v. Florida Prepaid Postsecondary Education Expense Board 527 U.S. 627 (1999).

Columbia Broad. Systems v. United States, 316 U.S. 407 (1942).

Commission for Public Education and Religious Liberty v. Nyquist, 413 U.S. 756 (1973).

Conway, David. 1987. *A Farewell to Marx: An Outline and Appraisal of His Theories*. Middlesex, England: Penguin Books.

Cook, Gail C.A., ed. 1976. *Opportunity for Choice: A Goal for Women in Canada*. Catalogue IC 23-15/1976. Ottawa: Statistics Canada and C.D. Howe Research Institute.

Cook, Gail C.A., and Mary Eberts. 1976. In Cook (1976).

Cordato, Roy. 1989. "Subjective Value, Time Passage, and the Economics of Harmful Effects." *Hamline Law Review* 12, no. 2.

"Court Ruling Raises Alarm on Title IX: ASU'S Dowd Calls Decision 'Idiotic'." 1997. *Arkansas Democrat-Gazette*, 22 April.

Crais, Robert. 1996. *Sunset Express*. New York: Hyperion.

Crawford, Jacquelyn S. 1977. *Women in Middle Management*. Ridgewood, N.J.: Forkner.

Crittenden, Danielle. 1998. *What Our Mothers Didn't Tell Us*. New York: Simon and Schuster.

Curran v. Mount Diablo Council of Boy Scouts of America, 952 P.2d 218 (Cal. 1998).

Cuzan, Alfred G. 1979. "Do We Ever Really Get Out of Anarchy?" *Journal of Libertarian Studies* 3, no. 2 (Summer).

Dale v. Boy Scouts of America, 734 A.2d 1196 (N.J. 1999)

Daly, George, and J. Fred Giertz. 1978. "Externalities, Extortion, and Efficiency: Reply." *American Economic Review* 68, no. 4 (September).

Daniel, Lamar. 1994. Remarks to the Office of Civil Rights, Gulf South Conference Meeting. Birmingham, Ala., 26 January.

Dauterive, Jerry W., William Barnett, and Everett White. 1985. "A Taxonomy of Government Intervention." *Journal of Southwest Society of Economics* 40, no. 1 (September).

Davis v. Monroe County Board of Education, 526 U.S. 629 (1999).

Dawkins, Richard. 1989. *The Selfish Gene*. Oxford University Press.

———. 1995. *River out of Eden: A Darwinian View of Life*. New York: Basic Books.

de Beauvoir, Simone. 1974. *The Second Sex*. New York: Vintage Books.

de Jasay, Anthony. 1985. *The State*. New York: Basil Blackwell.

———. 1988. *The State*. Indianapolis, Ind.: Liberty Fund.

———. 1997. *Against Politics: On Government, Anarchy, and Order*. London: Routledge.

DeLong, Sidney W. 1993. "Blackmailers, Bribe Takers, and the Second Paradox." *University of Pennsylvania Law Review* 141, no. 5 (May).

Democratic Party of the United States v. Wisconsin ex rel La Follette, 450 U.S. 107 (1981)

Demsetz, Harold. 1965. "Minorities in the Market Place." *North Carolina Law Review* 43, no. 2.

Denton, Margaret A., and Alfred A. Hunter. 1982. *Equality in the Workplace, Economic Sectors, and Gender Discrimination in Canada: A Critique and Test of Block and Walker ... and Some New Evidence*. Women's Bureau, Discussion Paper, Series A, No. 6: Equality in the Workplace. Ottawa: Labor Canada.

DiLorenzo, Thomas J. 1988. "Competition and Political Entrepreneurship: Austrian Insights into Public Choice Theory." *Review of Austrian Economics* 2, no. 1 (December).

———. 1997. "The Myth of Natural Monopoly." *Review of Austrian Economics* 9, no. 2 (September).

DiLorenzo, Tom, and Walter Block. 2001. "Constitutional Economics and the Calculus of Consent." *The Journal of Libertarian Studies* 15, no. 3 (Summer).

Dooling, Richard. 1996. *Blue Streak: Swearing, Free Speech, and Sexual Harassment*. New York: Random House.

"Drea Tells Firm to Stop Questions." 1980. *Toronto Globe & Mail*, 31 July.

Eastland, Terry. 1996. *Ending Affirmative Action: The Case for Colorblind Justice*. New York: Basic Books.

Ebeling, Richard M. 1991. *Austrian Economics: Perspectives on the Past and Prospects for the Future*. Champions of Freedom Series. Vol. 17. Hillsdale, Mich.: Hillsdale College Press.

———. 1993. "Economic Calculation Under Socialism: Ludwig von Mises and His Predecessors." In Herbener (1993).

Eckert, R. D. and G.W. Hilton. 1972. "The Jitneys." *Journal of Law and Economics* 15.

Ehrlich, Paul R. 1968. *The Population Bomb*. New York: Ballantine.

Ehrlich, Paul R., and Anne H. Ehrlich. 1990. *The Population Explosion*. New York: Simon and Schuster.

Ellison v. Brady, 924 F.2d 872 (9th Cir. 1991).

Ellsberg, Daniel. 1975. "The Theory and Practice of Blackmail." In Young (1975).

England, Paula. 1993. "The Separative Self: Androcentric Bias in Neoclassical Assumptions." In Ferber and Nelson (1993).

Entine, Jon. 2000. *Taboo: Why Black Athletes Dominate Sports, and Why We're Afraid to Talk About It*. New York: Public Affairs.

Epstein, Richard A. 1983. "Blackmail, Inc." *University of Chicago Law Review* 50.

———. 1985. *Takings: Private Property and the Power of Eminent Domain*. Cambridge, Mass.: Harvard University Press, 1985.

———. 1992. *Forbidden Grounds: The Case Against Employment Discrimination Laws*. Cambridge, Mass.: Harvard University Press.

———. 1995. *Simple Rules for a Complex World*. Cambridge, Mass.: Harvard University Press.

Evans, Hugh. "Why Blackmail Should be Banned." *Philosophy* 65.

Fanon, Franz. 1963. *The Wretched of the Earth*. New York: Grove Press.

Faragher v. City of Boca Raton, 524 U.S. 775 (1998).

Farron, Steven. 2000. "Prejudice is Free but Discrimination has Costs," *Journal Libertarian Studies* 14, no. 2 (Summer).

Favia v. Indiana University of Pennsylvania, 812 F. Supp. 578 (W.D. Pa. 1993), aff'd, 7 F.3d 322 (3d Cir. 1993).

Fein, Ellen, and Sherrie Schneider. 1996. *The Rules: Time-Tested Secrets for Capturing the Heart of Mr. Right*. New York: Warner Books.

Feinberg, Joel. 1988. "The Paradox of Blackmail." *Ratio Jurisprudence* 1.

———. 1990. *Harmless Wrongdoing*. Oxford: Oxford University Press.

Feiner, Susan F. 1995. "Reading Neoclassical Economics: Toward an Erotic Economy of Sharing." In Kuiper and Sap (1995).

Ferber, Marianne A., and Julie A. Nelson, eds. 1993. *Beyond Economic Man: Feminist Theory and Economics*. Chicago: The University of Chicago Press.

Ferrara, Peter J., ed. 1990. *Free the Mail: Ending the Postal Monopoly*. Washington, D.C.: The Cato Institute.

Financial Post. 1980. 15 May.

Fishel, Leslie H., Jr., and Benjamin Quarles, eds. 1967. *The Black American*. Glenview, Ill.: Scott Foresman.

Fisher, Dave. 1974. *Killer: Autobiography of a Mafia Hit Man*. New York: Simon and Schuster.

"Fleet agrees to loan program." 1995. *Boston Globe*, 27 September.

Fletcher, George P. 1993. "Blackmail: The Paradigmatic Case." *University of Pennsylvania Law Review* 141, no. 5.

Folbre, Nancy. 1993. "Socialism, Feminist and Scientific." In Ferber and Nelson (1993).

Foreman, David. 1990. "Only Man's Presence can Save Nature." *Harper's Magazine*, April.

Fortune, Timothy Thomas. 1969. *Black & White: Land, Labor, & Politics in the South*. New York: Arno Press.

Foss, Nicolai J. 1995. "Information and the Market Economy: A Note on a Common Marxist Fallacy." *Review of Austrian Economics* 8, no. 2.

Frank, Robert H. 1988. *Passion Within Reason: The Strategic Role of the Emotions*. London: Norton.

Frazier, E. Franklin. 1957. *The Negro in the United States*. New York: Macmillan.

———. 1967. *Negro Youth at the Crossways*. New York: Schocken.

Fried, Charles. 1981. *Contract as Promise: A Theory of Contractual Obligation*. Cambridge, Mass.: Harvard University Press.

Friedan, Betty. 1974. *The Feminine Mystique*. New York: Dell.

Friedman, David. 1972. *Laissez Faire in Population: The Least Bad Solution*. New York: Population Council.

———. 1979. "Private Creation and Enforcement of Law: A Historical Case." *Journal of Legal Studies* 8 (March).

———. 1985. "Discussion." In *Morality of the Market: Religious and Economic Perspectives*, ed. Walter Block, Geoffrey Brennan, and Kenneth Elzinga. Vancouver, British Columbia: The Fraser Institute.

———. 1989. *The Machinery of Freedom: Guide to a Radical Capitalism*. 2nd ed. La Salle, Ill.: Open Court.

Friedman, Milton. 1962. *Capitalism and Freedom*. Chicago: University of Chicago Press.

———. 1965. "Alleviation of Poverty and Social Welfare Measures." In Weisbrod (1965).

———. 1975. *There's No Such Thing as a Free Lunch*. La Salle, Ill: Open Court.

———. 1981. *Free to Choose*. New York: Avon Books.

———. 1985. "Capitalism and the Jews." In Block and Walker (1985).

———. 1992. *Money Mischief: Episodes in Monetary History*. New York: Harcourt Brace Jovanovich.

Friedman, Milton, and Rose Friedman. 1980. *Free to Choose : A Personal Statement*. New York: Harcourt Brace Jovanovich.

———. 1983. *Tyranny of the Status Quo*. New York: Harcourt Brace Jovanovich.

"GAO Study Shows Drop in Men's Participation, but Reason Is Unclear." 1999. *NCAA News*, 5 July.

Garrison, William Lloyd. 1833. *Declaration of Sentiment of the American Anti-Slavery Convention*. Boston: R. F. Wallcut.

Guardians Association v. Civil Service Commission, 463 U.S. 582 (1982).

Ginsburg, Douglas H., and Paul Shechtman. 1993. "Blackmail: An Economic Analysis of the Law." *University of Pennsylvania Law Review* 141, no. 5 (May).

Gordon, David. 1990. *Resurrecting Marx: The Analytical Marxists on Freedom, Exploitation, and Justice*. New Brunswick, N.J.: Transaction.

Gordon, Wendy J. 1993. "Truth and Consequences: The Force of Blackmail's Central Case." *University of Pennsylvania Law Review* 141, no. 5 (May).

Gore, Albert. 1992. *Earth in the Balance: Ecology and the Human Spirit*. New York: Houghton-Mifflin.

Gottfredson, Linda. 1987. "The Practical Significance of Black-White Differences in Intelligence." *Behavioral and Brain Sciences* 10.

———. 1988. "Reconsidering Fairness: A Matter of Social and Ethical Priorities." *Journal of Vocational Behavior* 33, no. 3 (December).

Gross, Michael, and Mary Beth Averill. 1983. "Evolution and Patriarchal Myths of Scarcity and Competition." In Hardin and Hintikkia (1983).

Gorlick, Vivian. 1978. "Why Women Fear Success." In *Essays in Feminism*. New York: Harper & Row.

Gornick, Vivian, and Barbara K. Moran, eds. 1971. *Women in Sexist Society*. New York: Basic Books.

Gorr, Michael. 1992. "Liberalism and the Paradox of Blackmail." *Philosophy and Public Affairs* 21.

———. 1977. "Nozick's Argument Against Blackmail." *The Personalist* 58.

Green v. Mansour, 474 U.S. 64 (1985).

Grier, William H., and Price M. Cobbs. 1968. *Black Rage*. New York: Basic Books.

"Group for Blind Suggests Job Quota." 1980. *Toronto Globe & Mail*, 21 August.

Grove City v. Bell, 465 U.S. 555 (1984).

Grubel, Herbert C., and Michael A. Walker, eds. 1978. *Unemployment Insurance*. Vancouver, British Columbia: The Fraser Institute.

Gunderson, Gerald. 1989. "Privatization and the 19th-Century Turnpike." *The Cato Journal* 9, no. 1 (Spring/Summer).

Gunderson, Morley. 1974. "Factors Influencing Male-Female Wage Differences in Ontario," Toronto: Research Branch, Ontario Ministry of Labour.

————. 1975. "Male-Female Wage Differentials and the Impact of Equal Pay Legislation." *Review of Economics and Statistics* 57, no. 4 (November).

————. 1976. "Work Patterns." In *Opportunity for Choice: A Goal for Women in Canada*, ed. G. Cook. Ottawa: Statistics Canada.

————. 1976b. "Time Patterns of Male-Female Wage Differentials." *Relations Industrielles/Industrial Relations* 31.

————. 1979. "Decomposition of the Male/Female Earnings Differential: Canada, 1970." *Canadian Journal of Economics* 12, no. 3 (August).

————. 1982. *The Female-Male Earnings Gap in Ontario: A Summary*. 1982. Employment Information Series, no. 22. Toronto: Ontario Ministry of Labor.

"Guns prevent crime in Kennesaw." 2001. *Augusta Chronicle*. http://chronicle. augusta.com/stories/032601/opi_046-7178.shtml.

Gwartney, James, Robert Lawson, and Walter Block. 1996. *Economic Freedom of the World, 1975–1995*. Vancouver, British Columbia: The Fraser Institute.

Gwartney, James D., and Richard L. Stroup. 1993. *What Everyone Should Know About Economics and Prosperity*. Vancouver, British Columbia: The Fraser Institute.

Gwartney, James D., and Richard E. Wagner, eds. 1988. *Public Choice and Constitutional Economics*. London: Jai Press.

Hafer v. Melo, 502 U.S. 21 (1991).

Hagen, J. 1977. "Finding 'Discrimination': A Question of Meaning." *Ethnicity* 4, no. 2 (June).

Haksar, Vinit. 1976. "Coercive Proposals." *Political Theory* 4.

Hall v. Gus Construction Company, 842 F.2d 1010 (8th Cir. 1988).

Hardin, Russell. 1993. "Blackmailing for Mutual Good." *University of Pennsylvania Law Review* 141, no. 5 (May).

Harding, Sandra, and Merill B. Hintikka, eds. 1983. *Discovering Reality: Feminist Perspectives on Epistemology, Metaphysics, Methodology, and Philosophy of Science*. Dordrecht, Holland: D. Reidel Publishing Company.

Hartsock, Nancy C.M., "The Feminist Standpoint: Developing the Ground for a Specifically Feminist Historical Materialism." In Sandra Harding and Merill B. Hintikka, eds. (1983).

Harris v. Forklift Systems, 510 U.S. 17 (1993).

Harrison, Paige M., and Allen J. Beck. 2003. "Prisoners in 2002." *Bureau of Justice Statistics Bulletin* (July). http://www.ojp.usdoj.gov/bjs/pub/pdf/p02.pdf.

Hayek, Friedrich A. 1948. *Individualism and Economic Order*, Chicago: The University of Chicago Press.

———. 1978. "Competition as a Discovery Procedure." In *New Studies in Politics, Philosophy, Economics and the History of Ideas*, Chicago: The University of Chicago Press, 1978.

Hazelwood School District v. United States, 433 U.S. 299 (1977).

Hazlitt, Henry. 1946. *Economics in One Lesson*. New York: Harper & Row.

Healy, Gene. 1999. "Liberty, States' Rights, and the Most Dangerous Amendment." *Liberty* 13 (August).

———. 2000. "Roger and Me." *Liberty* 14 (February).

Health Information Division, Department of National Health and Welfare. Unpublished material. Statistics received from Revenue Canada Taxation, September 1980. Ottawa, Ontario: Revenue Canada.

Held, Virginia. 1985. "Feminism and Epistemology: Recent Work on the Connection Between Gender and Knowledge." *Philosophy & Public Affairs* 14, no. 3 (Summer).

Hennig, Margaret, and Anne Jardim. 1976. *The Managerial Women*. New York: Simon & Schuster.

Hepworth, Michael. 1975. *Blackmail: Publicity and Secrecy in Everyday Life*. London: Routledge and Kegan Paul.

Herbener, Jeffrey, ed. 1993. *The Meaning of Ludwig von Mises*. Boston: Kluwer Academic Press.

Herrnstein, Richard, and Charles Murray. 1994. *The Bell Curve*. New York: The Free Press.

Hicks et al. v. Arkansas Department of Higher Education, No. Civ-00672, E.D. Ark. (2000).

Higgs, R. 1977. *Competition and Coercion: Blacks in the American Economy, 1865–1914*. Cambridge: Cambridge University Press.

High, Jack. 1984. "Bork's Paradox: Static vs. Dynamic Efficiency in Antitrust Analysis." *Contemporary Policy Issues* 3.

Hill, Christina Maria. 1973. "Women in the Canadian Economy." In Robert M. Laxer, ed., *(Canada)Ltd.: The Political Economy of Dependency*. Toronto: McClelland and Stewart.

Hobbes, Thomas. 1943. *Leviathan*. London: J.M. Dent.

Hoffmann, Carl, and J. Reed. 1982. "When is Imbalance not Discrimination?'" In Block and Walker (1982).

Holmes, R.A. 1976. "Male-Female Earnings Differentials in Canada." *Journal of Human Resources* 11.

Hoppe, Hans-Hermann. 1989. *A Theory of Socialism and Capitalism: Economics, Politics, and Ethic*. Boston: Kluwer Academic Publishers.

⸻. 1993. *The Economics and Ethics of Private Property: Studies in Political Economy and Philosophy*. Boston: Kluwer Academic Publishers.

⸻. 1996. "Socialism: A Property or Knowledge Problem?" *Review of Austrian Economics* 9, no. 1.

⸻. 1998. "The Private Production of Defense." *Journal of Libertarian Studies* 14, no. 1 (Winter).

⸻. 2001. *Democracy—The God That Failed: The Economics and Politics of Monarchy, Democracy, and the Natural Order*. New Brunswick, N.J.: Transaction.

⸻. 1992. "On Praxeology and the Praxeological Foundation of Epistemology and Ethics." In Herbener (1993).

Horner, M.S. 1968. "Sex Differences in Achievement Motivation and Performance in Competitive and Non-Competitive Situations." Ph. D. diss., University of Michigan.

⸻. 1969. "Fail: Bright Women." *Psychology Today* 3 (November).

⸻. 1970. "Femininity and Successful Achievement: A Basic Inconsistency." In Bardwick, et al, 1970.

Horowitz, Steven. 1995. "Feminist Economics: An Austrian Perspective." *Journal of Economic Methodology* 2, No. 2 (December).

⸻. 1996. "Money, Money Prices, and the Socialist Calculation Debates." *Advances in Austrian Economics* 3.

"How Selective Colleges Heighten Income Inequality." 2000. *Chronicle of Higher Education Review*, 15 September: http://www.prospect.org/webfeatures/2000/reich-r094 5.html (last visited December 3, 2001).

Hughes, Jean O., and Bernie R. Sandler. 1986. "In Case of Sexual Harassment, A Guide for Women Students." In *The Project on the Status of Education and Women*. Washington, D.C.: Association of American Colleges.

Hummel, Jeffrey Rogers. 1990. "National Goods versus Public Goods: Defense, Disarmament, and Free Riders. *Review of Austrian Economics* 4.

Hurley v. Irish-America Gay, Lesbian, and Bisexual Group, 515 U.S. 557 (1995).

Hutt, W. H. 1964. *The Economics of the Colour Bar: A Study of the Economic Origins and Consequences of Racial Segregation in South Africa*. London: Andre Deutsch.

————. 1973. *The Strike-Threat System*. New York: Arlington House.

Intlekofer v. Turnage, 973 F.2d 773 (9th Cir. 1992).

Isenbergh, Joseph. 1993. "Blackmail from A to C." *University of Pennsylvania Law Review* 141, no. 5 (May).

"It's Art vs. Sexual Harassment." 1996. *The Tennessean* (Nashville), 1 March.

Jackson v. Concord Co., 253 A.2d 793 (N.J. 1969).

Jaffe, Louis. 1965. *Judicial Control of Administrative Action*. Boston: Little, Brown and Company.

Jandoo, R. S., & W. Arthur Harland. 1984. "Legally Aided Blackmail." *New Law Journal* 27 (April).

Johnson v. Florida, 512 U.S. 997 (1994).

Jones v. Flagship International, 793 F.2d 714 (5th Cir. 1986).

Jones v. Wesco Investments, 846 F.2d 1154 (8th Cir. 1988).

Jongeward, Dorothy, and Dru Scott. 1976. *Women as Winners*. London: Addison-Wesley.

"Judge Blocks Cal State-Bakersfield's Plan to Cap Size of Wrestling Team." 1999. *Chronicle of Higher Education*, 12 March.

Katz, Leo. 1993. "Blackmail and Other Forms of Arm Twisting." *University of Pennsylvania Law Review* 141, no. 5 (May).

Katz v. Dole, 709 F.2d 251 (4th Cir. 1983).

Kaufman v. Applied Signal, 970 F.2d 178 (6th Cir. 1992).

Kentucky v. Graham, 473 U.S. 159 (1985).

Keyes, Ralph. 1980. *The Height of Your Life*. Boston: Little, Brown and Company.

Kimball, Meredith M. 1978. "Women and Success: A Basic Conflict?" In Stephenson (1978).

Kinman v. Omaha Public School District, 94 F.3d 463 (8th Cir. 1996).

Kirzner, Israel M. 1973. *Competition and Entrepreneurship*. Chicago: University of Chicago Press.

Klein, Daniel B., and G.J. Fielding. 1992. "Private Toll Roads: Learning from the Nineteenth Century." *Transportation Quarterly* (July).

————. 1993. "How to Franchise Highways." *Journal of Transport Economics and Policy* 27, no. 2 (May).

Klein, Daniel B., John Majewski, and Christopher Baer. 1993. "Responding to Relative Decline: The Plank Road Boom of Antebellum New York." *Economic History* 57, no. 4 (December).

Klein, Peter G. 1996. "Economic Calculation and the Limits of Organization." *Review of Austrian Economics* 9, no. 2.

Klitgaarrd, R., and R. Katz. R. 1983. "Overcoming Ethnic Inequality." *Journal of Policy Analysis and Management* 2, no. 3.

Knight, Frank H. 1956. *On the History and Method of Economics*. Chicago: University of Chicago Press.

Kotcher v. Rosa and Sullivan Appliance, 957 F.2d 59 (2d Cir. 1992).

Krecke, Elisabeth. 1977. "Law and the Market Order: An Austrian Critique of the Economic Analysis of Law." In McGee (1977).

Kuiper, Edith, and Jolande Sap, eds. 1995. *Out of the Margin: Feminist Perspectives on Economics*. New York: Routledge.

Kurkjiian, Stephen. 1995. "State warns that auto insurance shuld not be discriminatory," *Boston Globe*, 27 June.

Landes, William, and Richard A. Posner. 1975. "The Private Enforcement of Law." *Journal of Legal Studies* 4, no. 1 (January).

"Landlords Won't Rent to Man in Wheelchair." 1980. *Vancouver Sun*, 25 October.

"Landlords Close Doors to Thalidomide Victim: Deformity Makes Her an Unwanted Tenant." 1981. *Vancouver Sun*, 14 January.

Lawrence v. Texas, 539 U.S. 558 (2003).

Lester, Richard A. 1974. *Antibias Regulations of Universities*. New York: McGraw-Hill.

Levin, Michael. 1977. *Why Race Matters*. Westport, Conn.: Praeger.

———. 1982. "Is Racial Discrimination Special?" *Policy Review* 22 (October).

———. 1984. "Comparable Worth: The Feminist Road to Socialism." *Commentary* 74, no. 3 (September).

———. 1987. *Feminism and Freedom*. New York: Transaction Books.

———. 1996. "Why Race Matters: A Preview." *Journal of Libertarian Studies* 12, no. 2 (Fall).

———. 1997. *Why Race Matters: Race Differences and What They Mean*. New York: Praeger.

Lewin, Peter. 1998. "The Firm, Money, and Economic Calculation." *American Journal of Economics and Sociology* 57, no. 4 (October).

Lindgren, James. 1984. "Unraveling the Paradox of Blackmail." *Columbia Law Review* 84.

———. 1984b. "More Blackmail Ink: a Critique of Blackmail, Inc., Epstein's Theory of Blackmail." *Connecticut Law Review* 16, no. 4 (Summer).

———. 1986. "In Defense of Keeping Blackmail a Crime: Responding to Block and Gordon." *Loyola Los Angeles Law Review* 20, no. 1 (November).

———. 1989. "Blackmail: On Waste, Morals, and Ronald Coase." *UCLA Law Review* 36.

———. 1989b. "Kept in the Dark: Owen's View of Blackmail." *Connecticut Law Review* 21.

———. 1989c. "Secret Rights: A Comment on Campbell's Theory of Blackmail." *Connecticut Law Review* 21.

———. 1993. "Blackmail: An Afterward." *University of Pennsylvania Law Review* 141, no. 5 (May).

———. 1993b. "The Theory, History, and Practice of the Bribery-Extortion Distinction." *University of Pennsylvania Law Review* 141, no. 5 (May).

Lipsett v. University of Puerto Rico, 864 F.2d 881 (1st Cir. 1988).

Louw, Leon. 1980. "Free Enterprise and the South African Black." Address to Barclay's Executive Women's Club, Johannesburg, South Africa, 31 July.

Louw, L. and F. Kendall, F. 1986. *South Africa: The Solution*. Bisho Ciskei: Amagi Publications.

Lovell, Michael C. 1973. "The Minimum Wage Reconsidered." *Western Economic Journal* 11, no. 4 (December).

Lundahl, M. and E. Wadensjo. 1984. *Unequal Treatment: A Study in the Neoclassical Theory of Discrimination*. New York: New York University Press.

Luxton, Meg. 1980. *More Than a Labour of Love: Three Generations of Women's Work in the Home*. Toronto: Women's Educational Press.

Luxton, Margaret. 1973. "Urban Communes and Co-ops in Toronto." M. Phil. dissertation, University of Toronto.

Lynch, Michael, and Rick Henderson. 1998. "Team Colors." *Reason*, July.

Lyons, Daniel. 1975. "Welcome Threats and Coercive Offers." *Philosophy* 50.

Machan, Tibor. 1978. "Against Non-Libertarian Natural Rights." *Journal of Libertarian Studies* 2, no. 3.

———. 1990. *Capitalism and Individualism*. New York: St. Martin's Press.

————. 1982. *The Libertarian Reader*. Totowa, N.J.: Rowman and Littlefield.

Machan, Tibor, and Douglas Rasmussen, eds. 1995. *Liberty for the 21st Century: Essays in Contemporary Libertarian Thought*. Lanham, Md.: Rowman and Littlefield.

Mack, Eric. 1982. "In Defense of Blackmail." *Philosophy Studies* 41.

MacLeod, Neil. 1972. "Female Earnings in Manufacturing: A Comparison with Male Earnings." *Statistics Canada: Notes on Labour Statistics*, 1971. Ottawa: Information Canada.

Mainardi, Pat. 1970. "The Politics of Housework." In Morgan (1970).

Martin, James J. 1970. *Men Against the State: The Expositors of Individualist Anarchism in America, 1827–1908*. Colorado Springs, Colo.: Ralph Myles.

Mayor of Philadelphia v. Educational Equity League, 415 U.S. 605 (1974).

McChesney, Fred. 1991. "Antitrust and Regulation: Chicago's Contradictory Views." *Cato Journal* 10.

McCulloch, J. Houston. 1974. "The Effect of a Minimum Wage Law in the Labour-Intensive Sector." *Canadian Journal of Economics* 7, no. 2 (May).

McDonald, Lynn. 1975. "Wages of Work: A Widening Gap Between Women and Men." *Canadian Forum* (April/May).

McDowell, John M. 1982. "Obsolescence of Knowledge and Career Publication Profiles: Some Evidence of Differences among Fields in Costs of Interrupted Careers." *American Economic Review* 72, no. 4 (September).

McGee, Robert W., ed. 1977. *Commentaries on Law and Economics*. South Orange, NJ: Dumont Institute for Public Policy Research.

Meissner, Martin. "Sexual Division of Labour and Inequality: Labour and Leisure." In Stephenson (1978).

Meisner, M., E.W. Humphries, S.M. Meis, and W.J. Scheu. 1875. "No Exit for Wives: Sexual Division of Labour and the Cumulation of Household Demands." *Canadian Review of Sociology and Anthropology* 12.

Meritor Savings Bank v. Vinson, 447 U.S. 57 (1986).

Mincer, Jacob, and Solomon Polachek. 1974. "Family Investments in Human Capital: Earnings of Women." *Journal of Political Economy* 82, no. 2, part 2 (March).

Mises, Ludwig von. 1957. *Theory and History*. New Haven, Conn.: Yale University Press.

————. 1963. *Human Action*, 3rd ed. Chicago: Regnery.

————. 1966. *Human Action: A Treatise on Economics*. Chicago: Regnery.

———. 1969. *Bureaucracy*. New Rochelle, N.Y.: Arlington House.

———. 1969b. *Omnipotent Government*. New Rochelle, N.Y.: Arlington House.

———. 1969c. *Socialism*. London: Jonathan Cape.

———. 1972. *The Anti-Capitalist Mentality*. South Holland, Ill.: Libertarian Press.

———. 1981. *Socialism*. Indianapolis, Ind.: Liberty Classics.

———. 1990. *Economic Calculation in the Socialist Commonwealth*. Auburn, Ala.: Ludwig von Mises Institute.

———. 1991. *Two Essays by Ludwig von Mises*. Auburn, Ala.: Ludwig von Mises Institute.

Mitchell, Juliet. 1973. *Woman's Estate*. New York: Vintage Books.

Mitchell v. Helms, 530 U.S. 793 (2000).

Moore, G. 1961. "The Purpose of Licensing." *The Journal of Law and Economics* 4 (October).

Moore, Stephen. 1988. "Privatizing the U.S. Postal Service." In *Privatization: A Strategy for Taming the Federal Budget Fiscal Year 1988*. Washington, D.C.: Heritage Foundation.

Moore, Thomas G. 1990. "The Federal Postal Monopoly: History, Rationale, and the Future." In Ferrara (1990).

"More to an Interview than Meets the Eye." 1980. *Toronto Globe & Mail*, 19 July.

"More Women and Fewer Men Participate in Intercollegiate Athletics, Study Finds." 1999. *The Chronicle of Higher Education*, 9 July.

Morgan, Robin, ed. 1970. *Sisterhood is Powerful*. New York: Random House.

Morgan v. Hertz Corporation, 542F. Supp. 123 (W.D. Tenn. 1981), *aff'd* 725 F.2d 1070 (6th Cir. 1984).

Morris, Andrew P. 1998. "Miners, Vigilantes, and Cattlemen: Overcoming Free Rider Problems in the Private Provision of Law." *Land and Water Law Review* 33, no. 2.

Moylan v. Maries County, 792 F.2d 746 (8th Cir. 1986).

Mueller v. Allen, 463 U.S. 388 (1983).

Murphy, Jeffrie G. 1980. "Blackmail: A Preliminary Inquiry." *Monist* 63.

Murray, Charles. 1997. *What it Means to be a Libertarian*. New York: Broadway Books.

Murray, C. 1984. "Affirmative Racism." *The New Republic*, 31 December.

Narveson, J. 1987. "Have We A Right to Non-discrimination?" In Poff and Waluchow (1987).

———. 1988. *The Libertarian Idea*. Philadelphia, Penn.: Temple University Press.

National Academy of Sciences. 1981. *Women, Work, and Wages*. Washington, D.C.

National Collegiate Athletic Association (NCAA). 1993. *Final Report of the NCAA Gender-Equity Task Force*.

———. 1994. *Amendment No. 2-1, Principle of Gender Equity*. NCAA Convention (January).

Neimi, Beth. 1974. "The Female-Male Differential in Unemployment Rates." *Industrial and Labour Relations Review* 27, no. 3 (1974).

Nelson, Julie A. 1992. "Gender, Metaphor, and the Definition of Economics." *Economics and Philosophy* 8, no. 1.

New York State Club Association v. City of New York, 487 U.S. 1 (1988).

North, Gary. 1992. *The Coase Theorem*. Stone Mountain, Georgia: Publisher Services.

"Not Bigoted Enough." 1999. *Washington Post*, 23 August.

Nozick, Robert. 1974. *Anarchy, State, and Utopia*. New York: Basic Books.

Oakley, Ann. 1976. *Women's Work: The Housewife Past and Present*. New York: Vintage Books.

Oaxaca, Ronald. 1973. "Male-Female Wage Differentials in Urban Labor Markets." *International Economic Review* 14.

"Obese Are Victims of Bias: Professor." 1980. *Toronto Globe & Mail*, 5 August.

O'Brien, J. Patrick, and Dennis O. Olson. 1990. "The Great Alaskan Money Give Away Program." *Economic Inquiry* 28, no. 3.

Office for Civil Rights. 1996. *Clarification of Intercollegiate Athletics Policy Guidance: The Three-Part Test*. Washington, D.C.: U.S. Department of Education.

O'Leary, V. 1974. "Some Attitudinal Barriers to Occupational Aspirations in Women." *Psychological Bulletin* 81.

Oncale v. Sundowner Offshore Services, 523 U.S. 75 (1998).

Oppenheimer, Franz. 1914. *The State*. Trans. John M. Glitterman. Indianapolic, Ind.: Bobbs-Merril.

Ostry, Sylvia. 1966. "The Female Worker: Labour Force and Occupational Trends." In *Changing Patterns in Women's Employment: Report of a Consultation Held March 18, 1966*. Ottawa: Deptatment of Labour, Women's Bureau.

———. 1968. "The Female Worker in Canada." *Dominion Bureau of Statistics Census Monograph*. Ottawa: Queen's Printer.

———. 1970. "Labour Force Participation and Childbearing Status." In *Demography and Educational Planning*, Conference on the Implications of Demographic Factors for Educational Planning and Research, ed. Betty MacLeod. Monograph Series, vol. 7. Toronto: Ontario Institute for Studies in Education.

Owen, Robert. 1950. *A New View of Society*. Glencoe, Ill.: Free Press.

Owens, David. 1979. "Should Blackmail be Banned?" *Philosophy* 63, no. 246.

Paul Ellen Frankel. 1989. *Equity and Gender: the Comparable Worth Debate*. New Brunswick, N.J.: Transaction.

Pease, W. and J., eds. 1965. *The Antislavery Argument*. Indianapolis, Ind.: Bobbs-Merrill.

Pederson v. Louisiana State University, 912 F. Supp. 892 (M.D. La. 1996).

Pennock, J.R., and J.W. Chapman, eds. 1978. *Anarchism: Nomos XIX*. New York: New York University Press.

Pilon, Roger. 2000a. "In Defense of the Fourteenth Amendment." *Liberty* 14 (February).

———. 2000b. "I'll Take the 14th." *Liberty* 14 (March).

Pipes, Richard. 1999. *Property and Freedom*. New York: Alfred A. Knopf.

Piven, Frances Fox, and Richard A. Cloward. 1971. *Regulating the Poor*. New York: Random House.

Poff, D., and W. Waluchow, eds. 1987. *Business Ethics in Canada*. Scarborough, Ont.: Prentice-Hall Canada.

"Policies for the People." 1995. *Boston Globe*, 15 October.

Posner, Richard A. 1992. *Economic Analysis of Law*. 4th ed. Boston: Little, Brown and Company.

———. "Blackmail, Privacy, and Freedom of Contract." *University of Pennsylvania Law Review* 141, no. 5 (May).

Powell v. Ridge, 189 F.3d 387 (3d Cir. 1999).

"Preferred." 1980. *Toronto Globe & Mail*, 18 August.

Prosser and Keaton. 1984. *Prosser and Keaton on the Law of Torts*. 5th ed. St. Paul, Minn.: West Publishing Company.

"Pushing and Shoving for the State's Top Scholars." 1999. *Arkansas Times* (Little Rock), 27 August.

Rainwater, Lee. 1960. *And the Poor Get Children*. Chicago: Quadrangle Books.

Ray, Ratna. 1977. *Women in the Labour Force: Facts and Figures*. Catalogue L 38-30/1977-2. Ottawa: Labour Canada.

Read, Leonard. 1964. *Anything That's Peaceful*. Irvington-on-Hudson, N.Y.: The Foundation for Economic Education.

———. 1977. *Awake for Freedom's Sake*. Irvington-on-Hudson, N.Y.: The Foundation for Economic Education.

Reagan, Barbara B. 1975. "Two Supply Curves for Economists? Implications of Mobility and Career Attachment of Women." *American Economic Review* 65, no. 2 (May).

Reder, Melvin W. 1999. *Economics: The Culture of a Controversial Science*. Chicago: University of Chicago Press.

Reisman, George. 1996. *Capitalism: A Treatise on Economics*. Ottawa, Ill.: Jameson Books.

Reitman v. Mulkey, 387 US. 369 (1967).

"Report Biased Landlords, Male Students Are Urged." 1980. *Toronto Globe & Mail*, 18 August.

Revenue Canada Taxation. 1973. *Taxation Statistics, 1973 Edition: Analyzing the Returns of Individuals for the 1971 Taxation Year*. Catalogue RV 44-1973. Ottawa: Labour Canada.

———. 1980. *Taxation Statistics 1980 Edition: Analyzing the Returns of Individuals for the 1978 Taxation Year*. Catalogue RV 44-1980. Ottawa: Labour Canada.

Reynolds, Morgan O. 1995. *Economics of Labor*. Cincinnati, Ohio: South-Western.

———. 1998. "The Impossibility of Socialist Economy." *The Quarterly Journal of Austrian Economics* 1, no. 2 (Summer).

Ridley, Mark. 1993. *The Red Queen: Sex and the Evolution of Human Nature*. New York: MacMillan.

Robb, Roberta Edgecombe. 1978. "Earnings Differentials Between Males and Females in Ontario, 1971." *The Canadian Journal of Economics* 11, no. 2 (May).

Roberts v. Colorado State Board of Agriculture, 998 F.2d 824 (10th Cir. 1993).

Roberts, L. 1982. "Understanding Affirmative Action." In Block and Walker (1982).

———. 1979. "Some Unanticipated Consequences of Affirmative Action Policies." *Canadian Public Policy* 5, no. 1.

Roberts v. Colorado State Board of Agriculture, 998 F.2d 824 (10th Cir. 1993), *cert. denied*, 510 U.S. 1004 (1993).

Roberts v. United States Jaycees, 468 U.S. 609 (1984).

Robinson v. Jacksonville Shipyards, 760 F. Supp. 1486 (M.D. Fla. 1991).

Robson, R.A.H. 1969. "A Comparison of Men's and Women's Salaries in the Academic Profession." Report to the Royal Commission on the Status of Women. *C.A.U.T. Bulletin* 17.

Robson, R.A.H., and Mireille Lapointe. 1971. "A Comparison of Men's and Women's Salaries and Employment Fringe Benefits in the Academic Profession." Canadian Association of University Teachers: Studies of the Royal Commission on the Status of Women in Canada, 1. Ottawa, Ontario: Information Canada.

Rockwell, Llewellyn H., Jr. 1999. "The Right to Exclude." www.mises.org/fullstory. aspx?control=282&id=76. August 13.

Rosenbluth, Gideon and R.A. Holmes. 1967. "The Structure of Academic Salaries in Canada." *C.A.U.T. Bulletin* 15, no. 4 (April).

Ross, Peter S., Sheila Riordon, and Susan MacArtney, eds. 1989. *Resolving Global Problems into the 21st Century: How Can Science Help? Proceedings of the Fourth national Conference of Canadian Pugwash*. Ottawa, Ontario: CSP Publications.

Rossi, Alice S., and Ann Calderwood, eds. 1973. *Academic Women on the Move*. New York: Russell Sage Foundation.

Roth, Gabriel. 1967. *Paying for Roads: The Economics of Traffic Congestion*. Harmondsworth, England: Penguin.

———. 1987. *The Private Provision of Public Services in Developing Countries*. Oxford University Press.

Rothbard, Murray N. 1970. *Power and Market*. Menlo Park, Calif.: Institute for Humane Studies.

———. 1970b. *Man, Economy, and State*, Los Angeles, Nash.

———. 1973. *For a New Liberty*. New York: Macmillan.

———. 1978. *For a New Liberty*. New York: Macmillan.

———. 1978b. "Without a State." In Pennock and Chapman (1978).

———. 1982. *The Ethics of Liberty*. Atlantic Highlands, N.J.: Humanities Press.

———. 1983. *The Mystery of Banking*. New York: Richardson and Snyder.

———. 1983b. *For a New Liberty*. New York: Macmillan.

———. 1985. *For a New Liberty*. New York: Libertarian Review Foundation.

———. 1990. "Law, Property Rights, and Air Pollution." In Block (1990).

———. 1991. "The End of Socialism and the Calculation Debate Revisited." *Review of Austrian Economics* 5, no. 2.

———. 1993. *Man, Economy, and State*. Auburn, Ala.: Ludwig von Mises Institute.

———. 1994. *The Case Against the Fed.* Auburn, Ala.: Ludwig von Mises Institute.

———. 1997. *The Logic of Action Two: Applications and Criticism from the Austrian School.* Cheltenham, U.K.: Edward Elgar.

———. 1997b. "Buchanan and Tullock's The Calculus of Consent." In Rothbard (1997).

———. 1997c. *The Logic of Action, Vol. I: Method, Money and the Austrian School.* Lyme, N.H.: Edward Elgar.

———. 1998. *The Ethics of Liberty.* New York: New York University Press.

Royal Architectural Institute of Canada. Unpub.

Rubin, Lillian B. 1994. *Families on the Fault Line: America's Working Class Speak About the Economy, Race, and Ethnicity.* New York: HarperCollins.

Rushton, J.P. 1988. "Race Differences in Behavior: A Review and Evolutionary Analysis." *Personality and Individual Differences* 9.

St. Mary's Honor Center v. Hicks, 509 U.S. 502 (1993).

Salerno, Joseph T. 1990a. "Ludwig von Mises as a Social Rationalist." *Review of Austrian Economics* 4.

———. 1990b. "Postscript: Why a Socialist Economy is 'Impossible'." In Mises (1990).

Samuelson, P. M. 1970. *Economics*, 8th ed. New York: McGraw-Hill.

Scheuer v. Rhodes, 416 U.S. 232 (1974).

Schickman, Mark I. 1996. "Sexual Harassment: The Employer Role in Prevention." *Compleat Lawyer* 13, no. 1 (Winter).

Schmidt, Emerson P. 1973. *Union Power and the Public Interest.* Los Angeles: Nash.

School District of Grand Rapids v. Ball, 473 U.S. 373 (1985).

Sechrest, Larry J. 1999. "Rand, Anarchy, and Taxes." *Journal of Ayn Rand Studies* 1, no. 1 (Fall).

Seigan, Bernard H. 1972. *Land Use Without Zoning.* Toronto: Lexington Books.

Seligman, Daniel. 1992. *A Question of Intelligence: The IQ Debate in America.* New York: Birch Lane.

Seminole Tribe of Florida v. Florida, 517 U.S. 44 (1996).

Serbin, Lisa A. , and K. Daniel O'Leary. 1979. "How Nursery Schools Teach Girls to Shut Up." In J. Williams (1979).

Shavell, Steven. 1993. "An Economic Analysis of Threats and Their Legality: Blackmail, Extortion, and Robbery." *University of Pennsylavnia Law Review* 141, no. 5 (May).

Shelley v. Kraemer, 334 U.S. 1 (1948).

Sherman, Julia A. 1976. "Social Values, Femininity, and the Development of Female Competence." *Journal of Social Issues* 32, no. 3 (Summer).

Shugart, William F., II. 1987. "Don't Revise the Clayton Act, Scrap It!" *Cato Journal* 6.

Sierra Club v. Marita, 46 F.3d 606 (7th Cir. 1995).

Silberman Abella, R. 1984 *Equality in Employment: A Royal Commission Report.* Ottawa: Ministry of Supply and Service Canada.

Simmons v. Lyons, 746 F.2d 265 (5th Cir. 1984).

Simon, Julian. 1981. *The Ultimate Resource*. Princeton, N.J.: Princeton University Press.

Skoble, Aeon J. 1995. "The Anarchism Controversy." In Machan and Douglas (1995).

Smith, Adam. 1965. *An Inquiry into the Nature and Causes of the Wealth of Nations.* New York: Modern Library.

———. 1993. *An Inquiry into the Nature and Causes of the Wealth of Nations.* Ed. Kathryn Sutherland. Oxford: Oxford University Press.

Society of Management Accountants. Unpub.

Sommers, Christina Hoff. 1994. *Who Stole Feminism? How Women have Betrayed Women*. New York: Simon & Schuster.

Sowell, Thomas. 1975. *Race and Economics*. New York: David McKay.

———. 1975b. *Affirmative Action: Reconsidered*. Washington, D.C.: American Enterprise Institute.

———. 1975c. *Race and Economics*. New York: Longman.

———. 1976. *Patterns of Black Excellence*. Washington, D.C.: Ethics and Public Policy Center.

———. 1981. *Ethnic America*. New York: Basic Books.

———. 1981b. *Markets and Minorities*. New York: Basic Books.

———. 1981c. *Pink and Brown People*. Stanford, Calif.: Hoover Institution Press.

———. 1981d. "Weber and Bakker and the Presuppositions of "Affirmative Action." In Block and Walker (1981).

———. 1982. "Weber and Bakke and the Presuppositions of 'Affirmative Action.'" In Block and Walker (1982).

———. 1983. *The Economics and Politics of Race: An International Perspective.* New York: William Morrow.

———. 1984. *Civil Rights: Rhetoric or Reality.* New York: William Morrow.

———. 1987. *A Conflict of Visions: Ideological Origins of Political Struggles.* New York: William Morrow.

———. 1988. "Preferential Policies." In Anderson and Bark (1988).

———. 1990. *Preferential Policies: An International Perspective.* New York: William Morrow.

———. 1994. *Race and Culture: A Worldview.* New York: Basic Books.

———. 1995. *The Vision of the Anointed.* New York: Basic Books.

Spooner, Lysander. 1966. *No Treason.* Larkspur, Colo.: Pine Tree Press.

Stanley v. University of Southern California, 13 F.3d 1313 (9th Cir. 1994).

Stark, Rodney. 1998. "Socialization and Social Roles." In Rodney Stark, Sociology. Belmont, Calif.: Wadsworth.

"State warns that auto insurance should not be discriminatory." 1995. *Boston Globe*, 27 June.

Statistics Canada. 1970. *Annual Salaries of Hospital Nursing Personnel, 1970.* Catalogue 83-218. Ottawa, Ontario.

———. 1971a. *Salaries and Qualifications of Teachers in Universities and Colleges, 1970, 1971.* Catalogue 81-302. Ottawa, Ontario.

———. 1971b. *Census of Canada 1971, Occupation by Sex for Canada & Provinces.* Catalogue 94-717. Ottawa, Ontario.

———. 1971c. Census of Canada 1971. Catalogue 94-717. Ottawa, Ontario.

———. 1971d. *Teachers in Universities.* Catalogue 81-241. Ottawa, Ontario.

———. 1978a. *Salaries and Qualifications of Teachers in Public, Elementary, and Secondary Schools 1977, 1978.* Catalogue 81-202. Ottawa, Ontario.

———. 1978b. *Nursing in Canada: Canadian Nursing Statistics.* Catalogue 83-226. Ottawa, Ontario.

———. 1978c. *Corporations & Labour Unions Returns Act, Part II, Labour Unions.* Catalogue 71-202. Ottawa, Ontario.

———. 1979. *Income Distributions by Size in Canada, 1979.* Catalogue 13-207. Ottawa, Ontario.

———. 1979b. *Income Distributions by Size in Canada, 1979.* Catalogue 13-207. Ottawa, Ontario.

———. 1979c. *Teachers in Universities, 1978–1979.* Catalogue 81-241. Ottawa, Ontario.

————. 1979d. *An Analysis of Earnings in Canada.* Catalogue No. 99-758E. Ottawa, Ontario.

————. 1980. *The Labour Force.* Catalogue 71-001. Ottawa, Ontario.

————. 1980b. *Salaries and Qualifications of Teachers in Public, Elementary & Secondary Schools, 1979–80.* Catalogue 81-202. Ottawa, Ontario.

————. 1984. *Earnings of Men and Women, 1981 and 1982.* Catalogue 31-577. Ottawa, Ontario.

Steele, David Ramsey. 1981. "Posing the Problem: The Impossibility of Economic Calculation Under Socialism." *Journal of Libertarian Studies* 5, no. 1 (Winter).

————. 1992. *From Marx to Mises: Post-Capitalist Society and the Challenge of Economic Calculation,* La Salle, Ill.: Open Court.

Stein, A. H. and M. Bailey. 1973. "The Socialization of Achievement Motivation in Females." *Psychological Bulletin* 80.

Steindl, Frank G. 1973. "The Appeal of Minimum Wage Laws and the Invisible Hand in Government." *Public Choice* 14 (Spring).

————. 1974. "More on Minimum Wages and Political Clout." *Public Choice* 19 (Fall).

Stephenson, Marylee, ed. 1978. *Women in Canada.* Don Mills, Ontario: General Pub.

Stigler, George. 1971. "The theory of economic regulation." *Bell Journal of Economics and Management Science* 2 (Spring).

Stiglitz, J. 1973. "Approaches to the Economics of Discrimination." *American Economic Review* 63, no. 2 (May).

"Stop Provinces Reserving Jobs for Residents, Rights Chief Says." 1980. *Toronto Globe & Mail,* 4 June.

Strassmann, Dianna. 1993. "Not a Free Market: The Rhetoric of Disciplinary Authority in Economics." In Ferber and Nelson (1993).

Stringham, Edward. 1998. "Market Chosen Law." *Journal of Libertarian Studies* 14, no. 1 (Winter).

Strober, Myra H. 1994. "Can Feminist Thought Improve Economics? Rethinking Economics Through a Feminist Lens." *American Economic Review Papers and Proceedings* 84, no. 2 (May).

"Supreme Court Refuses a Motion to Force Grocery Clerk to Shave." 1980. *Toronto Globe & Mail,* 10 February.

Symons, Donald. 1979. *The Evolution of Human Sexuality.* Oxford: Oxford University Press.

Tannehilll, M., and L Tannehill. 1984. *The Market for Liberty*. New York: Laissez Faire Books.

Tepperman, Jean. 1970. "Two Jobs: Women Who Work in Factories." In Morgan (1970).

Texas v. Johnson, 491 U.S. 397 (1989).

"They're Biting the Hand that Won't Feed Them." 1980. *Toronto Globe & Mail*, 9 August.

Thirlby, G.F. 1946. "Subjective Theory of Value and Accounting Cost." *Economica* 13 (February).

Thomas v. Review Board of Indiana Employment Security Division, 450 U.S. 707 (1981).

Thompson, William. 1963. *Inquiry into Principles of the Distribution of Wealth Most Conducive to Human Happiness*. New York: August M. Kelly, Bookseller.

Tinsley, Patrick. 1998. "With Liberty and Justice for All: A Case for Private Police." *Journal of Libertarian Studies* 14, no. 1 (Winter).

Tooby, John, and Leda Cosmides. 1989. "Evolutionary Psychology and the Generation of Culture." *Ethnology & Sociobiology* 10.

———. 1990. "On The Universality of Human Nature." *Journal of Personality* 58, no. 1 (March).

Tooher, L.G. 1978. "Developments in the Law of Blackmail in England and Australia." *International and Comparative Law Quarterly* 27.

Toronto Globe & Mail. 1979. 14 September.

Trivers, Robert. 1985. *Social Evolution*. Menlo. Park, Calif.: Benjamin/ Cummings Publishing.

U.S. Census Bureau. 1998. "Money Incomes of Persons—Selected Characteristics by Income Level: 1995." In *Statistics Abstract of the United States, 1998: The National Data Book*. 118th ed. Washington, D.C.

———. 1999. "Historical Income Tables—People." *Table P-11, Marital Status— People [Eighteen] Years Old and Over by Median Income and Gender: 1974 and 1997*. Available at http:www.census.gov/hhes/income/histinc/pl1.html (last visited November 2, 1999) (on file with Oklahoma City University Law Review). Washington, D.C.

Vancouver Sun. 1984. 16 August.

Vaughn, Karen. 1994. "Beyond Beyond Economic Man: A Critique of Feminist Economics." *Journal of Economic Methodology* 1.

Volokh, Eugene. 1992. "Freedom of Speech and Workplace Harassment." *UCLA Law Review* 39: 1791.

―――. 1997. "What Speech Does "Hostile Environment" Harassment Law Restrict?" *Georgetown Law Journal* 85.

Waldron, Jeremy. "Blackmail as Complicity." Unpublished material (on file with author).

Walker, Deborah. 1994. "Economics of Gender and Race." In Boettke (1994).

Walker, Deborah, Jerry W. Dauterive, Elyssa Schultz, and Walter Block. "The Feminist Competition/Cooperation Dichotomy: A Critique." *Journal of Business Ethics* 55, no. 3 (December 2004).

Walker, Kathryn E. 1970. "Time Used by Husbands for Household Work." *Family Economics Review* 9 (June).

Walker, Michael, ed. 1976. *The Illusion of Wage and Price Controls*. Vancouver, British Columbia: The Fraser Institute.

Wall Street Journal. 1978. 22 June.

Waltz v. Tax Commission, 397 U.S. 664 (1970).

Warth v. Seldin, 422 U.S. 480 (1975).

Wasylycia-Coe, Mary Ann. 1981. "Canadian Chief Librarians by Sex." *Canadian Library Journal* 38, no. 3 (June).

"Wearing Nothing but a Seat Belt." 1980. *Toronto Globe & Mail*, 31 July.

Webster's New College Dictionary. 1973. H.B. Woolf, ed. Springfield, Mass.: G. & C. Merriam.

Weisbrod, Burton A., ed. 1965. *The Economics of Poverty*. Englewood Cliffs, N.J.: Prentice-Hall.

Welch, Finis. 1974. "Minimum Wage Legislation in the United States." *Economic Inquiry* 12, no. 3 (September).

―――. 1967. "Labor-Market Discrimination: An Interpretation of Income Differences in the Rural South." *Journal of Political Economy* 75, no. 3 (June).

West, E. G. 1974. "Vote Earning versus Vote Losing Properties of Minimum Wage Laws." *Public Choice* 19 (Fall).

West, E. G., and Michael Mc Kee. 1980. *Minimum Wages: The New Issues in Theory, Evidence, Policy, and Politics*. Ottawa: Economic Council of Canada and The Institute for Research on Public Policy.

Wharton, V.L. 1947. *The Negro in Mississippi*. Chapel Hill: University of North Carolina Press.

"While Footing the Bill: Football Also Creates Title IX Imbalance." 1996. *Arkansas Democrat-Gazette*, 14 November.

White Men Can't Jump. 1992. 20th Century Fox.

Whitehead, Roy, and Walter Block. 1999. "Mandatory Student Fees: Forcing Some to Pay for the Free Speech of Others." *Whittier Law Review* 20, no. 4.

———. 2008. "Christian Landlords and the Free Exercise Clause: Sinners Need Not Apply." *Oklahoma City University Law Review* 33, no. 1 (Spring).

Whitehead, Roy, and Kenneth Griffin. 1998. "The Supreme Court Finally Lays Down The Law On Employer Liability For Sexual Harassment." *The CPA Journal* (November).

Whitehead, Roy, Kenneth Griffin, and Pam Spikes. 1998. "Preparing For Same Sex Sexual Harassment." *The CPA Journal* (June).

Whitehead, Roy, Pam Spikes, and Brenda Yelvington. 1996. "Sexual Harassment in the Office." *The CPA Journal* (February).

Whitehead, Roy, et al. 1999. "Gender Equity in Athletics: Should We Adopt a Non-Discriminatory Model?" *University of Toledo Law Review* 30, no. 2 (Winter).

Whitney v. California, 274 U.S. 357 (1927).

Will v. Michigan Department of State Police, 491 U.S. 58 (1989).

Willett, Roslyn S. 1971. "Working in 'A Man's World': The Woman Executive." In Gornick and Moran (1971).

Williams, Juanita H., ed. 1979. *Psychology of Women*. New York: W.W. Norton.

Williams, Walter. 1977a. "Government Sanctioned Restraints that Reduce Economic Opportunities for Minorities." *Policy Review* (Fall).

———. 1977b. *Youth and Minority Unemployment*. Commissioned by the U.S. Congress, Joint Economic Committee, 95th Congress, 1st Session. Washington, D. C.: Government Printing Office.

———. 1978. "The New Jim Crow Laws." *Reason*, August.

———. 1979a. "Minimum Wage Maximum Folly." *Newsweek*, 23 September.

———. 1979b. "The Shameful Roots of Minority Unemployment." *Readers Digest*, October.

———. 1981. "On Discrimination, Prejudice, Racial Income Differentials, and Affirmative Action. In Block and Walker (1981).

———. 1982a. "On Discrimination, Prejudice, Racial Income Differentials, and Affirmative Action." In Block and Walker (1982).

———. 1982b. *The State Against Blacks*. New York: McGraw-Hill.

———. 1982c. "On Discrimination and Affirmative Action." In Block and Walker (1982).

———. 1989. *South Africa's War Against Capitalism*. New York: Praeger.

———. 1998. "The Legitimate Role of Government in a Free Society." In Bird (1998).

Williams, Walter E., and Walter Block. 1981. "Male-Female Earnings Differentials: A Critical Reappraisal." *Journal of Labor Research* 2, no. 2.

Wilson, E.O. 1975. *Sociobiology: A New Synthesis*. Cambridge, Mass.: Harvard University Press.

Wiprud, A.C. 1945. *Justice in Transportation: An Expose of Monopoly Control*. New York: Ziff-Davis.

Witters v. Washington Department of Service for the Blind, 474 U.S. 481 (1986).

Woolridge, William C. 1970. *Uncle Sam, The Monopoly Man*. New Rochelle, N.Y.: Arlington House.

Wright, Robert. 1994. *Moral Animal: The New Science of Evolutionary Psychology*. New York: Vintage.

———. 1994b. "Feminists, Meet Mr. Darwin." *New Republic*, 28 November.

Young, Oran, ed. 1975. *Bargaining: Formal Theories of Negotiation*. Urbana: University of Illinois Press.

Young Lawyers Section. 1979. *Demographic Survey, 1979*. Ottawa, Ontario: Canadian Bar Association.

Zaretsky, Eli. 1976. *Capitalism, The Family, and Personal Life*. New York: Harper & Row.

Name Index

SUBJECT INDEX